DEAN COLET ON THE HIERARCHIES
OF DIONYSIUS.

"As for John Colet, he hath never a word to shew, for he wrote no workes."
HARDING TO JEWELL.

"Hujus viri cogitationes, quacunque etiam lingua proditas, optarim."
ERASMUS JODOCO JONÆ.

IOANNES COLETUS SUPER OPERA DIONYSII.

TWO TREATISES ON THE HIERARCHIES OF DIONYSIUS,

BY JOHN COLET, D.D.,

FORMERLY DEAN OF ST. PAUL'S.

NOW FIRST PUBLISHED, WITH A TRANSLATION, INTRODUCTION, AND NOTES,

BY

J. H. LUPTON, M.A.,

SUR-MASTER OF ST. PAUL'S SCHOOL, AND LATE FELLOW OF ST. JOHN'S COLLEGE, CAMBRIDGE.

WIPF & STOCK · Eugene, Oregon

Wipf and Stock Publishers
199 W 8th Ave, Suite 3
Eugene, OR 97401

Two Treatises on the Hierarchies of Dionysius
By Colet, John and Lupton, J.H.
ISBN 13: 978-1-60899-608-7
Publication date 4/5/2010
Previously published by Bell and Dandy, 1869

PREFACE.

THE two Treatises now for the first time made public, along with a third one entitled *De Sacramentis Ecclesiæ*, are contained in a manuscript volume in the Library of St. Paul's School. This volume has been already described, in an edition of the work just referred to; so that, beyond mentioning that it is a fair copy, in one uniform hand, there is no need to give any further account of it here.

The original of the first Treatise, on the *Celestial Hierarchy*, is found in the manuscript marked Gg. iv. 26 in the Cambridge University Library; and this has afforded the means of correcting the text in some places, as well as of supplying one considerable omission.

The second Treatise, on the *Ecclesiastical Hierarchy*, is nowhere else to be met with, so far as I am aware. Although, therefore, this is the one on which the author evidently bestowed most care, yet the fact of its existing in but one copy (and that made, as I should infer, by a not very intelligent scribe), is a disadvantage, which may be pleaded in excuse of occasional errors.

One slight change in the spelling I have made

uniformly throughout; namely, by writing *æ* for the feminine termination instead of *e*. In other respects, the original is represented with tolerable fidelity.

I have now to tender my best thanks to the Court of the Worshipful Company of Mercers, for their permission to publish the contents of the School manuscript; to the Senate of the University of Cambridge, for allowing me to borrow the valuable manuscript before mentioned; and to the Librarian, Henry Bradshaw, Esq., for his great courtesy in previously affording me ready access to it.

To Mr. Seebohm, the author of *The Oxford Reformers of* 1498, my obligations are more than can be expressed in a Preface. I am indebted to him, less even for the information I have received, great though that has been, than for the high standard of work which he has set before me. That the life and writings of Dean Colet should have such an attraction, at the present day, for one possessing no local interest in his memory, is, I think, a happy omen for Colet's obtaining at length something of that recognition which is his due, but which his faithful adherence to his own maxim, *Si vis divinus esse, late ut Deus,* has hitherto prevented him from receiving.

St. Paul's School,
   March 17th, 1869.

CONTENTS.

INTRODUCTION.

	Page
§ 1.—Preliminary	ix
§ 2.—On the Biographies of Dean Colet	ix
§ 3.—On Dean Colet's Writings	xii
§ 4.—On Colet's connection with the Dionysian Writings	xv
§ 5.—On the Neo-Platonists of Florence	xix
§ 6.—On the Dionysian Writings	xxxii
§ 7.—On Colet's deviations from Dionysius	xlv

CELESTIAL HIERARCHY.

Dedication	1
Chapter I. On emanation from God	2
II. On the use of Symbols	7
III. On the Angelic Hierarchy	15
IV. On Angels as messengers	16
V. On the general and special meaning of the term	17
VI. On the nine Orders	18
VII. On the Seraphim, Cherubim and Thrones	20
VIII. On the Dominations, Virtues and Powers	24
IX. On the Princedoms, Archangels and Angels	27
X. On the mutual dependence of the Orders	31
XI. On the attributes of spiritual natures	33
XII. On the names Angels and Gods applied to men	33
XV. On similitudes	34
XVI. Supplementary; on distinctions in office, and on the fallen Angels	36

CONTENTS.

ECCLESIASTICAL HIERARCHY.

		Page
Chapter I. Introductory; on the earthly Hierarchy answering to the heavenly	. . . . . .	48
Chapter II. Part 1. Introduction to Baptism, or Illumination	.	59
,, 2. On the Sacrament of Baptism	. .	61
,, 3. Spiritual contemplation of Baptism	. .	70
III. ,, 1. Introduction to Synaxis, or Communion	.	77
,, 2. On the Ante-Communion Service, and celebration of Holy Communion	. .	78
,, 3. Symbolic truth of the Holy Eucharist	.	84
IV. ,, 1, 2. On the consecration of the Chrism	. .	95
,, 3. Spiritual contemplation of the sacred Chrism		100
V. ,, 1. Introduction to the [Sacrament] of Holy Orders	. . . . . .	102
,, 2. On Consecration and Ordination	. .	118
,, 3. Spiritual contemplation of Holy Orders	.	119
VI. ,, 1. Introduction to Initiation	. . .	126
,, 2, 3. On the Consecration of Monks	. . .	134
VII. ,, 1. Introduction to the Rites of the holy Dead	.	137
,, 2. On the ceremonies of Christian burial	.	140
,, 3. Spiritual contemplation of the rites of the holy Dead	. . . . .	141
,, 3 § 2. On Infant Baptism	. . . .	155
DE CÆLESTI HIERARCHIA	. . . .	163
DE ECCLESIASTICA HIERARCHIA	. . . . .	197
INDEX	. . . .	273

INTRODUCTION.

§ 1.

IN some respects time has not yet done justice to the memory of Dean Colet. With the present year three centuries and a half will be completed since he passed to his rest; and though the recollection of him has never faded away during that long interval, it has been but a faint and shadowy recollection. Men have seen him, not by his own light, but as reflected by Erasmus. As the founder of St. Paul's School, indeed, wise in his enactments, no less than liberal in his endowment, he has always been held in honour by some in each generation; themselves, too, neither few nor undistinguished. But whilst one and another of his contemporaries have enjoyed a European reputation, his fame has been considered to be only local. Those who knew enough of his history to describe him as the friend of Erasmus, doubtless meant by that term one whom Erasmus honoured with his friendship. They dreamt not that his words were not yet ended; that written, if not spoken, they would still be listened to; and that by those words chiefly, as the direct expression of his mind, his place must be finally awarded him among the thinkers of his time.

This comparative obscurity has been the result of several causes, chief among which I would mention the peculiar circumstances attending his biography, and the seclusion of his writings.

§ 2.—*On the Biographies of Dean Colet.*

THAT Colet was fortunate in having Erasmus to give the world an account of him, cannot be doubted. If his portrait be but a miniature, it is from the hand of a master, and it is drawn from the life. But the benefit must not be over-rated. Concerning much of Colet's history Erasmus was of necessity ignorant. He does not appear to have thought beforehand of writing such an account (there being but a few months' difference between their ages), nor, in consequence, to have collected any materials for it; and we find him writing from Louvain to Dancaster and Lupset, requesting them to send him such information as they could about their departed friend. The whole narrative is comprised in a single letter to Justus Jonas, the Wittemberg reformer, who seems to have been laudably anxious to gain an acquaintance with the eminent men of his time;[1] and of that narrative Colet occupies only half. The companion portrait, that of John Vitrier, a Franciscan monk of St. Omer, has but slight interest for Englishmen; of him far less is known[2] even than of Colet; and this indistinctness

---

[1] He had himself previously made a long and toilsome journey to see and become acquainted with Erasmus :—" per tot silvas latrociniis, per tot urbes pestilentiæ morbo infames, ad te grassati sumus, Erasme, Jonas et ego,"—writes his companion on the journey.—Knappii *Narratio* (1817), p. 3.

[2] Was he the same as the John Vitrarius, a Franciscan of Tournay, mentioned by Gieseler, whose doctrines were condemned by the Sorbonne in 1498? The question seems to me an interesting one. Erasmus tells us that he first met the Vitrarius he speaks of at St. Omer, when he had left Paris on account of the plague. This might probably be in the summer of 1500. After giving various particulars of Vitrarius's life and character, and of the truly Christian simplicity and uprightness which made him obnoxious to the rulers of his monastery, he says that he was sent by them to Courtray, to get rid of him, and that he died there. Now if a monk was thus sent from one monastery to another, as a punishment, ostensibly or otherwise, I see no reason why the John Vitrarius of Tournay, whose opinions were censured in 1498, might not have been sent to St. Omer, and be the very Franciscan whom Erasmus there met, and who afterwards died at Courtray. If this be so, then some little light will be thrown on the companion picture to Colet's. For there are given sixteen tenets of this Vitrarius of Tournay, as condemned by the Sorbonne, in D'Argentré (*Collectio*, i. p. 340); a few of which only are quoted by Gieseler. I have not space for more than two or three of these, as specimens :—(1.) " Il vaudroit mieux couper la gorge à son enfan, que de le mettre en Religion non reformée." (10.) " Les pardons viennent d'Enfer." (14.) " Il y a aucuns qui dient aucunes Oraisons de la Vierge Marie, à fin que à l'heure de la mort, ils puissent

INTRODUCTION. xi

in one half of the subject has diminished the clearness and effect of the whole.

After the lapse of nearly a hundred and fifty years, in 1661 preparations were being made by Thomas Smith, of Christ's College, Cambridge, an old Pauline, to publish some of Colet's Treatises;[1] but the design was never accomplished. The destruction of the School and its library, in the fire of 1666, probably put a final stop to it, if it had not been abandoned before.

At the end of another half-century, Mr. John Postlethwayte, the High Master of St. Paul's School, intended to have published a Life of Colet; but his death, in 1713, prevented that design also.[2]

Thus two hundred years had passed away, carrying with them into oblivion many reminiscences and traditions, if not actual memorials of Colet's own writing, which might have enriched the account of such a man. And meanwhile, little or nothing had been added to the sketch left by Erasmus. It had been translated and illustrated with notes by Smith, and repeated, in more or less modified form, by Holland and Fuller; his *Convocation Sermon* had been reprinted in the *Phœnix;* and some few additional particulars of his life and writings might be found in Anthony à Wood and Pitseus, in Polydore Vergil, Leland, and George Lily. But still Erasmus might be said to remain the only biographer of Dean Colet.

In the next few years, however, much was done in this direction. Dr. White Kennett, afterwards Bishop of Peterborough, the memorials of whose unbounded industry, as they stand amid the volumes of the Lansdowne manuscripts, I can never call to mind without veneration, had laboured hard in the mine of Erasmus's letters; and from thence, and

---

veoir la Vierge Marie. Tu verras le Diable, non pas la Vierge Marie." The violent spirit of these propositions perhaps does not well accord with the character of Erasmus's Vitrarius; but he might have been subdued by the censure passed on him in 1498.—See Gieseler, *Eccl. Hist.* (1855), v. p. 161.

[1] *A Sermon of Conforming, &c.* (1661), p. 2.
[2] Knight's *Colet*, (1823), p. 330.

from other sources, had gathered materials for a life of Colet, far more copious and varied than had yet been seen. These materials fill a folio volume (Lansdowne, 1030) of 181 closely-written leaves; and had the workman found time to complete his work, and to give shape and finish to his structure, Bishop Kennett would have been entitled to the name of Dean Colet's biographer. But more urgent duties called him away from the task; and, with his wonted liberality to other students,[1] he placed his collections in the hands of Dr. Samuel Knight, some time before March, 1721.[2] By Dr. Knight they were arranged and completed, and published in 1724. Nearly a century later, in 1823, this work was reprinted, with a few very brief additions; and here the matter rested, till the publication of *The Oxford Reformers of* 1498, two years ago, made Colet seem once more to live amongst us.

§ 3.—*On Dean Colet's Writings.*

IF for so long a space but scanty justice was done to Dean Colet by others, he had, or seemed to have, no writings to speak on his behalf. Although his Latin style is always forcible, and occasionally not wanting in elegance, there is

---

[1] "Far from engrossing any sort of knowledge to himself, he was exceedingly free, and communicative, and improving to all he conversed with, or that, far or near, desired his assistance and advice."—*Life* (1730), p. 190. This *Life*, which was anonymous, was assailed in a bitter pamphlet, entitled *Short Remarks, &c.*, which came out in the same year. Kennett's change of political principles, from Jacobite to Hanoverian, exposed him to long and violent hostility. The Rector of Whitechapel inserted his portrait, as Judas, in an altar-piece representing the Last Supper; an act of profanity which drew multitudes to the Church, till the Bishop interfered. The obloquy he underwent appears to me to have robbed him of some of the respect he deserves for his literary labours; and on this account I am desirous that his merit in the present instance should be acknowledged. See Nichols' *Lit. Anecd.*, i. p. 396 *n*.

[2] See the letter of Dr. Knight to Bp. Kennett, dated March 28th, 1721, prefixed to the MS. volume referred to; and Kennett's reply. No one can properly estimate the relative value of Bp. Kennett's and of Dr. Knight's labours, who has not well examined this important volume.

INTRODUCTION. xiii

in his extant compositions a certain inaccuracy of diction,[1] which he seems to have felt himself, and which, Erasmus thought, had restrained him from committing his reflections to writing. " And I wish," adds Erasmus, " that this had not been the case; for I should be glad of the thoughts of John Colet, in whatever language expressed."[2]

By his Will, dated Aug. 22nd, 1519, Colet thus disposed of such manuscripts as he had preserved :—" *Item*, the new testament, and oder of myne own making, wryten in parchement, as coments of Paulis Epesteles, and abbreviations, with many such other, I will shall be disposed at the disposition of myn executors, whiche disposition I leve to their discretion."[3]

It does not appear that anything was published by them; and some of the manuscripts, by purchase or otherwise, eventually came into the possession of Matthew Parker, a youth of fifteen at the time of Colet's death, afterwards Archbishop of Canterbury. He bequeathed to his own College of Corpus Christi the volume (No. 355) containing Colet's Exposition of the *Epistle to the Romans*, and a portion of his Letters to Radulphus on the Mosaic account of the Creation.[4] In Emmanuel College Library is another volume, the gift of Dr. Anthony Tuckney, containing a like Exposition of the *First Epistle to the Corinthians*.[5] The archetypes of both these, which are in the handwriting of

---

[1] The author of the Latin Essay, which gained the Chancellor's Medal at Oxford in 1866, entitled *Erasmus, sive Thucydidis cum Tacito comparatio*, threw his piece into the form of a dialogue between Warham, Colet, Erasmus and More; but he prudently avoided imitating Colet's Latinity too closely.

[2] *Epist. Jodoco Jonæ.*

[3] Kennett's MSS. vol. xv. (Lansdowne, 949), f. 29.

[4] Partly described in the printed Catalogue (1722), p. 69. For the Letters to Radulphus, see *The Oxford Reformers*, p. 36 *n*. Knight wrongly describes the volume as containing the same comments as that in the Emmanuel Library.—*Pref.* p. xv.

[5] For a description of this I am indebted to the Rev. Octavius Glover, B.D., the Librarian. Dr. Tuckney was successively Master of Emmanuel and St. John's College, Cambridge, and Regius Professor of Divinity, and died in 1670.

xiv INTRODUCTION.

Peter Meghen, are in the volume marked Gg. iv. 26 in the Cambridge University Library; a volume which appears to have been the property of Richard Holdsworth,[1] Gresham Professor of Divinity, who died in 1649, and which contains also the original of the *Treatise on the Celestial Hierarchy*, here published, the Letter to the Abbot of Winchombe, printed by Dr. Knight, and a short Treatise *De compositione sancti corporis Christi mystici*. There is also among the Gale MSS. in the library of Trinity College, Cambridge, a volume (O. 4.44) written on vellum, in a hand of Queen Elizabeth's time,[2] which has been thought to contain a copy of some of Colet's treatises; but this is now strongly doubted.

The above, omitting the manuscript in St. Paul's School Library, of which the remaining contents are here published, comprises all the extant writings of Dean Colet, so far as I am aware.[3] And when it is considered how large and im-

---

[1] Knight (Pref. p. xvi) says that it seems to be the "donation of archbishop Parker." But there is pencilled at the end of the volume, "Holdsworth Collection (1649) MS. 13." Dr. Richard Holdsworth, of St. John's College, was Master of Emmanuel College in 1637, from which he was displaced in 1645 to make room for the Dr. Anthony Tuckney mentioned above. Holdsworth died in 1649, and bequeathed his books to his college.—See Kennett's MSS. vol. li. (Lansdowne 985), f. 146.

[2] For these particulars I have to thank the Librarian, W. Aldis Wright, Esq. M.A.—Dr. Thos. Gale, the original owner of this MS. left it to his son Roger Gale, in 1702, by whom, at his death in 1744, it was bequeathed to Trinity Coll. Camb.—Nichols' *Lit. Anecd.* iv. p. 551. A note in Dr. Thos. Gale's writing gives his opinion that it is Colet's work, from its similarity to another volume, then in the Chapter House of St. Paul's, but now no longer discoverable.

[3] I must here express my obligations to Signor Ferrucci, the venerable Librarian of the Mediceo-Laurentian Library at Florence, for informing me that no record of Colet is to be found among the archives under his care; and to Robert S. Collet, Esq., of The Hale, Wendover, for a like courtesy.

I take no notice of the long list of works given in Bale and Pits; the latter of whom refers vaguely to Trithemius and Sixtus Senensis as his authorities. In Trithemius, so far as I can find, there is no mention of Colet at all; while Sixtus Senensis only says that he wrote comments on the Proverbs and St. Matthew (Ed. 1610, p. 254). Walch, in his *Bibliotheca* (1757), i. p. 309, makes him to have written on the Creed;

portant a section of his works has not yet seen the light, I mean his comments on the Epistles and on Genesis; and how that, till very recently, his Treatises on Dionysius were equally unknown; it will be felt that the means of forming a true opinion of Colet have not yet been supplied; and that, in the fate of his writings, as well as in the circumstances of his biography, he has been left in an obscurity altogether undeserved.

§ 4.—*On Colet's connection with the Dionysian Writings.*

AFTER the above summary of Colet's extant works, the reader's attention will naturally be directed to the present Treatises, which, with the *Treatise on the Sacraments* as a kind of sequel to them, form a separate class of Dean Colet's writings. The reasons for assigning an early date to them have been given elsewhere.[1] Whether or not Colet meant to describe them in his Will by the term "abbreviations," I cannot say; but it is obvious that they are the result of a careful study of two at least of the works of Dionysius, the so-called Areopagite. There is much originality in them; Colet often leaves his author far behind, and is found expatiating on the state of the Church in his own time; but still the title gives in the main a correct description of them; they are abstracts of the *Hierarchies* of Dionysius. It becomes accordingly an interesting question, how Dionysius should exert such an influence upon him.

A German essayist on Dionysius, Augustus Meier,[2] is

---

and Kemp, in his *Charismatum . . . Trias* (1677), reckons him among the writers on the Proverbs, the Apostles' Creed, and the Lord's Prayer: pp. 102, 276—7.

[1] *Treatise on the Sacraments* (1867), *Introd.* p. 4.—To what is there said about the Latin Edition of 1498, may be added the fact that it was edited by Jacobus Faber of Etaples, who was the frequent correspondent of Erasmus, and may therefore have been probably known to Colet.

[2] *Dionysii Areopagitæ et mysticorum sæculi xiv. doctrinæ inter se comparantur* (1845), p. 2.

probably right in saying, that mysticism chiefly springs up and flourishes, when the established forms of religion have begun to lose their hold on men; when the instinctive longing of the soul after the immortal and divine remains, but can find nothing to satisfy it in the external rites of a failing church. "From the hard and arid system of Peter the Lombard," says Milman,[1] "the profound devotion of the Middle Ages took refuge in mysticism." At such a period of transition as the latter end of the fifteenth century, even without taking into account reasons to be presently mentioned, it was natural enough for any educated Englishman to be attracted to the writings of Dionysius. And though Erasmus does not speak of Colet's having begun the study of that author till he had gone abroad, about the latter end of 1493, yet in his mention of Plato and Plotinus being carefully read by Colet while at Oxford, he shews that he had made a good preparation for such a study.

But I think that, in the present case, there are faint, yet perceptible, traces of a personal history, by following out which we can connect Dean Colet almost immediately with the Dionysian writings. Without attempting to surmise what turn may have been given to his thoughts by converse with Grocyn and Linacre, both of whom had returned from Italy before he started, it seems to me highly probable that he owed to Mirandola and Ficino, if not his first acquaintance with, yet much of his early preference for, those mystic writings; and that connecting links with Mirandola and Ficino may be found in Robert Gaguin, sometime ambassador in England of Charles VIII., and Germain de Ganay.

It was the sight of a letter of Erasmus's to Robert Gaguin, the French historian, that first introduced Erasmus to the notice of Colet.[2] The practice of handing letters about, as evidences of scholarship, seems at that time to have been common; and Gaguin had in this manner shewn to Colet one received by him from Erasmus. The fact would seem

---

[1] *Latin Christianity*, vol. vi. p. 439.
[2] *Erasmi Epist.* (1642), v. 3; dated 1497.

INTRODUCTION.

to betoken a certain amount of intimacy between Gaguin and Colet. Now Gaguin, a man of letters, and the enviable possessor of a well-stocked library,[1] was in correspondence with Ficino. In his collected *Letters* there is one addressed to the Florentine scholar, dated Sep. 1st, 1496,[2] in which he compliments Ficino on the extent to which his writings were then read in Paris. His translation of Plotinus, he says, and other treatises of his, were so popular and so highly esteemed, that many a French scholar was eager " to know by sight and to gaze upon a man, from whom issued forth such noble memorials of learning." One such he mentions by name, who had resolved on a journey to Italy for that purpose, with an ardour like that which carried Plato into Egypt, or brought the Spaniard from Cadiz to Rome, for the sake of beholding Livy. This being so, there seems nothing improbable in supposing that Colet, who had previously read Plotinus at Oxford, should be interested in the writings of Ficino, through Gaguin, and possibly enough through many other channels in Paris, and so be led up to the sources from which Ficino had drawn some of his varied learning.

Again, with respect to Germain de Ganay. He too was a friend and correspondent of Ficino's. In one letter[3] Ficino sends him word to expect shortly some of his works, which would have been sent off before but for the transcriber's slowness; and among them " the Areopagite, the highest of all Platonists." He was the friend also of the elder Pico della Mirandola ; on whose untimely death Ficino wrote to Ganay with the intelligence, as one who would be

---

[1] Thus Erasmus writes to ask the loan of Macrobius (Ep. iv. 26), of Trapezuntius and Quintilian (v. 16).

[2] *Roberti Gaguini* . . . *Epistole* (1498) f. xlv.—" Quibus omnibus plerique nostratium scholasticorum ardent te facie nosse et intueri hominem, a quo tam præclara doctrine monumenta prodierunt," etc.

[3] Dated Oct. 16th, 1494.—*Ficini Op.* (1641) i. p. 984 :—" Vidisses et Areopagitam simul, Platonicorum culmen, si nunc eo habitu, qui et ipsum et te decebat, accedere potuisset. Ex scriptoris et librarii negligentia impedivit accessum."

deeply affected by it.[1] This Germain de Ganay was Bishop of Orleans; and from a passage in a letter of Francis Deloine to Erasmus,[2] it appears that Colet, when abroad, spent some time there in study. Orleans would be naturally in the route from Paris to Italy; and we find, as a matter of fact, that Erasmus went that way on another occasion.[3] Now it is of course mere matter of presumption that Colet, staying there for purposes of study, would enjoy the society of its learned Bishop;[4] but there is at least nothing improbable in it; and if this were so, then by another channel would Colet be brought into communication with the writings of Ficino and Mirandola, and through them again be pointed onwards to Dionysius.

But, not to pause longer on these inconclusive, if interesting, traces of Colet's progress, the present Treatises prove beyond all doubt that he had read some, at least, of the writings of Mirandola and Ficino. From the *Apologia* of the former he quotes a passage of some length, with scarcely a verbal alteration;[5] whilst the identity of several phrases, and the general tone of thought, in another place,[6] betray a study of the *Dialogus inter Paulum et animam* of the latter. Now it is of course quite intelligible, that Colet may have

---

[1] *Mirandulæ Op.* (1601), i. p. 274. The letter is dated March 23rd, 1494, and addressed "Germano de Ganai, Parisii [*sic*] Præsidenti." According to Greswell (*Memoirs of Politian*, 2nd Ed., p. 357), this Ganay was Rector of the University of Paris; though in another letter of Ficino's (*Op.* 1641, i. p. 987, *b*) his brother John is styled "Parisiis Præsidens." Greswell criticizes the style of this letter somewhat severely.

[2] *Epistolæ*, i. 13 :—" Qui [Coletus] te, ut scribis, veteris amicitiæ ac consuetudinis commonuit, quæ mihi cum illo non vulgaris intercessit, *quum Aureliæ studiorum causa ageremus.*"

[3] " Nam nemini, cum olim essem Aureliæ, Italiam aditurus."—*Ep.* i. 14.

[4] There is still in the British Museum a beautiful MS. copy of Ficino's *Comments on the Romans* (Harleian, 4695), at the end of which is written, "Le livre appartient a maistre Germain de Ganay;" and after this, in a later hand, " en son vivant, Evesque d'Orleans, frere de Jehan de Gannay, chancelier de France, et freres de ma bisayeule maternelle."

[5] See below, p. 109, *n*.

[6] *Celestial Hierarchy*, p. 36, *n*.

been attracted to the study of Dionysius by many other causes than the influence of these two Florentine scholars. Soon after he started on his travels, there was published the great Ecclesiastical Dictionary of the day, the *Liber de Scriptoribus Ecclesiasticis* of John Trittenheim.[1] This included notices of the life and works, not only of ancient Fathers of the Church, but of eminent contemporaries; of Ficino, Mirandola, Reuchlin, and many more. Supposing now Colet to have taken up this new work of the learned Abbot of Spanheim, with the curiosity of a young student, and the deference naturally paid to the latest authority, how would he have found Dionysius spoken of? As the convert of St. Paul; of surpassing holiness and incomparable learning; as probably the first Bishop of Athens, and certainly the apostle of France; as the author, lastly, of many illustrious works.[2]

With such language as this passing current, as the best information of the day, on the subject of Dionysius, it is almost superfluous to enquire particularly how Colet's attention came to be turned to his writings. But still, as the evidence of his connection with the Florentine school is unmistakeable; and as that school had a very great influence, not only in making popular the study of the so-called Areopagite, but in infusing much of his spirit into the Christianity of the time, it seems desirable to notice, in passing, two at least of the great Neo-Platonists of Florence, Pico della Mirandola and Marsiglio Ficino.

§ 5.—*On the Neo-Platonists of Florence.*

THE Council of Florence, held under the presidency of Eugenius IV., which had for its chief object the reconciliation of the Greek and Latin Churches, and which closed its deliberations in April 1442, has generally been considered to be the means through which the Platonic philo-

---

[1] The first edition was published at Basle in 1494, and speaks of Pico, Politian and others, as still living.
[2] Leaf 2, *b*.

sophy was introduced once more into Europe.[1] But in reality Plato had been known to Italians a century before. Petrarch, who died in 1374, and to whose zeal in collecting manuscripts the cause of learning was in no small degree indebted, had procured several copies of Plato's works, partly in Latin translations, and partly in the original Greek.[2] His guide in this pursuit was Barlaam, a Calabrian monk, the fortunate possessor of still more treatises of Plato. Boccaccio succeeded to the study, and read Plato in the library of his friend Petrarch.[3] But the flame, if ever vigorous, seems soon to have died out. The Academy does not appear to have gained any fresh disciple of note in Italy, till the event referred to above, the Council of Florence, brought a number of learned Greeks to that country. The conversation of these men, especially of George, surnamed Gemistus or Pletho,[4] filled Cosmo de' Medici with an ardent desire to transplant the philosophy of Plato to Italian soil; and to his efforts must be ascribed the foundation of the Platonic Academy at Florence.

In some respects the Platonic revival is open to the charge of extravagance, and even childishness. In the enthusiasm of entering an unexplored country, so widespread and tempting, men were not likely to advance soberly and with measured steps. But we must remember what those days were, and how utterly new and untried many domains of knowledge still were. They were the days in which Politian, driven to take shelter from the rain in a chance workshop, could be urged by his fellow refugees to read aloud to them the works of a Roman poet, and could not

---

[1] "The synod introduced into Florence the lights of the Greek church, and the oracles of the Platonic philosophy."—Gibbon, ch. lxvi.

[2] This is stated by Bandinius, in his Preface to Corsius's Life of Ficino (1771), p. 184; where he quotes a passage from Petrarch himself, stating that he had sixteen books of Plato, or more; and that those were but a few, compared to the number he had seen in Barlaam's possession:—"Sedecim, vel eo amplius, Platonis libros domi habeo," etc.

[3] Bandinius, *ib.*; who refers, as authority, to Boccaccio's Commentary on Dante (1724), p. 231.

[4] The names both signify the same thing, so that there is no need to call him Gemistus Pletho.

INTRODUCTION. xxi

pacify them till he had read and explained the whole.[1] They were the days in which Poggio could rescue the only extant manuscript of Quintilian from the hands of a German grocer, just as it was about to be torn up, to make wrappers for his commodities.[2] We can judge leniently, therefore, of the excesses men might run into, when the fruits of the tree of knowledge were being showered down in such varied profusion at their feet; and of their inability to judge rightly at all times of the relative value of what they gathered. No doubt much nonsense was talked at the Banquets, revived, after twelve hundred years' interval, to honour the anniversary of Plato's birth;[3] and questions raised, far more trivial than that which occupied the company at the table of Hermolaus Barbarus in Rome, as to whether the old ship of Theseus, when its decaying timbers had all been gradually replaced, was the same ship or a different one.[4] But the freedom of thought thus fostered was as the healthy action of a child at play. It was the capricious but vigorous exercise of the mind, able at last to shake off the numbness which a previous system of education had brought on.[5]

---

[1] "Catullum autem plane universum Veronæ . . . intra officinam quampiam, quo nos pluvia coegerat, viris aliquot literatis pene cogentibus, enarravimus," etc.—*Politiani Opera*, (1533), i. p. 548.

[2] Varillas' *Secret History of the House of Medicis*, tr. by Spence, p. 234.

[3] See c. i. of the *Commentarius in Convivium Platonis* of Ficino. He gives the names of the nine guests who, in imitation of the nine muses, were assembled, one seventh of November, at the house of Bandinus, and who shared among them the parts of the interlocutors in the *Convivium*.

[4] The story is told by Alexander ab Alexandro, at the beginning of Lib. iii. of his *Geniales Dies*.

[5] No doubt there is much exaggeration in the *Epistolæ obscurorum Virorum*, but one cannot question the truthfulness of the slavish character of mind there pourtrayed. The very Grammar they had all been taught prepares one for the appeals to the *Catholicon* and the *Gemma Gemmarum*. Take, for instance, the first line of the universal *Alexander Dolensis*, and its commentary:—
"Scribere clericulis paro doctrinale novellis."
"Quia textus est planus, non indiget explanatione. Sed tamen pro forma servanda in sequentibus, sic construe: Ego magister Alexander paro scribere doctrinale, id est, librum dantem doctrinam, novellis cleri-

"From this period," says M. Delécluze, "freedom of thought in Europe took its rise; and from this crude medley of profound erudition and mystic philosophizing sprang the taste for the study of the moral sciences, and general literature, which opened the way to philosophy and the sciences."[1] And he adds that from such intellectual gatherings as those in the house of Bandinus at Careggi, came the first blows that were aimed at the scholasticism of the age.

The remarks above made will apply with special force to Mirandola and Ficino. In each we see a force of intellect, rioting in its own exuberance. At times they seem occupied with topics almost as trivial as those which amused the Della Cruscans of Florence three centuries later; and again, we seem to be reading, in the language of Cicero, arguments more sublime than the New Academy ever soared to.

Giovanni Pico, Count of Mirandola, was a few years older than Colet, having been born in 1463. In his twenty-fourth year he had already completed a course of reading so extensive, as to embolden him to publish at Rome a series of theses for disputation, enough to startle the most veteran dialectician there. Far outstripping Longfellow's Scholastic at Salern, who could say,

> "There, that is my gauntlet, my banner, my shield,
> Hung up as a challenge to all the field:
> One hundred and twenty-five propositions,
> Which I will maintain with the sword of the tongue
> Against all disputants, old and young,"

Mirandola could boast of nine hundred *Questions,* on all conceivable subjects, as the literary gages he had thrown down. It would be alike beside my purpose to stay to investigate these, and presumptuous to attempt to decide on the real knowledge which they indicate;[2] suffice it to say, that pro-

---

culis, i. scholaribus; quasi dicat, non pro provectis hoc opus scribitur, sed pro rudibus "—(*Ed.* 1482).

Who can compare this with Holt's *Lac Puerorum,* or with Lily's Grammar, and not feel that another generation had risen up?

[1] *Florence et ses vicissitudes* (1837), i. p. 239. The same testimony is borne by a writer in the *Quarterly Review* (Oct. 1862), in an article on *The Platonic Dialogues.*

[2] Villari, I think unjustly, speaks in disparaging terms of the learning

INTRODUCTION. xxiii

positions from Plotinus, Porphyry, Jamblichus and Proclus, find a place among the number at this early period of 1486.

The three great objects of Mirandola's literary labours were, as Ficino informs us,[1] the reconciliation of the Platonic philosophy with the Aristotelian; the explanation of the Holy Scriptures; and the confutation of astrology. The first of these objects he often alludes to in his extant letters. Thus, in one dated 1484, he speaks of having lately passed from the camp of Aristotle to that of the Academy, not as a deserter, but as a spy.[2] Six years later we find him writing to his Carmelite friend Baptista Mantuanus, and giving an account of his studies. "I am busily occupied," he says, "with the reconciliation of Plato and Aristotle. To that pursuit I give my whole mornings. My afternoon hours I give to my friends, to relaxation, at times to the poets and orators, and such lighter studies. Sleep and Holy Scripture share the night between them."[3] His nephew, John Francis Pico, makes repeated mention of this as an end which the elder Mirandola kept before him. In one passage of his great work,[4] for instance, after describing the increase of Aristotle's influence, which he attributes in part to the influx of the works of Averroes and Avicenna, rendered easier by the conquests of Ferdinand and Isabella, he details the efforts made by Pletho and Bessarion to call attention to Plato; and then contrasts his relative's endeavour to reconcile the two systems, with his own purpose of depreciating

---

of Mirandola. "These propositions," he says, "were after all very insignificant, and substantially contained nothing of any importance. . . . It must be confessed that his learning was not very profound, and that he was far inferior in erudition to Politian, and in philosophy to Ficino." —*History of Savonarola*, tr. by Horner, i. p. 81. In the case of one who died in his thirty-second year, an inferiority to Politian and Ficino, in the departments peculiar to each, may readily be allowed; and enough will still remain, as it seems to me, almost to justify the eulogy of Erasmus and of the elder Scaliger.

[1] Letter to Germain de Ganay, dated March 23rd, 1494.—*Op.* 1601, p. 275.
[2] *Op.* p. 250.   [3] *Op.* p. 243.
[4] *Examen vanitatis doctrinæ Gentium*, iv. 2.—*Op. Pars.* ii. p. 666.

heathen philosophy altogether, when brought into rivalry with the doctrines of Christianity.

In his love for Plato, Mirandola found a congenial spirit in one, who in personal appearance and fortune was most unlike him, Marsiglio Ficino. Born in 1433, and therefore thirty years his senior, Ficino yet addresses the other constantly as his partner in the search for wisdom;[1] and in the feeling letter in which he relates his death, speaks of him as "in age a son, in intimacy a brother, and in affection a second self."[2] To be near his friend, Mirandola hired an adjacent house, though one unequal to his rank, and resided in it for nearly three years.[3] It was through his entreaties that Ficino undertook the translation of Plotinus; an author whom Mirandola speaks of as worthy not only of constant perusal, but of being learnt by heart,[4] and who appears to have led Ficino naturally on to Dionysius, as a translation of some of his works was the next task he took in hand.[5]

There is one letter of Ficino's to Mirandola, unfortunately not dated, which describes so pleasingly the spirit in which they both worked, that I will give it entire. "You send me," he writes, "most welcome intelligence, my worthy friend, that you are daily advising many, and have already succeeded in persuading some, to abandon the irreligion of Epicurus, or lay aside some notions they may have gained from Averroes, and embrace the devout sentiments of our Plato touching the soul and God. For through this, as through an intervening road, they may finally reach the religion of Christ. Heaven speed you then, true fisher of men! For if they who persuade common minds seem to be catchers of fishes,—or minnows, as one may say—they who convince leading intellects are judged to be fishers

---

[1] "Conphilosophus suus."

[2] "Nam et ætate mihi filius Picus erat, et familiaritate frater, et amore prorsus alter ego."—Mirand. *Op.* p. 275.

[3] "Picus ille Mirandula . . . quum Florentiam venisset, ædes Marsilio vicinas conduxit, humiles admodum; quas tamen totum fere triennium habitavit."—Corsii *Vita*, p. 192.

[4] Corsius, p. 189, and Mirand. *Op.* pp. 79, 250.

[5] Corsius, p. 190.

of men. These perchance are the 'great fishes' named in the Gospel, which the net enclosed, yet for all that was not broken. Our net, Mirandola, is now the system of Plato; for if this be but rightly drawn beneath Christian truth, it breaks not, but remains whole while it is filled. You have read that no philosophers in former days embraced the Christian religion, but Platonists.[1] Rightly therefore with Platonic nets, so to speak, do you ever fish for the highest intellects for Christ. Would that our religion had were it but three such fishers in its service, that no great fishes might be left in the sea! But alas! unhappy, or rather, unfortunate that we are. 'The harvest truly is plenteous, but the labourers are few.' And the fewer we are, my dear Mirandola, the more frequently and the more zealously must we labour. Farewell."[2]

I said that it was unfortunate that this letter is not dated, as it would be desirable to know at what period of his life Ficino wrote in such terms. For the question that arises from it is one, in its wider extent, of considerable interest; as it amounts to this:—Were Mirandola and Ficino uniformly, through at least a considerable portion of their lives, men of such a religious spirit as the above letter would seem to imply; or were they almost wholly indifferent to Christianity, till a certain event arrested and changed their course, which event was the preaching of Savonarola?

Now far be it from me to detract from the just renown of that wonderful man. We seem to behold in him one set free from the ties that bind ordinary men to the earth, and able to hurl himself against the strongholds of iniquity. There was that fire of the Spirit in him for which enthusiasm sounds but a cold name, that can inflame the lukewarm, and fuse the stubborn, and, in Colet's language,

---

[1] So Bouillet, *Les Ennéades de Plotin* (1857), *Pref.* p. xxxi:—"Et, en effet, plusieurs des premiers Pères et des plus zélés Confesseurs de la foi, Saint Justin, Athénagore, Clément d'Alexandrie, étaient, on le sait, des Platoniciens convertis."

[2] Ficini *Opera* (1641), i. p. 956.

spread a "conflagration amid the forest of men." When he speaks, in his *Triumph of the Cross*,[1] of "men of science, skilled in all forms of learning, who, having drunk freely at the pure fountain of Holy Scripture, and tasted the sweetness of Christ, have abandoned their sciences, and only found happiness in His teaching," he is but describing the effects of his own words upon many in Florence.

But still I think it unjust to the fame of two illustrious men, to ascribe the formation of a Christian character in them to the influence even of Savonarola.

To speak first of Ficino. We are told by one writer, that the disposition of Ficino and others "to betake themselves to the fanciful theories of Plato, instead of to the cross of Christ for comfort, was probably a consequence of latent infidelity," engendered by the corruptions of the Church at that period.[2] And again, "Spondanus assures us that, under the preaching and influence of the celebrated monk Savonarola, he [Ficino] became in his latter days a humble and devout learner in the school of Christ."[3]

There are two facts which seem to me difficult to reconcile with this. One is, the all but entire absence of any mention of Savonarola in Ficino's numerous letters,[4] which

---

[1] Hill's Translation (1868), p. 123.
[2] Harford's *Life of Michael Angelo* (1857), i. p. 64.
[3] *Ib.* p. 70; where there is a reference to Schelhorn, *Amœnitates Literariæ*, i. p. 73. Schelhorn's authority is Henry Wharton (*Appendix to Cave*, 1688, p. 166), who says that Ficino "rei philosophicæ nimium deditus, religionis et pietatis curam posthabuisse *dicitur*, donec Savonarolæ, etc." In these questions one wants something like contemporary authority; and I suppose Wharton only drew from Spondanus (*i.e.* Henri de Sponde, a continuator of Baronius), who, in his *Annalium . . . . Continuatio* (1647), vol. ii. p. 230, writes :—" Cum interim Savonarola quamplurimos ad meliorem vitæ frugem reducere non cessaret. Inter quos fuit etiam Marsilius Ficinus, Canonicus Florentinus, philosophus ante Platonicus magis quam Christianus." For this no precise reference is given; but the whole account, by a marginal note higher up, seems to rest on the authority of Guicciardini and Abraham Bzovius. Bzovius, a Polander, was not born till the middle of the sixteenth century; and as for Guicciardini, I can only say that, after some search, I have not been able to find any such statement.
[4] Savonarola is, I believe, only mentioned once in Ficino's letters;

INTRODUCTION.   xxvii

is not what we should expect if Ficino owed so much to him; the other is the circumstance, that a distinct change of life is recorded of him by a contemporary biographer, and that change is not ascribed to the influence of Savonarola. Corsius, who was a disciple of Ficino's, speaks of a depression of mind to which he was subject in the early part of his life, fostered partly by peculiarities of constitution; and of the fruitless remedies by which he sought to alleviate it. He then speaks of a conviction growing upon him that he had forgotten Christianity in his Platonism, and of the works in which he sought to direct his philosophy to its right use, and concludes by describing him as having, "when he had now completed forty-two years of age, from a pagan, become a soldier of Christ."[1] Ficino was forty-two years old in 1475, the very year in which Savonarola, then aged twenty-three, left his home at Ferrara, to join the Dominican convent in Bologna. Three years later, in 1478, we find him thus writing to Hieronymus Rossius, touching his own treatise *On the Christian Religion*:—"If you find in it aught worthy of praise, give God the praise, without whose gift nothing is in truth worthy to be praised. If aught shall chance to displease you, take heed that you be not displeased on that account with Religion herself. Measure not the loftiness of things divine by the lowliness of my poor intellect; for the divine depends not on the human, but the human on the divine."[2]

No doubt there are many extravagances to be found in the writings of Ficino;[3] probably he was unable to shake

---

namely, in an epistle to Calcavanti, dated Dec. 12th, 1494 (*Op.* i. p. 987), shortly after the entry of Charles VIII. into Florence. At such a time it was most natural to call to mind the warnings which Savonarola had uttered.—See Trollope's *History of the Commonwealth of Florence* (1865), iv. p. 25.

[1] Corsii *Vita*, p. 188.

[2] In a letter in Ficino's own handwriting, prefixed to a copy of the *De Religione Christiana*, in the Library of St. Mark at Florence. The letter is dated Nov. 1st, 1478, and is quoted by Bandini, in his notes on Corsius, *ut supra*, p. 201.

[3] A list of them has been made out by Schelhorn, *Amœnit. Lit.* (1725), i. pp. 80, sqq.

off, even to his latest day, something of the superstitious belief in astrology, charms, and the like, which was then exceedingly prevalent;[1] but still in his case, as in that of Augustine, Platonism seems to have been as a porch to Christianity; and I believe the threshold was finally crossed, years before Savonarola preached in Florence.

In the case of Mirandola, as in that of his friend, a distinct change of life is recorded by one who knew him well. His nephew before-mentioned, in the *Life* prefixed to his collected works, distinctly says that the disappointment he met with, in finding his *Propositions* censured by the Pope, was the bitter lesson which sobered his thoughts, and turned him aside from the lure of youthful ambition, to listen to the voice of Christ. As Sir Thomas More translated this *Life*,[2] I will give the passage in his words:—"But as hymselfe tolde his nevewe, he judged that this came thus to passe by the especiall provision and synguler goodness of almighty god, that by this fals cryme untruely put upon hym by his evyll wyllers, he sholde correcte his very errours, and that this sholde be to hym (wanderynge in derknes) as a shynynge lyght, in whiche he myght beholde and consydre how ferre he had gone out of the way of trouth. For

---

[1] Some striking instances of this are given by Greswell (*Memoirs of Politian*, 2nd Ed. p. 350, *n.*). It is rash to question the opinion of Villari, when it coincides with that of Greswell. But I still think that they are both somewhat hard upon Ficino; the former in the character he gives of his work *De vita cœlitus comparanda*, and the latter in disputing the sincerity of the letter, in which Ficino explains to Politian what he meant to be the drift of that work. Villari describes it as "a treatise upon the influences of the stars, of stones, and of animals, together with long discourses on the occult virtues of agates, topazes, the teeth of vipers, the claws of lions, and so forth."—I. p. 64. Ficino himself describes the work as a medical one, and including, therefore, many specifics which he inserted as being popular, though he himself attached no value to them. But Greswell characterizes this as an attempt "to explain, or rather *to equivocate upon*, certain parts of his own writings that appear to favour the superstition in question."—P. 348. As this is partly a matter of opinion, the reader must judge for himself. Ficino's letter is in the *Epistolæ* of Politian (1522), p. 362.

[2] Published in 1510, under the title *Here is conteyned the lyfe of Johan Picus Erle of Mirandula*.

before this he had bene bothe desyrous of glory and kyndled in vayne love. . . . . But after that he was ones with this variaunce wakened, he drew back his mynde flowynge in riot, and turned hit to Chryst." This would be shortly after 1486. His letter of fatherly counsel to his nephew,[1] and the fervid language in which he conversed with him in the orchard of Ferrara, have been often quoted as examples of the warm and enthusiastic piety of Mirandola, and of the change which some cause or other had wrought in his character. That this change was "wrought in measure at least by Savonarola's influence," I should not seek to deny. There seems no doubt that Mirandola met Savonarola at Reggio, when a Chapter of Dominicans was held there, and that he was so impressed with what he saw of him, that he prevailed upon Lorenzo de' Medici to invite him back to Florence.[2] The younger Pico also mentions that, after his uncle's death, Savonarola spoke of that event in a sermon at Florence, and related how for two years he had exhorted Mirandola to enter a religious Order. "He was wonte to be conversaunt with me," he said, "and to breke to me the secretes of his herte, in which I perceyved that he was by privey inspyracion called of god unto relygion. Wherefore he purposed oftentymes to obey this inspyration, and folowe his callynge."[3] The great preacher then expatiated on the loss to Mirandola himself, through not pursuing the course he had marked out for him.

We may or may not be disposed to sympathise with

---

[1] Dated May 15th, 1492.—*Op.* ii. p. 819. It was translated by Gaguin, and published in 1498, under the title of *Conseil pourfitable contre les ennuys et tribulations du monde.* His words acquire a peculiar solemnity, when it is remembered that this same nephew was afterwards murdered, along with his son.

[2] This is stated by J. F. Pico in his *Vita Savonarolæ* (1674), vol. i. p. 20; and also by Burlamacchi, in his *Vita del P. F. Girolamo Savonarola* (1764), p. 15. The latter says that Mirandola "tanto restò preso dalla dottrina sua mirabile, *che non gli pareva poi poter vivere senza lui;* in modo che, trovandosi poi et ragionando di lui con Lorenzo de' Medici, amator grande degli huomini eccellenti, gli persuase che volesse con l'autorità sua operare che egli ritornasse in S. Marco."

[3] More's Translation, leaf C. 2.

Savonarola in this conclusion; we may estimate his influence over Mirandola more or less highly; but I think that in this case, as in that of Ficino, considering the express testimony of the younger Pico, it would be unjust to say that to Savonarola belongs the credit of raising Mirandola from Platonism up to Christianity; and that the religious characters of both of them were formed, before the second Amos began to inveigh against the sins of a second Samaria.[1]

It may be thought that an undue share of attention is being bestowed on these eminent men, connected but indirectly, as they are, with the history of Colet. But their writings are not only quoted in these present treatises, but also directed very materially the current of thought which at that time drew the rising generation of scholars along with it. Without even going beyond the bounds of their writings, we can trace the main stream in which the speculations of the age flowed. If the study of Cicero, which was eagerly pursued by Cicero's countrymen at the revival of letters, encouraged the study of Plato,[2] then Plato not unnaturally led the way to Plotinus. And to the Christian reader of Plotinus, the writings of Dionysius, then not doubted to be the Areopagite, would seem to bid him welcome. "His walls," says Creuzer, "are inlaid with Plotinian mosaic. . . . The rills that water his garden-plots, are drawn from the well-head of Plotinus."[3] We have seen above what a reader and admirer of Plotinus Mirandola was, and that his works were translated by Ficino. It is no surprise, therefore, to find Dionysius a familiar name with both of them.[4] And to the Platonist, who had made his way through Dionysius, what would seem so fitting a completion of his journey as St. Paul? To his writings, and perhaps

---

[1] See Stanley's *Lectures on the Jewish Church*, Part ii. (1865), p. 358.
[2] This is pointed out by Van Heusde, in his *Characterismi princip. Philosoph. vet.* (1839), p. 181.
[3] *Annotationes in Plotini de Pulcr.* (1814), pp. 198, 205.
[4] In Savonarola, too, there are passages which read very much like the *Celestial Hierarchy*. See especially the *Compendium Revelationum* (1495), leaves E 6 and 7 :—" Suspiciens igitur in cœlum vidi novem angelorum choros," etc.

INTRODUCTION.

also to the Epistles of St. John,[1] he would be inclined to turn, as most congenial to the habits of thought in which he had been trained. In reading, for example, the Epistle to the Hebrews, besides the mention of "ministering spirits," which would be so significant to him after Dionysius, he would hear familiar tones in such expressions as "the example and pattern of heavenly things:" "the holy places made with hands, which are the figures of the true:" "through faith we understand that the worlds were made by the word of God, so that things which are seen were not made of things which do appear." He would seem, in all this, to find again the *ideas* of his master Plato. And so we are not surprised to learn that Ficino wrote a commentary on part of the Epistle to the Romans, nor that he publicly lectured on St. Paul, as Canon of the church of St. Lorenzo in Florence;[2] nor finally that Colet, a student of Plato, Plotinus and Dionysius, lectured on St. Paul, on his return to Oxford.

The conclusion to which I would point, from this imperfect account, is, that the Platonic movement, in which Mirandola and Ficino were leading actors, was not an essentially pagan, as opposed to a Christian, movement; but that it directly conduced to the introduction of a purer and more intelligent Christianity. "The most zealous defenders of Christianity," says Van Heusde, "have esteemed the doctrine of Plato to be a prelude of the truest Christianity."[3] If it be a distinguishing feature of Plato's system, that he is ever prosecuting the search for truth, rather than laying down maxims as true; if he proceeds by analysis, and not, as moderns love, by synthesis; then was his method a most salutary one for the wants of that time. Men had long been under the sway of the opposite system: from the

---

[1] Gibbon, in ch. xxi. of his *Decline and Fall*, has some remarks, in his unenviable manner, about the doctrines of Plato gaining currency through St. John.

[2] Villari, i. p. 59; and the article *Ficino* in Herzog's *Encyklopädie*. I am indebted to Mr. Seebohm for this last reference, and for informing me that Ficino is quoted by Colet in his MS. Exposition of the *Romans*.

[3] *Characterismi*, p. 185.

dominant Aristotelianism they had had enough of doctrine and of definition. Weary of this intellectual thraldom, it was well for them that they had found an opener country, as it were, into which their minds could emigrate, and where their reason, confined no longer, could expatiate in purer air and ampler space. Those who think otherwise may relate how Ficino was said to keep a lamp ever burning in his study before an image of Plato;[1] or how Lorenzo de' Medici rejoiced at the discovery amid the ruins of Athens of a long-sought bust of the same philosopher.[2] But those distinguished men knew what Plato had done for them. And if Lorenzo could declare his belief that, without a Platonic training, a man could not easily be either a good citizen, or skilled in Christian doctrine,[3] it is only fair to presume that he looked on Christianity as after all the end; and that his encouragement of the Platonic Academy was something better than a revival of paganism.

In Colet's fondness for Dionysius, in his somewhat argumentative turn of mind, in his slight estimation of the schoolmen, we may see the influence of the Florentine philosophy; and he would probably have returned to England less armed than he was to search out and contend for the truth, and to be the great upholder of a spiritual Christianity, had he never met with the works of Mirandola and Ficino.

§ 6.—*On the Dionysian Writings.*

WHEN Paul "stood in the midst on Mars' hill," the scene was as memorable a one in the actual history of the world, as it is striking to the imagination of the poet.

---

[1] Villari, i. 59.

[2] *Laurentii Medici Vita*, by Nicolaus Valorius (1749), p. 18. Valorius was a disciple of Ficino's, along with his brother Philip. His work, though written in 1492, was not published till the above year, when it was edited by Mehus.

[3] Valorius, *ib.* p. 12 :—" Aiebat idem Ficinus Laurentium dicere solitum, absque Platonica disciplina nec bonum civem, nec Christianæ doctrinæ peritum facile quenquam futurum."

For though the Apostle seemed to leave Athens with but few tokens of success; though only " certain men clave unto him, and believed; among the which was Dionysius the Areopagite, and a woman named Damaris, and others with them;" yet, in the group there assembled, we see something far more pregnant with results than would be judged from the scanty list of converts. We see the contact of the new with the old; the light as of a new dawn beginning to chase away the shadows of the past.

Such as was St. Paul, standing on the spot where once Orestes was fabled to have been tried, looking on the one hand towards the Pnyx, and on the other towards the cave of the Eumenides, such in some degree are the writings that bear the name of Dionysius the Areopagite. As he spake of Jesus and the resurrection in the midst of Athens, where the air still seemed to echo with the appeal of the orator and the debate of the school; so do these writings present a bright centre of Christian truth, encircled, and at times obscured, by the oratory and the philosophy of ancient Greece.

As their external history has been elsewhere briefly traced,[1] and as an able and interesting account of them has recently appeared,[2] I shall confine myself almost wholly to two matters, namely, (1.) the question of date and authorship, and (2.) the subject of the *Hierarchies, Celestial* and *Ecclesiastical*.

1. First in order, in discussing the former of these topics, must be placed the opinion of those who maintain the writings to be the genuine production of the Dionysius converted by St. Paul. This opinion, of course, requires at the outset only to be stated; for, as the burden of proof rests on those who attack it, its probability or improbability will depend on the value of the arguments brought against it.

The chief reasons, then, from external evidence, urged against the writings being genuine, are summed up by

---

[1] *Dean Colet on the Sacraments* (1867), Introd. p. 8.
[2] In an article by Mr. Westcott in the *Contemporary Review* (May, 1867), entitled *Dionysius the Areopagite*.

Erasmus in the note on Acts xvii. 34, in his *Annotationes*. He there points out, after Laurentius Valla, that they are mentioned by none of the ancient Fathers, Greek or Latin.[1] Neither Eusebius, in his Ecclesiastical History, nor Jerome in his Catalogue of Ecclesiastical writers, specifies any such works; though the latter, who "left nothing untouched," includes two persons named Dionysius in his list. Whatever inferences may be drawn from these facts, the facts themselves seem unanswerable. Thus, while some have asserted that these writings are quoted by Origen, Peter Halloix himself, the zealous defender of their genuineness, frankly admits that the *Homilies*, where the quotation is found (*Homilia I. in Joannem*), are not Origen's.[2] And Bellarmine plainly says that Dionysius "was altogether unknown to Ambrose, Augustine, Chrysostom, and other Fathers, so far as can be gathered from their works."[3] And elsewhere he acknowledges that the citations said to be made by Chrysostom and Cyril of Alexandria, are not found in the passages referred to.[4] Nor does it seem a sufficient answer to say that the omission is accidental; inasmuch as, on some occasions, a reference to them would have been most appropriate. Thus how unaccountable seems all want of allusion to them, for example, when Dionysius, Bishop of Corinth, is treating of the conversion of his namesake by St. Paul.[5] And how strange the forgetfulness, in overlooking such a weapon as these writings would have furnished, when the arduous contest against the Arians was being waged.[6]

Hence the only way of escape from the conclusion these

---

[1] "Deinde mirum, si tam priscus autor fuit, et tam multa scripsit, a nemine veterum, seu Græcorum seu Latinorum, fuisse citatum," etc.

[2] *Quæstiones IV.*, appended to Migne's Edition of Dionysius, tom. iv. p. 893.

[3] "Ambrosio, Augustino, Chrysostomo, aliisque patribus incognitus fuit, quantum ex eorum operibus colligi potest."—*De Monachis*, ii. 5, quoted in Hakewill's *Apologie* (1630), p. 215.

[4] *De Scriptoribus Ecclesiasticis*, quoted *ib*.

[5] This is pointed out by Ussher, in his *Dissertatio de scriptis Dionysio suppositis* (1690), p. 285.

[6] Ussher, *ib* p. 281.

facts point to, seems to lie in assuming that the writings in question were sunk in utter oblivion for some centuries, and that, whether by accident, or from an excess of secresy on the part of the few that were initiated in them, they thus eluded observation till the time of Gregory the Great.[1]

When the nature of the treatises themselves is considered, such an assumption appears in a high degree improbable.

If we turn to the internal evidence, we find the arguments on the same side no less strong. In enumerating them, I shall purposely leave out all taken from the *Letters* ascribed to Dionysius, since such compositions are so often wrongly included in the works of ancient writers.

We find, then, in one passage,[2] a quotation from Ignatius:—" Scribit enim divinus Ignatius, 'Meus amor crucifixus est.'" Now, according to Eusebius,[3] these words were written by Ignatius when on his way to Rome to suffer martyrdom, about the ninth year of Trajan's reign. But Dionysius the Areopagite, if we are to believe his biographer, Methodius, suffered under Domitian, two reigns earlier.

We find again, in the same work,[4] a citation from " Clement the philosopher:"—" Si autem vult Clemens philosophus." If this were Clemens Romanus, there would be no difficulty in the matter. But it is urged that Clement of Rome had no pretensions to be called " philosopher;" and that the expression can only refer to Clement of Alexandria (fl. 194), in whose works the opinions cited by Dionysius are, in point of fact, to be found.[5]

Further, in the opening sentences of the *Ecclesiastical Hierarchy*, Timothy is addressed as " son:"—" Sacrorum filiorum sacratissime;" which, it is urged, is an unsuitable expression to be applied to one, who was a convert to the faith sooner than the Areopagite himself. To which may

---

[1] This is the opinion of Bellarmine, quoted by Hakewill, *ut supra*, p. 216.
[2] *De Divinis Nominibus*, iv. § 12.
[3] *Eccl. Hist.* iii. 36; quoted by Ussher, *ut supra*, p. 288.
[4] Ch. v. § 9.
[5] *Stromata*, lib. viii; quoted by Hakewill, *ut supra*, p. 222.

be added the further difficulty, that in both the *Hierarchies*, which are dedicated to Timothy,[1] there are frequent references to the Gospel of St. John. But this, according to the common account, was not written till a period later than the death of Timothy.

Moreover, the precepts laid down by Dionysius respecting Infant Baptism are said by him to be derived from " ancient tradition;"[2] and this, it is held, is language inconsistent with his being a contemporary of the Apostles.

Finally it is alleged that there is a like evidence of lateness of origin in the frequent mention of altars, temples, sponsors in Baptism, and the like;[3] in the general inflation and obscurity of style, savouring little of the lively realities of an Apostolic Christianity;[4] in the use of particular terms, which only after a lapse of time acquired the technical sense in which he employs them;[5] and in the very nature of the subject on which he wrote. Fault is found with his " curious speculations in the secrets of heaven, as if he had bin surveyor thereof, or had taken a muster of all the heavenly host of blessed spirits therein; whereas St. Paul himself, though hee had bin ravished up into the third heaven, even into the paradise of God, yet, returning back, neither durst nor did utter any such thing."[6]

Some of these objections admit of at least a partial answer. What seems irresistible is the cumulative force which they possess. Thus Halloix can maintain, with considerable ingenuity, that the quotation from Ignatius is an interpolation;

---

[1] It is observable that, in these inscriptions, Timothy is addressed as " Fellow-presbyter " by Dionysius. Now the word *Presbyter*, says M. Montet, is not once used in the body of the work, but instead *Hiereus* or *Hierarches.—Des Livres du Pseudo-Denys* (1848), p. 15.

[2] *Eccl. Hier.* vii. § 11. [3] Ussher, *ut supra*, p. 287. [4] *Ib.* p. 293.

[5] " A chaque page des livres de l'Aréopagite se rencontrent des mots qui, outre leur signification primitive, ont une signification historique, et qui n'ont pu être employés, dans le sens que leur donne l'auteur, qu'à une époque déterminée."—Montet, *ut supra*, p. 113. The author proceeds to specify several such terms, which he says are not earlier, in the sense referred to, than the Councils of Alexandria, Ephesus and Chalcedon (an. 451) respectively.

[6] Hakewill, *ut supra*, p. 222.

that the passages from St. John's Gospel were added by the author himself after the death of Timothy:[1] Chifflet can point out that "ancient" and "recent" are comparative terms, and that Dionysius, who lived to a great age, might properly speak of ".ancient tradition;"[2] and so on. But when each single objection can only be got rid of by what may fairly be called a stretch of probability, the cumulative force, as I said, appears but little weakened. And though some eminent names may even yet be counted as upholders of the theory of genuineness,[3] their opinions are not likely to do more than win for them the credit of ingenuity.

Assuming now that good reasons have been shown for rejecting the notion that these writings are really the Areopagite's, it remains to be considered at what time they probably appeared. The two chief opinions (omitting, for brevity's sake, all less supported hypotheses) are those which refer them to the third, and to the fifth centuries.

A principal supporter of the former theory is Baumgarten-Crusius, who thinks that the period of their composition was the age in which Christianity was employed in extricating itself from Gnosticism, and adopting a fixed system of doctrine. This period he judges to be the third century. From the general tone of the writings, he concludes them to be the offspring, not of the monastery, but of the school, and that school an Alexandrian one. In keeping with this view, he disputes the inferences drawn from the supposed lateness of certain words and phrases, and pronounces them to be mere Platonisms.[4] One singular theory is advanced by this author, which has had the effect of discountenancing, to some extent, his conclusions in general. He thinks that the writer, whoever he was, sought to embody in Christ-

---

[1] *Quæstiones, ut supra*, pp. 898, 932.
[2] Petri Francisci Chiffletii *Opuscula* (1679), p. 58.
[3] Baumgarten-Crusius mentions some such :—" Patrocinatur tamen scriptis, atque Areopagitica censet, G. Arnoldus . . . similiterque nuper Ewaldus: suo modo A. Kestnerus."—*Opuscula Theol.* (1836), p. 269, *n.* More recently the Abbé Darboy prefixed a defence of their genuineness to his translation of the Dionysian writings: Paris, 1845.
[4] See above, p. xxxvi. *n.* 5.

ianity the esoteric doctrines of the ancient Dionysian mysteries; and that hence he took the name of Dionysius. For this, he argues, is clearly a symbolic name, like Hierotheus, and others; since, had the writer merely wished to pass for a disciple of St. Paul, he would not have selected a name to disguise himself under, which, however celebrated in other respects, had no philosophic reputation attached to it.[1]

But the theory which has on the whole found most favour, is that which refers them to the latter end of the fifth, or the beginning of the sixth, century. Such is the opinion of Montet,[2] and of Gieseler;[3] and it is accepted by Mr. Westcott; who concludes his enquiries into the subject of date by saying that "the error cannot be great, if it be conjectured that they were composed A.D. 480—520, either at Edessa, or under the influence of the Edessene school."[4] Mr. Westcott agrees with Baratier in thinking that there is no ground for considering the writings to be a forgery, though he does not go so far as to acquit them of being pseudonymous.[5] In any case the real name of the author will probably still remain unknown. Time has in one respect dealt with these remarkable monuments of the Alexandrian mind (if such indeed they be), as it dealt with the Pharos, which was Alexandria's material monument. In the one case, as in the other, it has shewn the name outwardly inscribed on the work to be unenduring; but it has not yet, in the one case as in the other, revealed the name of the true artificer chiselled underneath.[6]

---

[1] *Opuscula*, ut supra, pp. 270—274. Not greatly differing in his conclusion, as to the date, is Bishop Pearson, who assigns the works to the fourth century.—*Vindiciæ Epist. Ignatii* (1852), i. p. 249.

[2] *Ut supra*, p. 116.

[3] *Compendium of Theol. Hist.* tr. by Davidson (1848), ii. p. 113.

[4] Art. in *Contemp. Rev.*, ut supra, p. 7.

[5] Baratier, in the third Dissertation appended to his *Disquisitio Chronologica* (1740), maintains that the writer was a Dionysius, i.e. Dionysius of Alexandria; and that all the expressions, which represent him as the Areopagite, are additions by over-zealous scribes, who wished to magnify their subject.

[6] "Le nom de l'auteur," says M. Montet, "restera probablement inconnu."—P. 133.

INTRODUCTION.

2. In approaching the study of the *Hierarchies* themselves, it is difficult to restrain a vague feeling of wonder. As none but a poet can understand a poet, so to read Dionysius aright, there is need of something of that old Dionysiac fervour, in which the mind of the devotee was transported beyond itself, and lost all individuality in an adoration of what it worshipped.[1]

To trace the first origin of mysticism, we should no doubt have to travel, as Meier says,[2] to the banks of the Ganges or the Hydaspes. But I think that, with a less remote search, a point may be reached, from which, though not as from a parent lake, the stream of the Dionysian writings, and others akin to them, may be deduced. I refer to that part of Plato's teaching in which he treats of the communication between God and man; and especially to the passage in the *Symposium*, where Diotima relates the birth and office of Eros, or Love. The child of Poros and Penia, himself neither a mortal nor an immortal, but a genius between the two, he is ever busied in "interpreting and conveying to the gods what comes from men, and to men what comes from the gods; on the part of the one, their prayers and sacrifices, and on the part of the other, their behests and requitals of the sacrifices of men. And being midway between both, he fills every void, so that the universe is firmly compacted together."[3]

The thought was one which appears to have worked in the minds of Mirandola,[4] and other leaders of the Florentine school, and which had been laid hold of and developed by the Neo-Platonists of an earlier generation.

---

[1] With words to this effect Ficino begins his translation of the *Mystica Theologia* of Dionysius. After speaking of the mental effect of the old Dionysian, or Bacchic, mysteries, he says " Hoc igitur Dionysiaco mero Dionysius noster ebrius exultat passim . . . . Idem profecto, ad id facile consequendum, necessarius omnino nobis divinus est furor."—*Op.* (1641), ii. p. 1.

[2] *Dionysii et Mysticorum doctrinæ* (1845), p. 1.

[3] *Symposium*, 202, E.

[4] See the passages quoted below, p. 9, n. 2, and p. 133, n. 2.—Dante and Ficino are among the commentators on the *Symposium*.

How does the Supreme Being communicate himself to man: by what stages of ascent can man raise himself up to God: these are the problems which have occupied the thoughtful in all ages. In the allegory of the birth of Eros, Plato shadowed forth one solution of them; and the *Hierarchies* of Dionysius seem to be chiefly a contribution towards the same result.

The writings of the Neo-Platonists all bear witness of the extent to which these problems absorbed men's minds. Thus, whilst Plato had spoken of the lives of the Musician, the Lover, and the Philosopher, as being three ways by which the human soul might rise to the Divine, so Plotinus had marked out three ways, almost identical with those, of reaching the same goal; namely, those of Music, Love, and Reason.[1] As the one who is "moved by concord of sweet sounds" may learn to withdraw his mind from the externals of music, and gradually drink in that harmony of the *intelligible* world, with which the mechanism of this sensible world vibrates in unison; so the Lover may rise from admiration of material beauty to the immaterial; and so lastly, by Reason, or Metaphysics, the mind may be wholly lifted above the sensible, and enjoy uninterrupted commune with the invisible and eternal.

In some passages Plotinus speaks of the Divine Vision, which the mind thus elevated can enjoy, in language that forcibly reminds us of Dionysius. "*He* is not unfortunate," he exclaims, "that findeth not beauty of complexion, or fairness of person, or power, or dominions, or a kingdom; but he that faileth of this Divine Vision alone; for the obtaining whereof it were meet to abandon kingdoms, and dominion over every land, yea and over every sea, and over heaven itself; if only, by forsaking and despising these, one might see and turn to that."[2] And elsewhere he has a striking comparison about man's purification to the truly beautiful. Just as a statuary, he says, chips away from the

---

[1] *Ennead I. De Dialectica*; quoted by Creutzer in his *Præparatio* to the *Liber de Pulchritudine* of Plotinus (1814), p. civ.
[2] *De Pulchritudine*, c. vii.

block of marble what are in his eyes but as excrescences on the fair image he sees beneath, and smoothes and polishes it till the beautiful countenance stands revealed; so should man labour upon himself, and "not cease fashioning his own image, till there beams forth for him a godlike splendour, and he sees Temperance moving in holy purity."[1]

The same notion of laying aside all that is extraneous, that the image of God may be restored in man, and he may return to what he feels his proper resting-place, is brought out in Porphyry, the immediate disciple of Plotinus. "We seem like exiles," he says, in a passage that calls to mind the *Intimations of Immortality*, "who have emigrated to nations of another race, and are not only banished from their own homes, but have become filled with foreign affections, and manners, and customs, and have gained an inclination for them. And just as he that means to return from thence to his own land, not only longs to be on his journey, but also takes pains to lay aside everything foreign that he has acquired, in order that he may be received back again; and calls to mind what he had forgotten that he possessed, without which it were impossible for him to be received again by those of his own country; so in like manner must we, if we would return from hence to what is truly our native home, lay aside all things that we have acquired from our mortal nature, along with our propensity for them . . . . and recall that blessed and eternal existence, and hasten to return to the colourless and unqualified."[2]

Still more clearly in Proclus, the last of the great Neo-Platonists, may we discern the thoughts, and almost the very language of Dionysius. "Beginning from beneath,"

---

[1] *Ib.* c. ix.—Compare with this what Dionysius writes in the *Cel. Hier.* iii. 3:—"Oportet igitur, ut arbitror, eos qui purgantur, puros effici omnino, etc.;" and what Colet has below (p. 96), "God portrays his own full image, if man will aim wholly and untiringly at it."

[2] *De abstinentia*, Lib. I. (Ed. Fogerolles, 1620), p. 59. This notion of *colour* and *quality*, as defects, will be illustrated by what Colet writes concerning ceremonies, "whereby men are drawn through manifold colours to the pure light itself, that is luminous to its innermost, and becomes not coloured in passing through dim signs."—P. 97.

he writes in one place,[1] when describing the successive hindrances to be overcome, in our ascent to the Divine, "we must shun the multitude of mankind, who go in droves, and must neither be partakers of their lives nor their opinions. We must avoid the manifold desires, which distract us in attending on the body, and which cause us to pursue first one external object and then another; now irrational pleasures, and now undefined and conflicting actions. For these fill us with regrets and troubles." And as the spiritual athlete is thus to shun that "multiplicity," which Dionysius, and Colet after him, speaks of so often, so is he bidden by every means to strive after unity.[2] The life of Proclus himself, as related by Marinus, was an exhibition of such a strife. And we are at once reminded of the familiar "purification, illumination and perfection," when we read of the three stages through which he passed—of virtues political, purgatorial and contemplative.[3] That theurgic state, to which his biographer declares that Proclus by this triple ascent attained, may correspond to the state of beatific vision, which the Christian philosopher sets forth as the highest elevation to which the mind of man can soar.

Not without reason, then, does Fabricius conclude, that Proclus and Dionysius "ploughed with one and the same Neo-platonic heifer."[4] And in reading the following pages the reader will hardly fail to be struck with the resemblance in tone between Dionysius and what has just been quoted. In the Jacob's ladder, which this author would describe as linking all earth with heaven, he will see something more real than any mere flight of fancy; he will see a mind labouring, cumbrously, no doubt, but powerfully, to make plain the way between God and man; and to teach how man, "rightly apprehending his own position in the chain of

---

[1] *De Unitate et Pulchritudine*, c. ii.
[2] *Ib.* c. iii.—Compare the *Eccl. Hier.* vi. 3. § 2, and p. 95 below.
[3] Marini *Procli Vita* (Ed. Fabricius, 1703), pp. 26—49.
[4] "Fateor tamen mihi longe videri credibilius, utrumque, et Proclum et larvatum illum Dionysium Areopagitam una eademque Neoplatonicorum vitula arasse, quam Proclum ex Dionysio profecisse, ejusque verba scriptis suis inseruisse."—Ib. *Prolegomena*, p. xii.

INTRODUCTION.

being, might elevate himself through the next higher order to communion with still higher orders, and finally with God himself."[1]

As to the outward system, or agency, by which Dionysius would bring about this result, it will be so readily apprehended from Colet's summary of it, as to require little to be said here.

Accustomed to the notion of emanations from the Divine Being, which had gradually been materialized and distorted by the successors of Plotinus, he seems to have adapted to these the various names for the angelic host which he found in Scripture, and thus to have laid the groundwork of his Celestial Hierarchy. And when it is considered how all but silent the Scriptures are concerning "Thrones, Princedoms, Pow'rs, Dominions," and the other "orders and degrees" which Dionysius recounts, it will readily be imagined that these are in fact little more than titles by which those emanations might be denoted; and that the orders themselves have only that slight individuality, which could be derived to them from the import of their names.[2]

The Ecclesiastical Hierarchy, in keeping with this, is looked upon as only a continuation of the Celestial. It is but the end which touches earth of the same heavenly ladder; the divine rays are the same, but refracted through another medium. As the imagination of Dionysius, and after him of Milton, beheld the angelic host in ninefold array

"Under their Hierarchs, in orders bright,"

so the Church on earth presented a faint, but true, reflection

---

[1] Gieseler, *Theol. Hist.* (tr. by Davidson), ii. p. 113. Compare below, p. 100, "Every descent of divinity is for the ascent of humanity, &c."

[2] "Some, as Proclus, Hermias, Syrianus, and many others, betwixt God and the rational soul place a great number of creatures . . . . Plotinus, Porphyrius, and generally the most refined Platonists, betwixt God and the soul of the world assigne onely one creature, which they call the Son of God, because immediately produced by him. The first opinion complies most with Dionysius Areopagita, and Christian Divines, who assert the number of Angels to be in a manner infinite."—Mirandola's *Plátonick Discourse* (tr. by Stanley, 1651), p. 217.

of it. In the words of Dean Milman, "The triple earthly sacerdotal order had its type in heaven, the Celestial Orders their antitype on earth. The triple and novene division ran throughout, and connected, assimilated, almost identified the mundane and supermundane Church. As there were three degrees of attainment, Light, Purity, Knowledge (or the Divine Vision), so there were three Orders of the Earthly Hierarchy, Bishops, Priests, and Deacons; three Sacraments, Baptism, the Eucharist, the Holy Chrism; three classes, the Baptized, the Communicants, the Monks. How sublime," he continues, "how exalting, how welcome to the sacerdotalism of the West this lofty doctrine! The Celestial Hierarchy were as themselves; they themselves were formed and organized after the pattern of the great Orders in heaven."[1]

This, however, will be so readily understood from the pages of Colet himself, whose orderly cast of mind appears to have found a peculiar pleasure in such symmetry of arrangement,[2] that no more need here be said upon the subject. I would only beg the reader not to lose sight, in the course of the various details, of what has been pointed out as the main object of Dionysius in his *Hierarchies*;[3] namely, to show the relation of the soul to God, and the means by which it may be raised from its earthly prison-house to the unclouded glory of the Divine presence.

---

[1] *History of Latin Christianity* (1855), vi. p. 405.

[2] Quite in keeping with this, we find him, in the opening of his sermon at the installation of Wolsey as Cardinal, in 1515, comparing the cardinalate to the order of Seraphim, "which continually burneth in the love of the glorious Trinity."—See the passage quoted by Mr. Seebohm, in his *Oxford Reformers of* 1498, p. 274.

[3] The term *Hierarchy* is defined by Dionysius himself to be "a sacred order, and science, and energy, which approaches as near as possible to the godlike" (*Cel. Hier.* iii. § 1); or, as M. Montet expresses it, "La hiérarchie est donc à la fois ordre, science et puissance, conforme autant qu'il se peut aux attributs divins, et reproduisant par ses splendeurs originelles comme un reflet des choses qui sont en Dieu."—*Ut supra,* p. 101.

§ 7.—*On Colet's deviations from Dionysius.*

ALTHOUGH it has been found convenient to speak of these Treatises as "abstracts" of the corresponding works of Dionysius, the term is not an altogether adequate one. Following his author faithfully, in the main, both in the arrangement of his subject, and in his conclusions and general tone of thought, Colet pauses at times to treat more fully of some passing topic than is done in the original.[1] Occasionally, too, he passes over a chapter of the *Hierarchies* altogether, that he may stay the longer at some halting-place of greater importance.[2]

But what it more concerns us to notice, is the way in which he corrects, or supplements, the Dionysian view of two subjects of the highest interest; namely, the work of man's Redemption, with its attendant mystery of the Incarnation; and the nature and existence of evil, as shewn especially in the working of evil spirits.

The former of these subjects is scarcely brought out, even by Dean Colet himself, with the explicitness which might have been desired. But his language is full and scriptural in its tone, when compared with that of Dionysius.[3] The latter speaks, indeed, of "God himself deigning to come to us, through his love of man;"[4] but his words in this passage are few and indistinct, and rather distantly allude to the fact, than declare it. In another place[5] he says more distinctly, "We have heard as a mystery that Jesus was made in substance as a man;" but he adds, "We know not how he was fashioned of the Virgin's substance by a law other than natural; nor how, with feet bearing a corporeal mass and weight of matter, he passed dryshod over this watery and fleeting existence." And he then goes on to say that "these topics have been elsewhere set forth;" referring apparently to treatises now lost. In any case,

---

[1] See especially his long discussion on Infant Baptism, p. 155, and *n*.
[2] See below, p. 34, *n*. 2.
[3] See below, p. 61, *n*.
[4] *Eccl. Hier.* ii. 2, § 1.
[5] *De Divin. Nom.* ii. 9.

neither in what he writes himself, nor in the mystical extract which he proceeds to quote from his preceptor Hierotheus,[1] is there anything explicit on the subject of the Incarnation and Redemption of mankind.

In truth, convenient as it may be to speak of these doctrines as "sufficiently set forth elsewhere," the Dionysian system hardly admits of the Scriptural doctrine of man's Redemption. The Orders of the two Hierarchies fill up all the space between God and the humblest human soul; the chain is too complete to admit of such an interruption as the work of a personal Saviour. "The office that Christ should have discharged," says Meier, "is discharged by this order of Hierarchies."[2]

But Colet speaks on this topic unequivocally, if briefly;[3] and in the *De Sacramentis Ecclesiæ* especially, which may properly be regarded as a sequel to these present writings, he brings into due proportion the facts both of the Incarnation and Redemption.[4]

In the other instance given, the difference between their methods of treating the subject is equally striking. Whilst Colet speaks of evil spirits as "incessantly waging war against men,"[5] and as "destined to be hereafter more miserable, after the last judgment,"[6] Dionysius denies that they are evil by nature;[7] denies, in fact, the existence of positive evil in the universe altogether. That, in some way or other,

---

[1] *De Divin. Nom.* ii. § 10.

[2] *Ut supra*, p. 19. He says also very truly, "De incarnatione disputat quidem Areopagita, sed ita ut revera negetur potius quam agnoscatur. . . . Ipsa Christi lux illuminare mundum nequit, nisi per hierarchias eo descenderit."—Compare below, p. 55, *n*.

[3] See below, pp. 61, 62.

[4] Compare p. 59:—" Qui ob id causæ solum assumpsit hominem, ut spiritalem et divinam in homine vitam ostendat hominibus, doceatque quam vestem nuptialem induat homo, si velit a Deo in uxorem duci." Also p. 65:—" Hic est Iesus, masculinus Deo, et femininus humanitate, per quam attraxit sibi reliquos homines in completionem conjugis suæ, etc.;" where there is still very prominent the Dionysian idea of God's *drawing man to him*, rather than of being propitiated on man's behalf.

[5] See below, p. 45.   [6] *Ibid*. p. 44.

[7] "Sed neque dæmones natura sua mali sunt," etc. *De Divin. Nom.* iv. 23.

INTRODUCTION.

there is that in the world which we call evil, Dionysius is of course unable to gainsay; but as he cannot account for the presence of an active antagonistic principle, after starting with a First Cause, perfectly wise, and good, and powerful, from whom all things proceed, he is driven back upon optimism. He maintains that even the Devils " are called bad, because of weakness in respect of their natural energy."[1] In other words, all things were created perfectly good; and if any beings discover opposite qualities, it must be through their failing to keep up to their proper standard of goodness. Evil is a failure, a defect, not an active intelligent power working in opposition to God.[2]

Very different is this from the language of Colet, referred to above, and from the equally strong expressions in the *De Sacramentis,* touching the mischief continually wrought in the world by those angels " who apostatized through their own wickedness; the one who, from an Angel of Light became an Angel of Darkness, the Devil, and his ministers."[3]

It may be observed, in conclusion, that Colet plainly held up the Dionysian writings, as a glass to his own times. Again and again does he revert from the ideal portrayed in the *Hierarchies* to the realities around him, and end with some indignant apostrophe upon the contrast they present.[4] It might have been expected that more attention would be given, in this *Introduction,* to such a phase of the subject; that, considering the disputes now rife on matters of ecclesiastical doctrine and ritual, an endeavour would be made to gather opinions on those points from the present Treatises.

---

[1] " Pravi autem dicuntur, quatenus in naturali actione sunt imbelles." —*De Divin. Nom.* iv. 23.

[2] See Mr. Westcott's Essay, above quoted, p. 21; and M. Montet (p. 86), who shews the similarity between this theory and the optimism of Plotinus.

[3] *De Sacramentis,* p. 39. And so further on in the same treatise:— " Sua sponte longe abiit a Deo, qui erat conjunctissimus, Lucifer ille factuosus, secum contrahens in suas partes magnam angelorum catervam; quorum culpa invenialis, et discessus irrevocabilis est, quod scienter et sponte commissus erat."—P. 50.

[4] Compare pp. 123, 126, 136, 151, and elsewhere.

But I consider this to be no part of my task. In translating what Dean Colet wrote more than three hundred and fifty years ago, I am anxious that his words should go forth with no suspicion of party bias attached to them; but that they should be received by some few, at least, of those fellow-citizens, whose forefathers gathered round him in St. Paul's, as words of honest truth and Christian love.

CELESTIAL HIERARCHY.

DEDICATION.

I KNOW thy lofty and angelic mind,[1] my worthy and cherished friend; a mind that deserves in truth not only to hear of angels, but moreover to be associated with them. Wherefore I would share with thee what within the last day or two I have read and retained in memory from Dionysius the Areopagite, in that treatise of his which is entitled *On the Celestial Hierarchy*, in which he discourses of the angels in a glorious and heavenly manner. For in what I have thus retained, and in what I have learnt in that treatise, this is the very first and chiefest principle, that, whatsoever benefit we have received from other sources, we should freely share and communicate in succession to others. Since herein we imitate the inestimable goodness of God,[2] who bestows and imparts himself in due order to all; and who gives whatever he gives, to the intent that it should in turn be straightway transmitted by the receiver to another, so far as is meet: that thus, by the gifts of God being distributed and dispersed from one to another, all alike may own that

---

[1] Erasmus, in the *Ciceronianus*, makes one of his characters to say "Fateor *Angelum* prorsus *angelica* fuisse mente," alluding to Angelo Poliziano; but the date of his death (Sept. 22, 1494) apart from other considerations, precludes the thought of his being the friend here mentioned.

[2] So Savonarola, in his sixteenth sermon on Job, makes Christ to say: "But if, on the contrary, you see men who do not diffuse and allow others to partake of the talents which I gave them, it is a clear sign that they in no degree share that goodness which is in me."—Villari's *Hist.* tr. by Horner, i. 333.

God is good, and may be themselves also united together through the divine goodness.

Accept therefore what my memory[1] has retained from that perusal of Dionysius, which I will compendiously and briefly touch upon, following the order of the chapters.

CHAPTER I.

On the Emanation from God the Father of all Spiritual Light and Grace; and on the means through which it is conveyed to Man.

IN the First Chapter it is said that from the Father of Lights there goes forth and spreads through all creation a bright and spiritual light, recalling all things to itself, so far as their several natures permit; that everything may be established in its own order and degree, and, according to the capacity of its nature, may be perfected in God. That light is one and entirely the same through all things, not changed by the change of objects, but rather, so far as is possible, drawing what is various and diverse to a likeness and unity with itself. In this oneness and identity of light in all cases there is a diversity of objects, and the light remains one and undivided in different objects; so that, without confusion, you may assign always variety to the objects, identity to the light.

---

[1] Colet's memory was a very retentive one, and formed the subject of a strange story in Wirtzung's "General Practise of Physicke" (1605) p. 120; part of which was quoted by Thos. Smith, in his edition of Colet's sermon, and after him by Knight. It sets forth that "there was by our time at Canterburie here in England a Canon, a Doctor of Divinitie and also in the law, named Johannes Coletus, to whom, by that time he was sixteene yeares old, was an experiment imparted by a Christened Jew, whereby he obtained such a marvellous strong memorie that he retained and kept all that he ever read in all his life time." Various instances of this strength of memory then follow, as well as the "experiment," or prescription itself, which is singular enough. The story is probably worthless, except to show, as I think it may be fairly taken to do, that Dean Colet's memory was a matter of common remark.

Now as for rational creatures, which have a capacity for the divine nature itself, that marvellous shining of the heavenly sun rarefies them, as it were, and lightens them by its touch, and lifts them up closely to itself, yea and draws them,[1] and even makes them one with itself. In this great happiness are all those spiritual natures, which we call by the common name of angels; on whom the light is shed forth in its untempered purity. For by reason of the singleness of their nature, they are not unmeet to be suffused with open and unallayed truth. But as for men, who occupy the last place among rational beings, and who are not themselves of a single and undivided nature (since there clings to their souls the heavy and wearisome mass of the body, in which the soul, degenerating from its simplicity, becomes in some degree corporeal, so as now to be unfitted and altogether unable to gaze upon the purely spiritual, and so weakened also by admixture of the body, as to be powerless to endure any strong light, but to shrink from it, as though sickly and feeble, and to shun it and stumble at it);—as for these men, I say, when our good and bountiful God would not have them wholly void of his light and truth and grace, it was brought about by the ministry of angels, that, to suit their nature and capacity, the ray of the heavenly sun and the truth of God should, as it were, abase itself a little to their condition; bodily, that is, and sensible; to the end that the mind of man, become well nigh corporeal in the body, might behold the radiance of so great a light without shrinking from it; and, with countenance now akin to it and more able to endure, might give it entrance, and under cover of sense, so far as is possible, might behold the truth, now

---

[1] In the MS. treatise by Colet " De Compositione Sancti Corporis Christi mistici," is a striking passage on the uniting and attractive power of the Spirit of God :—" Hoc divinum vinculum ecclesiæ in Christo Jesu vel spiritus ipse est Dei in Christo, vel ejus virtus conglutinans ; quæ est ejusmodi in ecclesia ferme cujusmodi coaguli virtus in lacte qua coagulatur, vel certe perinde se habet ut magnetis vis in ferro, qua trahitur ferrum et suspenditur. Omnes sumus tracti in spiritum Dei, ut ex spiritu Dei solo pendeamus, qui noster est quasi magnes, et horologii nostri temperatio."—*Camb. MS.* Gg, iv. 26, fol. 70 b.

rendered almost corporeal through the indication of corporeal signs and figures. And this naked truth, when she could not of her own self penetrate men's minds, recognizing the intimacy which the soul has with the senses, entered on another course, and through these senses, as through convenient means, sought to convey herself to men's souls; in order that, what could not be accomplished by the former method—the participation of truth by mankind—might by the latter at any rate be in some way brought to pass. And so, that which flows from God in a pure, simple and unmixed state upon the angels, to promote their stability, order and perfection, when it further proceeds to men, declining from its purity and simplicity, becomes by the ministration of angels to some degree perceptible to their senses. The very objects of sense, such as have the greatest resemblance, thus, so far as is possible, represent the truth; that man, placed midway between the material and the immaterial, may be led by the body to the spirit, by the senses to the understanding, by the shadow to the light, by the image to the truth; that finding truth at length, he may then wholly despise the flesh, and striving after the spirit may rest in spiritual truth alone. So, and by such ways, would the good God, of his marvellous loving-kindness, recall degraded men to his own loftiness, and restore them at length to truth and light itself; which is none other than our Jesus, blessed for evermore. For that great Creator, and unutterable cause of all order, is a glorious and mighty pattern to the first hierarchy, and to that holy princedom,[1] which is fired with such great love, which strives with all its might to represent God, and to move all that are beneath them to represent him in turn. And thus, as God teaches the first hierarchy, so does it the second, and the second the third. Then the third hierarchy of angels, seeing the ignorance of men upon earth (who are in the fourth place) and their unfitness for performing divine offices, purposely ordained for a time, by the will of God, that men should

---

[1] The word princedoms is used afterwards to denote the chief of the three orders in the third, or lowest, hierarchy of angels; but here it is only a further term to signify the highest hierarchy in general.

imitate the angels in their bodies and bodily actions; to the intent that they, who in spirit had been unable, through their bodily dulness, might at any rate in a figurative manner, in their flesh and body itself, so far as is possible, exhibit God. This corporeal and carnal hierarchy and order among men, purifying, illumining and perfecting, or rather significant of purification, illumination and perfection, was (under Moses the teacher of the Hebrews) the Synagogue; which imitated the angels by bodily objects and sensible signs, not by intellectual and spiritual. Yet Moses himself was not ignorant of the truth, after the pattern of which he disposed the Hebrews. Nor was he unaware himself, moreover, that there would one day be a Man, in whom not an angel but the Truth itself should speak; and who would, in spirit, advance men to the truth which he, Moses, had shadowed forth in their bodies. This is our most blessed Jesus, "the Sun of Righteousness," who has not only shown us what was the meaning of those shadowy ordinances of Moses, but has also enlightened our understanding to believe what is revealed. Meanwhile, however, it was brought to pass, that on earth there should be only visible that empty shadow of order and of some hierarchy; that the advancement and translation of mankind to an angelic state might appear to proceed in a just order; namely, from the shadow to the image, and from the image to the truth. Under Moses there was the shadow; in Christ there now exists on earth the luminous image; the reality we shall hereafter have in heaven. Under Moses the system of the Hebrews, and their Synagogue, was such as to contain a measure of light in very much shade. Whilst, on the other hand, we are here in the Church of Christ, there is very great light, but at the same time along with it some duskiness and shade; yet still so overpowered by the light, that it should rather be called colour than shade. For colour consists of darkness and light.[1]

In truth the Church, whilst we are here in the body,

---

[1] This definition of *colour* should be noticed in passing, as it will help to explain one or two subsequent passages.

neither is, nor can be, without sensible signs; but they are here in due measure, and are very needful for keeping weaker members in the Church, that they may be admonished by sense when they are receiving the Spirit within their soul. And the Spirit descends not upon men, so long as they are creatures of sense, except by means of sensible signs; which, during our life here, are the foundations and essential matter[1] of the Christian sacraments; and without which men cannot be initiated, and imbued with the reality of the sacred rites. This is the cause, as Dionysius relates, of the holy mystery of Communion; in which the sacred fellowship of Jesus in the spirit is profitably recognized.

All the other sacraments moreover have their own material form underlying them, meetly and fitly employed; through which those to whom the spirit is administered, learn that, whilst living here, they are but men, and are as yet by no means fitted for the unshrouded spirit. A time indeed will come, when the darkness and mortality of our body shall be wholly done away, and there shall be perceived by us, neither shadow nor colour, but the untempered and radiant light in all its naked simplicity; when what we now believe shall be realized and accomplished.

But, to return to Dionysius, the topic treated of and demonstrated in this chapter is, to speak briefly, the flowing forth from God of a common spiritual and divine light, and its gracious passage through all things, and reception by each, according to each one's capacity. On the Angels, who are of clear and transparent natures, the light is poured forth in naked simplicity; but for men, according to the wonderful goodness of God, it is administered[2] with folds and

---

[1] In the *Eccl. Hier.* ii. 3, Dionysius speaks of having shewn at length, in a work now lost, *De Intelligibilibus et Sensibilibus*, that "visible Sacraments are figures of what is spiritual:"—"Visibilia sacramenta intelligibilium imagines quædam [sunt]." On which Corderius remarks: "Itaque, secundum Dionysium, omne Sacramentum non tantum constituitur ex materia et forma sensibili, sed etiam ex natura sensibili et forma spiritali seu intelligibili." This he further illustrates by the analogy of the bodily framework and the soul in man.

[2] Perhaps, instead of "ministratam," the reading should be "instratam," "overspread."

coverings, so to speak; that it may not by its excessive brightness dazzle and offend the weak eyes of their mind; and that men may be more conveniently drawn, through fit sensible signs, to the truth signified.

CHAPTER II.

On the Use of Symbolic Acts and Words.

THEOLOGY, which is the revelation of divine truth, and the language of the prophets,[1] takes great count of human weakness; and when it would regenerate that weakness to a heavenly state, it makes the heavenly and spiritual natures to degenerate in some measure, and brings them down to the lowly state of men, to be objects of their senses to some degree; describing the condition of things divine and the ranks of the blessed spirits by poetic fictions. But this, not in that which is altogether fictitious, lest there should be too little authority in a mere fable, but in the persons of actually living men, and also in their actions with one another; that so there may first exist a sort of stage, and rude show, and indistinct representation, albeit not of the absolute truth itself, yet still of some figure of it that is to be; and that this latter may afterwards be more brightly manifested, and more clearly reproduce the reality itself; its shade being in some measure brought forth to the light, and the darkness that there was being as it were illumined with colours. For, as I have said before, the Synagogue of the Jews is as a shadow; the Church, in Christ, its Sun, as shade variously illumined. And this Church, like some object beautifully coloured by receiving the light of the Sun, was foreshadowed on earth by all that system and

---

[1] This term, like *Theologi*, is used by Dionysius to signify the authors of Holy Scripture generally, as "speaking forth" the revealed will of God. It is more fully explained by Colet below, at the beginning of chap. vi.

order established among the Jews by Moses. Which foreshadowing, when the "Sun of Righteousness," Jesus Christ, arose, he illumined by sending forth upon it the rays of His truth, in varied measure, according to its varying capacity; and caused it to be fit to gaze upon openly and in the day, by bringing forth the shadow to be a bright image, and transforming the Synagogue into the Church; day dispelling the darkness of night; to the end that men should no longer walk and live here in darkness and the shades of night, but in the light of God, under Christ their Sun, and in the spirit; that at length hereafter, being translated to the reality itself, in the day of days, and sabbath of sabbaths, they may rest together in happiness.

As those Jews trained themselves by the disposal of their bodies and of their actions after a certain principle, so it is the duty of Christians to follow out in soul and spirit, whatever was there signified, that not a single jot may pass away. These spiritual acts, whether of the shadow that preceded, or of the reality which followed, and which was a figure of the reality that is to be, arise from faith; that is to say, from the fact that men believe in Jesus Christ, who shewed openly at length what was the meaning and signification of the foreshadowing by Moses, and of all that hierarchy of the Synagogue (carried on, as it was, by bodies, not by souls), and what was its tendency. They who believe this gospel and good tidings, and also in consequence of their faith, perform with soul and spirit what is signified, like Jesus, who taught not in words only, but still more distinctly by action,—they truly are in the day, and walk, as it were, more brightly coloured, and in fair order among themselves; and in their actions one with another, spiritual and clear in a high degree, represent both more nearly and more brightly the true aspect of the heavenly spirits. Into this image, as St. Paul says, they are "transformed from glory to glory, even as by the Spirit of the Lord." And in this image[1] they will at length be in the reality itself; which now, as

2 Cor. iii. 18.

---

[1] That is, "by continuing in this image," which will gradually open out into the reality, as a river opens out into the ocean.

best they can, they spiritually represent in a figurative order and acts, believing in Christ, and eagerly looking for the full and perfect reality they will have with the angels. This is what St. Paul writes to the Galatians: "For we through the Spirit wait for the hope of righteousness by faith." Meanwhile we live by faith, "which worketh by love," in which is "the fulfilling of the law." This is the "short work which the Lord has made upon the earth."[1] Thus by God's wonderful dispensation of things, and care, as it were, of the human race, that it may be fashioned again for happiness, has there first gone before a faint shadow of the divine countenance, drawing men to a closer image of that same countenance, that at length they may be transformed into the reality of the selfsame countenance; to the end that no longer either in a shadow, or in an image, or in the Church here on earth, "as through a glass, darkly," but "face to face" they may behold the true countenance of God itself; then, namely, when "it shall have appeared what men shall be," as saith St. John, and "they shall see him as he is." Now, however, none seeth either God or things divine: we believe Jesus Christ, the "messenger of the great counsel:"[2] "the only begotten Son, which is in the bosom

Gal. v. 5, 6.

Rom. ix. 28.

1 Cor. xiii. 12.

1 John iii. 2.

Isai. ix. 6.

---

[1] In what sense the author uses this passage is not quite clear. The words themselves are quoted by St. Paul, from Isai. x. 23, where the Almighty "is represented, in the language of men, as making a short and summary *reckoning* (*logon*, i. e. *tale* or *account*), with the entire population of the land of Israel." See Peile on Rom. ix. 28. Through the influence of the Septuagint on the Apostle's quotation, that which in the Vulgate of Isaiah appears as "consummationem et abbreviationem," in the Vulgate of Rom. ix. 28, is "verbum breviatum." I suppose, therefore, that Colet, thinking chiefly of the term *verbum*, understood by it not any "work," (as in the E.V.), or summary visitation of God; but rather a revelation of the Eternal Word, "shorn of his splendours" (abbreviatum), a specimen only of the glory to be revealed in Him hereafter. In Wycliffe's version (Forshall and Madden, 1850), the verse stands thus; "Forsothe a word makynge an ende, and abreggynge in equyte, for the Lord schal make a word breggid on al the erthe."

[2] This expression, which Colet often recurs to, is from the Septuagint version of Isaiah ix. 6. The English version, "And his name shall be called Wonderful, Counsellor," agrees with the Latin, "Admirabilis, Consiliarius." A full discussion of the reading will be found in Bos's

of the Father, he hath declared him." He has declared it to be the time for the image of Moses' describing to come forth more clearly among men, and exhibit the countenance of God and the Trinities of the Angels. He has offered Himself as leader, and instituted a chorus, and a more radiant sacred dance, if one may say it,[1] that men, with hands joined in concert, may follow his steps, placing reliance on him in all things; whereby he signifies more closely and distinctly the state of heavenly things upon earth, and the imitation of God among men. Through such means and convenient methods, by the marvellous goodness and loving-kindness of God towards men, there is a recalling and drawing back to heavenly things; from the body to the spirit, from the spirit to God; that men, being in this life made spiritual in Christ, out of corporeal and carnal, may hereafter be most blessedly made godlike in God Himself. Men themselves are inwardly in a true and gradual progress to what is better; from clear to clearer; that they may discern more and more distinctly the truth of the Divine countenance and righteousness; being themselves more and more made righteous by the ray of justice and the Spirit of Christ. And this enlightening will go on, until in perfect clearness and full righteousness they behold righteousness itself, no longer "darkly" and obscurely, but most openly and clearly; nor "through the glass" of the church here (which Paul calls "darkly"), but through the church herself, then become the face and the truth, in reality "face to face." Which church is now an image of that which she will be, and even now presents a figure of that which she

---

edition of the LXX. In the Preface to the Latin Dionysius of 1498 and in the Scholia on c. iv. (towards the end of which the text is quoted), the variation in the reading is pointed out. Perhaps the strangest adaptation of the passage is that made by Mirandola, in his "XXXI Conclusions" respecting the Hymns of Orpheus, where he quotes as parallel to it the expression of Diotima in the *Symposium*, calling Poros the child of Themis, or Counsel :—" Ex iisdem dictis potest intelligi, cur in symposio a Diotima Poros consilii filius, et Jesus in sacris literis angelus magni consilii nominetur " (*Op.* 1601, p. 71).

[1] This metaphor is employed again, more briefly, in the beginning of the *Ecclesiastical Hierarchy*.

will then behold. And when this church has passed from the reflection as in a glass to the true face, then will she behold with her own true face the true countenance and face of God. That is plainly what Paul saith: "But then face to face;" that is, the true church will behold the true God in himself, after the example of Jesus, who now beholds him face to face. And as the renewal of that Spirit works in us, that we may be like him, we are daily more and more raised to his likeness. And this has Paul beautifully expressed when writing to the Corinthians: "But we all, with open face beholding as in a glass the glory of the Lord, are changed into the same image from glory to glory, even as by the Spirit of the Lord." For we are being changed, that we may be like Jesus in heaven, and that, along with him, we may with true countenance behold the true countenance of the Trinity of God. When Moses learned this from the angels, who showed him in what way they themselves exhibit the form and order of God, he endeavoured, according to the rule and direction of the pattern showed him, to fashion among men a representation of God, after the likeness of the angels; to the end that, by a certain system and order, men might imitate the angels in their life and actions, and present in themselves something of the divine plan; although, as was natural for the beginning of the matter, they did it somewhat ignorantly and blindly. But their heavenly Father was content with a commencement, however poor; foreseeing that there would be one to refine and enlighten their dull ignorance. Thus led he forth those uninstructed Hebrews, like boys, to school; in order that, like children playing with dolls and toys, they might represent in shadow what they were one day to do in reality as men; herein imitating little girls, who in early age play with dolls, the images of sons, being destined afterwards in riper years to bring forth real sons; imitating moreover boys, who mount mimic horses, armed with mimic arms, being destined one day to mount real horses in real armour.[1] "When I was a child," says St. Paul, "I under-

2 Cor. iii. 18.

1 Cor. xiii. 11.

---

[1] This noticing of children's ways quite agrees with what Erasmus

stood as a child; but when I became a man, I put away childish things." From childishness and images and imitations Christ has drawn us; who has shone upon our darkness, and has taught us the truth, and has made us that believe on him to be men; in order that we, "with open face beholding as in a glass the glory of the Lord, may be changed into the same image from glory to glory, even as by the Spirit of the Lord:" "God, who commanded the light to shine out of darkness, hath himself shined in our hearts, to give the light of the knowledge of the glory of God in the face of Jesus Christ;" that by faith we may discern more truly the countenance of him who has revealed what Moses pourtrayed concerning Christ and the Church. He that believes in this word, believes in that "short work which the Lord has made upon the earth."[1] For in Christ

Marginal references: 2 Cor. iii. 18.; 2 Cor. iv. 6.; Rom. ix. 28.

---

says in his *Letter to Justus Jonas* of Colet's fondness for children:—"In pueris ac puellis delectabat naturæ puritas ac simplicitas; ad cujus imitationem suos vocat Christus, Angelis eos solitus comparare." It is strange to observe in what an unquestioning spirit the anecdote of Erasmus about barbarity in schools ("Novi theologum quendam," etc., *Op.* i. 441,) has been assumed to refer to Dean Colet above all people. Mr. Seebohm has satisfactorily refuted this application of the story (*Oxford Reformers*, p. 144), and I will not impair the freshness of his arguments by repeating them. But it may be instructive to notice how widely such base coin circulates, before it can be finally detected and destroyed. Thus, in the present case, we have Tytler, in his *Life of Henry VIII.* (p. 42), relating how "the amiable Erasmus . . . has left us a picture of the manner in which Colet used to superintend the flagellations, and the good will with which Lilly administered them, which is at once ludicrous and revolting." And to the same effect we may read in the *Quarterly Review*, vol. xxxix. p. 104; *MacMillan's Magazine*, No. LXXI. p. 401; *Report of the Commissioners on Colleges*, etc. vol. i. p. 194; and many other places. And all this, because Dr. Knight says that "it will be a hard task to apply [the story] to any other than to them." Kennett, from whose collections Knight took the passage, speaks more diffidently: "I *think* there can be no other application of it." And he sets down the extract from Erasmus in an evidently half-jesting mood:—"I leave it as a task to be translated by some ill-deserving Paul's scholar."— *Lansdowne MS.* 1030, *fol.* 132 *b.* Such are the scanty materials from which this tissue of error has been spun.

[1] See above, p. 9. A somewhat unexpected illustration of what is there supposed to be the author's meaning, is found in the *Bibliotheca* of Sixtus Senensis (1610, p. 178), under the heading of "A specimen of a

are all things in full measure, which Moses sought either to teach in righteousness or to establish in religion; which things had first to be foreshadowed, then afterwards in due time to be set in clearer light; that at length, in the end of the world, they may all be made perfect. In these foreshadowings and signs, metaphors are borrowed from all quarters by Moses, a theologian and observer of nature of the deepest insight; inasmuch as there are not words proper to express the divine attributes. For nothing is fitted to denote God himself, who is not only unutterable, but even inconceivable. Wherefore he is most truly expressed by negations; since you may state what he is not, but not what he is: for whatever positive statement you make concerning him, you err, seeing that he is none of those things which you can say. Still, because a hidden principle of the Deity resides in all things, on account of that faint resemblance the sacred writers have endeavoured to indicate him by the names of all objects, not only of the better but also of the worse kind; lest the duller sort, attracted by the beauty of the fairer objects, should think God to be that very thing which he is called.[1] You ought to speak me-

---

Scholastic Lecture on Psalm cxvi." The passage from Isaiah x. 23, is taken as the text; and the Prophet's language is said to suggest four *causes* of the Psalm, namely, the Material, Formal, Active and Final. The Material Cause, that, namely, which furnished its *matter*, or subject, to the Psalm, was the "mercy and truth" of God, as displayed in the incarnate *Word.* This will explain Colet's use of *verbum.* By *abbreviatum* is said to be signified the shortness of the Psalm. The whole composition is a most singular one.

[1] The soundness of this reasoning is pointed out by Mr. Westcott, in his Paper on Dionysius in the "Contemporary Review" (May, 1867), p. 10. "And here Dionysius acutely adds, that those positive affirmations are to be preferred which, while they convey a partial truth, yet convey it in such a form, as to avoid any semblance of expressing a complete truth. Thus there is little danger in describing the angels under the similitude of beasts and birds, because no one could suppose that the likeness extended beyond the single point of comparison, while many may be deceived by the nobler imagery which describes 'the beings of heaven as creatures of light in human form, of dazzling brightness, and exquisite beauty, arrayed in glittering robes, and flashing forth the radiance of innocuous fire.'" The same principle is laid down by Marsilius Ficinus (whom Colet more directly quotes afterwards, at the

taphorically in such a way that you may be considered to have sought an expression from other sources, not to have spoken in accordance with the reality itself; and that it may be openly acknowledged that you are using, not what is strictly appropriate, but similitudes. On which account divine attributes are expressed, not only by the name of sun, sky, light, life, intelligence, mind, or whatever of such a kind be better, but also by the names of birds and four-footed beasts, and plants, of stones, and elements, and creeping things. For God is all in all; and what is worse dimly represents what is better: all things, furthermore, represent God, so far as they are able; from whom, and by whom, and in whom are all things.

This kind of writing did the sacred writers of old employ, both patriarchs and prophets, as being both necessary and useful. Necessary, inasmuch as otherwise they could not have spoken of God; and useful, because by it both the weaker sight is attracted and led on to behold brighter things, and the ungodly and profane is kept in darkness. The veil wrought by Moses is of such a kind as to conceal from the ungodly the precious things of God, and yet to teach the good somewhat; though it be not the truth itself, yet at least some shadow of the truth. And what Dionysius discourses touching divine things, he adjures Timothy[1] religiously to conceal and keep hidden, and not to divulge save to the worthy; that it be not profaned by the eyes of the uninitiated.

---

beginning of ch. xvi.), in a section headed "Rectius de Deo loquimur negando et referendo quam affirmando," at f. 54 of his *Epistolæ* (1495).

[1] At the end of c. ii.: "Tu autem, o fili," etc.

CHAPTER III.

On the Angelic Hierarchy, and its threefold Office of Purifying, Illumining, and Perfecting.

GOD, who is one, beautiful and good; Father, Son, and Holy Ghost; the Trinity which created all things; is at once the purification of things to unity, their illumination to what is beautiful, and their perfection to what is good. That God, by pouring forth his light which purifies, illumines and perfects, unspeakably deifies and makes godlike the threefold hierarchy of angels; among whom, though all things be shared by all alike (for purity and light and likeness to God are inseparably connected), yet there are, as it were, personal attributes; so that perfection is the property of the first hierarchy, illumination of the second, purification of the third. Likewise, in the first hierarchy, the office of perfecting is specially assigned to the order which is first; that of illuminating to the second; that of purifying to the third. In this threefold way the threefold hierarchy resembles the triune God. The whole endeavour of all spiritual beings is to represent God. God first by his power makes like himself those beings who are near him; then they make others like in turn. Thus there proceeds a diffusion of the Deity from order to order, from hierarchy to hierarchy, and from better creatures to worse, according to each one's capacity, for the rendering godlike of all; "to the praise," in St. Paul's words, of the glory of the grace of God." In this allotted task moreover are men, that they may be refashioned in a hierarchy representative of God. And when, in reducing them to order the angels were wearied out, then did Jesus Christ, who is himself Order, and the incarnate beauty of God, "fairer than the children of men," come to their aid, establishing in himself three hierarchies, and in each one of these the threefold virtues of purifying, illuminating, perfecting; in order that men also, being fellow-workers in Christ for the glorifying of

Eph. i. 6.

God, may at length form a finished hierarchy on earth, to be made equal hereafter to the angels in heaven.

> God makes us like himself.
> He bestows that we may bestow.
> In communicating what we have received, we become most like God.
> The divinest of virtues is a tender-hearted liberality.
> In benefiting others we become most like God.

CHAPTER IV.

On Angels, as Messengers of God to Man.

GOD created all things, because he is good; and because he is good he also recalls to himself all things according to their capacity, that he may bountifully communicate himself to them. There is nothing that does not in some degree partake of God; since it is from God that all have both their existence and their well-being. But that rational creatures may be better and happier [there labour] first angels, then men by the ministration of angels, through the infinite goodness of God, and, as St. Paul says, according to the "riches of God." The foremost and highest men have plainer visions, and on their minds comes a more untempered effulgence of the godhead. To the rest in succession, who are of duller natures, all things are suitably made known by signs; both the formation of character, and the worship of God, and the looking for truth. Of these things obscure tokens are contained in the law of Moses; on which account Dionysius calls it the image of a holier law.[1] There is, I repeat, a diffusion of the outpoured Deity, which renders godlike, as it goes forth from a higher hierarchy to a lower, and from order to order in each hierarchy, by the mutual service of its members, that they may become souls and spirits of God. The mystery of the Incarnation was learnt by the angels first, and then they

Rom. xi. 33.

---

[1] "At id quidem nos verius instruit, divinæ illam fuisse sacratiorisque legis effigiem."—Sec. 3.

taught men; Zechariah, Mary, Joseph, the Shepherds. In men again there is a mutual instruction from member to member, in Christ, which goes on from the first, through the intervening ones, to those which are last in the church; as St. Paul says, "by that which every joint supplieth." Eph. iv. 6. Thus from God, through the angels, that is from angel to angel, and from them to men, there is diffused a communication of the godhead. God himself also coming in the form of man, even Jesus, undertook the office of an angel, and is called the "messenger of the great counsel;"[1] and so Isai. ix. 6. far as he was man, he received continually the ministrations of angels; at his conception, at his birth, in his youth, before his death, and before his ascension. For before his resurrection he was mortal man, inferior, as it were, to the angels; who after his resurrection was at once immortal man and God of all.

CHAPTER V.

On the general and special application of the name of Angel.

ANGELS have their name of Messengers from the messages they bear; seeing that the higher announce the things of God to the lower, even down to men. But the greatest messenger to man was Jesus Christ; whence he is called by Isaiah "Wonderful Counsellor," and "messenger Isai. ix. 6. of the great counsel." Although the lowest spirits are, by a special name, called Angels,[2] yet inasmuch as their office can be discharged by all the higher ones (since a higher power can do all that a lower can) the names of the lower are suitable to the higher, though those of the higher are

---

[1] "This angel was Christ Jesus, who is called the angel of the great counsel, because he brought from the bosom of his Father the secret counsel of God, and preached his great love to the world."—Pilkington, *Exp. on Aggeus.*

[2] The third, or lowest, hierarchy being composed of the Princedoms, Archangels, and Angels.

by no means so for the lower. These names were not invented by man, but borrowed from Holy Writ. And the variety of them in the Sacred Volume of necessity betokens a variety of spirits in heavenly regions; the order of whom Dionysius has arranged. The lowest angels work upon our bishops and priests, and refine and raise them to what is spiritual; to the intent that they may become wholly spiritual, and may in turn spiritualize others beneath them, each according to his capacity; that from among men, so far as is possible, there may be in Christ a fourth and highly spiritual hierarchy, who will one day be true spirits and angels, their spiritualizing being continued by God in Christ, through angels and angelic men.

CHAPTER VI.

On the nine Orders in the Angelic Hierarchy.

GOD, who is One and Three, has arranged threefold hierarchies among the blessed Spirits, after the pattern of the order in his own being; and these are called by Dionysius at one time Functions, at another Distinctions,[1] and at another, Hierarchies. God, who is the founder of all things and of every order, alone of a surety knows all things exactly; and he made known by his angels to the prophets (whom Dionysius also rightly calls Divine Teachers, since he is rightly and truly a divine teacher who speaks out what is revealed by God);—he made known to them in some measure, I say, what they in turn, so far as was

---

[1] Colet's adoption of these terms is a slight proof of his having used the translation of Ambrosius, according to which the sixth chapter begins " Quot nempe et cujusmodi sint sanctorum spirituum *distinctiones*, et quo pacto sacræ illorum *functiones* peragantur," &c. In the later edition of Corderius, in place of the words in italics are " dispositiones" and " ordines." The most complete definition of the term *hierarchy* by Dionysius is at the beginning of Ch. iii., where he explains it as " Ordo sacratior et scientia et operatio."

ON THE NINE ORDERS.

allowed them, committed to writing. And this both is, and is called, Holy Writ, as it contains the holy revelations of God; and herein we learn the names of nine orders of blessed Spirits. The meaning and signification of these names was well understood by St. Paul, enlightened as he was by the Spirit of God. He taught Dionysius the interpretations of the divine word in these matters. And from his instruction and opening of the Scriptures, as well as from the authority of the Scriptures themselves, Dionysius professes to say all that he does concerning the heavenly Spirits; calling the Apostle Paul his master, guide, and teacher.[1]

In each hierarchy, he writes, there are three co-equal orders, resembling the three Persons in God, who is the Hierarchy of hierarchies. Of these hierarchies there are three; which being tripled form nine Orders,[2] called by the

---

[1] The expression of Dionysius in this passage is simply "eximius preceptor noster;" which the paraphrast Pachymeres says may refer either to St. Paul, or Hierotheus, whom Dionysius elsewhere calls his instructor.

[2] As Thos. Heywood's book, *The Hierarchie of the Blessed Angells* (1635) may be little known, I will quote a corresponding passage from his poem. It will serve also to illustrate what is set down from Mirandola, at the beginning of Ch. viii. below:—

"So in the three parts of the world are said
To be no lesse than ten distinct degrees.
And first of the super-celestiall, these
Th' Angels, Archangels, and the Principates,
Thrones, Dominations, Vertues, Potestates,
The Cherubims and Seraphims: then He,
(Above all these) the supreme Deity.
   In the celestiall, Ten; and thus they run;
Luna, Mercury, Venus, and the Sun,
Mars, Jove, and Saturne: Then the starry Heaven,
Crystalline, and Empyriall, make them even.
   In this below the moon, where we now live,
Are likewise ten degrees, to whom we give
These characters; first, the foure Elements,
Mystæ, Impressions, Herbs, Fruits, Trees and Plants,
Beasts, Reptile Creatures, and the tenth and last
Materia Prima: so their number's cast."

Heywood occasionally refers to Dionysius in the *Observations* inter-

following names :—Angels, Archangels, Princedoms, Powers, Virtues, Dominations, Thrones, Cherubim and Seraphim. Nor are these names of human invention, but derived from heaven by the Prophets of God and Theologians in the sacred volume.

CHAPTER VII.

On the Seraphim, Cherubim, and Thrones.

FIRST after the Trinity come the Seraphic Spirits, all flaming and on fire, full of the Deity they have received, and perfect. The word *Seraphin* signifies *fire*. They are loving beings of the highest order, reposing most sweetly in the divine beauty, being associated in happiness with the most loving Jesus, who is very God for evermore. In the contemplation of his blessedness they love, worship, and adore; and moreover learn fully from our most glorious Jesus what by their own nature they know not. These most blessed loving ones are filled with unutterable delight in cleaving to the divine beauty; in gazing upon Jesus they feel themselves steeped in every joy. This is what St. Peter says in his Epistle—"Which things the angels desire to look into."

_{1 Pet. i. 12.}

Next after them, in the second place, are the Cherubic Spirits; most glorious beings of light, shining in nature, beyond aught that can be conceived, with the multitudinous wisdom of God; who may be called loving Wisdoms, as those first may be called wise Loves.[1] For there is in each

---

spersed among his nine books; but his work is not, as might be supposed from the title, avowedly founded upon the former's. The Cabalistic names of the nine orders are given by Archangelus at p. 728 of his *Interpretationes* in *Artis Cabalisticæ Scriptores* (1587):—"Novem sunt angelorum hierarchiæ; quarum nomina Cherubim, Seraphim, Chasmalim, Arælim, Tarsissim, Orphanim, Issim, Malachim, Elohim."

[1] In this antithetical refinement, Colet goes beyond Dionysius. It is a passing token of his very methodical cast of mind.

both love and wisdom. But in the first, inasmuch as they are nearer to God, the very sun of truth, this exists in a far greater degree. Therefore that which is in them is named love. In those next after them all things are in a less degree; and they, as compared with the first, appear to be only Lights. Therefore they have the appellation of Knowledge. Such, then, is the difference between these Orders; namely, that in the latter is knowledge proceeding from love; in the former is love proceeding from knowledge. In the latter, love is knowledge; in the former, knowledge is love. For in the angels an intensity of knowledge is love; a less intense love is knowledge. Do not imagine either that the highest angels have not knowledge, or that the second in rank do not love; but consider that the latter have knowledge accompanied by love, the former love accompanied by knowledge. Conceive also that in this difference and personal attribute, so to speak, there is a certain compensation and equality; to the effect that, just as the first subsist by their fire of love, so the second by their light of knowledge; and the one represent the wisdom of God, as the others do his love.

In the third rank are those who, from their unity, simplicity, constancy, and firmness, are sometimes called Thrones, sometimes Seats;[1] who themselves also are wise and loving. But from their simplicity, they have the attributes of unity, power, strength, fortitude, steadfastness. Which very attributes the Cherubim and Seraphim also possess; but they are applied by a special appropriation to these, as representing the first Person in the Trinity, and the power of God, of which the scope seems to be the most extensive in the universe. For in them there dwells in greater measure the power of God, and his authority and strictness, and as it were his fixed and

---

[1] This being the term in Ambrosius's version:—" Altissimarum et elevatarum *sedium* nomine," &c.; for which Corderius has *thronorum*. The three properties of a Seat, or Throne, which suggest to Dionysius a meaning for the name as applied to angels, are, elevation from the earth, stability, and capacity of bearing those seated on it; as the angels, in this last respect, have strength to endure the immediate presence of the supreme God.

settled resolution and unchangeableness of purpose. Hence it is that God is said to sit on a throne, and to exercise judgment, and to give an unalterable decision. For by means of these angels, the images of his power, he will execute at the last judgment that which will abide by an immovable decree.

Steadfastness comes from simplicity, simplicity from purification. For when each object is purified back to its own simple nature, then, being uncompounded, it remains indissoluble through its unity. Whence it is clear that purification is assigned to the Thrones. Moreover, when a thing is purified, it is illumined, and after it is illumined, it is perfected. This last office is given to the Seraphs, the other to the Cherubs. Among them all, in every threefold manner, there is a striving with all their might to imitate God; who is Purification itself, the parent of unities; who is the very Illumination of those unities; who is lastly the very Perfection of the illumined. Power cleanses, clear truth makes serene, finished love makes perfect.

Dionysius records that even the highest angels, the Seraphs (which he counts a marvellous thing) look up to Jesus at the right hand of the Father, and lowly and reverently worship him; and beckon with angelic signs to show that they would gladly learn of him, and know more fully the meaning of his mysteries, chiefly of those which concern incarnate Deity; and that thus they learn from the bounteous Jesus what they may in turn teach others below them. For he notes that in the prophets angels are introduced,[1] some of whom teach others the majesty of Christ glorified, they, the teachers, having learnt from Jesus; to wit, that he, who after his resurrection from the dead ascended into heaven as glorified man, is the Lord of Sabaoth and of hosts, and of the heavenly virtues, yea, and the very Lord of glory. For "Who is this King of glory?" the lower angels, in David's Psalm, ask of the mid ones above them, who, as Christ ascends, have cried out to those beneath, bidding them

Ps. xxiv. 7—10.

---

[1] "Quosdam enim ex ipsis inducunt a prioribus sacramenta perdiscere," &c.—§ 3.

"Lift up your heads,¹ O ye gates, and be ye lift up, ye everlasting doors, and the King of glory shall come in." And to their question they make answer: "The Lord strong and mighty, the Lord mighty in battle; the Lord of hosts, he is the king of glory." He it is that has "ascended into the hill of the Lord," having "clean hands and a pure heart; who hath not lifted up his soul unto vanity, nor sworn to deceive his neighbour." He is followed by "the generation of them that seek him, that seek the face of the God of Jacob." The highest angels, as they contemplate Jesus, ask in doubt of one another: "Who is this that cometh from Edom, with dyed garments from Bozrah?" To whom Jesus makes answer, "I that speak in righteousness." Then the angels, encouraged by his condescension, ask, "Wherefore art thou red in thine apparel?" Jesus answers, "I have trodden the wine-press alone." Thus do they learn the mystery of the incarnation more fully from the glorified Jesus, and teach those beneath them; at once purifying, illumining, and perfecting. For these operations go on together. But those highest spirits, reposing² in the most blessed happiness, sing in sweetest concert, "Holy, holy, holy, Lord God of Sabaoth."

Ps. xxiv. 3—6.

Is. lxiii. 1—3.

---

¹ It may make the sense somewhat clearer here, to notice that in the Vulgate, from which Dean Colet quotes, the word *Principes* is used otherwise than the English version would lead us to suppose. It there implies "Lift up your gates, *ye princes*," by which designation the angels may be intended; not "Lift up your *heads*, O ye gates," which, as Hammond observes, is applicable to the raising of a portcullis. The former interpretation is seen in Wycliffe's version: "Ye princes, take up your gatis, and ye everelastynge gatis be reisid; and the kyng of glorie schal entre."

² Hakewill, in his *Apologie* (1630), v. 224, makes this a mark of discrepancy between Dionysius and St. Paul, whom he professes to be his teacher:—"This Dionysius, in diverse chapters of the same *Hierarchy*, teacheth that the higher orders of angels are alwayes assistant about the throne of God, never imployed in forraine messages; directly contrary to that of his Master, 'Are they not all ministering spirits,' not *some*, but *all*, 'sent forth to minister for their sakes that shall bee heires of salvation?'"

CHAPTER VIII.

On the Dominations, Virtues, and Powers.

THERE are nine orders of Angels, figures of the nine archetypes in God. And each one obtains a name corresponding to the property in God which it exhibits. Hence the first have love, the second knowledge, the third a throne, as their characteristic; since these recall the steadfastness, wisdom and love in God.

In the second Hierarchy, the first have the name of Domination, being an express image of the true and archetypal dominion in God. For the domination in them is simple and unmingled, and devoid of all subjection, ruling over all, useful to all, a true and unmixed liberty of bearing sway, after the form and pattern of God. And they not only strive to exhibit in themselves this divine domination, but they strive also most earnestly to draw all things everywhere to a true dominion, and to an imitation of the dominion in God; in order that whatever takes upon it the character of domination, may bear true lordship in God.

In what way we poor men are to imitate the domination of God, the Lord himself, Jesus Christ, in his human form has plainly taught us; by whom we learn that domination among men is a free subjection, and willing obedience to God and to men, that they too may obey God.

To the second Order the name of Virtues is applied; by which word Dionysius wishes to be signified a certain manly and masculine and unshaken strength in them, and an unconquered and unconquerable valour, and a marvellous imitation of the divine virtue itself, in which nothing is done feebly, nothing weakly, nothing cowardly.

In these Valours and Virtues is zeal and care and energy, that all things in God may be strongly and manfully valiant in chaste and masculine virtue; that in virtue also God may be everywhere displayed. Jesus Christ, the very "power of God and the wisdom of God," as St. Paul calls him, when in our human form, taught us poor men, made strong in him-

Cor. i.24.

self, valour and strength and unconquered virtue. He taught us, I say, that true virtue and strength among men was endurance ; and the very " power of God," Jesus Christ himself, whilst showing us an example thereof, endured gloriously unto death, even the death of the cross. This becoming weak even to death was the strength and fortitude of God. Whence St. Paul wrote to the Corinthians, " The weakness of God is stronger than men." 1 Cor. i. 25.

The third Order have the name of Powers assigned them, because they exhibit in themselves the divine unity, simplicity, power and authority ; and present in a manner the all-powerful state and majesty of the Father, ever imitating God in begetting each to something that is grander. And this they not only endeavour in their own persons, but also summon all things to a majesty productive of power, so to speak, fertile and fruitful in God ; summoning first those that are nearer to them, which then in turn diffuse to their neighbours what they have received.

For that which the nine Orders of angels derive is dispersed over all in a ninefold progression ; so that there is nothing in the world so mean, as to be wholly devoid of this ninefold beneficence. For as there is an efflux of the Divine Trinity upon all things, so is there an effusion at the same time of the triple natures of the three Persons ; so as for all things to consist, by a ninefold method, in God the tenth.[1]

Jesus Christ, a magnificent and productive power, by the authority of the Father in himself, produced a power-giving state, so to speak, out of all the powers among men ; that each of them should daily beget in itself a better state, after the example of Jesus ; and that everywhere, through the divine power, the church in Christ might be at unity in itself, shining with virtue, and bearing sway with supremacy.

---

[1] Thus Mirandola, in the Preface to his *Heptaplus*, arranges beings super-celestial, celestial, and earthly into ninefold orders, under a presiding tenth. What God, in the first, is to the Hierarchy of Angels, the *empyrean* (for which we sometimes find the *Primum Mobile*) is to the nine spheres—of the seven planets, the firmament of the fixed stars, and the crystalline,—and elemental matter, in the third, to the ninefold order on earth of three mineral, three vegetable, and three animal forms. —*Op.* 1601, p. 4.

Thus does God beam forth with firmness, wisdom and love in the Thrones, Cherubs and Seraphs; which threefold system of the divine ray goes forth, and causes that in the Powers, Virtues and Dominations there should be reflected his divine and firm power, his wise virtue, and most loving dominion; and that the Trinity of God, coequal in itself, should shine with softened lustre, filling now the second place under that first one.[1] But although it be lowered somewhat from the first state (whence it obtains fresh appellations), yet remember always that in every abasement there necessarily arise at the same time circumstances that compensate for all things; so that in a series of objects, however unlike and unequal, there is yet by God's providence, to a marvellous degree likeness and equality. Thus it comes that, just as in unlikeness there is a certain variety and pleasing beauty of likeness, so in this likeness of unlikeness[2] there is at the same time a steady and unshaken fixity of all things arranged in order; to the end that beauty should not waver unsteadily, and that on the other hand a fixity by no means beautiful might not displease.

Now, that an enlightenment and revelation from God proceeds in order from angel to angel, Zechariah the prophet teaches us; in whose discourse it is written that an angel learnt from another angel that which he had taught the prophet. "Behold," saith he, "the angel that talked with me went forth, and another angel went out to meet him, And said unto him, Run, speak to this young man, saying, Jerusalem shall be inhabited as towns without walls, &c." For purification, illumination and perfection descends from on high, through what intervenes, to the lowest. In like manner Zechariah saw that the restoration of the Jews to their native land from the Babylonish captivity, which he learnt from an angel, had been learnt by that angel from another more exalted. Thus, by the testimony of the sacred writers, does Dionysius prove[3] that one angel imparts to another a threefold ray.

Zech. ii. 3, 4.

---

[1] That is, the first Hierarchy, of Seraphim, Cherubim and Thrones.

[2] That is, in this similarity which may be traced in things apparently unlike.

[3] In § 2 of ch. viii.; referring, besides the passage above quoted from Zechariah, to Dan. viii. 16, and other texts.

CHAPTER IX.

On the Princedoms, Archangels, and Angels.

THE last hierarchy is that of the Princedoms, Archangels and Angels. These Orders also have in God himself their models which they represent. For what else is principality than an image of the true and exalted principality in God, and than a spiritual effort to draw all things throughout the world, which hold principality, to an imitation of the true and predominant principality of God; in order that whatever is in chief place may exercise lordship with all love, and may join love with lordship?

Angels, who hold the last place in the series of divine spirits, and one nearer to worldly and corporeal objects, and who obtain the name of Angels in a more special manner, from being chiefly and most manifestly occupied in the care of bringing tidings to the world,— they, I say, specially express the bountiful and profitable messages of God, and exercise themselves truly and holily in announcing, as far as they can, among one another, and then in turn to mankind, the things which come derived from God through a long series of angels. As their nature is more akin to our human minds, and more nearly connected with them, so is their life more familiar to us.

Midway between these Orders is interposed that of the Archangels, as it is called; who have by nature, power, office and operation, as well as by position, an existence of an intermediate kind between the Principalities and the Angels; representing and imitating in God a certain supreme and wise and virtuous power of bearing tidings.

These Orders, like the others in the remaining Hierarchies, are distinguished by their special properties, and yet at the same time (as Dionysius constantly owns) are coequal;[1] which I judge to be on account of their representation of

---

[1] " Porro sanctissimus archangelorum ordo equalis quidem celestibus principatibus dicitur. Est enim (ut diximus) ipsorum atque angelorum functio una, unaque distinctio."—C. ix. § 2.

the Trinity, in which the Three Persons are equal. Such attributes of the Deity, lastly, as are expressed in the order of Angels, it is their constant business to introduce among men, and to bring men also to an imitation of them and of God; that beneath themselves there may exist a threefold hierarchy, to wit, of men on earth, answering to that which there is among the angels. This was long assayed in vain by the angels; the unfitness of mankind being an obstacle, till there came to their aid the mighty Angel, the "messenger of the great counsel," as Isaiah calls him, Jesus Christ; of whose nativity the angels sang in gladness, "Glory to God in the highest, and on earth peace toward men."

Isai. ix. 6.

Luke ii. 14.

He, the Virgin's Son, established a hierarchy after the model of the angels, according to the pattern of his own truth, and built it up of those whom he would, as living stones; whom he not only arranged in order, but also quickened in himself, that as lively members they might be arranged in him who is Order itself.

Now, that the angels are leaders and officers of mankind, for their obedience to God, the writings of the prophets testify. For in Daniel, there is a Prince of the Persians, and a Prince of the Grecians, and Michael is called the Prince of the Jewish nation; for "the Most High appointed the bounds of nations according to the number of the angels of God."[1] Michael had, as Vicegerent, the province of the Hebrews, which was more obedient to him. In all the others, the wickedness of mankind so resisted, and every one so followed his own proper will and crooked desire, that nothing could be brought either into order or the semblance of order. Of this evil, as Dionysius says, each one's self-love and pride was the cause. But Michael found some shadow of truth at least among the Hebrews, and trained

Dan. x. 20, 21.

[1] The Scholiast on c. ix. briefly states that the original of this quotation cannot be found:—"Hoc oraculo caremus." So far as the wording alone is concerned, the nearest parallel is perhaps Deut. xxxii. 8: "When the most High divided to the nations their inheritance, when he separated the sons of Adam, he set the bounds of the people according to the number of the children of Israel."

them in figures, that after a time they might then be promoted to something higher. At length the glorious Christ, the Lord of all, not only called men forth from every nation to love and obey God, but moreover caused them to shew such loving obedience to the whole host of angels, now ministering more readily for the salvation of men in Jesus their Saviour; as for men to be everywhere converted and live, turning towards the life-giving ray of God, now that Jesus, the "Sun of Righteousness" Himself, had arisen. As Dionysius says, however, the spiritual light of God at all times shone upon the minds of men in the world, and men had always the choice of turning themselves towards the light, and nothing stood in the way but their perverse will. Before Jesus was born, Melchisedec from among the Gentiles turned to God, and merited to be called "Priest of the most high God." At the birth of Jesus also, angels announced "on earth peace, good will toward men."[1] But consider thus, that God's assistance concurs with the force of our own will; and that in grace men have free power; so as for our freedom towards good to spring from both together; so that, unless a man will, he receives not the light, and, unless he be enlightened, he wills not to receive it. Man's will is the cause why his soul receives it; and at the same time the light is the cause why his soul wills. The spirit, when warmed by grace, in its own freedom chooses the good, which in that same freedom it can refuse. Without grace indeed, there is no liberty; and yet in grace there is nothing but liberty. In the diffusion of the ray there is assistance for whoever will, to turn himself to God; and those do so turn, who are aided sufficiently to wish to turn. At the birth of Christ the Sun came nearer us, and the light poured forth upon men more efficaciously, and hence the conversion of men became more abundant; of those, namely, who, being

Hebr. vii. 1.

Luke ii. 14.

---

[1] As Colet has just spoken of men's "perverse will," it is possible he meant more in quoting this text than appears from the English version. For in the Vulgate it is "Et in terra pax hominibus bonæ voluntatis," *i. e.*, "to men of good will." Erasmus, in a long note on the passage in his *Annotationes* shews how untenable the Latin version is.

placed through grace in a freedom of choice, willed to turn themselves.

But let us dismiss these topics; for the mental vision grows dull, quite blunted by the hardness of the subject and of the enquiry; and let us return to Dionysius.

He affirms that the power and goodness of God are everywhere equal, but that the good will of men is not everywhere so; that an even ray of grace is shed abroad over all, but that men are not evenly disposed towards it;[1] that God has a like care for all mankind, and that there is one God of all, and that the angels placed in charge of their own territories throughout the universe are equal, and treat their provinces with equal care. For what happened to Pharaoh, king of the Egyptians? Did not a good angel, the Prince of that region, shew him a dream, the meaning of which Joseph, being taught by the angel, afterwards explained? In like manner, was not Daniel the interpreter to the King of the Babylonians, of the vision which an angel, the viceregent of that nation, set before his mind? What else then can be said, but that there is one God of all, and that he is alike good to all? For He is not an accepter of persons; but some men are rejecters of God.

Gen. xli.

Dan. ii. 19.

Dionysius affirms also,[2] that angels are everywhere distributed about, as officers of the world, with equal power, zeal and kindness; that the ancient Hebrews were in no respect a chosen people before the rest; that the lot of all is equal; that there is one common freedom to all alike; and that the Hebrews were more pleasing to God, because they more readily obeyed their vicegerent Michael. Now that the Jews had Michael for their commander, just as other nations had other Archangels, the language of Daniel plainly shews;

---

[1] "Neque enim coactam habemus vitam, neque liberi arbitrii gratia, divinitus indulta mortalibus, providentiæ divinæ luce et splendore obtunditur: ceterum dissimilitudo Spiritalium luminum facit, ut affluentissima paternæ benignitatis lux aut omnino capi participarique non possit . . . . aut certe ipsa lucis participatio pro suscipientium meritis varia sit; parva scilicet vel magna, obscura vel lucida."—C. ix. §. 3.

[2] Ch. ix. §§ 3 and 4; ending with the words "omnes autem angelos singulis prefectos nationibus," etc.

in whose tenth chapter it is written: "And there is none that holdeth with me in these things, but Michael your prince." And that God is a God for all alike, David also testifies, saying, God is "King over all the earth." And so St. Paul: "Is he the God of the Jews only? is he not also of the Gentiles? Yes, of the Gentiles also." Dan. x. 21. Ps. xlvii. 2. Rom. iii. 29.

But inasmuch as the Hebrews of old time were more obedient to the inspirations of angels, therefore in David it is written:—"For the Lord hath chosen Jacob unto himself, and Israel for his peculiar treasure." Ps. cxxxv. 4.

CHAPTER X.

Recapitulatory; on the dependence of the several Orders, one upon another.

OF the spirits who contemplate God, about whom we have just discoursed, the first Hierarchy both penetrates more deeply, and is more inflamed in God, than the rest; being wholly purified, wholly illumined, and wholly perfected. This chiefly works out firmness, knowledge and love in the human Hierarchy; that the first among men, being borne on high, may along with them have a pure, clear, and glowing vision of all things. This first shining and dazzling Hierarchy irradiates the second and next beneath it, that it being enlightened may illuminate the third; that the third in order may beautifully colour darksome men, and cause them in some measure to imitate and reproduce the beauty of God; for to Him all is set down as due. And as this diffusion goes on and advances, fresh names in turn arise in the distinctions of ranks. The gifts that have at length come down to men, from the bestowal of God, have, on account of their lowered condition, other appellations; and thus, when Jesus Christ arose, who as man shewed more clearly to us wretched men the divine plan, the ray proceeding from Him, which purifies, illumines, and perfects, is called the Gospel. And herein, in the case of men (those I mean, who are touched by the Gospel ray, which works in man's spirit simplicity, clearness and perfection), that simplicity, whereby a man steadfastly lives in God through Christ, is called Hope ; the clearness, whereby he has higher knowledge, is called Faith ; and the perfection, whereby he wills and does all things aright, is called Charity. In like manner, the other gifts of grace are styled by their own proper names among men, other than among the angels, in keeping with the littleness of mankind. Among all the angels, moreover, from the higher ones even down to us, there is a mutual and alternate announcement proceeding from above; as they receive and deliver in turn what they announce in a marvellous and most beautiful order. Since among the angels themselves there is an order of all ordinances after the pattern of the Order of all. They announce by means of their own gestures and angelic beckonings, in a manner inconceivable by the human mind ; not only a higher Hierarchy to a lower, but one Order in each Hierarchy to another. But every announcement is a receiving, informing, purifying, enlightening, perfecting, and representing of the divine truth; the light of which, as it goes forth in order and shines upon all, so distinguishes and marks each object in a wonderful manner, that everything shines forth in it in its own proper quality, and stands out and appears in its own nature, with its individual powers and office, exhibiting in its own degree some perfection in God, in whom all perfection is in its highest; nay, rather, who is Himself the proper perfection of every one, perfecting all things ; in whom there is nothing perfect but Himself. For He is the proper completion of everything, the drink that fills each according to its capacity, poured from the same cask. For all things drink of the wine that flows forth from the fount of God, which, being one and the same, makes all drunk[1] in equal measure, yet variously, according to the varied capacity of each.

---

[1] The English version of Psalm xxxvi. 8, does not convey the full force of the Latin, which Colet had probably in mind in this passage. It is more nearly "They shall be drunken with the fulness of thy House."

CHAPTER XI.

On the attributes of Spiritual Natures.

OF the individuals who share in the goodness of the same God, whom we call at one time Light, and at another Drink, there are, and stand distinctly forward, personal peculiarities, as it were; so that in unity there is a pleasing variety, and in variety there is an unbroken unity. The nature of Spirits is divided into existence, virtue and operation. For they exist that they may be strong, and they are strong that they may act. On this threefold condition all Spirits exist; and by reason thereof they share their names.

CHAPTER XII.

On the sense in which men are called Angels and Gods.

IN like manner, the priest of a human Church is called by Malachi "a messenger," which is, as Dionysius says, Mal. ii. 7. from his imitation of the angels, and announcement of the truth, and from his desire and office of purifying, illumining, and perfecting those who are committed to his charge. For, as I have before said, according to the opinion of Dionysius, all things are in all; but in the lower ones, of a more debased type; among men, most debased. Yet among these very men, especially on the part of those who are of the better sort, there is such an imitation of the angels, that men also may seem to be in some degree rightly able to be called

---

He may perhaps have also thought of Augustine's exposition of it :—
"For when shall have been received that ineffable joy, then shall be lost in a manner the human soul; it shall become Divine, and be drunken with the fulness of God's house. Wherefore also in another Psalm (xxiii. 5) it is said, *Thy cup inebriating, how excellent it is!*" (Tr. in *Library of the Fathers*, Oxf. 1847.)

34   *CELESTIAL HIERARCHY.*   CH. XV.

angels. Nay, more, they are even called gods in Holy Scripture, by a metaphor, and by their resembling the Deity as far as possible. For those who with all piety are led to this end along with the angels, are along with the angels called gods. That the angels are called gods the expression in Genesis bears witness, which was spoken to Jacob by the man that wrestled with him: " As a prince hast thou power with God and with men, and hast prevailed." The angel there called himself a god. And David speaks of " a great King above all gods." To show that men are so called,[1] in Exodus, " the Lord said unto Moses, See, I have made thee a god to Pharaoh." And David writes, " I have said, Ye are gods; and all of you are children of the most High;" which our Saviour himself, in St. John, teaches, is to be explained of those men to whom the words of God were delivered.

Gen. xxxii. 28.
Ps. xcv. 3.
Ex. vii. 1.
Ps. lxxxii. 6.
John x. 34.

We may conclude, therefore, that, as is the matter, so at the same time are the names, derived to mankind from above.

CHAPTER XV.[2]

On the similitudes by which the nature and operation of Spiritual Beings are made known to us.

THE Angels, when taught, teach others; they turn towards God; they are steadfast in themselves; they pour down influence from above. These properties of the

---

[1] In the margin opposite this there is written in a smaller hand, "Deus stetit in synagoga deorum: in medio autem deos dijudicat;" being the first verse of Ps. lxxxii.

[2] It will be noticed that the thirteenth and fourteenth chapters of Dionysius are passed over by Colet without remark; possibly because he thought their contents unimportant. The subject of chap. xiii. is the question why the office of *purifying* Isaiah from his sin (Is. vi. 7) should be assigned to one of the Seraphim, theirs being the special office of *perfecting*; whilst chap. xiv., which is a very brief one, treats of the infinity in number of the heavenly hosts, as gathered from Dan. vii. 10. Aquinas has arguments based on both chapters.

angels are made known to us by the inspired writers by figures and similitudes; and they most willingly employ the symbol of fire, the power of which is known to us as most resembling those other, and by which the heavenly spirits are most fully made plain to us. Out of this world of sense and darkness, accordingly, fire is adopted in the first instance, that it may be taught us what things are done in the bright world of angels. For this fire, by its light, has great likeness to that true light itself, which is unapproachable. Those writers also use very largely the excellent nature of man, because this is most akin to us; and thus, by borrowing similitudes from all its parts, they make angels as it were men. Moreover, by means of many other objects of various kinds, such as are familiar to us, they signify to men the natures, powers, actions, properties, likeness, difference, simplicity, firmness, steadfastness, strength, obedience, order, beauty, light, wisdom, pleasantness, beneficence, vigour, swiftness, subtilty, freedom, chieftancy, potency, authority, equity, government, fertility, fruitfulness, quickening, sanctity, religion, worship of God, happiness, blessedness, reign, abundance, plenty, riches, glory, the contemplation, in fine, and the joy, of those blessed spirits. These objects of sense and metaphors were sought on all sides and from every quarter by the ancient divines, those great prophets, with wonderful sagacity and love; that by this way and method they might both teach feeble men what are the things of God, and might preserve the dignity of things divine.[1]

---

[1] This appears to have been originally intended by Colet to be the close of his abstract of the *Celestial Hierarchy*, in uniformity with the fifteen chapters of Dionysius; for at the end of this paragraph is written, in the Cambridge MS., "Finis Dyonisii celestis hierarchiæ." The closing sentence in the same MS. was at first "Hæc et plurima alia quæ theologi prophetæ excogitant in angelis, undique petitis translationibus, quam melius et religiosius possunt denotant, ut Deum et divina doceant homines, quæsita simul eruditione hominum, et servata divinarum rerum dignitate," in place of " Quas quidem . . . . . conservent," as it now stands.

CHAPTER XVI.[1]

Supplementary; on the distinctions in nature and office of the Celestial Orders, and their representatives on earth; on the fallen Angels, their state and operations.

1 John i. 5.
John i. 5.

GOD, the boundless good, filling to the full within, and encompassing to infinity without, is very "light, and in him is no darkness at all." Wherefore, when it "shineth in darkness, the darkness comprehended it not." This very Divine principle also is abstracted in itself from matter, place, time, degrees, cause. It is so abstracted, that all things may seek it as the end in which they may be made perfect; by which all things were created; and by which also all things are disposed in beautiful order after the pattern of itself. God is therefore the beginning from which are all things, and the mean through which they are beautifully ordered, and the end, lastly, by which all things are

---

[1] The portion from this point to the end appears to be in some respects a distinct or supplementary treatise. In the Cambridge MS. it stands by itself, occupying ff. 148 *b*.—151, whereas the last chapter ended on f. 165. But from its similarity of subject, as well as from its following consecutively on in the School MS., I have marked it as an additional chapter of the *Celestial Hierarchy*. It is an interesting fact that many expressions in it are plainly taken from Ficino. Among the letters of Marsiglio Ficino, which were printed in 1495, is one thrown into the form of a dialogue between the Apostle Paul and a human soul, on the subject of the apostle's being "caught up into the third heaven." The following sentences from part of St. Paul's answer (fol. 52), if compared with Colet's Latin, will show clearly the connection between Colet and Ficino :—" Et si nihil usquam reperio extra *immensum bonum quod universum et omnino intrinsecus imbuit, et infinite extrinsecus ambit;* tamen quicquid reperio," &c. . . . . Hoc cum ex se et sui gratia efficiat omnia, et perficiat, certe ad sui ipsius exemplar, tanquam medium, cuncta disponit. Est ergo principium, medium, finisque cunctorum. . . . . . Seraphici finem ipsum propius attentiusque quam reliqua contemplantur. Cherubini in fine principium [*sic*]. Throni in fine medium speculantur," and so on through the rest of the nine Orders, as in Colet.

completed and perfected. This is what St. Paul says in his Epistle to the Romans, in these words: " For of him, and through him, and to him are all things: to whom be glory for ever." Since of himself, and after his own pattern, and by his own grace, he forms, disposes, and perfects all things. In so far as he fashions by his power, he is the Father; in so far as he disposes by his wisdom, he is the Son; in so far as he graciously perfects, he is the Holy Ghost. Hence comes existence, order, and aim among things; hence all things both are, and are beautiful, and are good. This existence, beauty, and goodness are wholly in the Beginning; and in it is an undivided essence, in which all things are the same; and this First Cause, through its infinite power, begets in the depths of itself an infinite offspring, that is infinite in the infinite. This is the eternal, beautiful Son of the eternal, omnipotent Father, between whom of necessity there springs an eternal and infinite love. And these three, on account of their common infinity, are both equal one with another, and most like, and their essence is one and undivided. In case of these, a man may not rightly speak otherwise than of three Persons and one God, the beginning, middle, and end of all. In whom, saving only relationship, whatever is in each, is in all. For the Father is Power, wise and good; the Son is Wisdom, powerful and good; the Holy Ghost is Goodness, powerful and wise. By this Trinity in Unity all things whatever are powerfully, wisely, and well established; and in them there is universally, in like manner, propagation and love, essence, sense and aim. For all things consist in themselves of beginning, middle, and end; and exist steadfastly in themselves, and are resplendent in beauty, and do well in Him, from whom they received being, form, and goodness.

Rom. xi. 36.

Upon that unspeakable Trinity the blessed spirits, whom we call angels, unceasingly turn the eyes of their mind. And all of them indeed gaze earnestly upon the three Persons, but severally in a varying manner; yet so that all contemplate everything, and all the hidden principles of things.

The Seraphs, who turn their looks with more nearness

and intensity on the End,[1] gaze upon all things in the End lovingly and sweetly; as also they do upon the Beginning and Middle, both the power of God and the Wisdom. But they contemplate the End itself more attentively than they do the rest.

The Cherubs also gaze upon the End along with the Seraphs; but in that End more the middle, while the Thrones behold more the beginning in the End.

And so these three orders of the first Hierarchy turn rather towards the good End, and the Holy Spirit of God. But among these who are so rapt by the force of the End and of the good, as to be occupied about God alone, although, in the contemplation of that End, the Seraphs, as gazing on the End most chiefly, are called Flames and Loves, the Cherubs, as gazing on the middle in the End, and on order and beauty, are called Knowing; whilst the Thrones, as gazing chiefly on the beginning in the End, and on power and steadfastness, are called Standing; yet still all this third and highest Hierarchy, inasmuch as it is especially bent upon the third Person, in which each order chiefly marks that which is peculiar to it, is therefore on the whole so situated with respect to the other two Hierarchies, supposing it to be compared with them, as the first Order in it is to the remaining two.[2] And although in this sacred Principality there are orders which have love, wisdom, and steadfastness in case of the End and goodness of God, yet this trinity on the whole, as compared with the other Hierarchies, certainly can and ought to be considered as loving.

In like manner the second Hierarchy, which as a whole is directed towards the Middle, and in the Middle, and in order and wisdom, beholds all things, albeit in a triple and

---

[1] This term is used to denote the Third Person of the Blessed Trinity, as the terms Beginning and Middle denote the other two. So in like manner they are described by the attributes of Power, Wisdom and Love respectively, corresponding to the Father, the Son, and the Holy Spirit. A glance at the table which follows, p. 41, will make this clearer.

[2] That is, as the Seraphim are to the Cherubim and Thrones; distinguished chiefly by the attribute of love.

CH. XVI.   *DISTINCTIONS IN OFFICE.*   39

varying method, whence in it also three orders are stationed; this second Hierarchy, I say, when compared with the others, may be designated on the whole as knowledge.

Finally the third, which as a whole is principally turned to the Beginning, in which its members discern and adore all things, but on account of their diverse nature in a threefold order, may on the whole, as compared with the preceding, be rightly named Thrones and Seated.

Moreover all the spirits that are in the second Hierarchy, although they admire all things, yet do they more nearly, and so to say more readily, gaze upon the very Middle, and pattern, through which all things are made. But the Dominations observe the end in that Middle; the Virtues the middle in that Middle; the Powers the beginning in that Middle. This middle Hierarchy gazes on all things in the Middle; and, as compared with the others, may on the whole be called Knowledge. It is occupied chiefly in that method and wisdom, through which all things are finished beautifully and in order.

The third Hierarchy depends in the highest degree on the Beginning; and in it are the Principalities, intent on the end in that Beginning, the Archangels, intent on the middle in that Beginning; and the Angels, intent on the beginning in that Beginning.

Thus the last order of each Hierarchy tends towards the beginning: Angels to the Beginning itself; Powers to the beginning in the Middle; Thrones to the beginning in the End. The middle Hierarchy tends towards the Middle; and in each Hierarchy all the middle Orders towards the middle; the furthest in each towards the end.

Accordingly the first[1] Hierarchy, the one more remote from God, seems, in the power of God, to attend to the being of each one; the mid one, in God's system, to attend to the form of each; and the last and highest one, the perfection of each. Further, in the first, those Spirits who are of the first Order most care for the being of each; those of the second, for form in being; those of the third, most for

---

[1] Or lowest, reckoning upwards.

perfection in being. In the mid Hierarchy, those of the first Order most care for being in form; those of the second for form itself; those of the third for perfection in form. In the third and highest, those of the first Order care most for being in perfection; those of the second for form in perfection; those of the third for perfection itself.

Thus by the ministry of angels all things have their being, form, and completion.

Moreover for the work of founding a church of Christ for a time beneath the angels, out of men that shall be purified, illumined and perfected under Jesus Christ, the angels are ministering spirits. The first Hierarchy purifies, and as it were begets men again to exist by hope in God. The mid one reveals and illumines, that men by faith may have clear insight in God. The last inspires love, that men by love may be made perfect in God. But in the first Hierarchy, the Angels chiefly make it their business that men may be purified and established in hope; the Archangels produce light and faith in hope; the Princedoms love in hope. In the mid Hierarchy the Powers work hope in faith; the Virtues faith itself; the Dominations love in faith. The Thrones, moreover, in the third, work hope in love; the Cherubs faith in love; the Seraphs love itself, the perfectress of all.

After this manner does this threefold Hierarchy, triply, in a triune God, constantly work out a threefold Christianity among men, subsisting by faith, hope, and charity. The Thrones, and in them the Powers, and in them again the Angels,[1] diligently work out, in the power of God, purification, and a pure and simple and steadfast hope; that man may come forth from multeity to simplicity, from base despair to pure hope in God, and may stand firm in it, and by hope in the powerful ray of God, may at length have a spiritual existence in God and Christ. Next the wise Cherubic spirits, and in them the Virtues, and in them again the Archangels, in the

---

[1] These being the first, or lowest, Orders in the three Hierarchies, as the Cherubim, Virtues, and Archangels are the middle ones, and so on, reckoning downwards.

CH. XVI.   *DISTINCTIONS IN OFFICE.*   41

all-disposing wisdom of God, reveal the reasons of things, and the fair verities of the Word of God; and by revealing illumine man, now hoping in God, in the faith of Jesus Christ, who is very Reason, and the Word, and the Messenger of truth; in whom every announcement of light comes in order from the angels midway down to men; that being now purified to hope, they may believe on that Word of God.

The Jews seem to have had hope rather than faith, before the coming of Christ. The Christians in like manner, during the lifetime of Christ upon earth, faith rather than charity, which is the gift of the Holy Ghost.

Lastly the Seraphic spirits, in goodness and love and the Holy Ghost, wholly inflamed with love itself; and the Dominations, wholly inflamed with wisdom; and the Princedoms, wholly inflamed with the power of God, one in another in order, the lower in the higher, and all in the heat of the Spirit of God, fill men, now clear and bright by faith, fully and weightily and sweetly and perfectly with the love of God; that so, being purified by Angels, Powers, and Thrones, illuminated by Archangels, Virtues and Cherubs, they may finally be perfected in the Spirit of God by Princedoms, Dominations, and Seraphs.

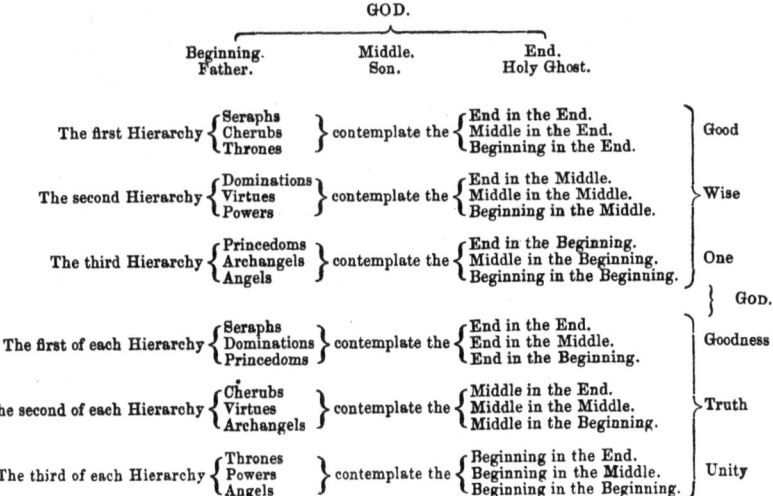

GOD.

Father.	Son.	Holy Ghost.
Power.	Wisdom.	Goodness.
{ Thrones. Powers. Angels.	Cherubs. Virtues. Archangels.	Seraphs. Dominations. Princedoms.
Faith.	Hope.	Charity.
{ Jews.	Christians under Christ.	Christians after the Ascension under the Holy Spirit.

GOD.

Father.	Son.	Holy Ghost.
First.	Second.	Third.
Beginning.	Middle.	End.
Unity.	Beauty.	Goodness.
Centre.	Radii.	Circumference.
Prayer.	Fasting.	Almsgiving.
Hope.	Faith.	Charity.
Repentance.	Baptism.	Eucharist.
Thought.	Word.	Deed.
Root.	Stalk.	Ear.
Fire.	Light.	Heat.[1]

As there are nine Orders of angels, so are there in like manner of men, through Christ in God, and by the ministry of the angels. And in these, all things are in all; since all hope, and believe, and love God in Christ. It neither is, nor can be, otherwise in this threefold Ecclesiastical Hierarchy.

In the last place are those who are specially in the state of hope; the second are those who believe in hope; the third are those who love in hope; the fourth those who

---

[1] I have not thought it worth while to set down in English the whole of the long list of triplets, as it stands in the Latin, but have selected a few merely as a sufficient specimen. With this list the Cambridge MS. (Gg. iv. 26) ends, at fol. 171 b; the last leaf of all containing only a few hasty lines, apparently as rough hints for some other composition, such as "Seraphim in amore Dei ardent," etc.

hope in faith; the fifth are those who especially believe; the sixth those who love in faith; the seventh, as it were Thrones, are those who firmly hope in love; the eighth are those who believe in love; the ninth and last are those who especially and wholly love.[1]

Those who are without hope, faith, and love, are in a state of all disorder, coldness, darkness and death. Among them there is no order, but an everlasting wandering. Still, there are degrees of disorder, unhappiness and misery. And agreeably thereto set down on the other side nine bands of men, under the Devil, the prince of darkness, and under his ministering satellites; who, in their state of utmost confusion and defect, and privation of all goodness, are distributed into nine most horrible troops: set down, I say, beneath them, nine bands of men, who under their chieftain the Devil, beneath the standards of death, in the armour of darkness, are all fighting with the sword of impiety and hatred; each one, alas! most miserably, to his own everlasting destruction.

According to the testimony of Solomon, the angelic, and every spiritual nature, was created at the same time as the corporeal. For he says, "He that liveth for ever created all things in general." Those spirits were created as inhabitants of the empyrean heaven,[2] which shines like fire above the firmament. They were created in innocence; but a great part, of their own will, not long afterwards, wishing in a guilty pride to exalt themselves, fell from the highest to the lowest. Our Saviour Jesus Christ bare

Ecclus. xviii. 1.

---

[1] It may make this somewhat clearer to notice that the three successive bases or foundations here referred to are Hope, Faith and Love, whilst the same three virtues form the three ascending gradations on each foundation.

[2] So Milton speaks of " th' empyreal host Of Angels;" and elsewhere describes the spheres in their ascending order:—
"They pass the planets sev'n, and pass the fix'd,
And that crystalline sphere whose balance weighs
The trepidation talk'd, and that first mov'd."
Beyond these was the empyrean heaven, the dwelling-place of God and his Angels. See *Par. Lost*, iii. 481 (with Bp. Newton's Comment) and Cary's Dante, *Paradise*, ii. 112.

witness to this, when he said, "I beheld Satan, as lightning, fall from heaven." Satan also stood not fast in the truth. The remainder, looking up to God, partly through their own will, partly through grace working with them, happily remained in the truth; not through their own merits, but through grace being made blessed in God. On the other hand Lucifer with his followers fell not through God's disdain, but by his own proper fault. These wretched and lost angels inhabit the dense and murky atmosphere around us,[1] and are harassers of men, lest they should grow sluggish through neglect and apathy; being destined to be hereafter more miserable after the last judgment. St. Paul teaches us that we have our wrestlings against "the prince of the power of the air." For they unceasingly endeavour to render us like themselves, that we may feel a like punishment with them. But during our life here angels are delegated, by the mercy of God, to the protection of mankind. For each one has his own angel as his guardian aud preserver, and also as his constant monitor and instigator to what is good; otherwise weak man would neither be able to persist in the good, nor to oppose the evil. It is the opinion of some that, according to their advance in labouring, will be their advance in blessedness; which these disputants call *accidental merit*.[2] All the angels have a care of us; but those to whom we are entrusted as guardians

---

[1] "And by *Tartarus* here (2 Pet. ii. 4,) in all probability is meant this lower caliginous air, or atmosphere of the earth, according to that of St. Austin concerning these angels, *Post peccatum in hanc sunt detrusi caliginem, ubi tamen et aer.*"—Cudworth, *Intel. Syst.* (1678), p. 817.

[2] I am not sure whether the passage which Colet had in view was Art. iii. of *Quæst.* xciii. in the Supplement to the *Summa* of Aquinas. The concluding words are: "Quamvis etiam ex ipso genere actus possit aliquis gradus in merendo considerari; non quidem respectu præmii essentialis, quod est gaudium de Deo; sed respectu alicujus accidentalis præmii, quod est gaudium de aliquo bono creato." There is a similar line of argument in Lib. iv. Dist. xlix. A. of the *Sentences* of Peter Lombard. The chief texts on which both rely are John xiv. 2, and 1 Cor. xv. 41. It will be noticed that Colet speaks with but scanty respect of the author, or authors, from whom he quotes.

provide for us with more earnest care.¹ Wherefore they act most rightly who daily worship and pray to their own guardian angel with some special prayer.

The Devils, unclean spirits, possessed of reason, subtle, envious, strive to injure the human race, long to beguile them, delude their senses and corrupt their affections. Whether sleeping or waking, they unsettle the world and disturb the elements. As hypocrites, they often "transform themselves into angels of light;" in the form of Idols they arrogate to themselves the majesty of God; in their pride they aim at empire. They are incessantly waging war against men, both by openly assaulting them, and by secretly plotting against them. If victorious, they exult; if conquered, they go away in confusion, so as not again to venture to tempt in the same case and to the same sin. Of these malignant natures David makes unceasing complaint in his hymns; and as though ever in danger, implores aid for himself, and invokes curses upon those evil spirits. " Be pleased, O Lord, to deliver me: O Lord, make haste to help me. Let them be ashamed and confounded together that seek after my soul to destroy it. Let them be driven backward and put to shame that wish me evil. Let them be desolate for a reward of their shame." Again in another Psalm: "Make haste, O God, to deliver me; make haste to help me, O Lord. Let them be ashamed and confounded that seek after my soul." In truth he does scarcely anything else in all his Psalms than pray to God in Christ, that among so many and great enemies he may come off victorious, and be saved in God. To this perilous war men are called by God through Jesus Christ. But we must not proceed to it rashly or heedlessly, but weigh our strength first, and look beforehand to the risk. Yea and before each one becomes a Christian, or a priest and religious in Christianity, let him first consider carefully with himself what he will be able to do; lest, if he be vanquished, the Devil, now become

2 Cor. xi. 14.

Ps. xl. 13-15.

Ps. lxx. 1, 2.

---

¹ This opinion concerning guardian angels was held by Origen. See the passage quoted by Jewel, *Replie* (1611), p. 156.

an open enemy, should deal more harshly and miserably with him, than if he had remained a subject and tributary of Satan. For this cause Jesus Christ, the leader and captain in this war, when summoning his fellow-soldiers to him, as St. Luke relates, although he would have all men to be saved, yet (that they might not in avoiding Scylla fall into Charybdis, nor in search of safety rush into greater condemnation) admonished the multitudes to beware and look heedfully to what they were about to undertake; willing rather that they should live as servants to the Devil, than be slain in open war as enemies; and be condemned with a less rather than with a greater condemnation. And so he said to them: "What king, going to make war against another king, sitteth not down first, and consulteth whether he be able with ten thousand to meet him that cometh against him with twenty thousand? Or else, while the other is yet a great way off, he sendeth an ambassage, and desireth conditions of peace." When we have made profession of any better life in Christ, then the Devil prepares himself with a more numerous and better equipped army, that he may assault and vex us; and if he conquer us in rebellion, as a tyrant he will more cruelly torment us; so that, as St. Paul writes to the Hebrews,[1] "It had been better not to have known the way of righteousness, than to turn back again."

<small>Luke xiv. 31, 32.</small>

<small>2 Pet.ii.21.</small>

The Devils are by nature subtle, observing the natural world with keen eye, skilful by long use and experience, diviners of the future, moreover, and at times well versed in former revelations. But, evil themselves, they use all for what is evil; plotting before everything the everlasting destruction of mankind. Enduring not, in their envy, the glory which men are to have in Christ, they suggest evil under the guise of good; and if at any time they prompt aught that is good, they do it for an evil purpose. True good they always dissuade; and if ever they have dissuaded evil, it is that they may lead into greater evil. At times

---

[1] By a slight fault of memory, Colet here quotes as from St. Paul the text referred to in the margin. The circumstance, trivial in itself, will help to show how full his mind was of St. Paul.

they harm men's bodies, and shatter their limbs, and bring on them diseases: before their senses they place vain phantoms, and overwhelm the mind with false images. On which account St. Peter wrote to us, "Be sober, be vigilant; because your adversary the devil, as a roaring lion, walketh about, seeking whom he may devour." 1 Pet. v. 8.

By divine grace, and by the assistance of the angels, by continual prayers and atonements, we may both resist the Devil and overcome him; especially by imitating our leader Christ, who overcame when tempted, and broke the power of the Devil.

END OF THE CELESTIAL HIERARCHY.

ON THE

ECCLESIASTICAL HIERARCHY.

CHAPTER I.

Introductory; on the existence of a Hierarchy in the Church on earth, answering to the Celestial; on Jesus its Head and pattern for imitation; on the system of figures through which God conveys knowledge to man, and on the light of tradition which illustrates them.

HOLY Scripture teaches us that the human priesthood has within it from above a divine wisdom and operation. In this human priesthood are all those who are consecrated to God in Christ. The sense of Holy Scripture is entirely spiritual; which sense was fully shewn by Jesus to his disciples. And from this source we must believe that by the appointment of the Apostles, there grew up in the growing church sacrifices, rites, and ceremonies. Jesus himself, after his resurrection, declared what the meaning of Scripture was with regard to the condition and state of the new church in Him. That spiritual sense, therefore, which requires the spirit of prophecy for it to be understood, is the wisdom and meaning of our whole Christian Church thus built up. For it was of Christ that Moses spake. And to this Pope Leo also, a weighty authority, who succeeded to the helm of the Apostles, has borne witness, in a sermon on the fast of Pentecost,[1] in these words:—" We

---

[1] The passage occurs at the beginning of the second sermon " De jejunio Pentecostes."—See Sancti Leonis Magni . . . . . Opera (1753), vol. i. p. 316.

must not doubt, dearly beloved, but that every Christian observance is of God's teaching, and that whatever has been devoutly received as customary by the Church, proceeds from the tradition of the Apostles and from the teaching of the Holy Spirit, who now also rules over the hearts of the faithful by his ordinances, to the end that they should be both obediently kept, and wisely understood, by all." Thus Leo the First, who sat on the papal throne four hundred and fifty years after Christ.[1] This is the way of elucidating the Scriptures, not so much by words as by acts, not so much by teaching and writing as in reality, according to the appointment and command of the Apostles, that Saint Dionysius undertakes to write of to Timotheus. Before which, he conjures him[2] seriously and in many words, not wickedly to disclose to the multitude the principles of sacred rites, and things most holy, and the mysteries of God and of divine worship, nor to impart them to any but men like himself, of the greatest holiness, keeping in mind that precept of Jesus Christ: "Give not that which is holy unto the dogs, neither cast ye your pearls before swine." He bids him rather keep all in sacred and serious privacy; and store them up and tend them religiously, with all love and reverence, in the deep of his own heart; imitating herein Jesus, the author of all priesthood and sacred rites, who taught the mysteries to none but his own disciples, and that too apart; and taught not all even to them, who were not yet perfect and spiritually minded, nor able to bear all. That same Jesus now, as Light unspeakable, at the right hand of the Father, shines more brightly and more fully upon the angels, beings of far higher nature than man, and bestows on them a more abundant revelation; then in turn 'through them on such men as tower aloft by severance and separation from the body, and approach more nearly the

Matth. vii. 6.

---

[1] He succeeded Sixtus III. in 440, and died in 461.

[2] "Sed observa diligentius ne sancta sanctorum efferas, neu prophanis luminibus violanda permittas," etc., sec. 1; but more fully at the end of Ch. ii. of the *Cel. Hier.*, where is the passage from St. Matth. vii. 6.—See above, p. 14.

angelic nature, in purification, illumination and perfection. Notable in which kind was John the son of Zebedee, who by the revelation of an angel on the Lord's day saw many things, which he wrote down for the seven churches; for the right understanding of which there is need in truth of the same revealing angel; which things that divine penman has called the Apocalypse. Through the angels men have a revelation, under seemly figures, that[1] * * * * * * * * * * * * * there is a recognition of degree, and of devotion to God, and means by which men are established in different states of being in Christ, that in different ways they may be illumined in him, and when so illumined, may be perfected. And in all these, in Christ, there is a truly single principle, so to speak, and what Dionysius calls an intensity,[2] and all strive for the same object, according to the strength of the grace given them. For "there are diversities of gifts, but the same Spirit." "The manifestation of the Spirit is given to every man to profit withal;" to "one after this manner, and to another after that." The endeavour of all is that they may be perfected by the divine agencies, and as far as is possible made like to God. He that attains this in the highest degree is the Bishop, and rightly holds the first place in the ministry, to the end that he should transmit that which he has received. And the greater he is, the more should he serve in the office of love and ministration. Then, in the next place, those who are second perform this task, and transmit what they have received to the third. And thus the work goes on in order, and the imbuing of men with truth in Christ proceeds; all striving upwards, and delivering to those beneath them what they have drawn from above, that they may be perfect members in Christ, through a yearning love of God and their neighbour. Through the love of God they receive, through the love of their neighbour they give, that

1 Cor. xii. 4, 7.

1 Cor. vii. 7.

---

[1] One leaf is here wanting from the manuscript.

[2] "Nostros item varios et inconstantes motus honestarum amore rerum, in eum intento nosque intendente, constringit et complicat, et in unam ac divinam perficit vitam."—C. i. sec. 1.

so, being fashioned in righteousness by love on either hand, they may be ministers of the grace of God, from whom are all things in Christ. For in him each one ought to be so ready to give what he has received, as to appear to have received it for no other reason but to give; that in the giving there may be set forth the receiving, and the love of God in the love of our neighbour; since we then declare that we love Him, if, as St. John teaches in his Epistle, we love our neighbour. "If a man say, I love God, and hateth his brother, he is a liar." 1 Joh. iv. 20.

In this mutual love consists all order, duty and office in the Church; and the whole Ecclesiastical Hierarchy in it rests on the love of God and of our neighbour; in receiving and giving; in an imitation of Jesus its head, who is all love; in a desire for each one's sanctifying himself with the fire of love, that he in turn may sanctify others; so that, in this office of sanctifying, the whole Church may copy Jesus, to the end that at length they may be made wholly like him; as St. John writes:—"Every man that hath this hope in him, purifieth himself, even as he is pure." 1 Joh. iii. 3. And again he says:—"He that saith he abideth in him, ought himself also so to walk, even as he walked." Ib. ii. 6. In this ecclesiastical chorus Jesus has himself begun the sacred dance; that all may follow him with linked hands.[1] He was the fulness of righteousness, that all in him should jointly imitate his righteousness, which consists in giving and in loving, because from love we have received. For what other perfection is there in the angels, than the giving what they have received? In this giving they more resemble God than in receiving. For there is no perfection in receiving. God receives nothing; but he gives in the highest degree, and by giving he is in the highest degree set forth. Wherefore St. Paul says that "it is more blessed to give than to receive." Acts xx. 35. In Christ therefore, in whom are all things, who is the highest principle and limit of order and of our hierarchy, who has received nothing from us, who gives all things, who has placed us in a course of truth,

---

[1] See above, p. 10.

who has raised us above the law of Moses to the light of the gospel and of revelation, who has made us to know by faith and to act on our faith, who by his Spirit has brought us forth into a better state; that in the law of the Spirit we should rightly imitate the blessed angels, in whose virtue we begin to be spiritual; that being at length perfected we may be spirits; the endeavour to imitate whose super-celestial life of bliss made St. Paul say that "our conversation is in heaven;"—yet in this happy state in Jesus Christ, because we are as yet men to outward view, whilst at any rate this our nature is strange to us, its powers and operations are both profitably declared and assured to us by a groundwork of sensible signs; that they may be reminders to us, and inducements to the things which are not seen. For so long as we are in a world of figures, and "see through a glass darkly," no training or fashioning or forming of us, no working and imitating spiritual beings, can dispense with corporeal figures. For as long as we are in the body, our sacraments and ecclesiastical system must be in some degree corporeal. Under Moses the legal hierarchy was wholly corporeal and figurative; under Christ, in whom we are now imitating the truth which spirits possess, there has been established an ecclesiastical hierarchy, partly corporeal, partly spiritual. But in the hierarchy triumphant, all will be spiritual, since our animal bodies will have been all transformed into bodies spiritual. Then shall we burst forth from these signs and allurements of grace to the open face and truth; that with the angels we may then truly, and in our true nature, behold truth herself "face to face." All ought to aim at one object, and as far as possible to assume its form. Now the one prize of our Church is Jesus, towards whom we all run, that we may wholly obtain him. Him ought every one to represent in himself, and to have a taste and savour of; albeit not all in the same manner and in equal measure, yet each so far as he can, and so far as is given to each: "according as God hath dealt to every man the measure of faith," each as he thinks that he is able, should strive to represent that which is our Head and undivided. And though he represent not all of it in the highest degree, yet must he do so in as high a degree as he can, lest he should seem to be loth to do all he can, and thus to misuse his grace, which is given to every one according to the "manifestation of the Spirit;" and lest he should seem of choice to be feeble, when he can be strong; which sort of wilful faintness is damnable. For he wickedly effaces the image, who does not reproduce it so far as he is stamped with it. For we are all sealed with one signet, and have received the impress of one king, like his coin, that we should represent the one on whom all things depend; in accordance with whose seal and impression we must act. And in that first and undivided one, Jesus Christ, in whom we have been alike signed with his image and mark, that we should be Jesuits[1] in him; we are alike signed, I say, by him, being in him consecrated to a priesthood, to offer sacrifices to God in him, and to present a holy oblation, even as he presented, who, as St. Peter writes, "suffered for us, that we should follow his steps." If we be in him, as St. John testifies, "we ought ourselves also so to walk, even as he walked." In Christ should every one offer himself as a whole burnt-offering to God, that he may be all on fire with love upon the altar of the cross. "Hereby perceive we the love of God, because he laid down his life for us; and we ought to lay down our lives for the brethren."

1 Cor. xii. 7.

1 Pet. ii. 21.

1 John ii. 6.

1 John iii. 16.

But let us now discourse of the Ecclesiastical Hierarchy.

Every hierarchy is a system and summary of things sacred. In the Christian hierarchy the office and duty of the Bishop is, to comprise in himself and possess all sacred things. For the Bishop is a veritable sacrament, and a summary of all that follows after him in the Church. He apprehends and represents fully and clearly in himself the whole priesthood; so that there is nothing in any inferior minister given by

---

[1] The name of *Jesuates* had been given to an order of "Apostolic Clerks," founded by John Colombini of Sienna in 1368. The followers of Ignatius Loyola (who was twenty-five years younger than Colet) did not formally receive their title till 1540.

God that exists not in Christ our Bishop[1] more substantially, and clearly, and in a yet more perfect manner. Nay, it follows that through him all spiritual and divine gifts must be transmitted to all the orders of the Church; and that from him nothing goes forth in the Church which is not first contained in him, the Bishop; and that nothing praiseworthy and divine exists in any one beneath the Bishop that is not recognized as having proceeded from him. For in truth if he were wanting in anything proceeding from God that is found in any inferior person, such as holiness, wisdom, justice, he assuredly is not the one to occupy the seat of the Bishop.

The creator and founder of our hierarchy is that same one and all-powerful Jesus. Through him the Father with the Holy Spirit, the adorable Trinity, of his goodness, is the cause that there exists this human hierarchy, warring under Christ its leader, beneath the standard of truth, with spiritual weapons. That is the cause also of its well-being and perfectness. For it was the will of the good God that man should be saved; and that cannot be unless men be made godlike, and refashioned to a divine condition, and become gods, by being made like unto God, that they may represent God. For to that as their end all things strive earnestly and most ardently, that they may be fashioned after the divine image. To that end, all who are called in Christ are consecrated to God, that whilst living here they may represent God so far as they are able. And how far men are able, Jesus, who is God and man, has taught us. For he willed to be made man, that he might show among men a godlike way of living;[2] to whose likeness all, in him, ought to strive. For "he that saith he abideth in him, ought himself also so to walk, even as he walked." He is the head both of the celestial and the human hierarchy; in whom the world had a pattern for imitation, and now the angels also in heaven

1 John ii. 6.

---

[1] There appears to be a confusion here between an earthly bishop and Christ himself, the "Bishop of our souls," as it is to the former that the concluding words of the paragraph must refer.

[2] The reader will notice here, what has been pointed out more fully in the Introduction, how the Dionysian system throws into the background

have an ensample, with love of whom each one ought to be inflamed, so that being moved towards him, he may behold nothing but him, may turn his eyes to no other quarter, may in no wise look back again; but, as St. Paul writes touching himself to the Philippians: "Forgetting those things which are behind, and reaching forth unto those things which are before, he may press toward the mark for the prize of the high calling of God in Christ Jesus;" that by imitating him he "may win Christ," "being made conformable to his death," that at the resurrection he may be fashioned like him in glory, that at length by death he may "apprehend that for which also he is apprehended by Christ Jesus" for God: that so all that are in him may by every means be brought to the one only principle of his perfection; that, being formed by him, they may represent him in the best degree they can; being constantly sustained, nourished, renewed, and refreshed by him every day, and being carried on "from glory to glory," until they are wholly transformed after his likeness. To him, I say, should they be brought, being zealously inflamed with love, that in him they may offer and sacrifice themselves as whole burnt-offerings and incense of a sweet savour to God, with the fire of love; and there should be a flight from these lower things as eager and anxious as if one thought that the enemy and death were ever pressing on behind. The reality of the emblem by which he is guiding his steps, and the highest object, should ever be set before his eyes; to it he should rise and run and fly; it should he seize, and taste, and feed on, and be wholly brought to very Christ in God. This wholesome strife, indeed, there ought to be on the part of every one in the Church; that all men should in all things have an appearance, a sound, a savour, taste, and representation of Christ.

Phil. iii. 13, 14, 10.

---

the atonement of Christ. It sees in him "an ensample of godly life," rather than "a sacrifice for sin" also. Thus Meier:—"Christus igitur esse non potest nisi illuminator generis humani; et, homo si factus est, præceptor et magister, solo prophetico munere functus. ...... Quo enim Christus munere debuerit fungi, hierarchiarum ille ordo fungitur." *Dionysii* etc. p. 19.

God renders godlike, by imparting himself to the angels immediately and singly; to men indirectly, and by a manifold system of images, of which Holy Scripture is full (which Dionysius calls the substance[1] of our priesthood), the Old Testament especially; and the New, added thereto, and written by evangelists and apostles, is not wanting in such figures. These books, in the time of Dionysius, were placed by the authority of the early Church among the sacred and canonical writings, and were approved with all reverence. To these was added a more hidden system of wisdom, not committed to writing by the Apostles, but sacredly and religiously kept in their minds and bosoms. This did they, as worthy, learn from Jesus Christ, and afterwards handed down only to those that were worthy and like themselves, charging them not to commit the matters to writing, lest divine things should be held cheap, and "that which is holy be given unto the dogs, and pearls to swine." The sublime mind of St. John so shadowed forth by similitudes of his own that which in this kind he saw, as that scarce any but himself can understand,[2] unless he be moved by the same spirit of prophecy. For ordinances commonly practised in the Church, and transmitted from the Apostles themselves to us, were by them not committed to writing, but were entrusted to the practising of the common sort, whilst the

Matt. vii. 6.

---

[1] The passage is in the *Eccl. Hier.* I. § 4:—"Substantia enim sacerdotii nostri Scriptura sacra est, nobis divinitus tradita." As he goes on to attach an apparently equal importance to the oral traditions, "quæ ex animo in animum . . . . . sine litteris transfusa sunt" (which Colet refers to as the "more hidden system of wisdom"), Corderius alleges the passage as a strong argument—"pulchrum et irrefragabile argumentum"—against those who would make Scripture only the rule of faith and manners.

[2] Colet speaks just afterwards of what he seems to regard as the fruitless speculations of commentators on the Apocalypse. As he almost certainly quotes Alcuin in another passage (*Eccl. Hier.* ch. ii. pt. iii.), it is possible that he may have had in view, when he thus wrote, Alcuin's own Commentary. The *uncertainty* of interpretation which seems to have dissatisfied Colet, could not be better illustrated than by the choice of three reasons which Alcuin gives for the number of the twenty-four Elders in ch. iii. 4 of the Revelation.

reasons of them were retained by the chief men only in the Church.

These reasons they disclosed not, save to those whom they knew to be of purer natures, and advanced to the episcopal rank; and by them were the undisguised principles of things and of the sacraments understood. By the wisdom of the Apostles it was brought about, that a draught of the same should be given to the common people, under a figurative system, as it were; that being untaught they might drink and feed on coarser food. For, as saith St. Paul, "there is not in every man that knowledge." Holy bread, according to our Saviour's testimony, is not to be "given to the dogs." Of the fine flour[1] of sincerity the bread of the priests alone is made. But that on which common men feed must needs have somewhat of the bran of figures and images; lest by the naked verity their eyes should be overmuch dazzled, or they be stirred up to vain thoughts. Hence Sacraments and ceremonies, whether purgatorial or illuminating or perfecting, were instituted for the common people by the Apostles themselves, of excellent inner meaning, and denoted by the choicest images. The reasons of them, however, were committed not to writing, but to the minds of the holy Bishops; that, just as the signs follow their course among the common people, so the reasons of them should follow in the minds of the Bishops. The unfolding of these reasons has at length been attempted, after very many years, by William, Bishop of Mende;[2] who in this pursuit divines

1Cor.viii.7.

Matth. vii. 6.

---

[1] Lat. *semela*, Pliny's *similago*.

[2] Guillaume Durand, born at Puy-Moisson about 1232, was raised to the Bishopric of Mende in 1287; and after declining the Archbishopric of Ravenna, died Nov. 1, 1296. His great work, the *Rationale divinorum officiorum*, was one of the earliest books printed. In the British Museum is a fine copy, printed on vellum, by John Fust and Peter [Schoyffer] of Gernszheim, 1459. It was often reprinted in the 15th and 16th centuries. A translation of the first Book, with notes, was published by two English clergymen, Messrs. Neale and Webb, in 1843; and the whole work was translated into French in 1854 by Charles Barthélemy.

"Le protestantisme," complains M. Barthélemy (*Préface* p. vi.), " avaite porté un rude échec à la sainteté des traditions ; vint la renais-

and conjectures as he can, much as they do, who tell us what the Apocalypse of St. John means. In all subjects of this kind, whether written with such a material nature in the emblems, or accommodated to manner and custom, we need either a revealer to whom the truth has been revealed, or else the same prophetic spirit by whom they were ordained, that he may disclose them : otherwise the vision of man must needs be baffled. But whatever things are in frequent use in the Church, we must believe to have been instituted by the Apostles as symbols and signs of divine principles. The reasons of these were retained by men taught of God himself, and they, to use the words of Dionysius, veiled the heavenly sacraments in visible signs, setting before the ignorant simplicity in the midst of distraction, what was spiritual amid what was bodily, things divine amid things human, things far off amid what was near, and things strange amid what was familiar; and as they wrote but little touching these at the first, they committed the greatest part to the memories of men. For when they went forth preaching the gospel and proclaiming Christ, such as they met with and found willing to believe, them they instructed with

---

sance, païenne dans les arts, dans les lettres, dans les mœurs ; enfin le dix-huitième siècle, avec son rire perfide autant qu' insensé, et qui, après avoir brisé tous les liens qui rattachaient l'homme à Dieu, le courba vers la terre et lui arracha, dans les funestes étreintes du philosophisme, l'abjuration de ses souvenirs, seule planche de salut qui lui restât."

There is some truth in this; and the poetic taste of the late Dr. Neale, aided by his fellow-translator, discovered something that is valuable, as well as merely curious, in Durandus. But, though there are signs, I think, of Colet having drawn an expression or two from him elsewhere, it can cause little surprise to find that he speaks of his labours, in the present passage, with no great apparent respect. What, for instance to a man of Dean Colet's strong sense, could have seemed the value of the following piece of symbolizing, which occurs in Bk. 1, ch. iv. on *Church Bells:*—" Moreover, as the rope begins from the wood on which the bell hangs, by which wood the Cross of our Lord is understood, it is a fit sign of Holy Scripture coming down from the wood of the Cross. And as the rope consists of three strands, so also does Scripture consist of a threefold strain, namely, History, Allegory and Morality. And so the descent of the rope from the wood, in the hands of the priest, is the descent of Scripture from its mystery in the mouth of the preacher."—" Ad hæc cum funis etc."

further doctrine, so far as seemed good, and arranged them in order; placing over the Church presbyters and elders for the younger to obey, and leaving certain sacramental pledges in words and signs according; to be to the people a kind of supports, as it were, and buttresses, and convenient reminders of a higher and simpler truth; that by these the multitude of Christians might be kept together in religion, and religion be guarded from the profane. The Bishops, however were brought into open light; and these possess the real meanings of the signs. The common people of the Christians are coloured by them; the people of the Jews had but the shadow. In the Christian religion, Dionysius, as a Bishop, knew the mysteries of the sacraments; and when commencing to write of these to Timotheus, he adjured him not to divulge them except to men holy and like himself, men of the episcopal order, learned and good; on condition that they too should not divulge them except to such like; lest "that which is holy be given" (against the injunction of the gospel) "unto the dogs, and pearls unto swine."

CHAPTER II.

PART I.

Introduction to the Sacrament of Illumination, or Baptism.[1]

THE object of our Christian religion is nothing else than our becoming like God. "Be ye perfect," saith our Saviour, "even as your Father which is in heaven is per- Matth. v. 48.

---

[1] Each Chapter of the *Eccl. Hier.* with the exception of the first, which is introductory, is divided into three parts, or sections; the first being a kind of preface to the subject treated of, the second relating the ceremonies with which the sacrament under consideration was solemnized, and the third containing a *Theoria*, or spiritual contemplation of them. The Scholiast on Ambrosius's version makes this harmonize with the threefold system of "purification, illumination and perfection," of which Dionysius is full:—"In cujus prima parte quasi accedentes purgat, preparatque ad sacratiorem intelligentiam; in secunda illuminat; et in tertia de spiritu litteræ perficit et consummat." P. 45. a.

fect." Now we become like him, by working out and executing his commands. We shall become altogether like him if we have loved him; and we shall love him if we have kept his commands. "If a man love me, he will keep my words." Love is the source of all things. From love we believe, from belief we hope. Love precedes faith, as hope follows it. Thus Polycarp writes to the Philippians :—[1] "By love we are begotten again to a new and spiritual being in God." When beloved by God, we are born again in him full of faith and hope, so as in Christ to cry Abba, Father. First must you be begotten again in God, that you may then grow up to a better state. We are begotten again to God by his Spirit, who warms and purifies us, that we may believe in Christ and hope in him. When from love we believe, and hope for that which we believe, then are we born again sons of God; this is the baptism with the Holy Ghost and with fire. This spiritual meaning is shadowed forth and signified by figures, so as for the spirit to be clothed with what is bodily by the one, and bodies to be made spiritual by the other. By these we are admonished to be mindful of the divine regeneration, by which we are "born, not of blood, nor of the will of the flesh, nor of the will of man, but of God;" and to consider that we must live, not according to man, but according to God our Father, in whose household we are, being not of the world but of God; and to live in this world, not so as to please men, but God. For what else is the object of our new birth, than that we should be what we were not? Is not the birth of the one a decay of the other? Are we not begotten again that we may die to the world and to men, and live unto God? that so our conversation may be in heaven and we may not be satisfied in the world with food and raiment? It was the will of the Apostles that this perfection of a new life, to which we are begotten again by the Spirit of God, should be signified by figures; that through figures men may approach to the truth, and through them also truth may come down

Joh. xiv. 23.

Joh. i. 13.

---

[1] I have not been able to verify this quotation.

to men; that so figures and sacraments may be means towards the truth, and towards men's being brought to the truth by the Spirit of truth.

CHAPTER II.

PART II.

On the Sacrament of Baptism.

WHILST men were altogether unlike God, and like themselves, it pleased the good God to be like man, that he might render men like God.¹ "The Word was made flesh, and dwelt among us." "He who was in the form of God, made himself of no reputation, and took upon him the form of a servant, and was made in the likeness of men. And being found in fashion as a man, he humbled himself, and became obedient unto death, even the death of the cross." "He hath made him to be sin for us, who knew no sin, that we might be made the righteousness of God in him." This was the eternal Son of God, whom the Father "sending in the likeness of sinful flesh, and for sin, condemned sin in the flesh; that the righteousness of the law might be fulfilled in us, who walk not after the flesh, but after the Spirit," in the acknowledgment and worship of the true God. His office on earth the Bishops everywhere discharge, and in him act as he acted, and with like zeal strive

Joh. i. 14.
Phil. ii. 6—8.

2 Cor. v. 21.

Rom. viii. 3, 4.

---

¹ It is observable how Colet here expands, and brings into due prominence the work of Christ's atonement, as compared with Dionysius. The latter, in the passage corresponding to this, briefly says that the Bishop, desiring the salvation of men by their being made like to God, "proclaims to all the gospel, truly so called, how that God, in mercy to those on earth, of his own natural goodness, deigned himself to come to us, in keeping with his love to man, and by a union with himself to assimilate, as fire does, what is so united, according to men's several capacity for being made godlike." This, with the quotation of St. John i. 12, which follows, is all that Dionysius has in this place corresponding to what Colet dwells on so fully and scripturally. It has been elsewhere said that the work of the atonement is left very much in the background in the system of Dionysius.

for the purification and illumination and salvation of mankind, by constant preaching of the truth, and diffusion of gospel light, even as he strove. St. Paul says, "God was in Christ, reconciling the world unto himself, not imputing their trespasses unto them, and hath committed unto us the word of reconciliation. Now then we are ambassadors for Christ." Acting in Christ's stead, they fan the fire which Christ came to send upon the earth, that they may increase it. "I am come," he saith in St. Luke, "to send fire on the earth, and what will I, if it be already kindled? I have a baptism to be baptized with, and how am I straitened till it be accomplished!" He baptized, as John testified, "with the Holy Ghost and with fire." For fire purifies, illumines, and perfects. That fire of the spirit does this in the souls of men. For the increasing of this wholesome conflagration amid the forest of men, the Bishops are ministers and vicars of Jesus, and they seek the kindling of mankind in God. Now this fire is, I doubt it not, the holy love of God, which Bishops worthy of love diffuse over the world,[1] being themselves lovers of men in God, that they may in turn love God again, and being born anew by the love of God, may live in God, believing in the Son whom he hath sent, and placing all their hope in God. For love is the source of begetting; holy love, of begetting holiness; and the love of God, of godliness. Now the messenger of this goodness, compassion, love and tenderness of God, was his lovely Son Jesus Christ, who first in wisdom brought down love to men, that they, being born anew by love, might in turn love their heavenly Father along with him. To them that acknowledge, admit, hear and receive the "messenger of the great counsel," Jesus, "gave he power

---

[1] Erasmus has a fine passage on what the episcopal office is, and what it is not, in his *Enarratio in Psal. I.*:—"Nam juxta Paulum præcipuum ac peculiare munus Episcoporum est, docere plebem Christianam, nec docere Platonem, aut Aristotelem, aut scholasticas quæstionum argutias, sed *Christi doctrinam, simplicissimi simplicissimam.*" The whole is too long to quote. The words in italics might have suggested the line of Tennyson,

"Not preaching simple Christ to simple men."

to become the sons of God;" that the sons of men, now believing in Christ, might be happily born anew the sons of God. Whilst he lived as mortal man in the flesh, he performed the office of Bishop himself, teaching the duty thereof in actual practice. And at that time there was salvation in believing on him who was present. When, however, after he had shewn the form of a Bishop, our good and patient High Priest offered himself as a propitiatory sacrifice to God, then there began to be like salvation for such as believed on those who discharged the work of Jesus in his stead; who in Jesus' stead preach him as he preached himself. "For we preach not ourselves," says St. Paul, "but Christ Jesus the Lord; and ourselves your servants for Jesus' sake." Therefore, as St. Luke records, did the Saviour say to those whom he sent to preach the gospel: "He that heareth you heareth me; and he that despiseth you despiseth me; and he that despiseth me despiseth him that sent me." For God was in Christ, and Christ in his Apostles and in the successors of his Apostles, for the reconciling of the world to God. Every Bishop accordingly in the church, as the blessed martyr Ignatius has testified in his Epistle to the Magnesians,[1] acts the part of God and Christ; and Ignatius bids all obey him as the Lord himself. Under the Bishop, priests occupy the place of the Apostles. Under these, deacons are ministers for the faithful people. The office of the Bishop is, like Christ, to preach constantly and diligently the truth he has received. For he is as it

2 Cor. iv. 5.

Luke x. 16.

---

[1] This is rather the general sense of the letter in question than an exact quotation from it. Ignatius commends a "fellow-servant Zotion," because that he "subjectus est Episcopo ut gratiæ Dei, et Presbyterio ut legi Jesu Christi." And he adds, "Sed et vos decet non concuti ætate Episcopi, sed secundum virtutem Dei Patris omnem reverentiam ei tribuere." And again, "Subjicimini Episcopo et adinvicem, ut Christus Patri secundum carnem."—*Epistolæ* (Oxon. 1708) pp. 59 sqq. Indeed the precept occurs in almost every one of the extant Epistles. This is incidentally shewn by the younger Pico's quoting the Epistle to the *Trallians* in evidence of the same principle :—" Ita namque scribit beatissimus Ignatius Episcopus et martyr ad Trallianos : Sicut Episcopus forma est Patris omnium, presbyteri vero sicut consensus Dei, et conjunctio Apostolorum Christi." (*Op.* 1601, *pars* ii. p. 198).

were a messenger midway between God and men, to announce to men heavenly things, as Christ did; to render others such and suchlike as God has rendered him; to proclaim unceasingly that precept of the Apostle's, "Be ye followers of me, even as I also am of Christ." For the life of man upon earth consists in an imitation, and advance towards the likeness, of God who is in Christ Jesus. The bishop, exhibiting in himself the form of Christ, and preaching and exhorting and admonishing all men to desire to be fashioned after that form, that, being like Christ they may be saved in him, must needs move some, by reason of the power of the word of God. For it, as St. Paul writes to the Hebrews, "is quick and powerful, and sharper than any two-edged sword, piercing even to the dividing asunder of soul and spirit, and of the joints and marrow, and is a discerner of the thoughts and intents of the heart." He who is influenced by the ray of God's Spirit, who walks by the word of God, begins to be born again of the Spirit as a son of God. For he begins to repent of his life spent without God; since the first effect of the Holy Spirit is a repentance for the life which is being done away with, and a laying aside and casting away of it for ever. Hence the forerunner of Christ, St. John, used to cry "Repent ye." Christ also after him cried aloud to man with yet grander tones, "Repent: for the kingdom of heaven is at hand." For he that repents not of past evil, cannot wish for future good. And he who has not laid aside what he repents of, cannot put on the better habit that he may wish for. Whoso wishes to change his raiment, must strip, that he may clothe himself and abolish in himself all that is old, that he may savour of what is new. That which is preached by the Bishop is a new thing, and requires vessels thoroughly new, with the old flavour scoured away; lest like new wine poured into old bottles, it should burst them and itself be spilled. He that will walk becomingly in Christ, in the new and spotless robe, which the hand and finger of God has wrought, must have stripped off and wholly thrown aside the old and soiled garment of mortality, which man has fashioned for himself. For "no man putteth a piece of

new cloth unto an old garment;" or, as St. Mark speaks, Mark ii. 21.
"No man also seweth a piece of new cloth on an old garment;" for, as St. Luke adds, the new patch "agreeth not Luke v. 36. with the old." If a man be journeying towards immortality, he must do nothing save what tends towards immortality. He must "cast off the works of darkness, and Rom. xiii. put on the armour of light." He must follow the High 12. Priest, his captain; he must be a soldier bound by oath in the Christian army. Having come out from the world, signed with the cross of Christ, he must declare battle against the foes of truth, against the prince of darkness. "We wrestle not," writes the Apostle to the Ephesians, Eph. vi. 12. "against flesh and blood" (that is, against men whose salvation, not whose death, is to be sought; as the Lord saith in Ezekiel, 'I have no pleasure in the death of the wicked; Ezek. but that the wicked turn from his way and live'), "but xxxiii. 11. against principalities, against powers, against the rulers of the darkness of this world, against spiritual wickedness in high places."

He who declares this war against the enemy of light, through love of the prize which is set forth for the conquerors, ought humbly and yet courageously to come to the Church, and ask of some one that he may be brought to the captain of the army, that is, the Bishop; that by the soldier's oath in Christ he may be bound in him to fight, and may avow himself the enemy of the world, and the servant and soldier of Christ; and being sworn by his oath (St. Paul calls those to whom he writes his "fellow-soldiers") may ask for spiritual weapons, may ask to be stationed in lawful combat. The other then, whoever he be to whom such a one comes by the guidance of the divine spirit (for no man, saith our Saviour, cometh unless he be Joh. vi. 44. drawn; and at the preaching of St. Paul in Antioch of Pisidia, as St. Luke writes, "as many as were ordained to Acts xiii. eternal life believed");—he, I say, to whom there comes the 48. one who is foreordained and drawn into the true Church, when he is asked by him to lead him to the Bishop, that he may be admitted to the number of warriors in Christ Jesus, is bound to act thus:—Though he that hears the man's

F

prayer desire nothing more than that as many as possible be believers and take upon them a spiritual warfare in Christ, yet first of all, reflecting and concluding with himself how great a matter is the profession of the Christian warfare and name, and how great moreover is man's infirmity, he should shudder within himself, and be afraid for that man, lest he should be rashly taking on himself more than he can perform. For it fares ill with those who do not war in Christ Jesus; but a thousand times more unhappy are they who act not up to the part assigned them, who are faint, and cold, and desert their post, and fall away to the place from whence they came. Then, as our Saviour says in St. Matthew, "the last state of that man is worse than the first." As it is in the second Epistle of St. Peter, "If, after they have escaped the pollutions of the world, through the knowledge of the Lord and Saviour Jesus Christ, they are again entangled therein and overcome, the latter end is worse with them than the beginning. For it had been better for them not to have known the way of righteousness, than, after they have known it, to turn from the holy commandment delivered unto them. But it is happened unto them according to the true proverb, The dog is turned to his own vomit again, and the sow that was washed to her wallowing in the mire."

It was, indeed, a custom and the usage of all those who introduced any one to the Church of Christ, into the temple of God, for the heavenly warfare, first to hesitate and shrink in thought. At last, however, they led them in, with good faith and hope in God, and with an utterance of many prayers, that the issue might be prosperous, and all end well and happily for the one who wished and desired to be initiated in the Christian rites. But the Bishop, inwardly rejoicing over the gain in Christ, returns thanks to God, and along with the rest of the priesthood sings hymns in festal strain. And then, on the Bishop asking his will, he who is introduced makes answer, with an abhorrence of the way in which he has wandered, that he seeks to be placed in the way of righteousness, and in the path of truth: he bewails his former condition, and longs for the newness of

Matth. xii. 45.

2 Pet. ii. 20—22.

Jesus Christ. And the Bishop, perceiving this repentance to be genuine, and commending the singleness of his will, assures him at the outset, that, if he seeks to direct his course towards God, he must betake himself wholly and throughly thither, and be entirely purified and perfected. Then, setting before him the right way of living, and the road he is to enter upon, and afterwards asking whether it is his wish freely and of his own accord to enter upon it, on perceiving the man to be offering himself wholly for that end, he lays his hands upon him, and signs him, according to custom. When he has next committed him to the priests, for them to inscribe in the register[1] of Christians his name, and the name of his introducer (whom Dionysius calls Sponsor; the same, I suppose, as we now in our country call Godfather), he straightway consigns him to the priests and deacons to be unclothed. When uncovered and stripped, he is usually placed with his face towards the west. They bid him then thrice eschew[2] Satan, and with mouth, look, breath, hands, avow a renunciation for ever of all that is the devil's; finally, they bid him utterly renounce his own self. And when he has done this, and eschewed Satan, and renounced all that is his, and lastly denied himself (according to that precept of the Saviour's, who said to all his disciples, as St. Luke relates, "If any man will come after me, let him deny himself, and take up his cross, and follow me"), they Luke ix. 23.

---

[1] On this custom, and on the employment of Sponsors for adult persons, see Bingham's *Eccl. Antiquities* (1855), vol. iv. pp. 151, 156. With respect to the use of such Sponsors for the adult, he says, "These are spoken of not only by Dionysius, and the author of the *Apostolical Constitutions*, but by many other more unquestionable writers. . . . . St. Austin often mentions them; but then he also acquaints us, that it was no part of their office to make responses for their pupils in baptism, as it was in the case of infants, and sick persons, who could not answer for themselves." Erasmus in his *Annotationes* alludes to the custom, in his note on Luke i. 4.

[2] The expression in the original, "ut *exflet* Sathanam," for which *insufflare* and *exsufflare* are elsewhere used, to render the *emphusesai* of the Greek, is more forcible than the term I have adopted. It denotes a spitting, or blowing out of the breath, to imply a detestation and defiance of Satan.

then turn the man towards the east,[1] and bid him thrice both in thought and words to profess Christ and the things that are Christ's. On his doing thus, the Bishop blesses him, and commends him by prayers to God, laying his hands upon him the second time. Then, after his remaining clothing has been stripped off, the Bishop with the consecrated oil first signs him thrice with the sign of the cross, and then delivers him to the priests to have all the rest of his body anointed.[2] The Bishop meanwhile, after consecrating the water, the mother of adoption,[3] in the manner appointed by the Apostles, and in the lawful form, has the man brought to him; and when his name has been read aloud from the book, the priests also proclaiming his name in response, with a threefold invocation of the Trinity, he thrice dips and plunges the man in the water, that he may thrice emerge. When he is come from the water, and now brought to light, as it were born again to God, they clothe him with a new white robe, and bring him back, thus clad, to the Bishop. The Bishop then again signs him with the ointment, and receives him as a partaker of the Holy Communion; in order that, being now in the mystical body, he may daily go forth towards Christ and proceed onwards, that he be not pronounced slothful in the march he has undertaken, and the form of life he has professed.

---

[1] In the *Apostolical Constitutions*, ii. 61, the reason given for turning towards the East, in prayer during the Holy Communion, is the recollection of paradise: "in memoriam veteris possessionis Paradisi ad Orientem positi, unde primus homo contempto mandato, serpentis consilio obtemperans, expulsus fuit."

[2] From this passage a slight argument may be drawn for the comparatively late date of Dionysius. Bingham says, "It is plain from Tertullian that neither of these [unctions] were given before baptism, but when men were come out of the water, then they were anointed with the holy unction, and had imposition of hands, in order to receive the Holy Ghost. Whence I think Daillé's conjecture very just and reasonable, that the unction preceding baptism is *of later date*, and not as yet adopted among the ceremonies of baptism in the time of Tertullian. But the writers of the following ages speak distinctly of two unctions, the one before, and the other after, baptism."—*Antiquities* (1855), vol. iv. p. 158.

[3] The Font is thus called by Dionysius.

Such was the custom and ceremony of Baptism and the washing of regeneration in the primitive Church, instituted by the holy Apostles; whereby the more excellent baptism of the inner man is signified. And this form differs very greatly from the one we make use of in this age. And herein I own that I marvel, how it is that in one and the same old-established religion, there should be so dissimilar a sacred rite; since it would seem that we ought to be more careful in preserving our ceremonies, than the Jews were in theirs, in proportion as ours are more perfect than theirs. For, as St. Paul writes to the Ephesians, "There is one Lord, one faith, one baptism, one body;" so in like manner there ought certainly to be one manner and rite of the sacraments, without adding to, or taking from, the ancient and venerable institution of the Apostles; the changing of whose ordinances in sacred things is in truth a grievous crime. For they, being fully taught by Jesus Christ, knew well what are convenient symbols and appropriate signs for the mysteries; so that one may suspect either rashness or neglect on the part of their successors, in what has been added to, or taken from, their ordinances.[1]

Eph. iv. 5.

---

[1] It is interesting to compare with this the complaint which Erasmus makes of the innovations in the Service of the Mass which had been made in his day. He says, "In multis ecclesiis publice consecratur aqua, et canitur responsorium, pro missæ introitu. Psalmus qui totus cani solet abbreviatus est. Ante evangelium canuntur prosæ, nonnunquam indoctæ, et prætermittitur symbolum fidei. Ante canonem missæ, canitur præfatio aucta; sub consecrationem canitur Sanctus: quum ostenduntur mysteria, canitur cantio implorans opem beatæ Virginis, aut S. Rochi, et supprimitur precatio dominica. Hæc impia non sunt, sed recedunt a gravitate pristini cultus, et si nullus obsistat, tendunt ad superstitionem."—*Annotationes*, in Luc. ii. 14.

CHAPTER II.

PART III.

On the Spiritual Contemplation of Baptism.

BESIDES the purification of life, which is fitly signified by the above washing of water, there is also an elevation in it, and an indication of a higher meaning. For as invisible things are the archetypes of sensible things, so are sensible sacraments the tokens of things invisible; and they are joined to spiritual sacraments, as body to soul. The good and bountiful God is the "Sun of Righteousness," that shines upon spiritual natures, diffusing Himself alike and equally over all without ceasing, and that stands at the doors and windows of the soul, knocking that he may be admitted. Under these rays of the heavenly sun are two kinds of men; one, that will not have all the wisdom it can; the other, that would be wise even above its power. The former, basely and wilfully pleased with evil and darkness, refuses the light; the latter over-proudly exceeds the measure of its light; whence it follows that these not only receive not what they would, but also lose what they have possessed. For, as St. Paul admonishes us "not to think of ourselves more highly than we ought to think, but to think soberly," lest, "professing ourselves to be wise, we become fools;" so if, on receiving the divine light, you trust in yourself, and begin to form plans with yourself, you then extinguish all. Increase what you have, by the same means as you received it; I mean, trust believingly in God, nowise in yourself. Suffer the heavenly ray to increase in you; be subject to it, humble and patient; this is to lay yourself open to the light. If, relying on yourself, you boast in any wise in the light, you are inclosing yourself against the entering in of the light, and walking in your own darkness, knowing not whither you go. The Bishop who is illumined by Christ, like the sun, shines from the pulpit with the light of truth, and makes the word of the gospel to stream forth alike on all. He cries, "Awake, thou that sleepest, and arise from the dead, and Christ shall give thee light." His words are

Margin notes: Mal. iv. 2. — Rom. xii. 3. — Rom. i. 22. — Eph. v. 14.

CH. II. 3. CONTEMPLATION OF BAPTISM. 71

"pure words, even as the silver which is tried, and purified seven times in the fire." The Bishop himself is made fire by God; he has the light of truth, the warmth of goodness; in loving-kindness he teaches all. Ps. xii. 7.

He now who has learnt that he is in darkness ("all things that are reproved, are made manifest by the light: for whatsoever doth make manifest, is light"), when he, I say, recognising his own state, is being enlightened, he then seeks to be carried onwards still higher in the light, and goes to some believer more illumined than himself. Eph. v. 13.

But in this material order of things be mindful also of a spiritual order. To apply thus to a believer[1] is humility, and a subjection of the heart to the heavenly ray. And when this is done submissively and sincerely, such a man is at once touched with the divine light, and sealed to the lot of the Saints. For he receives a portion of the light, as a sign and token that he is of the Lord's flock. This marking, as it were, of the sheep of God the Shepherd, is called by St. Paul in his Epistle to the Ephesians, "the earnest of our inheritance." "In whom ye also," he says, "after that ye heard the word of God and of truth, the gospel of your salvation, received it: in whom also, after that ye believed, ye were sealed with that Holy Spirit of promise, which is the earnest of our inheritance until the redemption of the purchased possession, unto the praise of his glory." This marking is signified by the laying on of the Bishop's hand. For as he is touched by the hand of the Bishop, so is he at the same time touched and sealed by the right hand of God, which is the Son of God, whose finger on man's head is the Holy Spirit. Then is the man happily among those who are enrolled for salvation; of which the inscribing of his name in the list of the faithful by the priests is a figure. Eph. i. 13, 14.

In the primitive Church there were enrolled all who through grace had been sealed to the faith. But this afterwards, from the influx of a multitude of men to the name, rather than to the reality, of Christianity, began, like many other customs which had been general, to be kept up in the purer branch of the Church alone.

---

[1] See above, p. 65.

The godfather, whom Dionysius calls *Sponsor*, is also enrolled: the name is inscribed both of him who offers himself, and of him who offers another, to God; because our Father in heaven "rejoices more over the recovery of the hundredth sheep, than over the ninety and nine which went not astray."

Matth. xviii. 13.

He, being newly admitted into the singleness of Christ, must profess a single and undivided mode of life—the life above, only. For, as saith Dionysius, it is not lawful that he, who has received a share in that which is one, should have a divided life. He must needs proceed in one direction only. For "no man, having put his hand to the plough, and looking back, is fit for the Kingdom of God." "No servant can serve two masters: for either he will hate the one, and love the other; or else he will hold to the one, and despise the other." He cannot be divided and single. Christianity is a profession of singleness; and man is drawn to it, as from multiplicity to simplicity. A single Christ endures not a double coat.[1] If you would be in his wedding garment, you must take order to come to him naked, that you may put it on; and to lay aside your former manner of living, that you may enter on that which is Christ's. This is the meaning and significance of the divesting himself of all garments by him who betakes himself to Christ; of his spitting and blowing towards the west, and renouncing with a solemn avowal whatever is of iniquity. The meaning of his turning to the east, when now quite stripped, and exposing himself to the rays of the risen "Sun of Righteousness," is that he, being now purified and single, should receive the single and pure ray, and put on the robe of light and righteousness, which the grace of the Holy Spirit in Christ has woven; that, shining in the light with the bright raiment of righteousness, he may walk in heavenly majesty through this gloomy vale, "by the armour of righteousness on the right hand and on the left;" holding out to all his

Luke ix. 62.
Luke xvi. 13.

2 Cor. vi. 7.

---

[1] This would seem to be an allegorical interpretation of the "two coats" in St. Matth. x. 10, St. Mark vi. 9. Erasmus, in his *Annotationes* on the latter passage, does not mention any such interpretation, but has a long and exceedingly sensible note on the folly of justifying mendicancy by any such texts.

CH. II. 3. CONTEMPLATION OF BAPTISM. 73

undefiled hands, full of goodness; he himself being ever good and like himself, unable to do anything save to benefit; towards the guilty, guileless; in troubles, of patience unconquered; that so by a continual doing good he may seem to have kept untarnished his robe of righteousness. This is the white robe which is put on by every one that is washed in the laver of holy regeneration, the robe of a holy and unspotted righteousness. In this we must walk always towards the east, for the earning of light ever more and more; with no looking back towards the west, the region of death, lest, like Lot's wife, we be "turned into a pillar of salt." Gen. xix. 26.

His being anointed all over by the priests, signifies the contest and wrestling that we have "not against flesh and blood, but against the rulers of the darkness of this world, against spiritual wickedness in high places," in the armour of God, which is signified by that anointing, even the Holy Spirit, that our limbs may be rendered more vigorous. You must strive, that you may conquer; you must conquer, that you may be crowned. Fight in him, who fights in you and prevails, even Jesus Christ, who has declared war against Death, and fights in all. He it is who overcomes in us, and we in him, when anointed with the Holy Spirit; who, when he shall have subdued and overthrown the empire of Death, in the kingdom of light is himself to be all in all. It is the rule of combat that we should imitate our leader, who is "the Lord strong and mighty in battle." Nor may Christians undertake any other manner of warring than he has himself taught; for we have no enemies and opponents except sin (which is ever against us), and the evil spirits that tempt to sin. When these are vanquished in ourselves, then let us, armed with the armour of God, in charity succour others; even though they be not for suffering us, even though in their folly they see not their bondage, even though they would put their deliverers to death. So to love man, as to die in caring for his salvation, is most blessed. Eph. vi. 12.

Ps. xxxiv. 8.

The threefold immersion, with an invocation of the Trinity, is a beautiful image of death,[1] and of the putting off the flesh,

---

[1] "Datur igitur baptismus in mortem Jesu; aqua pro sepultura;

and of carnal thoughts from the mind, and all sins; from which he that believes in Christ professes to be separate, and dead to them for ever. "He that hath died to sin, hath died once; but he that liveth, liveth unto God." As death is a putting off of the body, so spiritual baptism is a putting off of the life of the body. And this is signified by the plunging of the whole man beneath the waters, by which men are admonished that they are dead with Christ, and as it were buried with Christ three days. This is the meaning of that triple immersion; that, with the putting off of Christ's body, all our bodily life should be put off, that we may rise again in righteousness; preparing to die in Christ the righteous, that at length we may in the same body also rise again to glory. We must first come forth to a life of righteousness; then we must rise to a life of glory. Death destroys death; grace begets righteousness; righteousness brings forth glory. That we may die unto sin, it needs that a righteous one die for us. And that we may live unto righteousness, it needs that we be sustained by the grace of the righteous one rising again. And again, that we ourselves when dead may rise again in righteousness, it needs that we be reanimated by the virtue and power of God. They truly rise again, who having put off their sins in the washing of regeneration, in the death of Christ, walk with perseverance unto the end, in the white robe of righteousness without spot; and who baffle not the anointing of confirmation, which is finally used by the Bishop,[1] to signify that a man is confirmed in grace and

Rom. vi. 10.

---

oleum pro Spiritu sancto; sigillum pro cruce; unguentum est confirmatio professionis .... demersio significat quod commorimur, emersio quod resurgimus."—*Apost. Constit.* iii. 17.

[1] "To Signation succeeded Imposition of Hands, or that which most properly we term Confirmation, which was, The Minister laid his Hands on the Head of the Party baptized, anointed and signed, and prayed that the Holy Ghost would be pleased to descend and rest upon him. This immediately followed Signation, as that did Unction. So saith Tertullian, 'The flesh is anointed that the soul may be consecrated; the flesh is signed, that the soul may be fortified. The flesh is overshadowed with the imposition of hands, that the soul may be enlightened by the Spirit.'"—King on the *Primitive Church,* ii. p. 82 and Tert. *De Resurrect. Carnis,* p. 31, there quoted.

perfected. To the one who is thus perfected as a member of Christ in his kind, for his union with the Body, and his nourishment as a member, the sacred food of the Eucharist is administered; by which it is understood that he is both in the Body, and is fed and spiritually nourished in that Body. No one is perfectly a member of Christ, until he has been a partaker of the Holy Communion and the food of life; by participation in which he grows to be one with the Body. In the early Church all who were baptized and at the same time confirmed by the holy anointing, were invited without delay to the Communion of the heavenly food.

It is to be observed, that Dionysius speaks of Confirmation in such a way as to teach, not that it is a distinct sacrament, but something for the completion of baptism; so as for it and baptism to be only one sacrament. It is also no less to be remarked, that it was customary in the primitive Church for all the baptized to communicate at once, in order, by a common nourishment, to be reckoned to be of the mystical body of Christ. Otherwise, although baptized, they are not considered to be of the body. For such communicating gathers and binds together by a common nourishment, and perfects by a final completion. On this account it was at one time given even to baptized infants;[1] about whom we read thus in ancient Sacramentaries:—" If a Bishop be present, the child must be at once confirmed, and afterwards

---

[1] Aquinas lays down that children, being as yet devoid of reason, should not have the Eucharist administered to them; and says that the contrary has been wrongly inferred from Dionysius, inasmuch as he is speaking of the baptism of *adults*, who then received the Communion:— " Non intelligentes quod Dionysius ibi loquitur de baptismo adultorum." *Pars* iii. **Qu.** lxxx. **Art.** ix. But he takes no note of the fact that Dionysius, in the last chapter of the *Eccl. Hier.* § 11, speaks distinctly of children as partaking of this Sacrament:—" Illud vero quia pueri quoque, qui necdum possunt intelligere divina, sacri baptismatis *altissimorumque communionis sacrosanctæ signorum* participes fiant, videtur quidem prophanis, ut dixisti, rationabiliter irridendum." In Cyprian *De Lapsis* (*Op.* Ed. 1617, p. 145) is a strange story of what befel a little girl on receiving the sacramental cup, which shows that in that time and country the practice was not unknown. And so Pamelius, in his note on the passage, infers from the words, quoting the authority of Dionysius; but thinks that the custom of young children communicating survived no

receive the Communion. If a Bishop be not present, then, before the infant suck, or have tasted anything, let the priest give it the communion of the body and blood of the Lord, before mass, even though the emergency be pressing; that it may now be a man in Christ, purified, illumined and perfected. The washing purifies, the anointing with the unction which follows illumines and makes bright, the Eucharist fulfils and perfects in perfect Christ, in whom all things are perfect, in whom can be nothing which is not perfect.

Gracious God! here may one perceive how cleansed and how pure he that professes Christ ought to be; how inwardly and thoroughly washed; how white, how shining, how utterly without blemish and spot; in fine how perfected and filled, according to his measure, with Christ himself; that in him he may afterwards be vigorous and strong, a member of him whole and sound. For Christ, the head of the Church, is health and perfectness itself; "from which," as St. Paul writes to the Colossians, "all the body, by joints and bands having nourishment ministered, and knit together, increaseth with the increase of God;" to the intent that in every one, being simple, still and firm, God may be reflected; that with steadfastness, clearness and perfectness men in Christ may now recognize and worship God; and that each one may so savour of and represent Christ alone in himself, as for Christ to be seen to be all in all. Wherefore if, after bap-

<hr>

later than St. Augustine's time, who alludes to it in his *Epist.* 107 *ad Vitalem.*

By " ancient Sacramentaries " I imagine that Colet is referring to Alcuinus, who in his chapter *De Sabbato sancti Paschæ* treats of the rites of Baptism, and after describing the baptism of an infant, writes:— " Postea vestiatur infans vestimentis suis. Si vero Episcopus adest, statim confirmari eum oportet chrismate, et postea communicare; et si Episcopus deest, communicetur a Presbytero dicente ita: Corpus Domini nostri Jesu Christi custodiat te in vitam æternam. Amen. . . . . Sed et hoc providendum est, ut nullum cibum accipiant, neque lactentur antequam communicent " (Hittorpius *De Officiis*, 1624, p. 259). Alcuin, a north-countryman, died in 804. From the wording of the last sentence, I think that something has been left out in the transcript of Colet's Latin, and that the sense should be:—" Nor let it taste anything before Mass, even though the emergency be pressing."

tism, we "be risen with Christ, let us seek the things which are Christ's, where Christ sitteth on the right hand of God: let us set our affections on things above, not on things on the earth." Being dead, let us seek our life, which is "hid with Christ in God," which is the glory that shall appear to us, when Christ, in whom we have hope, shall appear in glory. Meanwhile, may Jesus Christ himself bring it to pass, that we who profess Christ may both be, and set our affections on, and do, all things that are worthy of our profession.

Col. iii. 1—4.

CHAPTER III.

PART I.

Introduction to the Sacrament of Synaxis, or Holy Communion.

THIS communion in the body and blood of Christ is the consummation of all the sacraments. All the sacraments indeed lead to a communion, but in no degree compared to this, in which there is a wonderful communication and fellowship, since many, by participation in one, become themselves one. For this, men are prepared by other sacraments, which go before, that by this they may be fulfilled. All the sacraments have for their object the developing of unity, likeness and simplicity among men.

Towards this we are brought by other sacraments; by the Eucharist and Synaxis we are perfected. Wherefore, whatever great mystery is being performed, it is wont to be completed by this sacrament; without which all the mysteries in which men are initiated, are undeveloped and imperfect. And since the effect of them all is, that men may be formed into one body, by being themselves united to one, and since the *synaxis* especially attains this end, it has on that account had this name specially allotted to it;[1] just as to the sacra-

---

[1] The passage of Dionysius on which this is based formed a point of dispute between Harding and Bishop Jewel. The former argued that the words of Dionysius, "This most worthy Sacrament is of such excellencie, that it passeth all other Sacraments, and for that cause it is

78 ECCLESIASTICAL HIERARCHY. CH. III. 2.

ment of regeneration the name of Illumination is peculiarly fitted. In all the sacraments there are the three qualities of purifying, illumining, perfecting; but perfection is the attribute of the *synaxis*, illumination of the sacrament of regeneration. For in the latter first man receives light, whereby he begins to perceive the truth. Hence baptism is called by Dionysius the sacrament of illumination. For he who is touched by the heavenly ray is recalled and looks back. This is signified by the laying on of the bishop's hand. He looks back upon the light by returning to God;[1] as David says, "In thy light shall we see light."

Ps. xxxvi. 9.

CHAPTER III.

PART II.

§ 1. *On the ante-Communion Service;* § 2. *On the celebration of Holy Communion.*

§ 1.

THE Bishop first offers at the altar a holy prayer, which I suppose to have been the Lord's Prayer. He censes the altar with incense, and then the whole temple. Next, returning to the altar, along with the rest of the priests, he sings hymns and psalms of David. The ministers and deacons, one after another, then read from Holy Scripture the Lessons, as they are called. They then drive away from the temple the Catechumens and the Energumens and the

---

alonely called the Communion. For albeit every Sacrament be such as gathereth our lives, that be divided asunder many waies, into that one state, whereby we are joyned to God, yet the name of Communion is fit and convenient for this Sacrament specially and peculiarly, more than any other"—implied that the Communion, or Synaxis (i. e. *Gathering*) was so called by way of distinction, from its gathering and uniting us *to God*. Jewel shews that there was another equally sound reason for the name, which was, that it joins Christians together in a common fellowship.—*Replie* (1611), p. 20.

[1] This seems to be the general sense of the passage, but I cannot understand the Latin *resiliente in Deum*.

Penitents, seeing that they are not worthy to be present at the mysteries. The Catechumens are those who, not having been as yet initiated in the sacred rites, nor baptized, are being instructed for baptism. For *Catechize* signifies *instruct;* whence those who are being instructed, that they may duly approach the mysteries, are called by a Greek word *Catechumens.* Concerning these St. Paul says in his Epistle to the Galatians, "Let him that is taught[1] in the word, communicate unto him that teacheth, in all good things." The Energumens are those who are driven and harassed by evil spirits,[2] in whom dwells largely the power of darkness; from whose force and working and operation they are called Energumens. For the Greek word *energeo* signifies *I work.* Under this name are not only those who are hurried away to a demoniac fury and pitiably distracted; but moreover all men of the deepest guilt, who either disguise or deny their religion, as Apostates; or, when they have made profession of Christ, yet lead a life of the greatest enormity, and stained with notorious crimes, such as are fornicators, poisoners, murderers, blasphemers, and all such like; who, though nominally Christians, lead the life of profane heathens, and, though called after Christ whom they falsely profess, are in reality the subjects, nay the servants of darkness. In them the princes of darkness and "spiritual wickedness in high places" have more power than Christ; and they are but a few degrees removed from those, who are goaded on to madness by evil spirits and the satellites of the devil. For they are in the very state, and under the very influence, of the devil; and the life of those wicked ones, whoever they be, in the devil, is a kind of madness. And for them to be utterly deranged, and altogether out of their

Gal. vi. 6.

Eph. vi. 12.

---

[1] "Him that is taught" being expressed by the single term *Catechumen.*

[2] "The word Energumens," says Bingham, "in its largest signification denotes persons who are under the motion and operation of any spirit, whether good or bad; but in a more restrained sense it is used by Ecclesiastical writers for persons whose bodies are seized or possessed with an evil spirit."—*Antiqq.* Bk. iii. c. iv. § 6.—A form of prayer for them is given in the *Apostolical Constitutions*, viii. 8.

minds, nothing is wanting, except that, for the completion of their madness, some few steps be taken by the evil spirit, who commenced that falling off from light. In the falling off to what is worse, there is a commencement made by the devil as prime mover, and this tends towards completion; just as, in growing perfect towards what is better, there is such a beginning from God. And as the latter ends in a heavenly enthusiasm, so does the former in a devilish madness. But the heavenly enthusiasm is wisdom and health in Christ; and such as have fallen away from him towards themselves, into a lapsing towards darkness, and such as are pleased with their own ways, because they are then forsaken by God, and are straightway easily led on by evil spirits to every kind of guilt, may be called Energumens, that is, Demoniacs. He that is not moved by the Spirit of God, to be a child of God, is necessarily moved by the spirit of the devil, to be a child of the devil. For on either hand man is being drawn unceasingly, to follow which he will. And towards whichever side he inclines, there are constantly present those that advance his steps when thus drawn, and perfect him when advanced. It is man's own part to choose whither he will go, and to listen to prompters, good or evil, and to follow the inspirations of the one or the other. But towards whichever quarter he tends, on all hands are spiritual beings, that guide him whither he wills.[1]

When therefore the heavenly mysteries in Christ are being solemnized, none may be present, save those who are moved by the Spirit of God, who are wholly in life. But the profane, such as all Energumens may be called, should be driven far away from the sacred rites and mysteries. For, as David has sung, "holiness becometh the house of God." All these accordingly, whose wicked life has declared them to be in the power of the devil (for "by their fruits ye shall know them,") used in the primitive Church to be kept far off from the sacred rites; that this honour might not be

Psal. xciii. 5.

Matth. vii. 20.

---

[1] In illustration of what is here said may be quoted the striking dream, related in Epist. viii. § 6 of Dionysius, which Mr. Westcott has given in an English version at p. 3. of the *Contemp. Rev.* for May, 1867.

bestowed upon the devil, namely, that some of his subjects should be present at them.

The *Penitents* were those who repented of this wandering and lost life, and who with change of purpose had returned to the Church. These, in humble prostration at the feet of the Church, implored the mercy and grace of God, bewailing their sins, and suing for the pains and penalties of their sins, that they might publicly deplore their errors, for an example to all, and by temporal punishment might avoid eternal death, and purchase again eternal life. The Church, which acts the part of Christ, which has whatsoever it looses or binds on earth, loosed or bound in heaven, which "hath no pleasure in the death of the wicked, but that he turn from his way and live," when such have discharged the penance assigned them, and are sufficiently penitent, receives them lovingly again into the Church, and cherishes them, and, so far as can be, preserves them in the same. But meanwhile, so long as they are disciplining themselves in the allotted penance, they are esteemed to be not as yet sufficiently purified; and along with the Catechumens and Energumens, are driven far away and shut out.[1]

§ 2. When these are excluded, and the gates of the temple watchfully guarded by the door-keepers and porters, that no profane person may enter, then, each deacon and minister discharging his own office, the chief deacons along with the priests who are about the bishop at the altar, diligently wait upon him, and place on the altar the holy

Ezek. xxxiii. 11.

---

[1] " Dionysius Areopagita saith, ' That after the reading of the Old and New Testament, the Learners of the Faith before they were baptized, Madmen, and they that were joyned to Penance for their faults, were shut out of the Church, and they only did remain which did receive.' Chrysostom witnesseth also that these three sorts were shut out from the Communion. Therefore Durant writeth, ' That the mass of the Learners is from the *Introite* until after the *Offertory*, which is called *missa, misse*, or *sending out:* Because, when the Priest beginneth to consecrate the sacrament, the Learners be sent out of the Church. The miss or *sending out* of the Faithful is from the Offering till after Communion; and is named *missa*, a *sending out*, because, when it is ended, then each Faithful is sent forth to his proper Business."—Guest to Sir Wm. Cecyl, in Strype's *Annals of the Reformation* (1709), App. p. 38.

bread and the cup of blessing. Meanwhile, as the whole body of clergy chant together the laud and confession[1] of the sacred office, the bishop, having the bread and the cup now before him, utters a sacred prayer, which I believe to have been the Lord's Prayer. Then, after a benediction has been pronounced by the bishop on all together, they all in turn salute and kiss each other. Next, after reciting the mystic names[1] of the saints, the bishop stands along with the priests, with washed hands, at the middle of the altar, closely surrounded by the priests and chosen deacons, and proceeds to utter the other things that tend to the praise and confession of the sacrament, and at length by the sacramental words to complete the divine and saving act. When this is done, he displays to them all, with all reverence, the consecrated sacrament; and then, turning to the altar, he first partakes thereof, and afterwards invites all the rest to partake and communicate in the same sacrament; that in one sacrament all may be made one with the bishop. When all together have partaken, the bishop makes an end by giving thanks; understanding well what is the meaning of those sensible signs, and seeing the reason of the whole

---

[1] It might seem as if two distinct portions of the Service were here intended, corresponding to the *Gloria in excelsis* and the *Credo* of the Roman Office. But the Greek words (which I give, as the Latin version fails in closeness) are *proomologetheises hypo pantos tou tes ecclesias pleromatos tes catholices hymnologias*, and appear to signify only the singing of a hymn, as a confession of faith, by the whole assembled congregation, previous to the placing of the bread and wine upon the altar.

[2] I am uncertain whether, by *mysticis verbis sanctorum*, Colet meant what I have given, or "the mystic words of the holy books." In any case it is clear what the custom referred to was. "Sometime before they made oblation for the dead," writes Bingham, "it was usual in some ages to recite the names of such eminent Bishops or Saints or Martyrs, as were particularly to be mentioned in this part of the Service. To this purpose they had certain books, which they called their holy Books, and commonly their *Diptychs*, from their being folded together, wherein the names of such persons were written, that the Deacon might rehearse them, as occasion required, in the time of Divine Service. . . . It appears from this author [Dionysius] that these *Diptychs* were then read before the Consecration, immediately after the Kiss of Peace." —*Eccl. Antiqq.* xv. iii. § 17. A further account of the custom may be found in Rock's *Hierurgia* (1851), p. 477.

matter; although others, more ignorant, cannot look beyond the objects of sense. Still, what they do in sincerity, is for their salvation. Knowledge leads not to eternal life, but charity. Whoso loveth God is known of him. Ignorant love has a thousand times more power than cold wisdom. But it is the part of the bishop, and of him whose task it is to perform the divine office, to have both the highest love and the highest knowledge; that he may thoroughly understand the meaning of the sacred rites he performs. To this beyond doubt all priests are obliged and bound, whose part it is to perform the office of the divine sacrament; that they may have more understanding than the people in that heavenly mystery. 1 John iv. 7.

In the primitive church, as St. Jerome[1] proves by good evidence, they whose office it was to make the Body of the Lord, were the chief of all; and at first all, as being equal in virtue of this office, were on a level in rank. For rank is known by office and action. The most excellent office, demanding the most excellent and perfect men, is the consecration of the Lord's Body. None can be chosen and selected to a more excellent office out of the whole priesthood. Still, from the number of the priests, though equal in office and rank, the first disciples and followers of the Apostles, immediately after the apostolic age, made choice of one, and placed him at the head, for the settling of disputes and appeasing of strifes, and for putting an end to contentions by his opinion and sentence; that the Church might abide in harmony. To him an authority was deputed by the universal Church, that those who were at variance should rest in his decision. And he is not so

---

[1] In his Epistle to Evagrius (Op. 1553, v. i. p. 329,) he says:—" Quid enim facit, excepta ordinatione, Episcopus, quod presbyter non faciat?" and more to the same purpose. Hooker, reasoning from this Epistle, writes:—" That, where colleges of presbyters were, there was at the first equality among them, St. Jerome thinketh it a matter clear: but when the rest were thus equal, so that no one of them could command any other as inferior unto him, they were all controllable by the Apostles, who had that episcopal authority abiding at the first in themselves, which they afterwards derived unto others."—*Eccl. Pol.* Bk. vii. § 5.

much superior to the other priests in office and dignity, since he performs no act more exalted than does every priest, as in a kind of administration and authority in quelling disputes; that the priests, who perform all acts alike with him, may have an end put to all their dissensions, and may all acquiesce in him, as in a central point of decision. He then began to be specially called Bishop; a name which under the Apostles belonged to all priests, until there was chosen the one whom I have just mentioned, and for the reason above given.

But now we must set forth the wisdom, and contemplation of the truth, and the very principle of this mystery in its depths, which no priest ought to be ignorant of.

CHAPTER III.

PART III.

On the symbolic truth of the Holy Eucharist.[1]

FIRST of all, chants and lessons from the sacred writings are heard by the people, and by all the Church together, that they may learn a holy life in the records where it is taught. This is what St. Paul writes to the Ephesians; bidding them "be filled with the Spirit; speaking to themselves in psalms, and hymns, and spiritual songs, singing and making melody in their heart to the Lord, giving thanks always for all things unto God and the Father, in the name of our Lord Jesus Christ." And to the Colossians:—"Let the word of Christ dwell in you richly in all wisdom; teaching and admonishing one another in psalms, and

---

[1] As Dean Colet has given a title to this section, "Significa veritas sacræ Eucharistiæ," I have retained it, instead of the more uniform heading of "Spiritual Contemplation of," &c. A glance at the Latin will shew that Colet prefixed no headings systematically to his chapters; and indeed in the MS. the division into chapters altogether is sometimes scarcely distinguishable, and has had to be now made by comparison with Dionysius.

hymns, and spiritual songs, singing with grace in your hearts." Hence has been derived the custom of passages from the sacred writings being read in the Church; that men may learn from them how to live well. For Holy Scripture is the mistress of life and the rule of truth. Likewise the people and the ignorant multitude are well and fitly admonished, in the setting forth of one bread and cup, and in the participation of the same sustenance by all, that all, being fed and nourished by one, should grow together into one, in concord and brotherly agreement, under God their Father, at the table of God. They are bidden also to understand, that, as the bread is one, and the cup one and alike, which they all taste, so they themselves also ought to be all one and alike among themselves, and bound together in a union of charity, which is the "bond of peace." For this Communion affords a solemn representation of that holy supper of the Lord with his disciples, in which he gave himself for them to eat, that all might be united in him, and being incorporated together might form one body with him. This hallowed and life-giving supper St. Matthew the Evangelist describes, when he informs us that at the paschal feast Jesus set forth the bread and cup before his disciples. For "as they were eating," he says, "Jesus took bread, and blessed it, and brake it, and gave it to the disciples, and said, Take, eat; this is my body. And he took the cup, and gave thanks, and gave it to them, saying, Drink ye all of it; for this is my blood of the new testament which is shed for many for the remission of sins." That which was given by Jesus Christ to his disciples, is in turn distributed after the same form by all episcopal persons to the faithful; that, in memory of that supper, they may be united in Christ with those who were first united in Christ; that so the life-giving work which was begun may go on advancing, by the operation of the sacred mysteries, towards the fulness of Christ, in whom are both the dead and the living, and all that shall believe hereafter. For they are sustained in Christ by the Holy Communion and the heavenly food, in the exalted company of God, being banqueters now not at the unclean table of devils, but at the spotless table of God.

Matth. xxvi. 26-28.

This sacrament contains other and far loftier subjects of thought; but were there nothing else in it, its setting forth of the Lord's Supper, and of our common training and brotherly union, conveys for men of less elevated perceptions a most useful admonition towards living together in honesty. But let us now take a loftier scope.

The Bishop acts the part of God, as he burns at the altar, in the sight of God, with a sweet odour of incense, which is a sign of the Almighty's most fragrant love. For as God pours forth abundantly his sweet goodness, and Jesus his compassion, that it may return again to him along with a great salvation of mankind;—to him, I say, who, though stationary in himself, yet marvellously extends himself to others, that by his fragrant grace he may draw them together to himself,—like as Peter's net, which when let down into the sea is brought back by him into the ship full of fishes— in well-nigh the same manner, that what is least may imitate what is greatest, does the bishop and vicar of God, the head of the Church, the more vital part, communicate bountifully and divinely to others himself and his own divinity, or rather the godhead of Christ which is in him, without in any wise departing from himself, or lessening his own majesty; that as many as possible may be made godlike with him in Christ. This assuredly the fuming of incense, beginning from the altar, and thence proceeding through the whole temple, and returning to the place whence it set forth, signifies in sacred and solemn manner to the unlearned; that herein, if they are able, they may perceive that sweet-smelling grace is diffused far and wide over all from the high place of God; in order that, being captivated by the fragrance of the heavenly sweetness, they may eagerly follow the grace[1] on its return to the same place whence it set out that it might

Luke v. 5-7.

---

[1] The metaphor here is a somewhat bold one; the notion being, that as the outward senses of the worshipper follow the incense in its course from the Bishop at the altar, through the congregation, back to the Bishop again; so his mind may be drawn by the grace which comes forth from God, and may ascend back again, as it were, with that grace, to the Holy of Holies whence it proceeded. Dionysius in the *De Div. Nom.* iv. § 14, compares the love of God to a circle, which, after running its endless course through mankind, comes back to himself.

CH. III. 3. EUCHARIST SYMBOLICAL. 87

thither return. Now the grace in the Eucharist is what is called fruitful grace, which, when ministered by the Bishop, passes on from him to others, that it may return to him again, with others drawn along to him. So too the Bishop himself by signs, as it were, goes forth and imparts himself to others; whilst none the less withdrawn in himself, and self-contained, in entire and unmingled contemplation of the mysteries. The chanting of Psalms, and reading of the canonical scriptures from the sacred volume, neither can nor ought to be wanting to the celebration of the mysteries in the Church. For in them is contained all wisdom and goodness, all natural science, all metaphysical speculation, all instruction in good manners, the record of all the past dealings of God, the anticipation of all things to come; in a word, all belief and love for the true and good; so that there is nothing left, but what should be read and listened to and impressed on the ears of men. Nor would the Apostles have men hear anything else from the Church. For St. Paul once and again enjoins, when writing both to the Ephesians and Colossians, that they should admonish and comfort one another, " in psalms and hymns and spiritual songs, singing in their hearts to God." Accordingly the chanting of psalms, and singing, ought to have a suitable part in the solemnizing of the mysteries and sacrifice in the Church; that the minds of the hearers may be soothed by harmony, and being composed by the concord of divine music, may be sweetly drawn to a state of complete unison and concord; that so, being tranquillised in mind, they may be more able to receive the grace of God. The repeating of Psalms and Scriptures, during the performance of the sacred rites, seems to have been instituted by the Apostles, that we, learning that Christ, who according to the Old Testament was to come, has come, and being glad, may go on in the preparation of this faith to become subjects of further grace, which the celebration of the rites secretly and marvellously works in pious believers. This is said by Dionysius[1] to be the cause of the chanting of Psalms and

Eph. v. 18.
Col. iii. 16.

---

[1] In § 4 of the *Contemplatio;* where there is also a summary of the contents of Holy Scripture that is worth attention.

Scripture, during the performance of any of the mysteries. Whence it may be seen that chanting in the Church is of very ancient date in our religion.

Now there are four kinds of men: one, that refuses the word of truth; another, that receives it, but is not yet initiated,—the class that are called Catechumens; a third of those who, though initiated, have not yet set themselves sufficiently free from the power of evil spirits, whom the ancients called Energumens; a fourth, of those who repent of not having lived according to their profession. All of these hear the Scriptures read and the Psalms chanted; that, admonished by the heavenly teaching, they may come to themselves again, and return to perfection. But when the performance of the sacred rites is at hand, they are driven out of the temple. For it was the design of the ancient ordinance, that no one should take part in the sacred rites, unless wholly perfected. Christ was perfect; and from him flow all things for the consecration of man to God in him; but these are poured only upon those who are perfected in the holy mystical body of Christ. Therefore all the profane, imperfect, shortcoming, back-sliding, are kept far away from the mysteries; for these are but an unshapen offspring, of whom their mother the Church is in travail, and whom she has not yet brought forth to the light. And so, lest their eyes be over dazzled by the splendour of the mysteries, the Church takes thought for their weakness, and bids them to be absent, till they have grown stronger. For the sacred things of God require no common light of faith. Apostates, who have been initiated in the rites; bad Christians, living in no wise according to their setting forth;[1] Energumens, as they are properly called, who are distracted by an evil spirit, by which the perfect are by no means harassed (these rather command every evil spirit); and in a word all the host of the profane is dispersed, and dismissed from beholding the sacred rites; yea, even those who repent of having sinned, until they be fully purified. Thus then there are left in the

---

[1] Lat. *ex profectione*. Perhaps it should be *ex professione*, "according to their profession."

temple only the pure, the enlightened, and the perfect, wholly without spot; namely, the most holy Bishop, the priests, deacons, ministers and holy people. And these all, with eyes bent on the sacred mysteries, sing together the Creed of our religion, *I believe in one God*. For in it are contained all things that belong to our salvation in Christ; and these must be rehearsed with the utmost devotion, that in the giving of thanks for our salvation, we may seem to God also to be mindful of the divine compassion.

When the sacred bread, covered, is placed upon the altar, and the cup of blessing, those present salute each other in turn with a mutual kiss, and call to memory the names of the departed in Christ. The mutual salutation of the living, and commemoration of the dead,[1] which takes place on the setting forth of that one bread, whereof all may partake, signify the unity in Christ of both living and dead; their agreement, likeness, and uniform way of living according to the fashion of Christ; which all profess to imitate who worthily partake of his sacred rites. Moreover whilst rehearsing the names of the saints, we call to mind how great was their virtue of whom we keep a recollection; that by their example we may be roused to a like virtue. In the few, whose names are heard, are implied the rest, whose names cannot be repeated for multitude; and these are rehearsed in undoubting hope, as certainly living; for they, as our Saviour has borne witness, are "passed from death unto life," and are held in mind of him who well "knoweth them that are his," as is written in the Book of Life. On the setting forth of the Saviour under the forms of bread and wine, the commemoration of the saints follows straightway; that they, being united in Jesus, may be felt to be something that is one with him. Joh. v. 24. 2 Tim. ii. 19.

The washing of hands on the part of the bishop and priests, signifies that they are wholly clean, and need no washing, except as regards their extremities; as saith our Saviour, "He that is washed needeth not save to wash his feet, but is clean every whit." The fingers are washed, Joh. xiii. 10.

---

[1] See above, p. 82.

that if any taint of sin, however slight, remain, it may be utterly scoured away,[1] and that the Bishop with those about him may in all sweetness and purity enter on the most holy rites, so as purely and devoutly to conduct and complete the divine office in the sacrament. For it is hard to live so chastely and uprightly, as that no tinge of passion, though slight, appear to cloud our brightness. Hence Jesus washed the extremities of St. Peter's feet. Hence the Bishop, when about to perform the sacred rites, washes the extremities of his hands; a custom derived from that washing of feet; that even the remaining taint of sin, whatever it be, on the tips of his fingers, may be removed by the water of grace. At which act it is now the custom to repeat "I will wash mine hands in innocency." But no one is so innocent as not to have need to wash the tips of his fingers at least, if he be performing any sacred office; that is, to lay aside the slight passions, from which it is hard to keep aloof, and the relics of sins that have been, as it were, rooted out.

Ps. xxvi. 6.

And here let every priest observe, by that sacrament of washing, how clean, how scoured, how fresh he ought to be who would handle the heavenly mysteries, and especially the sacrament of the Lord's body; how such ought to be so washed and scoured and polished inwardly, as that not so much as a shadow be left in the mind whereby the incoming light might be in any wise obscured; and that not a trace of sin remain to prevent God from walking in the temple of our mind. Oh! priests, Oh! priesthood,[2] Oh! the de-

---

[1] This is the reason given by Dionysius:—"Enimvero pontificis illa sacerdotumque . . . . . ablutio coram signis sacratissimis agitur, ut ostendatur sub Christo nos arbitro degere, *cunctas nostras secretissimas cogitationes* inspectante;" words which might have suggested our introductory prayer, "Cleanse the thoughts of our hearts," and so on.

[2] This apostrophe at once calls to mind passages from the writer's Convocation Sermon, to which I am persuaded that Dean Hook has awarded less than justice in describing them as "rhetorical phraseology." (*Lives of the Archbishops*, vi. p. 295.) This passage, as well as another afterwards referred to from his Exposition on 1 Corinthians, will shew that Colet had thought too long and deeply about such topics to be likely suddenly to "become rhetorical" about them in 1513. Nor

testable boldness of wicked men in this our generation, Oh! the abominable impiety of those miserable priests, of whom this age of ours contains a great multitude; who fear not to rush from the bosom of some foul harlot into the temple of the Church, to the altar of Christ, to the mysteries of God. Abandoned creatures! on whom the vengeance of God will one day fall the heavier, the more shamelessly they have intruded themselves on the divine office. Oh! Jesu Christ, wash for us not our feet only, but our hands and our head.

These mystic washings are pointed at by the brazen laver, and the washing appointed for the priesthood in the Old Testament (as it is described in Exodus), and are typified by them, as they are by other emblematic purifications in the same passage. By which we ought to be admonished, as well as by our own holy emblems, how purified and cleansed in mind we should be to stand by the altar of God, where God himself, even Jesus Christ our judge, is present as a spectator; where the observers are the angels, in whose sight, and under the all-seeing eye of Jesus, we perform his most sacred office; if rightly, to our everlasting salvation; if unlawfully, to his despite in our wickedness, and to our own eternal condemnation.

Ex. xl. 30.

The Bishop then, wholly and inwardly washed, returns to offer holy praises, to consecrate the sacrament, to show it openly, and lastly to communicate also in it. This very thing all together do along with the Bishop, being joined to him by this common participation. To shew the meaning and significance of which acts, let us trace the matter somewhat nearer to its source.

---

had they faded from his mind, when in 1518 he exhibited to Cardinal Wolsey his Statutes for the Reformation of Residence in St. Paul's Cathedral. See the documents in the Appendix to Dugdale's St. Paul's (1716), pp. 32-3, and 45, especially the passages where he enters into the meaning of the terms *Canonici* and *Residentes*. The renewed contrast of *deforming* and *reforming*, and the repeated *Proh dolor!* and *Proh scelus!* which sound like Colet's battle cry, all shew that the Convocation Sermon of 1513 was but an audible passage in a great sermon which began many years before, and was not ended till his death.

When, directly after the Creation, foolish human nature was allured by the seductive enticements of the enemy, and fell away from God into a womanish[1] and dying condition, and was rolling headlong down with rapid course to death itself, then at length, in his own time, our good and tender and kind and gentle and merciful God, giving us all good things at once in place of all that was bad, willed to take upon him human nature, and to enter into it, and rescue it from the power of the adversary, overthrowing and destroying his empire. For, as St. Paul writes to the Hebrews, "Forasmuch as the children,"—that is, servants—"are partakers of flesh and blood,"—that is, men forsaking God —therefore also God himself "made himself of no reputation and took upon him the form of a servant," and "himself likewise took part of the same" flesh and blood—that is, human nature;—"that through death he might destroy him that had the power of death, that is, the devil; and deliver them who through fear of death were all their lifetime subject to bondage:" that he might destroy, I say, that enemy, not by force, but (as Dionysius says) by judgment and righteousness, which he calls a hidden thing and a mystery.[2] For it was a marvellous victory, that the Devil, though victorious, in the very fact of his conquering should be conquered; and that Jesus should conquer in the very fact of his being vanquished on the cross; so that in reality, in the victory on each side, the matter was otherwise than it seemed. And thus, when the adversary that vanquished man was himself vanquished by God, man was restored, without giving any just cause of complaint to the Devil, to the liberty and light of God. There was shewn to him the path to heaven, trodden by the feet of Christ, whose foot-

Heb. ii. 14, 15.

Phil. ii. 7.

---

[1] This is a common term of disparagement with Colet, as *masculine* is of praise. Thus in the *De Sacramentis Ecclesiæ*, p. 76, "Quod est in ecclesia Christiana detestabile, ut aliquis scilicet sponte langueat *mulieretque*, quum sumus vocati in *virilem* dignitatem, non ut turpe aliquid et carnale *muliebriter* agamus." See also the beginning of Ch. vi. pt. i. below.

[2] "Non viribus veluti prævalens, sed, juxta nobis *traditum mystice* eloquium, in judicio et justicia."—Pars iii. sec. 11.

steps we must follow, if we would arrive whither he has gone. A suffering Christ, I say (most marvellous!), and dying as though vanquished, overcame; cast out, he became the caster out; when there was heard that voice of the Father, "I have both glorified it, and will glorify it again;" which voice was uttered for the sake of others. Then Jesus, shewing what kind of glorifying that was, said: "Now is the judgment of this world; now shall the prince of this world be cast out. And I, if I be lifted up from the earth, will draw all men unto me. This he said, signifying what death he should die." By that death we have been rescued from the dead, and are the servants of God; and we celebrate the memorial of that death, when initiated in the sacred rites of him, who, when about to die, commanded and said, "This do in remembrance of me." Likewise St. Paul, "As often as ye drink this cup, ye do shew the Lord's death, till he come." During the sacrifice, that remembrance of his death does truly fashion us after the image of Christ, and the sacraments lead and draw us away from the world, and station us apart, yea and bind us to God, that the form of God may be reflected in us. Joh. xii. 28—33.

Luke xxii. 19.
1 Cor. xi. 26.

Wherefore, to return to our subject, when the Bishop with his priests has made mention of what Jesus the Son of God did for us, he then proceeds to complete what remains, with meet symbols appointed by God. He makes heartfelt excuse for himself, and declares himself unworthy to approach so great a mystery; he prays that he may worthily consecrate, may rightly distribute to the church standing by, and that the Church may duly participate. In the primitive Church, at the Mass, the subordinates of the priest partook together with him of the offered Christ; before whose eyes he places the consecrated sacraments, and divides the holy bread into pieces,[1] and distributes it along with the

---

[1] The passage of Dionysius as rendered by Ambrosius, is *in frusta concidens*; as rendered by Corderius, *in multa diviso*, which is the more literal. In any case it will be observed how little countenance is here given to the Roman practice of using wafer-bread, and of dividing one wafer only into three parts. Jewell takes advantage of this in his controversy with Harding :—" As M. Harding is deceaved in the maner of

cup; thus multiplying one to many, that he may unite many in one. He sought, whilst abiding undivided, in a manner to multiply himself; that many, by jointly partaking in the one true Word of God, may be united in him, and be made like him, wholly sanctified in him. As Dionysius writes, we ought to regard the life of Jesus in the flesh, which was all for us, and to imitate the example shewn us, and that life, if we would be partakers together of his glory. He came forth from his secret place before the eyes of men; the invisible became visible; the one, in a manner, many: that he might draw all things to his own purpose. This is the mystery signified by the taking of the one bread and cup from their hidden and secret place, and by the displaying and distribution and joint participation thereof; and as these sensible signs, though one, are multiplied, for union, so may we understand that the invisible, even Jesus, is multiplied and divided, though one, that as many as possible may be united in him;—those, namely, who imitate the sinlessness of Jesus (that I may use the expression of Dionysius),[1] and who sin not, even as he sinned not. The Bishop partakes first, because he is nearer to God, and ought to be by far the holiest and wisest of all. For the unworthy receiving of that so great a sacrament comes of ignorance. Let Bishops therefore learn the mysteries of God, and promote worthy priests to the sacred offices; lest, through our long unworthiness, the condign vengeance of God be at length called forth upon us. May God, of his great pity, make us worthy of his mysteries!

---

breaking, so is he also deceived in the quantity of the Bread; imagining it was a little thin round cake, such as of late hath beene used in the Church of Rome, *which,* Durandus saith, *must be round like a Pennie; either because Judas betraied Christ for some like kinde of Coyne; or because it is written, Domini est Terra et plenitudo ejus: The earth is the Lord's, and the fulnesse thereof.* But indeed it was a great Cake, so large and so thicke, that all the Congregation might receive of it. . . . . So Dionysius: Velatum Panem in multa concidens, et unitatem Calicis omnibus impertiens: Dividing the bread, that stood covered, into many parts, and delivering the unitie of the Cup unto all the people."—*Replie* (1611) p. 329.

[1] "Sanctamque ejus impeccantiam imitando," etc.—§ 12.

CHAPTER IV.

PARTS I. II.

On the consecration of the Chrism.

IN all the Sacraments there is a derivation of the one to the many, of the single to the manifold, and of the invisible unity to sensible signs; that by these kindred principles men may be taken and led from multiplicity to unity. Thus it is clear, that all the sacraments are opportune means between God, who is one, and men, who are many; that the many may be made godlike in God.

The consecration of the Chrism,[1] which the priestly office employs for almost all its services, has well-nigh the same ceremonies as the Communion; namely, incense, psalms, lessons, chants. During the consecration of it also, Catechumens, Apostates, Energumens and Penitents are dismissed. The concealment and covering of the Chrism indicates and signifies the keeping secret in the religious

---

[1] This rite occupies an important place in Dionysius, and is placed by him on a level with the Holy Eucharist. His term for the sacred unguent, or Chrism, is *muron;* and he speaks of it as used in Baptism, in Confirmation (or the completion of Baptism), and in the consecration of the Altar. But this actual reference to its use is very brief, and occupies a small space in comparison with his meditation on it as symbolical of Christ. Below, in the Seventh Chapter, he speaks of the anointing after death; but nowhere, I believe, does Dionysius make any allusion to what is called Extreme Unction. In the Discourse ascribed to Cyprian *De unctione Chrismatis* much is said about this Chrism, and its consecration on the Thursday in Passion-week. One passage reminds us of what Colet writes below:—" Ut, sicut Christus a chrismate dictus est, eo quod singularis excellentiæ oleo unxerit eum Deus; ita et participes ejus quotquot sunt, consortes sint tam unctionis quam nominis, et dicantur a Christo Christiani." In the later Latin Church there were three kinds of unguent employed, "oleum sanctum, oleum chrismatis, et oleum infirmorum; that is, holy oil, chrism oil, and sick men's oil;" which were kept in separate flasks in a vessel called a Chrismatory.—See Peacock's *English Church Furniture* (1866) p. 161 n.

mind of divine inspirations; which ought neither to be unbecomingly displayed, nor rashly made common, lest, in that case, they lose their precious odour. The fragrance of the substance, and the brightness of the divine grace, ought alike to be shielded by the covering of a religious custody. For nothing is either more precious or more fragrant than the gift instilled by God into the mind of man. And if a man hold fast to this instilling, the degrees of grace are intensified, so as for his mind at length to become not unlike the pattern of God. God portrays his own full image, if man will aim wholly and untiringly at it. But let him not make public the share of the divine nature which he has received, lest the fragrance of the odour of the heavenly gift grow poor and faint.

By their own private right, things divine choose to be kept secret; for if they be divulged they lose their divineness. For God wills not to communicate himself to many; since there are not many to whom he can communicate himself. If you make public his secret gifts, their brightness, beauty, virtue, fragrance is gone; and you ought so to conceal them, as not only to refrain from publishing wisdom, and what you know by revelation, but even from "doing your works" publicly, according to our Saviour's injunction, "to be seen of men." For as God is in secret, so are divine men retired, secret, solitary, and inwardly self-contained, being widely separated from the multitude; and so is their whole wisdom and life and works hidden, being seen of God and the angels, not of men. They "seek and set their affections on things above, where Christ sitteth on the right hand of God, not on things on the earth. They are dead, and their life is hidden in Christ." Hence they love solitude; and, like God, all their good deeds they desire to do in secret, that God may be praised, not themselves; and that their works may "shine before men," not themselves, and "their Father which is in heaven may be glorified," not they themselves. If you would be godlike, lie hidden, as God does; be manifest in heaven, and in heaven let your conversation be. If you be in the truth itself, you need not sensible sacraments; you possess the grace of God itself, which

Mat. xxiii. 5.

Col. i. 1—3.

Matth. v. 16.

is the object of all sacraments. So did the monks in Egypt[1] once possess it, not having in use all the sacraments that we have, in order to be drawn towards God; because that, being already drawn to God, they needed them not.

That we may understand that what is divine ought to be secret and covered, the Chrism, by which every priestly office is performed and fulfilled, is shrouded by the wings. For the sacred Chrism is almost on a level with the Eucharist; and in use and necessity is equal to it. In the consecration of it there are the same solemn ceremonies, whereby also men are drawn through manifold colours to the pure light itself, that is luminous to its innermost, and becomes not coloured in passing through dim signs; and in the case of the Chrism, as in that of the Eucharist (in which latter the truth of God is beheld in signs by the bodily eyes) the simple truth, as it streams forth from the Sun of Righteousness, is beheld by the spiritual eye. They that cannot look on the sun itself, the radiance of whose powerful light blinds the vision, made delicate in the shade, yet can endure tempered hues.

The ointment and sacred Chrism I describe is compounded of many varied and fragrant materials, that men, anointed with it, may have a good and sweet odour, refreshing and pleasant to the nostrils. This Chrism is Jesus Christ himself, our heavenly anointing and fragrance; in whom an odour, rising from a blending of all virtues, breathes with unspeakable pleasantness on spiritual men,[2] and refreshes

---

[1] I do not know whether Colet is referring to anything more special, in this, than the solitary asceticism in which the lives of the earliest monks were spent, and which of necessity debarred them from many religious rites. "Monachism certainly took its rise in Egypt," says Dr. Burton (*Lectures* &c. 1845, p. 227), who traces the origin of it to the ancient Therapeutæ. In the persecution under Decius many fled to such retreats as the cavern St. Jerome describes (*Epist.* iii. 1) in the Thebaid, which in the days of Antony and Cleopatra had been the resort of coiners

[2] Compare with this figure what Ignatius writes to the Ephesians: "Wherefore our Lord received the anointing on his head, that he might breathe upon his Church incorruption." *Propter hoc, unguentum* etc. (Ed. 1708) p. 53.

the nostrils of their mind. This very Jesus, our Chrism, saturates us with himself; and anoints us with his own life-giving oil of gladness, that we may be vigorous, strong, shining and sweet. This is the oil, of which St. Paul thus writes in his second Epistle to the Corinthians:—"Now he which stablisheth us with you in Christ, and hath anointed us, is God; who hath also sealed us, and given the earnest of the Spirit in our hearts." This Spirit of Christ it is which is the true Chrism; and where that is, it breathes the sweetest of odours. This is the "unction from the Holy One," which "teacheth all things," as St. John writes: we are Christians in Christ, that is, anointed in anointing itself. God is all softness, gentleness, sweetness, pleasure, delight, savour, fragrance, harmony, light and exulting joy. Jesus, God and man, sates with every pleasure our spiritual senses; and through excess of pleasure transports to ecstasy his bride, the soul, which unites with him; that, in the pleasure of God, it may be all pleasure; no longer now feeling pleasure, but being itself pleasure, affording rather pleasure to others. This softness filling the touch, and savour regaling the taste, and fragrance delighting the smell, and harmony soothing the ears, and light refreshing the eyes, is Jesus, our spouse, wholly delectable. He that stands nearer to him has the more fragrant odour. We ought all to be diffusers and followers of this fragrance, that we may be as a sweet-scented temple of God, ourselves sweet-scented; that, we being made odoriferous in Christ with a pleasant odour, the whole temple may be redolent of God. And so our Chrism is Christ, with whom we have been saturated and made fragrant.

Twelve Seraphs' wings cover Christ and the Chrism, and guard them from the profane. Those spirits themselves also first, and without ceasing, derive their fragrance from Jesus. Therefore they are portrayed around Christ and the Chrism. All things come to us in succession from Jesus through the angels, who constantly and unceasingly refresh themselves in the fulness of Jesus, and rejoice uninterruptedly, singing evermore *Holy, Holy, Holy*; through unspeakable joy being unable to refrain themselves; so do they rejoice most highly in the highest.

When you read of twelve Seraphs' wings, understand two Seraphs;[1] the six wings of one of which and the six wings of the other conceal what is deep and profound, disclose what is midway, and lean towards the things of God that are midway. They in turn cry aloud to one another, that they may in turn impart glory. They stand by the anointing Jesus, that we may understand that Christ, by being incarnate, withdrew not from his own majesty and from the angels; and that he who was anointed and sanctified "above his fellows," was the very one who anoints and sanctifies. Christ Jesus is the very anointing which the angels adore; and therefore this is rightly employed in all sacred rites. To the spiritual nostrils it is such as the word of God is to the ears, and the Eucharist to the eyes. Ps. xlv. 7.

The Soul { sees / hears / smells } God in the { Eucharist. / Word of the Gospel. / Sacred Unguent. }

In these three, Jesus Christ is the very sacrament of the { Eucharist. / Gospel. / Anointing. }

The signs of the cross also, made with the sacred unguent, are ever a sacrament to us of Christ and our Chrism being crucified and dead for us. In the baptistery the oil is poured on the baptized in the form of a cross, by which it is signified that the Anointed himself was crucified and died for those who are baptized in him; and that the baptized die on the Cross of Christ, and sink in his death, that they may come forth to his life. This indeed is what St. Paul writes to the Romans:—"Know ye not, brethren, that so many of us as were baptized into Christ Jesus, were baptized into his death" and cross, who was in the flesh for us, that we in the flesh might lay aside our sinful life, and be sunk in the waters of his death, "being buried with him by baptism into death." In this baptism, by faith in the cross of Christ, we are as it were crucified along with him, Rom. vi. 3, 4.

---

[1] The expression in Dionysius is merely "duodecim sacris alis circumtectum;" but in the next section this is explained to refer to the Seraphim, as seen in the vision of Isaiah.

and die to obtain that life for which Christ died. Therefore the Apostle says, "Being buried with Christ by baptism into death; that, like as Christ was raised up from the dead by the glory of the Father, even so we also," coming forth washed, "should walk in newness of life." Jesus is our sanctifying death; therefore is he present as crucified at the waters of our baptism. He too is our altar; therefore that same Chrism is poured on the altar, during its consecration.[1]

^{1 Cor. i. 30, 31.}

Christ is in all, and is our all; "who is made unto us wisdom and righteousness and sanctification and redemption; that, according as it is written, He that glorieth, let him glory in the Lord." He is in truth all our Sacraments, whether purifying, illumining or perfecting. He is our temple, our altar, our priest, our sacrifice and sanctification; and he sanctified himself for us, that we may be sanctified in him, our very Lord Jesus Christ.

CHAPTER IV.

PART III.

On the spiritual contemplation of the sacred Chrism.

GOD is in Christ, Christ in the sacraments, the sacraments in men, for their temporal death here, that men by those same sacraments may be initiated in Christ and God, for their eternal life. Every descent of the divinity is for the ascent of humanity: every descent is for mortification, that there may be a resurrection to life. God was made man, that he might die for men, and ordain sacraments of mortification for them that believe in him; mortification, I say, of

---

[1] This custom is mentioned by Dionysius in § 12. Bingham says that it seems to have arisen in the sixth century: "For the council of Agde, *An.* 506, is the first public record, that we meet with, giving any account of a distinct consecration of altars; and there we find the new ceremony of *Chrism* added to the sacerdotal Benediction. . . . But as this ceremony was new, so was the consecration of altars, as distinct from Churches, a new thing also."—*Eccl. Antiq.* viii. ix. § 10.

faithful men, that they may live immortally in God. All the sacraments, as Dionysius the Areopagite teaches, work our assimilation to God; and this cannot be, unless at the same time they work our mortification in ourselves, that God may live in us. In the sacraments therefore we ourselves die, that Christ may live in us.

Through death we pass to life; through the death of death, that is, to the life of life. Through sacraments of mortification, in all of which there is the death and cross of Christ, we pass to Christ himself the giver of life; that in them we being crucified, dead, and "buried with Christ," may stand forth purified, illumined and perfected in him; rising again, as it were from the dead, living in Christ, purified by his sacraments, in which is the virtue of the death and cross of Christ; by which sacraments we "crucify the flesh with the affections and lusts," that the virtue of the Spirit may live in us. All things were first in Christ, and from him come all things to us. In him is humility, death, sanctification of himself, an ensample to others, that they may die righteous. In St. John he says, "For their sakes I sanctify myself, that they also might be sanctified through the truth." He, the holy one, sanctified others, that they, being holy, might sanctify yet others: he gave an ensample of holiness to men. From him flow all things, which are previously in himself. He, being purified, makes pure; being sanctified, he sanctifies; being perfected, he makes perfect. He is our *Telete*, that is, our sanctification and perfection. Since the Chrism makes perfect, it was therefore called *Telete* by our forefathers. Extreme Unction[1] is the consummation of our Christianity. In anointing there is an emblem of Christianizing: from the fulness of anointing, Jesus is called Christ; in whom all that are his are anointed.

Gal. v. 24.

Joh. xvii. 9.

---

[1] As will be noticed in Ch. vii, the "Extreme," or final, Unction of Dionysius is an anointing after death.

CHAPTER V.

PART I.

Introduction to the Sacrament of Holy Orders.

THE function of the priestly office consists in drawing all things to order, honour and glory. The whole Hierarchy is parted into three divisions; and the office of every Sacred Order is distributed into *Teletæ*, that is, *Perfections*. In those who make perfect and those who are perfected consists every function of the priestly office; that the higher, when perfected, should perfect the lower, and these in turn whoever are still lower; that so the first Orders may consist of those who are perfecting, the second of those who are being perfected and also perfecting, the third and last of those who are perfected. In the conveyance of the divinity and of divine principles to man is comprised the whole priestly office and task; that what is received may be handed down, for the perfection of all.

The triune God himself is the true *Telete*, and Perfection that perfects all things; and he carries on a threefold perfection of mankind. Hence beneath the Trinity of the Godhead there are three Hierarchies of spirits; and each of these is threefold, with three distinct Orders. All those Orders receive the all-glorious Trinity openly and clearly, and transmit it from the first, through the midmost, to the lowest angels; receiving and diffusing the divine light downwards. This bountiful diffusion of the heavenly light and goodness, by which all things are perfected, proceeds through those pure spirits even as far as men. But in the earlier ages before this time, when men were but children, and of tender faculties, the unmixed ray of divine truth and righteousness entered a great number and variety of shadows, under the ministry of Moses; and by these the pure light of God, becoming degenerate, as it were, passed into many different colours; that the delicate sight, which could not endure the pure and untempered light of truth and righteousness, powerful in its force and working, might for a time gaze upon

INTROD. TO HOLY ORDERS. 103

colours, of softer and fainter brilliancy, so to say; until at length the eye, become stronger and able to bear the light, should be able to look upon the truth without any shadows. This is the hierarchy and legal priesthood ordained by holy Moses, subordinate to the angels. For Moses, when, under the angels, he was exposed to the pure light itself on Mount Sinai, not daring to entrust that light to men's weakness, abated that which he beheld upon the mountain to the lowly gaze of men, by veils, appropriate indeed (knowing as he did how to accommodate each to each), but yet very coarse, and woven of thick thread. He set before their eyes a meadow, so to speak, of truth and righteousness; that they might look down upon the truth in the painted flowers of the Mosaic Law; unable as they were to look up to the Sun of righteousness exalted in the heaven. For when the whole world lay utterly without light, nay more, without a symbol of it, nay even without so much as a shadow of the truth, the heavenly order had to be faintly outlined at the first, as on blank canvas;[1] and men had to be trained in cheerless shadows, by a mutual working on one another, in a labour and service foreshadowing the true. This is what St. Paul, in his Epistle to the Colossians, calls "rudiments;" Col. ii. 8. and this foreshadowing was to wait for the illumination that should come, that at length in God's own time a splendid

---

[1] There is the same figure in the *De Sacramentis Eccl.*, p. 48 :—
"Non potuit enim imago Dei depingi in terrâ in hominibus, nisi prius adumbraretur. In media mundi tabula et hominum quasi carbone infuscavit atrum quiddam Moyses; depinxit clarius in toto mundo noster Jesus." How much Colet's thoughts were occupied at times by the Mosaic writings, may be seen from *The Oxford Reformers*, pp. 25-36, where a summary is given of his letters to Radulphus on the account of the Creation. The reference to Macrobius, by the way, which is there alluded to (p. 35), may be supplied by observing the last words with which the MS. abruptly breaks off: "Honestissimo et piissimo figmento," etc. Colet was no doubt going to quote, when he mentioned Macrobius, the passage in Lib. i. c. 2, of the *Comment. in Somn. Scip.*;
—"Aut sacrarum rerum notio sub figmentorum velamine, *honestis* et tecta rebus et vestita nominibus, enuntiatur; et hoc est solum *figmenti* genus, quod cautio de divinis rebus admittit.' Macrobius had been previously distinguishing the various kinds of mythical composition, and their uses.

image might stand forth, able to express more brightly and manifestly the truth which is in heaven. On this canvas of the world the work of God has so proceeded; from the shadow to the image, from the image to the reality. In this theatre of the world the Legal Hierarchy was the representative of the Christian. Now the Christian drama is representing the citizenship in heaven.

These are the three in their order; one appearing beneath another, the image of that above it:—namely, the Heavenly Hierarchy, the Christian, and the Mosaic.

$$\begin{cases} \text{God, the cause of all order.} \\ \text{Order Himself, the founder of all order.} \end{cases}$$

The $\begin{cases} \text{Heavenly} \\ \text{Christian} \\ \text{Mosaic} \end{cases}$ Hierarchy is $\begin{cases} \text{Luminous truth.} \\ \text{A bright image of the truth.} \\ \text{A shadowing of the image.} \end{cases}$

The World is the material of the work, and, as it were, the canvas of the picture.

The human race is the material, the clay, for God to fashion what he will. Out of these men he moulds, and by a structure of shadows, with Moses for his minister, prefigures on earth the Heavenly Hierarchy. Then, with Jesus for his minister, he fashioned out of whom he would under that state of shadows, a bright image; that heaven might plainly appear upon earth. One day all will be heaven, and all things truth. Thus, what suddenly fell, has been revealed again in a long order; and what the creature suddenly demolished, the Creator in a long succession of time is building up again; that he may restore all things in Jesus Christ. He is advancing men from nothingness to shadow, from shadow to image, from image to truth; that in the truth all things may be made true. But when men were to be recalled to God, that they might contemplate him as the angels do, so debased were they for such lofty contemplation, that it was necessary to draw them first a certain height by figurative systems; that, gaining a footing there for a time, they might then be lifted higher, and thence finally be raised to the truth itself. After the fall of man there was darkness on the earth. The Sun of righteousness and truth, screening his rays by means of the angelic hierarchy, cast a shadow of that same hierarchy upon the earth. At length in his own good time the Sun himself descended, by his own immediate presence to brighten with colours that shadow of the angelic hierarchy, and to shed upon it the light of his truth; that thence a tinged reflection of the angelic city also might be more clearly seen upon earth. And at length, when the shadow is taken away, the unclouded light will one day appear in the glory of Christ, "who is our life," hidden in the heavens; which "shall appear, when he shall have appeared, in glory." Meanwhile "the whole creation groaneth and travaileth in pain together until now, waiting for the adoption" of God. *Col. iii. 3, 4. Rom. viii. 22, 23.*

The
- Heavenly / Christian / Individual — Hierarchy is typified by
  - Anagoge, to wit, the more hidden depth.
  - Allegory.—The whole.
  - The Moral sense.—The part.
- Mosaic Hierarchy is wholly typical in its acts of
  - The Heavenly truth.
  - The Christian image.
  - The righteous life of a Christian man.

The act is a shadow of three things
- Light.
- The Whole.
- The Part.

From this order, any one may perceive the reasons of the four senses[1] in the Old Law, which are customary in the

---

[1] From the tenour of Colet's rejoinder to Erasmus, on the subject of Christ's agony in the Garden, it has been thought that he rejected the theory of fourfold senses much more decidedly than would appear from this passage. As the subject is an interesting one, I will endeavour to state it clearly for the reader, though at the risk of being prolix.

From the *Bibliotheca* of Sixtus Senensis (Ed. 1610, p. 134) may be gained a full view of the method, as it was regarded by its advocates. He says that there are two chief lines of Scriptural interpretation, (1) the *Historical* (which Colet calls the Literal), and (2) the *Mystic*. This latter again is subdivided into the *Allegorical, Tropological* (or Moral) and *Anagogical*. Sometimes, he argues, the same word or phrase may bear, in different passages, all four significations. Thus take the term "waters." In Gen. i. 9, "Let the waters under the heaven," &c. it is in its *literal* sense. In Isai. xliii. 2, "When thou passest through the waters I will be with thee," it is in the *moral* sense. In Ezek. xxxvi. 25, "Then will I sprinkle clean water upon you" (understood of baptism) it is in the *allegorical*. And lastly in Jer. ii. 13, "They have forsaken me, the fountain of living waters," it is in the *anagogic* or elevating sense;

Church. The *literal* is, when the actions of the men of old time are related. When you think of the image, even of the Christian Church which the Law foreshadows, then you catch the *allegorical* sense. When you are raised aloft, so as from the shadow to conceive of the reality which both represent, then there dawns upon you the *anagogic* sense. And when from signs you observe the instruction of individual man, then all has a *moral* tone for you.

In the writings of the New Testament, saving when it pleased the Lord Jesus and his Apostles to speak in parables, as Christ often does in the gospels, and St. John

---

by which, that is, our thoughts are raised from the earthly to the heavenly. Mirandola goes to great lengths in this direction. Thus he says in a passage of his *Heptaplus* that the Waters above the Firmament, the Firmament itself, and the Waters under the Firmament, signify the three Hierarchies of Angels (Op. 1601, p. 18). Erasmus, who may fairly be classed as one of the same school in this respect, goes so far as to say, that we might as well read the story of Livy as the Book of Judges, or many other parts of the Old Testament, if we leave out of sight their allegorical meaning (*Enchiridion*, 1523, leaf g). Savonarola in his sermons, besides the literal interpretation, " divided almost every passage in the Bible under four other heads, namely, *Spiritual, Moral, Allegorical, Anagogical.*" (Villari's *Hist.* tr. by Horner, i. 114.) So also Bishop Longland, a friend of Colet's, when preaching before the University of Oxford, on the occasion of Hen. VIII.'s founding a new College there in 1525, took for his text Prov. ix. 1, 2; and explained the words " She hath also furnished her table," to betoken the four dishes, or courses, of History, Morality, Allegory and Anagogy, which Wisdom set forth on the table of her Scriptural banquet. (*Concio*, 1525, fol. 23).

These extracts may serve to shew the principle as it was maintained by some at that period, and those too, men whose opinion Dean Colet would respect.

The opposite view may be taken as it is held by a learned scholar of Dean Colet's school, Whitaker, the opponent of Bellarmine. In his *Disputation on Holy Scripture* (Parker Soc. 1849, p. 405) he says : " As to those three spiritual senses, it is surely foolish to say that there are as many senses of Scripture as the words themselves may be transferred and accommodated to bear. For although the words may be *applied* and *accommodated* tropologically, allegorically, anagogically, or any other way; yet there are not therefore various senses, various interpretations and explications of Scripture, but there is but one sense, and that the literal, which may be variously accommodated, and from which various things may be collected." He then goes on to explain even the well-known text in Gal. iv. 24 (" Which things are an allegory") on this principle;

throughout in the Revelation, all the rest of the discourse, in which either the Saviour teaches his disciples more plainly, or the Apostles instruct the Churches, has the sense that appears on the surface; nor is one thing said and another meant, but the very thing is meant which is said; and the sense is wholly literal. Still, inasmuch as the Church of God is figurative, conceive always an *anagoge* in what you hear in the doctrines of the Church; the meaning of which will not cease, till the figure has become the truth. From this moreover conclude, that, where the literal sense is, there the allegorical is not always along with it; but, on the other hand, that, where there is the allegorical sense, the literal sense is always underlying it.[1]

---

though he is driven to admit, that "the whole entire sense is not in the words taken strictly; but part in the type, part in the transaction itself. In either of these, considered separately and by itself, part only of the meaning is contained; and by both taken together the full and perfect meaning is completed."

It seems to me that this last admission concedes as much as Colet, in the guarded sentence with which he ends the paragraph, has assumed; and that there may be a middle ground on which the contending parties could unite. The keen mind of Thomas Aquinas appears to me to detect the truth, when he writes:—" The author of Holy Scripture is God; in whose power it is, not only to accommodate words to have a meaning (as man also can do), but facts themselves as well. And so, whereas in all other sciences words are significant of things, the science of Theology has this peculiar property, that the very things implied by words have themselves also a significance" (*Summa, Pars* I. Art. X. *Conclusio.*) Without going so far as to maintain, with some expositors, that the very names of places, such as Bethesda, Bethsaida, and the like, were given, in the workings of Providence, to harmonize with events afterwards to be transacted there, I yet am unable to think that the meaning of such an act as the lifting up of the Serpent in the wilderness, is exhausted in the record of it as an historical fact. Doubtless the only meaning of the writer who narrates it, is the simple literal meaning which his words bear; but the act itself I would look on as a word spoken in the then unknown language of God, whose meaning in later times became revealed.

On such a principle as this, I think it possible that what Colet wrote to Erasmus, as against the scholastic system of interpretation, may be reconciled with what he lays down in the text.

[1] " Sensus enim Historicus, veluti substratum fundamentum, non excludit, sed sustinet sensum mysticum."— Erasmus, *Exposit. in Psal.* lxxxvi.

Or one may view the matter thus:—that in the night of this world and gloom of mankind, the patriarchs and prophets were stars shining in the absence of the Sun: that Moses, and seventy elders, were chosen, to whom, along with Moses, the Spirit was communicated. Concerning these is that expression of St. Peter in his second Epistle:—
2 Pet. i. 19. "We have also a more sure word of prophecy; whereunto ye do well that ye take heed, as unto a light that shineth in a dark place, until the day dawn, and the day star arise in your hearts." The day is that of the truth of Christ, in which we Christians walk. One may consider also that the rest of the people were as images of the stars shining in the waters; for these perceived not the truth except in fleeting signs. And that which is specially called the day of the Lord, is the day when the Lord of lords in his majesty shall gain the summit of the hemisphere, and illumine all things.

Day beneath the Sun.—The day is that true day of the Lord, when the Sun of Righteousness enlightens all things.

In Night
- Stars shining in heaven, under Christ; namely, saints illumined by the Sun.—Conversation in heaven.
- Stars shining in the water, under the Law; a watery image of the Church.

Night of darkness, wholly without light, before the Law.

For whilst we are living here, in the hours of morning and forenoon, we are journeying towards the mid-day sun, to sup with our Lord. Starting from a northern region, we are travelling towards the south.

The Day
- Of the Lord in its fulness, when all clouds are dispersed and all enemies subdued, and God shall be all in all.
- Begun in Christians: men beholding the rising of the Sun of Righteousness.

The Night
- Prophets, shining as stars in the heaven; understanding the meaning of the symbols.
- The people, shining in the water; clinging to the symbols.
- The Gentiles, wholly without light, wandering " in the vanity of their mind."

Moses[1] in truth received from God upon Mount Sinai not only the Law, which he left to them that came after, written down in five books, but also the hidden and true explanation and interpretation of it, and its spiritual meaning when unfolded. This God commanded him not to commit to writing in any wise, but to disclose and entrust it to Joshua the son of Nun only; who should in turn communicate it to the chief priests, that were likely to maintain a sacred, strict and religious silence. But the written law he was bidden by God to publish to the people; in which, through a simple history, there is shown at one while the power of God, now his wrath against the wicked, again his mercy towards the good, everywhere his justice towards all; that the people might acknowledge and reverence a powerful and good and righteous God. In which Law also the multitude are trained, by wholesome and divine precepts, to live well and happily, and to the service of the true religion. And thus, in the written Law, is seen only in how vast a series of events is visible the goodness and power of God; how each one should live; in what manner he should worship God. But as for those more hidden mysteries, and such as lay concealed beneath the rugged bark of the Law and its rude covering of words; to wit, those secrets of the divinity on high; if they had been disclosed to the foolish multitude by the men of old time; what else, I ask, would it have been, than to "give that which is holy unto the dogs, and to cast Matth. vii. 6.

---

[1] From this point to the mention of Sixtus IV., what Colet writes is an almost verbal transcript from the *Apologia*, or *De Homine*, of Pico della Mirandola. I mention both treatises, because the nephew of the elder Mirandola states that this passage appeared in the beginning of the *Apologia*, published in the author's lifetime, and also at the end of the *De Homine*, which he had kept reserved in manuscript. The first edition of the latter is, I believe, 1530.—*Op.* 1601, p. 207. The passage is much less correctly printed in the *De Homine* of 1530 (fol. b. 7) than in the *Apologia*, as edited in 1601. How it came to pass that Colet should transcribe this portion of Mirandola's treatise, without citing the author's name; whether it be a token that he never contemplated the publishing of his own treatise; or whether the omission be simply due to the copyer of the original manuscript; are interesting questions, but to which I have no means of furnishing an answer.

pearls before swine?" Wherefore those wise ancients divulged not the profound contemplation of the most secret things in the Law, and the hidden depth of its more recondite truth, save to wise men only, unknown to the multitude; among whom alone St. Paul writes to the Corinthians that he "speaks wisdom." This was a sacred custom among all the wise men of old time, to guard their mystic doctrines from the uninitiated multitude by abstruse riddles.[1] Jesus, the Teacher of Life, revealed many things to his disciples; and these they would not write down, lest they should become common and public. Dionysius relates, that the more secret Christian mysteries were conveyed by the authors of our religion from mind to mind, without writing, by the intervention of the spoken word alone. In the same way, agreeably to the command of God, the true interpretation of the Law, revealed and given by God to Moses, was called by a Hebrew term *Cabala*, that is, in Latin, *Receptio;* because that teaching was *received,* as of hereditary right, by one from another, not by means of written memorials, but by an orderly succession of communications. But after that the Jews were restored from the Babylonish captivity through Cyrus, and, after the rebuilding of their temple under Zerubbabel, turned their mind to the restitution of the Law, then Ezra, the ruler of the Church, after revising the book of Moses, plainly perceiving that the custom instituted by their forefathers, of transmitting the teaching from hand to hand, could not be preserved, through the exiles, massacres, flight and captivity of the Israelitish race; and that the result would be, that the secrets of heavenly doctrine vouchsafed to him would perish, since, without the intervention of their commentaries, these could not be long preserved in memory;—determined that the wise men who then survived should be

---

[1] In his *Conclusiones*, Mirandola endeavours to point out various instances of such esoteric meaning; as for example the doctrine of a Trinity in the number of the Graces, the Fates, and the three sons of Saturn. (*Op.* 1601, p. 71.) Many more such instances may be found, taken from Proclus (an author whom Colet is said to have studied) and other writers, in Cudworth's *Intellectual System* (1678), pp. 301 sqq.

called together, and that each should bring forwards as much of the mysteries of the Law as he retained in memory; and that by the aid of scribes this should be collected in seventy volumes; that being about the number of wise men in the Sanhedrim. Concerning which Ezra himself thus speaks, in his fourth book and thirteenth chapter:— "And it came to pass, when the forty days were fulfilled, that the Highest spake, saying, The first that thou hast written publish openly, that the worthy and unworthy may read it: but keep the seventy last, that thou mayest deliver them only to such as be wise among the people: for in them is the spring of understanding, the fountain of wisdom, and the stream of knowledge. And I did so." These are the books of the *Cabala* and of *Reception*;[1] which are kept with such religious care by the Jews, that none but those who are forty years of age may touch them. In these books all our doctrines plainly appear. Pope Sixtus IV. provided with great zeal a translation of them into Latin, by the aid of some learned man; and in his lifetime three books were under perusal.

2 Esdr. xiv. 45—48.

And thus it is plain that, besides the Law which was given by God to Moses on Mount Sinai, and which he left written and contained in five books, there was revealed by God himself to Moses also a true explanation of the Law, with a display of all the mysteries and secrets contained

---

[1] "It is originally Hebrew, *Kabalah*, signifying *Reception*, from the root *Kibel, to receive by tradition*. . . . We find no Cabbalistic writings but what are evidently posterior to the destruction of the second Temple. The most celebrated of them are (1) the *Sepher Jetsira*, or *Book of Creation*, which some Jews ascribe to the patriarch Abraham, but which was actually written by Rabbi Akhiba, who lived soon after the destruction of Jerusalem; and (2) the *Sepher Zohar*, or *Book of Splendour*, which was composed or invented by Rabbi Simeon Ben Jochai, who is said to have been a disciple of Akhiba, and who flourished in the second century of the Christian era."—*Encycl. Metrop.* under *Cabala*.

Mirandola included a number of propositions from the Cabala among the nine hundred on which he offered to dispute publicly in Rome. See the *De ascriptis numero noningentis* . . . 1486, last leaf but three, and elsewhere. These were afterwards reproduced and commented on by Archangelus, a minorite, in the *Artis Cabalisticæ Scriptores* (1587), pp. 732 sqq.

under the bark and rugged surface of the words of the Law; and that Moses received a twofold Law on the mount, the literal and the spiritual. The literal, it is evident, he committed to writing, and according to God's command delivered to the people; the spiritual Law he communicated to wise men only, seventy in number, whom Moses at God's command had chosen for the guardianship of the Law; and he enjoined upon them not to write it, but to reveal it by word of mouth to their successors, and these in turn to others. From this successive *reception* it was called *Cabala*; but this knowledge afterwards came to be put into writing; and those books openly contain all the secret things and mysteries which are veiled in the literal Law. These secret things, as Origen[1] perceives, are called by St. Paul "the oracles of God," giving life to the Law; without which life-giving spirit the Law is dead. That explanation and spiritual sense of the whole literal Law, which Moses, as we have said, received from God, was what we call the *Anagogic* sense. For as there is with us a fourfold method of explaining the Bible, and a fourfold sense, namely, the Literal, Mystical and Allegorical, Tropological, and Anagogical; so was it with the Hebrews. But the *Cabala* follows the Anagogic sense,[2] which was delivered to Moses from the mouth of God, and which is the loftier and more divine; drawing and leading us up from earthly to heavenly things; from the sensible to the intellectual; from things temporal to

Rom. iii. 2.

---

[1] "Sed et hoc ipsum quod dicit, *Quia credita sunt illis eloquia Dei*, considerandum est quia non dixerit *litteras* esse creditas, sed *eloquia Dei*. Unde via nobis datur intelligendi quod his qui legunt et non intelligunt, et qui legunt et non credunt, littera sola sit credita, illa de qua dicit Apostolus quia *littera occidit;* eloquia autem Dei illis sint credita, qui intelligentes et credentes his quæ Moyses scripsit, credunt et Christo, sicut et Dominus dicit: *Quod si credidissetis et ipsi Moysi, crederetis utique mihi; de me enim ille scripsit.*"—Orig. Comment. in Ep. ad Rom. L. ii. § 14.

[2] "The Cabalists therefore, which are the anatomists of words, and have a theological alchymy to draw sovereign tinctures and spirits from plain and gross literal matter, observe in every variety some great mystic signification; but so it is almost in every Hebrew name and word."—Donne's *Essays in Divinity*, by Jessopp, p. 122.

things eternal, from what is lowest to what is highest, from the human to the divine, from the bodily to the spiritual. The Jews pursue what is earthly, sensible, temporal, low, human, corporeal; all which things are in "the letter that killeth." They that are called to the Spirit of Christ, pursue what is heavenly, intellectual, eternal, above, divine, spiritual; in a word, that which was revealed by God to Moses, and by Moses also delivered to the seventy chosen ones: and this is the heavenly and exalted sense. To this divine truth men are called more closely in Christ; that they may set their affections higher, and live better, than the Jews: and this is the Anagogic sense. Towards this sense Dionysius writes[1] that they were guides, who learnt the more sacred meaning of the holy tabernacle; whom we may understand to have been the seventy wise men, whom Moses chose, to teach them the explanation of the Law. And that we may with faith and charity believe the heavenly things, Jesus Christ will be our leader; who has brought us out from Egypt, and even beyond the worldly promise and the earthly Jerusalem, and has appointed us under himself to be a more glorious Hierarchy, which stands towards the legal Hierarchy in the relation of end and perfection. The end again, and final perfection, of this hierarchy of ours, is the celestial and supernal; between which and the legal, as Dionysius records, this of ours is intermediate; and, as becomes what is so, comprises in itself, in some degree, both extremes; having from the one above it a spiritual and enlightened understanding, and from the one below it a

2 Cor. iii. 6.

---

[1] His words are "Duces vero ad eam ii sunt, qui sanctum illud tabernaculum a Mose sacratius didicerunt;" which the Scholiast explains as Colet does; "Per eos . . . . intelligit eos septuaginta qui post Mosen legis tenuerunt intelligentiam." In St. Prosper the inner, or figurative, meaning of the Tabernacle is explained in an extremely fanciful manner. Thus the joining of the sides and ends is a token that "mercy and truth are met together;" the covering of eleven curtains of goats' hair signified that the world was in a state of penitence, as guilty before God; and of this he finds a symbol even in the number of the eleventh Psalm (twelfth in the E. V.) which begins in accents of mourning:—" Help, Lord; for the godly man ceaseth; for the faithful fail from among the children of men."—*De Promiss.* Pars ii. c. 2.

carnal and corporeal and sensible symbolism. For, so long as we are men, even the most spiritual of us cannot altogether dispense with symbols. The lower Hierarchy resembles the higher in measure, as it can. All things that are in the heavenly Hierarchy, are also in the Christian, in a figurative manner; and all things that are in the Christian have gone before in the Legal, in a shadowy manner.

Heavenly		Angelic. Enlightened.		Higher.
Christian	{	Angelic; enlightened.—The spirit; God.—Heaven	}	Middle.
		Human; shadowy.—The flesh; man.—Earth.		
Legal		Human. Shadowy.		Lower.

We may consider therefore that there are in the Christian Church three Hierarchies, and these moreover threefold; so as for there to be among us, as among the angels, nine Orders, in imitation of the angelic degrees; the shadows of which preceded in the literal Law. All the office of these is in the work of sanctification, that men may be made like to God, who is holy; and among them are various classes of holy ones : the first and highest, those who sanctify; the last, those who are sanctified; and others, midway between these, who are at once sanctified and sanctifying. But all are ministers of God, for the diffusion of the divinity, for the full sanctification at length of mankind. All strive to imitate the angelic Orders; that the first triad may purify, the second illumine, the third perfect and complete; that the whole Church may be purified, illumined and perfected in God. Purification consists in the putting off whatever was ours, even our cause of greatest trust in ourselves; that we may turn to God, and hope in him. Illumination consists in faith in what is revealed, which is our wisdom. Perfection consists in the fulness of charity, which is " the fulfilling of the law" and of righteousness. The highest purify, illumine and perfect; the lowest are purified, illumined and perfected, being now initiated in the sacred rites, baptized and confirmed. The intermediate ones also are both receiving and bestowing purification; being themselves already enlightened, and illumining the purified for their completion. Com-

Rom. xiii. 10.

pletion and purification are the work of the highest in the Church; in whom there ought to be the greatest power of establishing men in hope, and of illumining them in faith, and lastly of perfecting them in love. By them, namely by those chief ones in the Church, the same is done as by the intermediate ones; and by these latter the same as by the lowest. For by all alike there is carried on together men's purification, illumination and perfection. For these three operations, wrought as they are by one cause, cannot be separated; but the same acts are performed by the intermediate ones as by the lowest, only after a more glorious scale, and finally by those last and highest on the most glorious. The whole of this divine working, among the heavenly beings, tends towards their assimilation to God, towards the representation of the Trinity, its unity, beauty and goodness. Hence there are three operations; purification, illumination and perfection. The effect of purification is unity, simplicity, power, constancy, stability; which in them is one single faculty, as it were, whereby they stand firm in God. The effect of illumination is a fair variety, truth, order, beauty, wisdom, clearness; all which terms have a certain identity of meaning, and in the angels signify a manifold knowledge of the divine word. Lastly, the effect of perfection is goodness, mercy, love, perfection,[1] charity. In us also these operations have their proper effects, after the likeness of the unity, truth and goodness which are in the angels. For our unity, which is the object aimed at by our purification, is hope, which is our simplicity and stability. Our truth is faith in the all-embracing truth which was in Jesus Christ. Our goodness and perfection is a love of the good. Towards these results every office and function in the Church of Christ is directed. And among them we may conceive of three kinds of those who hope, and three of those who believe, and three of those who love. Not that there is any one in the Church who does not love, or does not believe; for all things are in all; but because these qualities are dis-

---

[1] "The effect of perfection is . . . perfection."—It will be seen that this inexactness of expression is in the Latin.

tinguished according to degrees, and vary according to the greater or less participation in the divine ray; which indeed is one and the same, working everything in all; but according to a distinction of degrees there is a various assignment of names, and each has his own special attribute. Each one in his degree, in proportion to the gift bestowed upon him, discharges his office; all labour together in drawing men away from this world, and consecrating them to God. "Now," says St. Paul, "being made free from sin, and become servants to God, we have our fruit unto holiness, and the end everlasting life."

<small>Rom. vi. 22.</small>

In Dionysius three ecclesiastical orders are named; those of Bishops, Priests and Deacons.[1] The office of the Bishops is the widest, having all the power of a lower order, and having moreover its own proper duty, which is, to make the offering of the Eucharist. Whence it appears that Dionysius styles those Bishops, whom the later Church calls Priests; and those generally Priests, who are now called Deacons. The office of Priests, with him, is to initiate in the sacred rites those who have been purified by the ministers, and to supply those things which are customary; but to leave the setting forth of the mysteries to the Bishop. For he would have the ministers to sift and separate men from the world and from themselves, and as it were to strip and divest them entirely of their old habits; that they may have nothing to hinder them from being illumined by the sacraments; but having the dust shaken and wiped off, may be pure as a fresh-scoured tablet, fitted now to have the heavenly image depicted on them. When thus prepared by the ministers, they are offered to the priests. When the latter discern them to have no spot, and no savour of their old foulness, and to be most fully disposed to be fashioned and formed in Christ; that "as they have borne the image of the earthy, so they may also bear the image of the heavenly," the priest depicts that image upon them, as it were, with the sacraments; initiating them also in most holy symbols, with which, at least for the faithful,

<small>1 Cor. xv. 49.</small>

---

[1] The terms in the original being *Hierarchai*, *Hiereis* and *Leitourgoi*.

the Spirit of God works. Here they are illumined in the hands of the priests, that they may be perfected and completed by the Bishop. All completion is the part of the Bishop, who is counted as himself complete. He bestows the Eucharist, and confirms with the sacred Chrism, and manifests to the worthy the mysteries of the signs; that, if they be deemed fit persons, they may be perfected in all things under the Bishop's hands, and coming forth from him perfect, may go to the station and degree of their office, as the wisdom of the Bishop rightly determines. By the deacons and ministers men are brought in purity into the Church; by the priests they are advanced with illuminating sacraments; by the Bishop they are perfected with perfecting mysteries. The Bishop, skilled in all the sacred rites, and a contemplator of heavenly things, duly orders the Church under him; that every one in him may perform something of divine work, in imitation of God and the heavenly spirits. For, as Dionysius teaches, every action in the Church, on the part of every one, ought to imitate the action of God. For, as he also says,[1] the functions of priests are figures of the divine workings. For the society of the Church is founded on earth by Christ after the pattern of the celestial hierarchy of angels, who unceasingly imitate God; and in Christ all things are arranged by the office of the Bishop. The Bishop sustains the part of God and Christ upon earth, to the end that every one in the Church may diligently occupy himself to the best of his power in some divine working, for the common good of the whole society; that he may be recognized as one sound and perfect member in the mystical body of Christ. "According as God," saith St. Paul, " has dealt to every man the measure of faith." "Now there are diversities of gifts; but the manifestation of the Spirit is given to every man to profit withal;" to wit, that the Church may be perfected at length in the Spirit, and in immortality. For to this it is called, and must needs aim at this with all its power, if it

Rom. xii. 3.

1 Cor. xii. 4, 7.

---

[1] " Quia tamen divinarum actionum imagines sunt sacerdotales distinctiones," etc.—C. v. Pars i. § 7.

would hereafter be an immortal Church; preserving its order, with offices clearly marked out beneath the Bishop, beneath [the Angels], beneath God.

CHAPTER V.

PART II.

On the Consecration of Bishops, and Ordaining of Priests and Deacons.

WHEN one is being consecrated a Bishop, he prostrates himself before the altar, and has the right hand of the Bishop, and the Gospels,[1] laid upon his head. There is an invocation of the Trinity over him; he is signed with the cross; he is named by the whole priesthood, and kissed. The same ceremonies take place, according to the ancient custom, at the ordination of a priest, with the exception of the laying of the gospel upon his head. The same again, in case of a deacon: save that he bends one knee only in submitting himself to consecration. The Bishop alone bears the gospels on his head. All, when consecrated, are bidden to the communion of the Eucharist.

---

[1] This custom seems to have been in use in all the ancient Churches. In the *Apostolical Constitutions* two Deacons have the office of holding the Gospels over the head of the one being consecrated a Bishop; whence Vasquez infers that this ceremony is not, like the imposition of hands, an essential part of the Sacrament. His argument is given in the notes of Corderius. The ancient form of Ordination of Priests is thus gathered by Bingham from the Canon of the Council of Carthage, and from Dionysius:—"The person to be ordained kneeled before the Bishop at the altar; and he, laying his hand upon his head, did consecrate him with an holy prayer, and then signed him with the sign of the cross; after which the Bishop and the rest of the clergy gave him the kiss of peace. The author of the *Constitutions* speaks also of imposition of hands and prayer, but no more. From which we may reasonably conclude, that the words which the Roman Church makes to be the most necessary and essential part of a Priest's Ordination, viz. *Receive thou power to offer sacrifice to God, and to celebrate Mass both for the living and the dead*, were not in any of the ancient Forms of Consecration."—*Eccl. Ant.* Bk. ii. c. xix. § 17.

CHAPTER V.

PART III.

On the spiritual contemplation of the Sacrament of Holy Orders.

NOW, that we may state the meaning of these visible signs, and that our spiritual eye, as well as our bodily, may perceive its proper objects, this first approach to the Bishop, and prostration at the altar, tells and admonishes us of subjection to God and to his Bishop. For bending the knee is a token of subjection and obedience; and by the use of this term St. Paul, in his Epistle to the Philippians, affirms that all things are subject to Jesus; saying, "Wherefore God also hath highly exalted him, and given him a name which is above every name: that at the name of Jesus every knee should bow, of things in heaven, and things in earth, and things under the earth. Wherefore, my beloved," be obedient. There is, and ought to be, in the Church, this subjection of every inferior person to a higher, for his own sanctification to God in Christ; in whom also is the supremacy of the higher for the sanctification of the lower, under whatever name they bear sway; be it among the people also, as fathers, masters, husbands. This is the teaching of St. Paul, in his Epistle written to the Ephesians, and in that to the Colossians; in which he enjoins on sons, servants and wives subjection and obedience; which we must understand in all cases to mean, with a view to their sanctification by the former. Therefore St. Paul notably uses in all these instances, and enforces, the expression "in the Lord." To the Ephesians it is: "Let the husbands love their wives, as Christ loved the Church, and let them give themselves for their wives, that they may sanctify them with the washing of grace by the word of life; that they may present them to themselves as glorious wives, not having spot or wrinkle or any such thing, but holy and without blemish." The laying on of the Bishop's hands upon his head, sets forth that

<small>Phil. ii. 9, 10, 12.</small>

<small>Eph. vi. 1. Col. iii. 18.</small>

he who is consecrated to God, whoever he be, is wholly laid hold of by God; that in him he may be and do all things, and by his power also hope to be defended and kept safe. For the hand signifies the power of God in man. And "if God be for us, who can be against us?" He is defended, be it observed, "against spiritual wickedness in high places." "For," as the Apostle writes more expressly to the Ephesians, "we wrestle not against flesh and blood, but against principalities, against powers, against the rulers of the darkness of this world, against spiritual wickedness in high places." The being signed with the sign of the cross is a declaration and protest that we bear the cross of Jesus, that we may be his disciples. For he has said "Whosoever doth not take up his cross, and follow me, cannot be my disciple."

<small>Rom. viii. 31.</small>

<small>Eph. vi. 12.</small>

<small>Luke xiv. 27.</small>

Now for men to take up and receive the cross, is in reality to put off wholly and for ever, through faith in the death of Christ, their sinful life, and to bury it along with Christ's mortal flesh; and then, with eyes fixed upon Christ, to imitate constantly his most holy life; that, "being made conformable unto his death, they may attain unto the resurrection of the dead," after the same manner as St. Paul writes touching himself to the Philippians:—"This one thing I know; forgetting those things which are behind, and reaching forth unto those things which are before, I press toward the mark for the prize of the high calling of God in Christ Jesus." To the Galatians he also writes; "They that are Christ's have crucified the flesh with the affections and lusts." This is the import of the sign of the cross, imprinted on the man who professes Christ, that, after he has received the stamp of the sacred cross from the Bishop, he should say with St. Paul: "I am crucified with Christ; nevertheless I live: yet not I, but Christ liveth in me." In him truly a man is a member, that he may be conformable to the head; and a branch in the tree of Christ, that in all things he may savour of the root; in order that no longer now by his own will, which has been crucified, but by the life-giving sap drawn from the root, which is Christ, he may in all things, so to speak, live Christianlike. Let each one then seriously recollect what is the meaning of the

<small>Phil. iii. 10, 11.</small>

<small>Phil. iii. 13, 14.</small>

<small>Gal. v. 24.</small>

<small>Gal. ii. 20.</small>

impression of the sign of the cross; how it is the very death for ever of the sinful character in man, that it may never revive again. For, as the Master of Life has taught us, his cross must be taken, and he himself must be followed; that is to say, our own special life must be forsaken, and his must be copied. [Matth. x. 38.]

The one who is consecrated by the Bishop is next proclaimed by name;[1] which signifies, no doubt, the election and lot of God; by whose will and pleasure all that is rightly done, is done in the Church. This gives me an opportunity of saying something concerning God's choosing by lot; if I first state what is meant by *lot*, a word often used in Scripture. Now the word *sors* (*lot*, or *chance*) denotes the accidental issue of anything; whence comes the verb *sortior*, that is, *I draw lots*, or *take by lot*, or *decide* or *choose* anything *by lot*. They who make any election by lot, are called *sortilegi* (*divineis*); as are those who by means of lots foretell what is going to happen. The word *sors* is sometimes understood however of *inevitable necessity;* sometimes of *judgment*. It is used also of *inheritance,* whence men speak of *consortes* and *consortia* (*joint heirs* and *joint-inheritance*). Among the Christians, at any rate those of the primitive times, and the Apostles, the sacrament of the *lot* was a great one; and the casting of the lot, with men, was a token of most undoubted election with God. With men who look for all things from God, and who believe that God works along with their tokens, the lot is an argument, and

---

[1] The words of Dionysius are. "At vero sanctam et consecrationum et eorum qui sacrantur prædicationem pontifex resonat; id insinuante mysterio quia sacrator ille divinus divinæ est electionis expositor." He makes this to correspond to the declaration of Aaron by lot, as chosen to the priesthood, in Numb. xvii. 8; to the declaration of Christ, as chosen a Priest after the order of Melchizedech; and to the declaration of Matthias, as chosen to fill up the number of the twelve Apostles. He then has a few words on *Lots*, which Colet here expands. According to Bingham, "in the Apostolical and following ages there were four several ways of designing persons for the ministry, or discovering who were most fit to be ordained; the first of which was by casting Lots, the second by making choice of the first-fruits of the Gentile converts; the third by particular direction and inspiration of the Holy Ghost, and the last in the common and ordinary way of examination and election."—*Eccl. Antiq.* Bk. iv. c. i. § 1.

token, and sacrament as it were, whereby is perceived on whom the divine will and sure election has fallen. "The lot is cast into the lap;" says Solomon; "but the whole disposing thereof is of the Lord." Accordingly, Matthias was chosen by lot to the apostleship, as St. Luke writes; after many prayers had been first made, invoking the Holy Spirit, that the will of God in the election might be solemnly proved by the sacrament of the lot. The words in the Acts of the Apostles are as follows: "And they appointed two, Joseph called Barsabas, who was surnamed Justus, and Matthias. And they prayed, and said, Thou, Lord, which knowest the hearts of all men, shew whether of these two thou hast chosen, that he may take part of this ministry and apostleship, from which Judas by transgression fell, that he might go to his own place. And the lot fell upon Matthias, and he was numbered with the eleven apostles." *Sors*[1] (*lot*) has also at times the signification in Scripture of *fated necessity*, of *judgment*, and of *inheritance*; whence the terms *consortes* (*joint heirs*) and *consortia* (*joint inheritance*). For those whom the predestination of God points out as sons and heirs of his inheritance, are called "heirs of God, and joint-heirs with Christ."

Now in the Church of Christ, of which the soul, as it were, is God himself, all things ought to be done by God himself; men in the meantime believing and awaiting. Whatever is done, either in the case of one who is being called into the Church, or promoted to any rank and position of honour, or is done in pursuance of his duty by the same person when so promoted; whatever, I say, is done either in forming or ordering or completing the Church, is nought, unless it be done at the prompting of the Spirit of God. "Except the Lord," says David, "build the house, they labour in vain that build it: except the Lord keep the city, the watchman waketh but in vain." In his work, which is the Church, it is right that He should govern all things. And if the mind of man rashly interfere therewith, all things must needs be disordered and confused. In men there is nothing else to be required than instant prayer and supplication, unwaver-

---

[1] This is a repetition of what has been said a little before.

ing faith, and steadfast hope, which, as St. Paul says, Rom. v. 5. "maketh not ashamed." And since the actions and operations of God are hidden, we must believe that it was not without a divine injunction that the apostles, and apostolic men in the primitive Church, occasionally resorted to lots; that by them they might be informed of the decree of God, as to whom they should appoint, in accordance with God's will, to any office and duty; believing that the will of God was unmistakably there where the lot fell. And as soon as the lot fell upon any one, all, as with one mouth of God, would appoint him together; believing undoubtingly that he who was appointed on earth, was also appointed by God in heaven. For whatsoever is loosed and bound on earth, by our Saviour's testimony, is loosed and bound in heaven; seeing that, where any are gathered together in him, he is in the midst. This is the meaning of what Dionysius says, that the sacrament of *nomination* betokens the choice and approval of God in heaven. And this nomination of any one, whether to be a member of Christ's Church, or to any ministry in Christ Jesus, may not lawfully be performed, unless it be done by the highest and holiest men, and in the most solemn places, and moreover with long and religious fastings, vows, sacrifices and prayers; that it may appear to be the work not of puny men, but of the mighty God. Matth. xviii. 18.

Wherefore one may here express an abhorrence of the detestable custom, which has now for a long time been growing in the Church, and is at the present time deep-rooted, almost to the destruction of the Christian commonwealth, whereby temporal princes, void of reason, and, under the name of Christians, open enemies and foes of God, blasphemers of Christ, overthrowers of his Church, not with humble and pious, but with proud and rash, minds; not in consecrated and holy places, but in chambers and at banquets; appoint Bishops to rule the Church of Christ; and those too (heinous crime!) men ignorant of all that is sacred, skilled in all that is profane; men to whom they have already shamelessly sold those very bishoprics.[1] Out upon

---

[1] The allusion is in too general terms, I fear, to afford any clue to the exact date when this was written. According to Roscoe, "The practice

this wicked generation! these abandoned principles! this madness of princes! this blindness and folly of ecclesiastics! a blindness whether more to be had in derision or wept over I know not.¹ All order is being overthrown, the flesh waxes wanton, the spirit is quenched, all things are distorted and foul. Unless Christ have pity on his Church, death, which is already almost at the door, will seize on all. For how shall that endure, which is managed with destructive counsels and murderous hands? The gracious Jesus, ascribing nothing to himself, humbly referred all things to the Father. "If I honour myself," he says in St. John, " my honour is nothing: it is my Father that honoureth me;" of whom not himself but the Father said, " Thou art a priest for ever after the order of Melchizedek." But these wicked princes, nominally Christians, but in reality ministers of the Devil, arrogantly claiming for themselves the things that are God's, destroy by their guilty passions the edifice and temple of God, which the blood of Christ reared up. God will one day render unto them according to their works. But let me now return to the matter of which I was speaking.

John viii. 54

Ps. cx. 4.

All those sacred rites, as I have said, are a sacrament of nomination in heaven. By the name of *sacrament* are not only designated the seven best known in the Church; but moreover whatever is distantly signified by a sensible token

---

of selling benefices was commenced by Sixtus IV. He was the first Roman Pontiff who openly exposed to sale the principal offices of the church: but not satisfied with the disposal of such as became vacant, he instituted new ones for the avowed purpose of selling them."—*Lorenzo de' Medici*, p. 219, Bohn's Ed. Sixtus IV. died in 1484. In the *Oratio de reformandis moribus* addressed by the younger Pico to Leo X. (1513-1522) language is used as strong as any employed by Dean Colet:— " Qui auctionibus sacrorum pudendisque licitationibus invigilaverint, dent pœnas temerariæ mercaturæ," and the like.—*Op.* 1601, *pars* ii. p. 887.

¹ In Colet's Exposition of the First Epistle to the Corinthians (Camb. MS. Gg. iv. 26, fol. 91,) is a passage to some extent verbally identical with this. He is speaking of the scandals caused by the litigious spirit of the clergy, which brought them constantly into the secular courts; and exclaims against the " Homunciones, *quorum stulticia haud scio ridendane sit magis quam deflenda*, sed certe deflenda, quoniam ex ea ecclesia calamitatem sentit ac pene eversionem."

and visible marks, is called a sacrament.[1] In the choosing by lot of Matthias a great sacrament is noted by Dionysius; as he says that in it the Apostles had an indication[2] of the one on whom the secret election of God fell. And so in the sacrament of joint election, when performed by fit persons, there is disclosed (as is undoubtingly believed) the election of God in heaven. By Him, the one whom he wills is designated in the Church; and whosoever is not designated by him, let him believe himself to be not what he professes. Would that the Bishops that are nominated by temporal princes, being such as I have said, would listen to this!

In the common salutation and kiss given to him who is elected, is implied the sense of likeness, love and joy, felt by all in the one thus made like themselves, and by him also in those to whom he is made like.

But what is the meaning of laying the holy Gospels on the head of the Bishop at his consecration? It is this, that the Bishop should keep in his head and in his heart all things sacred and divine, and should be by far the wisest of all in heavenly things, and far the most excellent in every virtue and holy act, after the pattern of Christ set forth to us in the Gospels; whom in a manner he points to, when he receives the holy Gospels upon his head; that, so far as he can, he should shew forth Christ within him in his life, by sanctity and goodness, and by the wisdom of His truth and religion.

The Deacon, bending one knee, has the sacrament of the purified; the Priest, bending both, has that of the purified and the illumined; the Bishop, besides the bending of both knees, has the holy Gospels on his head, as a sacrament of purification, illumination and perfection; because he rightly

---

[1] The opinion of Bishop Jewell, *Treatise of the Sacraments* (1611), p. 263.
[2] "The author of the *Ecclesiastical Hierarchy*, under the name of Dionysius, fancies that God answered their prayer by some visible token: but if so, this had not been choosing by lot, as the Scripture says it was, but a quite different method of election."—Bingham, *Eccl. Ant.* iv. 1. § 1.

displays the mysteries of the Gospel, that men may be filled with them, and be perfected according to their capacity.

Thus does the whole system of the Church, by purification, illumination and perfection in Christ, labour for man's steadfast simplicity, and wise order, and perfect goodness, after the glorious example of the angels; that, above the chaos of confusion and of the world, there may arise a bright array of some simple and perfect men in God; to be a city set on a hill, the light of the world and the salt of the earth; such as may shine beneath Christ, their sun, with faith, hope and charity, and may illumine and give life to the world. But alas! smoke and noisome blackness have now for a long while been exhaling upwards in such dense volume from the vale of benighted men, as well-nigh to overwhelm the light of that city; so that now churchmen, shrouded in darkness, not knowing whither they go, have foolishly blended and confounded themselves with all [?]; so that in the world again there is nothing more confused than the mass of men. In this world the seal of Christ, which he stamped upon it, has been almost effaced and destroyed by the promiscuous jostling of mankind, in the universal disorder. I beseech thee, merciful Jesu, of thy almighty power, speedily scatter the darkness in thy Church, and restore order and tranquillity!

CHAPTER VI.

PART I.

Introduction to the subject of Initiation into the rites of the Church; and specially the Consecration of the Monk.

AS there have been ordained by God those that shall purify, illumine and perfect, who are the agents, and herein, so to speak, *males*,[1] with masculine vigour; so on

---

[1] In Colet's Treatise *De Sacramentis Ecclesiæ* this idea is a very prominent one. See p. 72 (Ed. 1867)—" Masculinior pars [ecclesiæ] cum femininiori agit assidue, ut a tota simul sacrificium et proles offeratur," and elsewhere.

the other hand there must needs be, to correspond to them, others to be purified and illumined and perfected; to be, as it were, the subject-matter of the Church, the *female*, united to the masculine element, that it may be perfected in the male. In this latter division are Catechumens, who must be assisted in delivery; Apostates, who must be recalled; Energumens, who must be exorcised; Penitents, who must be made clean. In these offices the Deacons are engaged, whose duty it is to purify, and bring forth, so far as they can, a simple unity in men; that those who are falling back, and slipping away, and tossed about, may stay themselves on God, on the central point of hope; that, hoping in God, they may at length be rooted in him. And as there are different persons to be purified, so are there different ministers. To Catechumens, striving to come forth from the world, a hand is held out by Catechizers, who lead them by constant instruction to God. The enemy unceasingly assaults the Church, that he may demolish what God through his ministers builds up. And so he overthrows and destroys some as Apostates; others he shakes and harasses as Energumens. On the other hand, the ministers of God should be earnest in labour and diligence to repair the mischief caused by the enemy, and to restore the Church in all its strength; both by summoning men away from the city of the Devil, and by recalling those who have seceded from the city of God, and by strengthening those who have been shaken. Thus against the Apostates of the one side there are the Catechumens of the Church; against the Energumens of the one, whom the enemies are vexing that they may fall, are the Church's Penitents, whom her ministers are purifying, that they may stand. In truth, the Church with ceaseless toil labours to preserve what is her own; and to regain what was lately hers, I mean the Apostates and Energumens; just as, on the other hand, the Adversary strives to retain what is and was his own, namely the Catechumens and Penitents. Thus, with mutual inroads, and frequent conflicts, and alternate losses, those armies of God and the Devil contend for the mastery; spirits against spirits, and spiritual men against carnal men. Evil spirits

Gal. v. 17. love the flesh; the good long for the spirit. "The flesh," says St. Paul, "lusteth against the spirit, and the spirit against the flesh." But inasmuch as, by our Saviour's testimony, "the spirit is willing, but the flesh is weak," (Mark xiv. 38.) therefore at times the flesh is overcome by the spirit, and darkness by light, and death by life, and the Devil by God; through our Lord Jesus Christ, to whom "all things shall be subdued, that God may be all in all." (1 Cor. xv. 28.)

The Church of God, which is situated on a hill above the world, in pure air and bright atmosphere, has supplied to it also from the vale of this world's misery the material of its own happiness. For the Church by its lower portion, which is masculine and active, raises upwards the higher and more passive portion of the world; much as the rays of the sun refine and rarefy by their heat the surface portions of water, and so raise them on high; that from it first it may fashion for itself a body, as it were; which body, though coarser and more corporeal than the spiritual part of the Church, is yet more spiritual than the mundane body as a whole. From this body in turn, and more material part of the Church, when sound and healthy, I mean from the highest and clearest quarter of it, and from among such as have now almost become spiritual, who are as it were the purer, clearer and more vital blood of the Church;—from among such men, I say, in the passive portion of the Church, the most advanced are drawn into a spiritual state, that they may at length be active portions and spirits; but at first only purifying spirits, whose whole duty and office consists in the purification and renewal and support of the body; that is, of the humbler and more material portion of the Church. For between it and God, the soul of the Church, come spiritual men, as the agents and workers of all. Just as in man, between his soul and body, there intervene pure, subtle, bright and fiery spirits, generated from the heat of the heart and the subtler blood; so in like manner between God and the Church of assembled men, are some of the assembled men themselves, from the clearer portion of the Church and its diviner blood, so to speak; spiritual men, begotten of the warmth and love of God, who are midway between God and the rest of mankind, depending on God through them. And moreover, just as the spirits that come between man's soul and body are of a threefold kind; —for some are natural, others vital, others animal;[1] of which the last are chiefly subservient to the soul, the vital to the senses, and the natural to generation, nutrition, growth, evacuation, reparation, healing and suchlike processes in the more corporeal part of man—so, after almost the same manner, there are in Christ, between God and the portion formed by the people, three kinds of spiritual men. Some of these, like the animal spirits, are the especial servants of God, the Church's soul; some chiefly tend the lower part of the Church, to repair, nourish, foster, increase, cleanse and preserve it; some, midway between these, are the ministers of the senses, as it were, and enlighten them to perceive the spiritual properties of the sacraments in the Church. The first in order,[2] which are nearer to the carnal portion of the Church, quicken the flesh by their purifying virtue, washing away men's sinful mortal nature, that they may live by hope in God. The second, who spiritualize the senses, illumine those who are purified and hoping in God; that with faith they may have a perfect sense of the sacraments of the Church, and every sacred symbol, and rejoice therein with the fullest belief. The third and highest are those who are intent upon God with all their affections, and have a clear understanding of the simple meaning of each sense. These take such as have by faith had a sense of the symbols and sacraments; and as many of them as come to them in a fit and ripe state they make contemplators of the simple meanings of the mysteries and objects of sense, according to their capacity; in order that, what they have long had a sense of, under priests, they may now, under the Bishop, understand with the most perfect love; and being filled with the mysteries, so far as they are capable, may be made perfect.

---

[1] I use the word here in its strict sense, as Johnson explains it:—"*Animal* functions, distinguished from *natural* and *vital*, are the lower powers of the mind, as the will, memory, and imagination."

[2] That is, the first, reckoning upwards; in reality the lowest.

For light is an ethereal and unsubstantial thing, unless it be intensified, as it were, with heat; and the sight of sensible things is well-nigh empty and vain, unless men be filled with a love of the mysteries that are made intelligible. By the vision of the mysteries, by love and worship, all things are completed and perfected. Therefore the highest ones, who perfect, are the Bishops; the intermediate, who illumine, are the Priests; the lowest, who purify, are the Deacons. Those who are purified so as to have a single hope in God, that they may stay themselves on him, and in hope may now breathe again in him, and, being born again in a new creation, may now [become] an entirely new creature;[1]—those, I say, are in the lowest degree, and vestibule, as it were, of the Church, and are as its bones, thick and solid, possessing but little sense in themselves, but steady in hope, depending on God in all that they do in the world for the support of the higher Church.

These are in truth purveyors of the necessaries of life, ministers of no learned understanding, but receiving that which is supplied by a gracious God and bountiful nature, and ministering that supply to others; so as to be ministers in temporal things to the ministers of spiritual things: for all things are God's. None has anything of his own to give; none possesses what he has not received. "The earth is the Lord's, and the fulness thereof." All things, temporal as well as spiritual, are rightfully his who created them all. What is temporal is of the earth; what is spiritual is from heaven. The humbler and more earthly portion of the Church is the minister of temporal things, by the help of God, and in a simple manner: the heavenly and more exalted portion bestows what is spiritual, as a minister of the great bounty of God. These latter are ministers to the corporeal and duller portion of the church, for their eternal life; liberally affording them spiritual food; whilst the humbler portion, depending in hope on God, and as-

---

[1] This may have been what Colet meant; but I think the repetition of "creatura nova" in the Latin, taken along with the occurrence of the hiatus, betokens some error in transcribing.

siduously gathering from the earth wherewith to feed the Church, ministers temporal life to the more spiritual portion. Thus by mutual services and benefits the Church, while militant here, and while partly temporal, partly and chiefly spiritual [is sustained], on each hand, both on the higher and lower region, in the riches of God, both temporal and spiritual; the servants and ministers of God religiously exerting themselves to sustain it in each kind of life, temporal and spiritual; the higher portion receiving temporal life from the lower, and the lower receiving spiritual life and strength from the higher; that so the whole Church, seeking only what is necessary in this world, and that too without overmuch care, and for the passing day, may strive for spiritual life here, for life eternal hereafter. In this lowest part of the Church are the Catechumens, as they are called, now under instruction; the Penitents who have been recalled; the Energumens who have been exorcized; and the Apostates who have been reclaimed. It is the business of these, by bodily work and labour in the earthly bounties of God, to earn the bodily sustenance of the Church; that they may exercise themselves in earthly matters in all simplicity and truth; being now ministers of God in these terrestrial things, for the refreshment of the perishable and corporeal part of the Church. These are they whom St. Paul, in his first Epistle to the Corinthians, when recommending concord to the whole Church, likens to the less honourable members of the body; which, in proportion as they are less comely than others, are the more necessary, and receive the greater care for their preservation from injury. From this sort of men, if at any time any of those who form its higher and clearer region, have at length through the assiduous labour of the deacons become more godlike, every stain of sin being thoroughly scoured away, so as now to be judged by the discerning deacons to be open and transparent, and capable of receiving a measure of light, they are then presented to the priests, that they may be suffused by them with fuller light, and shine with greater faith. These have now offered to their view the things seen by faith; that, being now purified, they may discern with unclouded eye

1 Cor. xii. 23.

the sensible sacraments in which they had been initiated by the priests; and being now initiated in the Christian rites, and signed with holiest signs, may contemplate in spiritual sense without hindrance the bright and heavenly figures in Christ, being themselves also full of light through the same images, and displaying in all humility the marks and impresses, stamped on them through human ministration indeed, but by the seal of God; and being most worthy witnesses of a loftier and singler light and truth. These enter the gate alone of God's temple, and contemplate the profaner ornaments of His House, not being admitted as yet to the more hidden treasures and those stored up in the inner shrine of God, which are sacredly and religiously guarded by the Bishop in his ark of wisdom; and which it is not lawful to disclose except to those who are perfected by the love of God and of divine things, and who are now finished Christians. Dionysius includes these, when illumined by the priests with the sacraments, and now allowed to be present at, and beholders of, the sacred rites, under the name of holy people; and these are strongest in faith. Others meanwhile, such as during their purification cannot be present at the sacred rites, if they be not such as they cannot easily be, must for the time occupy themselves in preparing the sustenance of the Church, namely of those initiated in the sacred rites and the holy people.[1] For one that is higher in the Church can do whatever a lower member can, though the converse does not hold. The highest and purest part of the holy people, which has now aspired as it were to the region of fire, and is heated with love so as readily to be inflamed, should be delivered by the priests to the Bishop, that he may in due season impart to it the last strokes for perfection, and fill it to the full, so far

---

[1] I have endeavoured to express what appears to be the sense of the passage. But there seems unquestionably something wrong in the Latin. I would suggest that the similar ending of two lines with "non possunt" has led the copyer to insert a "non" too much after "cujusmodi;" whilst "iniciati sacris" etc. seems an explanation of "ecclesiæ;" though not in grammatical agreement with it.

as its capacity goes, with the simple naked mysteries, that by the sight of them it may be fragrant[1] with love. These are above the people, and are called by Dionysius *Monks;* being the clearer portion of the people, now inflamed with love, so as, like fire, to cling to the heavenly orbs.[2] And in this station let them make progress, that they may be able to be promoted to the rank of ministers; so that they who are highest among the passive ones may be lowest among the active. What the Bishop is among spiritual persons, such are the Monks, single and lonely, among the lay; and such as are the priests among the one, such are those that are reckoned in the holy people among the other. Such lastly as are the Deacons among the one, such among the other are those who are under the hands of purifiers.

Spirit
{ Bishop.   Monk.   Perfection.
  Priests.   Holy People.   Illumination.
  Deacons.   Those under Purification.   Purification.

Body
{ Monks perfected.   Bishop, perfecting with goodness.
  People learning.   Priests, illumining with learning.
  Penitents under purification. Deacons, purifying.

---

[1] Lat. "fragret." But possibly the reading should be "flagret," "glowing" with love; a phrase which is elsewhere used.

[2] That is, to the Orders of the Clergy. The metaphor here used recalls passages in the *Commento sopra una Canzona de Amore, composta da Girolamo Benevieni*, of Mirandola. An English translation of it was published by Thos Stanley in 1651, under the title of *A Platonick Discourse upon Love*. Mirandola expands at length the allegory of the birth of Eros from the union of Poros and Penia, as related in the *Convivium*, and speaks of the flame of love that raises us "from this terrene life to the eternal."

CHAPTER VI.

PARTS II. III.

On the Consecration of the Monk.

THE Monk takes his rise from the purest portion of the people, being now wholly single and at one in himself, and altogether and thoroughly given up to one God, so far as any one of the people can be given up and surrendered.[1]

As those who are illumined by baptism have their own rite of consecration, that they, the holy people, may behold the sacred emblems; so those of the people who are completed in unity, and raised to another degree of perfection, have a signing of that event with ceremonies; in order that an outward and sensible form may be a reminder and token of spiritual progress. In order therefore that any monk may make profession of the unity which he has lately attained, and his undivided principle of living, he goes to some one of the priestly order (who seem to me to have held the position in the early Church which Deacons do with us), and stands behind him before the altar, with mind upraised towards God; one, single, and solitary. After the priest has given God thanks, he turns towards the man, and hears him renounce for ever by a most rigid vow all division and dissipation of life; he hears him promise to centre himself on one, and keep a single eye, that his whole body may be full of light; to strive towards one quarter only; to serve God alone. On this great profession he receives the sign of the holy cross; that what he declares himself to renounce

---

[1] " Inversion strange! that unto one who lives
For self, and struggles with himself alone,
The amplest share of heavenly favour gives;
That to a Monk allots, in the esteem
Of God and man, place higher than to him
Who on the good of others builds his own."
Wordsworth, *Eccl. Sketches.*

may be felt to be dead in the cross of Christ, never more to live again for him. His hair is shorn,[1] that by the shaving off of everything divided and superfluous he may appear as clean as possible in the sight of God. He changes his apparel, on changing his life; that to a simpler life a simpler garb may correspond. This custom was observed in every holy change, that, when the inner man was changing from one spiritual habit to another, the outer man should also do the same; that the outward habit might answer to the inward. Hence the life of man is called by the holy Apostles a garment and vesture. The kiss is significant of a sweet uniting. Lastly he is admitted to the Eucharist, but in a way more sacred than the rest of the people; he being now acquainted with the mysteries. Thus the monk, as it were a unit of the people, is duly completed and perfected. 1 Cor. v. 4.

I know not by what rashness of the Bishops, in later ages, this ancient custom fell into disuse, of initiating and consecrating not only monks, but all other Orders whatsoever; a custom that owing to its apostolic institution had the highest authority, and was most religiously observed in the early Church; nor by what rashness on the part of mankind another custom, with new signs and ceremonies, grew up and prevailed so greatly, that now, in the present Church, not even a trace appears of a matter of venerable antiquity, and of the sacred institution of the Apostles. And had not St. Dionysius, (who seems to me to be such in our Church as was Ezra in the synagogue of Moses, who willed that the mysteries of the Old Law should be committed to writing, lest in the confusion of affairs and of

---

[1] The reason given for this practice by Dionysius is:—" Porro tonsura crinium vitam mundissimam indicat, et nulla figura fucatam, et quæ nullis fictis coloribus inductis animi deformitatem exornet; sed ipsa in seipsa non humanis venustatibus sed singularibus et unicis ad Dei exactissimam similitudinem properet."—*Eccl. Hier.* vi. p. iii. It will be borne in mind, that the shaving, or more strictly cutting off, the hair, referred to by Dionysius, was a very different thing from the formal *tonsure* of the Latin Church in later times. The short-cropped hair was looked on as a decent remove from long flowing locks on the one hand, and from the shaven heads of the priests of Isis on the other.—See Richardson's *Prælectiones Ecclesiasticæ* (1726), vol. ii. p. 291.

men the record of so much wisdom should perish)—had not St. Dionysius, I say, in like manner, as though divining the future carelessness of mankind, left written down by his productive pen what he retained in memory of the institutions of the Apostles, in arranging and regulating the Church, we should have had no record of the ancient custom. Now to have thus departed from ancient usage is a thing truly to be mourned over; since we ought to be much more zealous in preserving the institutions of our forefathers, than were the Jews in retaining their traditions; in proportion as ours are clearer and more excellent than theirs, and symbols of greater and purer truth. For it were strange if the Apostles did not best know their meaning and fitness, having all things revealed to them by the Spirit; so that it could not be but that they wisely understood what to adjust fittingly, each to each, and how by a just propriety to pourtray spiritual verities under their special signs. How it befell, without grievous guilt, that these became afterwards wholly changed, I know not; since we must believe that it was by the teaching of the Holy Spirit that they ordained all things in the Church. For the words of our Saviour in St. John are these:—"Howbeit, when he the Spirit of truth is come, he will guide you into all truth: for he shall not speak of himself; but whatsoever he shall hear, that shall he speak; and he will shew you things to come." It is because their most holy traditions have been superseded and neglected, and men have fallen away from the Spirit of God to their own inventions, that, beyond doubt, all things have been wretchedly disturbed and confounded. And, as I said before, unless God shall have mercy on us, all things will go to ruin.

Joh. xvi. 13.

CHAPTER VII.

PART I.

Introduction to the rites of the holy Dead.

IT is to be undoubtingly believed, that those who have been born again in Christ, whose life of sin has been destroyed, and who have lived righteously that they may die in righteousness, even as Christ died in righteousness, in return for their repelling iniquity and maintaining the righteousness of God in themselves, will, at their departure from this life, have the reward of their righteousness first in their holy soul, and then, in due time, in their flesh as well, which was the soul's companion on the road to God and its comrade in the war; so that every righteous man, with his full individuality in Christ, may be blessed both in body and soul in glory. Jesus, who knew all truth, declared this to the Sadducees, who did not believe in a resurrection; saying, "When they shall rise from the dead, they neither marry nor are given in marriage; but are as the angels which are in heaven." Mark xii. 25. Supported by this hope, the good, who have led here a holy life in Christ, die willingly and joyfully; being glad, in part, at having escaped the danger of a fall, on which they might perhaps chance, were their life further prolonged; and in part rejoicing in the highest degree at the prospect of the reward of labour done, and the crown of glory for their Christian warfare, which is doubtless laid up in store for them that strive lawfully. Over the happy departure, yea and death, of those saints, their friends and relations together rejoice with many congratulations, and pray for a like consummation in Christ of their own lives; that, having kept the path of righteousness even unto death, they may in death itself exchange a temporal and troublesome life for a happy and immortal one, and may live everlastingly in Christ. Rejoicing through this hope in the departed, and being fully persuaded that he has journeyed to Christ, they carry forth the corpse with exultation, and bear it to the priest, and set it before him, to be committed to holy sepulture.

For nothing is more unbecoming our Christian profession, in which there is a most sure hope of resurrection and of glory after the likeness of Christ, than, after the manner of the heathen, to bewail the dead with as many tears, as if our belief were that it had fared ill with them, and not that they were living in the highest bliss with Christ. Yet this too is what they now practise almost everywhere in the Church, to its discredit; but most of all in Italy,[1] where men shamefully give utterance to womanish outcries at the funerals of their friends and relatives. But this is doubtless the custom of those only, who have lived a life here so unlike that of Christ, that, through consciousness of their abandoned course, they have nothing to look forward to at his hands; and so are pained and grieved that they must depart hence; either in despair of any future life, or in expectation of eternal misery. These are addressed by St. Paul in this manner, in his Epistle to the Thessalonians: "I would not have you to be ignorant, brethren," he says, "concerning them which are asleep, that ye sorrow not, even as others which have no hope. For if we believe that Jesus died and rose again, even so them also which sleep in Jesus will God bring with him."

1 Thess. iv. 12, 13.

---

[1] This is interesting as one of the very few allusions which this Treatise contains to the personal history of the writer; as there can be little doubt that Colet is here speaking of what he had witnessed with his own eyes, during his travels in Italy. The remark in the text receives confirmation, by the converse opinion which Polydore Vergil, an Italian, formed of funerals in England. He was struck by their quietness. After speaking of the custom of the people of Marseilles in ancient times, who kept the day of the funeral without indulging in lamentations, he goes on to say that a like custom then prevailed in England, where the people seemed to reflect "that it was useless to give a loose to their natural sorrow as men, by any foolish lamentations of God's pleasure to share with us his immortality. And this the more, as by death we bid adieu to the toils and dangers which we enter upon from our very birth."
—" Quod Angli hodie," etc.—*De Rerum Invent.* (1644) p. 448.

In the *Funus* and *Exequiæ Seraphicæ* of Erasmus are several allusions to the excessive outward display at funerals in his time.

This indeed bad Christians despair of; and, despairing, die in misery. But the good, for many causes, die joyfully; both because they are weary of this stormy and troublesome life, and wish for security, and desire rest, and long to be with Christ: as St. Paul said in his own case, "I have a desire to depart, and to be with Christ." Likewise the brave martyr Ignatius was wont to say, "My Love is crucified;" meaning Christ, with whom he desired to be in heaven.[1] The absurd notions that have arisen among men, even since the time of Christ, from hearing the teaching of philosophers, such as Dionysius mentions, are to be utterly rejected by Christians of lofty soul and who hope for better things. I mean, either that souls perish along with their bodies; or that they survive, but destined not to resume their bodies; or that they survive and migrate into other bodies; or exist in some Elysian fields or other, full of all pleasantness and delight.[2] All these poor and hazy notions were dispelled by the brightness of Christ, which revealed the truth for us to believe in.

Philipp. i. 23.

---

[1] The passage occurs in the Epistle of Ignatius to the Romans, and is quoted in the *De Divinis Nominibus*, where it would seem to be understood by Dionysius in the same sense as Colet here employs it :—"Atqui visum est plerisque ex tractatoribus nostris divinius esse amoris quam dilectionis nomen. Scribit enim divinus Ignatius, Amor meus crucifixus est."—c. iv. § 1. In each case then the *Amor* of Ignatius is referred to Christ. Yet this does not seem to be the natural sense of the passage:— "Meus enim amor crucifixus est, et non est in me: aqua autem alia viva manet in me, intrinsecus michi dicens, Veni ad patrem." Thus it stands in the Latin Dionysius of 1498, f. 115. It follows the striking sentence in which Ignatius calls himself, in view of his approaching martyrdom at Rome, "the Lord's corn, soon to be ground by the teeth of wild beasts," and would have his disciples even caress the beasts of prey, that they might give him a speedy tomb. And then he presently adds, "For my love is crucified, and is not in me. But there abideth in me instead a stream of living water, that saith to me from within, 'Come to the Father.'" Hence by "my love," he would seem naturally to mean all human passions. But the reading and sense of the passage are much disputed, as may be seen from the notes to the Venice Dionysius of 1756.

[2] Dionysius makes no mention of Elysian fields, but adduces four opinions as deserving to be rejected by the Christian:—(1) that of those who held that the soul perished along with the body, an opinion referred by Maximus to Bias; (2) that of those who held that the union between

CHAPTER VII.

PART II.

On the ceremonies of Christian Burial.

IF the dead body be that of a priest, it should be placed before the altar, during the time that the obsequies and funeral service are being performed. But if it be that of one of the people, let the corpse of the deceased be placed before the chancel, whilst the obsequies and sacred rites of the dead are going on; in the spot where it is usual for the people to stand, in the midst of all, that all alike may behold the sacraments of God. The chancel or sanctuary is the enclosure which is parted off by rails, and separates the priesthood from the people; in which the choir of priests celebrate the holy services; the place which by those of our time also is now called the Choir.

The chanting and giving of thanks is begun by the priests. Passages to assure men of a resurrection are read by the deacons. A eulogy is spoken over the departed, on the Archdeacon's[1] having first dismissed the Catechumens. The one also who is just dead in Christ is pronounced blessed.

---

soul and body was for ever sundered by death, for which Plato is made responsible; (3) that of Metempsychosis, and (4) that of those who made a sort of material paradise for the blessed (which Colet perhaps sums up in the term "Elysian fields"); which last opinion is thought by Pachymeres to have been that of Papias, Bishop of Hierapolis.

[1] The office of Archdeacon appears originally to have been nothing more than that of Deacon. Whether the name at first indicated the senior Deacon in a Church, or one elected by the others to a kind of presidency, is disputed. The admonition or address, spoken of here as delivered by him to the people, formed a proper part of his duty. "It was his Business also, as the Bishop's substitute, to order all things relating to the inferior clergy, and their ministrations and services in the Church: as what Deacon should read the Gospel, who should bid the Prayers, which of them should keep the doors," and the like.—Bingham's *Antiqq.* B. ii. c. xxi.

All that are present are admonished by the Archdeacon to take care to die well in Christ. The Bishop utters pious prayers and supplications over the departed; as it were exhorting him with words whispered in his ear; and commends him to God. He then gives him the kiss of peace along with his relatives and the whole Church, and anoints him with oil.[1] When the funeral rites have thus been duly performed, and the customary service done, the remains are then committed to interment, amid the other saints of his own order.

In these funeral obsequies there is nothing but hope, joy, gladness and congratulation over the dead in Christ Jesus; for that he is believed to have entered the assembly of the saints, and the life of the blessed in heaven; where in his Christ he will happily enjoy everlasting life.

CHAPTER VII.

PART III.

On the spiritual Contemplation of the rites of the Holy Dead.

BUT now let us see what is the meaning of the sacred rites and ceremonies of the dead. Every action of ours here in the Church is a sign of the things that are done in heaven. For we are established in faith, and believe that as we act on earth, in our imitation of the arrangement of things divine, so it is in heaven. Christ said to St. Peter, eminent in faith, that what he loosed or bound on earth should be loosed and bound in heaven. Our whole Christian life is a struggle, that we may be made like to God, as much

Matth. xvi. 19.

---

[1] Bingham says that these two ceremonies "are in a manner peculiar to this author [Dionysius], and the former of them expressly forbidden in some other Rules of Burial. But the Hymns and Psalmody, and proper portions of Scripture and prayers, made a part of the Burial Service in all Churches."—*Ib.* xxiii. iii. § 11.

as can possibly be. God himself was made man, in a certain measure unlike himself. For, as St. Paul writes, he "made himself of no reputation, and took upon him the form of a servant," that he might make mankind like to his Father. And when Jesus taught his disciples heavenly piety on the mount, he ended his sermon with this sentence, namely, "Be ye therefore perfect, even as your Father which is in heaven is perfect." But in this striving towards God by Christ, each one attains so far as the strength given him admits of. As the Apostle wrote to the Corinthians, "Every man hath his proper gift of God; one after this manner, and another after that." Our deserts are according to the measure of our faith; our rewards are in proportion to our deserts.

<small>Phil. ii. 7.</small>

<small>Matth. v. 48.</small>

<small>1 Cor. vii. 7.</small>

The diversity and order here in the Church militant is an image of that order which the Church triumphant is destined to have in heaven. And so, because the priest is esteemed more righteous than the layman, he is placed after death, during the obsequies, in the midst of the choir among the priests. A layman deceased, or the holier monk, is set among the lay people outside the chancel rails,[1] and in front of the choir, in the quarter of the people; that we may by this arrangement be admonished and believe that another and far holier place is assigned in heaven to the priests than to the laity. For this order in the Church is derived from that heavenly order; the Apostles, endued with the Spirit of God, arranging all things in a right and heavenly manner, and having learnt all truth from the Holy Ghost the Comforter. In the strength of God, we that have been enrolled in the Christian army, fight, conquer, go forth, die righteous in Christ; then to receive the glory of the righteous, each according to his righteousness. The Church rejoices over the righteous in death, and with festal procession commits

---

[1] As early as the time of Eusebius we have mention of the chancel rails, *cancelli*, as separating the clergy from the rest of the congregation. But Bingham notes that the custom varied in different times and places; the demarcation not being so strict in the Alexandrian Church in the third century, nor in the French Church (by the second Council of Tours) in the sixth.—*Eccl. Antiq.* Bk. viii. ch. vi. § 8.

the departed conqueror in sure hope to God, to receive his crown. The songs that the Church sings at the services of the dead, are songs of joy, for the consolation and encouragement of the living; that they, through hope that the dead have journeyed to God, may long for a like end for themselves; that so they themselves may have glory, and the Church rejoicing. As for weeping, tears, wailings, they are a disfigurement in the Church, and becoming those men alone, who have but little faith that the righteous after death will have the glory of Christ who rose from the dead. Now had they believed that Jesus Christ, because he died in righteousness, rose again in glory, and that after the same likeness all the righteous will rise again in him, through the power of God, doubtless they would not bewail so piteously the death of friends. For "precious in the sight of the Lord is the death of his saints." But the death of sinners is the worst death. Wherefore, if there were aught to be grieved over, one ought to grieve over the death of the unrighteous; since it fares worst with them, whose "worm dieth not." But in the Christian Church, which through faith and hope is of good courage in God, nothing is baser and fuller of disgrace, than much weeping for the dead; those at least whom men have known to have been not unrighteous in Christ. [Ps. cxvi. 15.] [Mark ix. 44.]

The Church in her customary rites rehearses the praises of departed saints; gives thanks for him that is dead; brings forth from the Scriptures the joyful hope of a resurrection; exults at the present gain of a friend and brother, in that by a holy death he is released from evils; rejoices in hope of the benefit that the just shall have. The Church, elect, wise and dutiful in Christ, does this, to show Christian men that no day can be more joyful, than the one in which any righteous man dies; especially if he die even suffering violence for righteousness' sake. That man will have so great glory, as for the whole church to exult through gladness. When his own most holy death was at hand, Jesus thus addressed his disciples concerning it, as St. John relates:— "Ye have heard how I said unto you, I go away and come again unto you." And, because he saw them sorrowful, he [John xiv. 28.]

added, "If ye loved me, ye would rejoice, because I go to the Father;" that they might rejoice at the death of Jesus. Thus also should the whole Church and every individual in it rejoice over the righteous man who has died with Christ for glory; that he may seem to have discharged the duty of Christian piety, and to have loved his departed brother also. Every one should rejoice, I say, at his brother's gain in death, and give great thanks for him: otherwise he would be judged to be a friend and lover not of his brother in Christ, but of himself in the world; and despairing, not hopeful.

Now the reason that the Catechumens are sent away and excluded from holy funerals is, that they are without the light of regeneration, which is given by God in baptism through the ministration of priests, and blind as yet, so as to be unable to gaze on the spectacle of the mysteries. Others however, who have been illumined, and have blinded themselves by their own wickedness, Apostates and Penitents; Energumens also, who, being too weak as yet, are unable to bear the malicious assaults of the devil; these, although they are not suffered to be present at other sacred rites, may yet be present at obsequies and funeral rites; in order that by the office of the Church, and by the hope of a future life which they perceive in the solemnities, they may be admonished to repent and desire the life to come. It is the custom also, as I have said, in the ceremonies and offices of the dead, for the Bishop at a funeral to pray for the deceased one, by the side of the bier, and salute him as though possessed of sense, and for all the rest in order to join in the salutation. He prays to God that he would forgive the departed whatever sins he has fallen into when alive through human infirmity, and mercifully pardon him, and receive him into his own bright region of the living; that he may rest in happiness in the bosoms of the patriarchs, where is joy and glory everlasting, and that too so great and substantial, as for St. Paul to assert, when writing to the Corinthians, that neither "eye hath seen, nor ear heard, neither have entered into the heart of man, the things which God hath prepared for them that love him." O! how great

1 Cor. ii. 9.

will be the pleasure, and how exulting the delight for those "children of men," who have "put their trust," gracious God, "under the shadow of thy wings;" as sang thy royal prophet David! "They shall be abundantly satisfied with the fatness of thy house, and thou shalt make them drink of the river of thy pleasures. For with thee is the fountain of life; in thy light shall we see light." The Lord himself, as it is in another Psalm, "is our refuge, and our portion in the land of the living." Ps. xxxvi. 7—10.

Ps. cxlii. 5.

But, some one asks,[1] what need is there for prayers to be made for one departed? For all is over with him, either for good or for ill. For, according to the deserts of his life, he goes by the just judgment of God either upwards or downwards. After death there is no room to any one for further desert.

Dionysius in answer shows first that prayer does not profit any one, either living or dead, unless both he that is prayed for and he that prays be worthy. He that is worthy to pray is the saint. He that is worthy to be prayed for is none but he, who wishes and uses every effort above all things to be holy, and who, acknowledging his own unworthiness, fears to approach the divine majesty with prayers, and to appear in his sight, unless there intercede one whom he thinks to prevail more with God, who may supplicate along with him; and who lastly in all humility seeks for himself one from the chief orders in the Church, to be a mediator between God and himself; in reliance on

---

[1] In what follows, on the subject of prayers for the dead, Colet fairly represents the guarded language of Dionysius, though, as usual, he discusses it at greater length. Dionysius (ch. vii. §§ 6, 7.) distinctly lays down the two great principles, that the prayer of the Bishop over the departed Christian is declaratory, rather than intercessory; and that it avails those only who are fit objects of God's mercy. The Roman doctrine of Purgatory, it need hardly be said, is not in Dionysius. Thus Stillingfleet can aver, in his argument with T. C., that the one who is prayed for in Dionysius "is said to be *replenished with divine joy, and not fearing any change to the worse, but knowing well that the good things possessed shall be firmly and everlastingly enjoyed*; as he speaks at his entrance upon that discourse. And if this be in effect to teach Purgatory, as you would have it, you must set your Purgatory a great deal higher than you do."—*Rational Account* (1665), p. 648.

whose intercession, and by the help of whose prayers, he himself, jointly using the strongest and most earnest entreaties, may at length be heard. Prayer undertaken in this way and method is a thing of all the most powerful and efficacious; so that, if supplication continue without ceasing, with hope and in humility (according to the teaching of our Saviour himself, by the example of the one who asked for loaves at midnight; and of the poor woman, who sought a decree from the unjust judge), it cannot assuredly fail to be heard. But if any one neglect his own cause, and be himself cold at heart in the matter of his own salvation, and be an evil liver after his accustomed manner, not beginning and striving himself first and foremost to regain the favour of God, but to commit to others the task of praying for him (as the custom of worldly men now is) on payment of a scanty fee,[1] with an expectation that he can be saved by the prayers of others; he assuredly is of the number of those who are unworthy to be prayed for, and is also the most foolish person of all mankind. For he thinks that, whilst negligent himself, the diligence of others can be of service to him, and that he who takes no pains himself to be saved, will be saved by means of others. He acts just as the sick man, who whilst living sumptuously would be cured by the physician; and, to use the simile of Dionysius, like one who, having put out his own eyes, would fain gaze upon the sun.[2] He is foolish and mad, who does nothing himself when he has the power, and yet hopes that he can obtain benefit by the working of others; and who trusts that he can by the help of others be reconciled to the Prince from whom he has been estranged, though doing nothing himself to win back the Prince's favour to him. Whoever therefore are so minded, as not first and foremost to use their own efforts that it may be well with them, are in the number of those

Luke xi. 5; xviii. 2.

---

[1] It is noticeable that in Dean Colet's Will, dated within a month of his death (Aug. 22nd, 1519), there is no desire expressed for masses for the dead, or any similar observance. A copy of the document is in Kennett's *Collections*, vol. xliv. f. 234 (Lansdowne, No. 978).

[2] "Nam profecto idem sit, ac si quis, sole suos radios sanis largiente oculis, sibi oculos eruens solaris luminis particeps fieri postulet."—§ 6.

whom prayer in no wise profits, and who are unworthy to be prayed for. But for those who strive with all their might to be saved, the prayer of saints cannot but be profitable. This opinion is supported by St. John in his canonical Epistle:—"If any man see his brother sin a sin which is not unto death, he shall ask, and he shall give him life for them that sin not unto death. There is a sin unto death: I do not say that he shall pray for it." He who prays is undoubtedly aided by the prayer of others; but he who does not pray, though he can, is nothing aided. The one who is himself an evil liver, trusts in vain, as Dionysius judges,[1] in the prayers of the good. 1 John v. 16.

The prayer of the Bishop over the departed, that he may be in glory, is not so much a petition that it may be so, as a declaration that it is so. For the Bishop, as Malachi calls him, is "the messenger of the Lord of hosts," and the interpreter of the will of God, moved by the divine Spirit. Accordingly the prayer in question is a declaration, from the sacred mouth of the Bishop, how it fares beyond doubt with the dead; in order that the Church may learn by the words of the Bishop what reward there is for the righteous that are dead in Christ, and may believe the Bishop, who hangs on the words of God, and who possesses the Holy Spirit ("Receive ye," saith He, "the Holy Ghost"), when faithfully saying somewhat in his ministration on God. For he speaks not of himself, but of the Spirit; and that which he believes in the fullest faith to be the case, and testifies of on earth, is done in heaven, where it takes place before it is revealed for men's belief. He, as Dionysius says, is the messenger and interpreter of the will of God, and says and does all things as he is counselled by God. Those whom God would have compassion on, the Bishop in God, as the diviner of His will, has compassion on. As for those on whom the Bishop has not compassion, it is a sign that the Spirit of God counsels him not to have compassion on them; Mal. ii. 7.

John xx. 22.

---

[1] And to the same effect his scholiast Maximus, on ch. vii. § 6, "Nota, quod solis dignis misericordia Dei prosint justorum orationes, sive vivant, sive mortui sint; non quidem peccatoribus et juste condemnatis, et hic et post mortem."

and that on such God himself in heaven has not compassion; for he moves, by his Holy Spirit, his minister the Bishop at his will; that he may execute on earth by the Bishop's office that which has been decreed in heaven. For all things are derived from heaven and from God; and He it is who works in all; and men are true ministers in him of his will from whom they have the Spirit, so as to be instruments, as it were, of the operation of God, and not to do anything of themselves, but God to do all things in them. It was for this purpose that, when the God-man Jesus Christ, after his resurrection, entered in to his chosen disciples, when the doors were shut, and said to them once and again "Peace be unto you;" it was for the purpose, I say, of making them fit instruments for himself of his will, to execute on earth what he did in heaven, that "he breathed on them, and saith unto them, Receive ye the Holy Ghost: as my Father hath sent me, even so send I you. Whose soever sins ye remit" (as executors, that is, of the will of God, whose Spirit they have received) are remitted unto them; and whose soever sins ye retain, they are retained;" provided it be done according to the Spirit given unto them, and to a just dispensation of the will of God; otherwise that which we are called on to believe is the work not of God but of man. Wherefore St. Paul, when writing to the Corinthians, after saying that they, the Apostles, and all who bear such an office, are "ministers of Christ, and stewards of the mysteries of God," subjoins close after, "Moreover it is required in stewards that a man should be found faithful." For not all are righteous ministers, nor due dispensers, nor moved by the Holy Spirit with wisdom from God; but in self-reliance do what they themselves wish in their own spirit, which is at enmity with God. But they who through Christ are chosen of God, are drawn upwards and depend on Him, and are instruments, as it were, in his hand, ever turned thither, and to that quarter, and to that object whither God directs them; and these are declarers and manifesters and executors of the will of God, and of his mind, which first determines and fashions all things. These assuredly do not act of themselves, but God in them; nor are they themselves the authors of any work, but God; and whatever they have done, we must believe to have been done by God. These are to be esteemed and reverenced in the place of God, as God himself; that is, not they themselves, but God in them; in whose Spirit they are counselled from above how to think and do and say all things. Concerning men of this kind is that saying of Jesus in St. Luke, "He that heareth you heareth me; and he that despiseth you despiseth me; and he that despiseth me despiseth him that sent me." For God is in Christ, and Christ in them that are truly his; especially in the heads of the Church, if they are truly Christ's. "Seek ye a proof," says St. Paul, "of Christ speaking in me?" These do all things by the Spirit of Christ, as Christ by the Spirit of God; these, being exalted in God, receive the verities revealed to them, and believe what is revealed; and that which has been shewn them by the secret promptings of the Spirit of God (whose motions none know but those that are elevated in God) in undoubting faith they do and say. This is the noble faith, by which St. Peter acknowledged Jesus to be "the Christ, the Son of the living God," and made confession in words. This is the faith, to which God assigns so great power, that whatever it has bound on earth shall be bound in heaven; and what it has loosed on earth shall be loosed also in heaven. Now all things no doubt have been bound in heaven, before they are bound on earth; and the things are loosed there first, which are afterwards loosed here. For God depends not on men, but men on God. Nor does he afterwards ratify our deeds, so to speak, but men execute the previous decisions of God; and by the ministry of men that is at length disclosed on earth, which had been before secretly determined by God in heaven. That which, when revealed and believed, is published by the lawful minister of God, has been disclosed at the fitting time, and by the office of God's servant; and we must believe him as the messenger and interpreter of God. Hence it is that Dionysius calls the Bishop, who is highest and nearest to God in the Church, the messenger and interpreter of God;[1] who,

Luke x. 16.

2 Cor. xiii. 3.

Matth. xvi. 16.

---

[1] "Venerandus antistes (ut scriptura ait) interpres est judiciorum divinorum; angelus enim domini omnipotentis est."—§ 7.

in faith in God who reveals it, binds on earth that which has been bound in heaven, and looses on earth that which has been loosed in heaven: that is, he shews to the Church the binding and loosing of God, so far as is declared to him, and gives notice of it under the will of God.

For it must be heedfully marked, lest Bishops should be presumptuous, that it is not the part of men to loose the bonds of sin; nor does the power pertain to them of loosing or binding anything. Since God alone looses and binds; and in his own sight in heaven does He loose and bind all things. They that are chief in the Church, as are the Bishops, receive by revelation what has been there loosed and bound, and declare what they have received, and by their words execute the design of God, not their own. And if they do not proceed according to revelation, moved by the Spirit of God in all things that they do or say, then are they of necessity foolish and mad of themselves, and abuse the power given them, both to the blaspheming of God and the destruction of the Church. Hence may we see how high, how exalted, how wholly conversant in heaven the Bishop should be; he especially who is the highest, whom we call the Pope;[1] that what by his authority he diffuses over the Church, quickening it to life eternal, he may draw wholly from God, and digest it when so drawn, and rightly and lawfully distribute it through all the members thereof; that these, being refreshed by the divine nourishment, may jointly live in the Bishop, who in the fullest degree lives in God. And this, to the end that all things should go forth from God to his Church, for the recalling of all things to himself, who himself in a sound and holy Church is all in all; who quickens, illumines and perfects the Bishop, especially him who is the highest; that he in turn may faithfully and sincerely be a minister of the wisdom and the will of God in all things, for the life and salvation of all; seeking

---

[1] This picture of what the Pope should be gains force by contrast, if it be remembered that at the time when Colet, in all probability, wrote, the notorious Alexander VI. (Roderic Borgia) was reigning. It will be observed that the Dionysiac system has no place for a Pope, as a power distinct from, and bearing sway over, the order of Bishops.

nothing but the advantage of men in God, and the approval of himself by God, in his stewardship of the mysteries of God. If he be a lawful Bishop, he of himself does nothing, but God in him. But if he do attempt anything of himself, he is then a breeder of poison. And if he also bring this to the birth, and carry into execution his own will, he is wickedly distilling poison, to the destruction of the Church. This has now indeed been done for many years past, and has by this time so increased as to take powerful hold on all members of the Church;[1] so that, unless that Mediator who alone can do so, who created and founded the Church out of nothing for himself (therefore does St. Paul often call it a "creature")—unless, I say, the Mediator Jesus lay to his hand with all speed, our most disordered Church cannot be far from death. Men slacken and draw again, loose and bind, not, through faith in God, what has been bound in heaven, but what they themselves wish; and hence all things on earth are in confusion. They are not executors of the will of God, but doers of their own. They do not testify what God wills, as they ought to do (for their office is nothing else than an attestation of the will of God); but they set forth what they themselves desire. They consult not God on what is to be done, by constant prayer, but take counsel with men; whereby they shake and overthrow everything. "All" (as we must own with grief, and as

Rom. viii. 19.

---

[1] The connection of this with the subject of "binding and loosing" lately mentioned, shews that Colet has in view the abuses of Papal Indulgences. More than a hundred years before, the system had been satirized by Chaucer, whose Pardonere is made to say:—

"And who so findeth him out of swiche blame,
He wol come up and offer in Goddes name,
And I assoyle him by the authoritee
Which that by bulle ygranted was to me.
By this gaude have I wonnen yere by yere
An hundred mark, sin I was pardonere."

And after Colet's death Erasmus continued the attack upon it in his Colloquies *De votis temere susceptis* and *Confessio Militis*. John Vitrier, the Franciscan, whose picture is made by Erasmus the companion one to Colet's, was of the same opinion:—"Damnabat stultam eorum fiduciam, qui, nummo in scrinium conjecto, putarent sese liberos a peccatis."
—Erasm. *Ep. Jod. Jonæ.*

Phil. ii. 21. I write with both grief and tears) "seek their own, not the things which are Jesus Christ's;" not heavenly things, but earthly; what will bring them to death, not what will bring them to life eternal.

But, to return to my subject, the true Bishop, and lawful overseer, and faithful steward of the mysteries of God, does nothing except after God. He is the hand, the minister, the instrument of God; whom we must believe even as God himself. Wherefore in the Funeral Service, whilst he is praying for eternal life for the saints that are dead in Christ, he is reverently speaking forth the sure will of God; faithfully and effectually asking for that to be done, which he fully knows will be done; that by words of intercession, which at all times beseem a Bishop, he may testify to the congregated Church the justice and grace of God towards men, towards those namely who die well in Christ. For the Bishop is the testifier of God's will, and as it were the mouthpiece and utterance of the mind of God, expressing the things that have been foreordained of God, which he perceives by faith. It is God himself who does all things well in all.

The custom of the Bishop and all the Church next saluting the departed, and bidding him, as it were, a last farewell, is a token of his being not dead altogether, but one who is passing to another region, to his own true and proper country. The corpse when kissed is anointed by the Bishop with oil, to imply that he has finished his conflict. And here must be noted the ancient custom, instituted by the Apostles themselves, that those who were to be initiated were first instructed in the creed, were prepared, and stripped; and, when now initiated, were anointed with oil for the conflict;[1] whilst at last, as noble warriors on their death, they received their final and completing anointing.

There is frequent use of ointment in the Christian Church, which has its name from anointing, and is called Christian. Now the Chrism is a mixture of different perfumes, with the addition of oil, or balsam, or some other oleaginous matter.

---

[1] See above, p. 68.

The Church in this particular has its own peculiar composition. And this Chrism is a sign of the Holy Spirit,[1] whereby all are strengthened in Christ; and is designed for that conflict which we enter on, under Christ our leader, with "spiritual wickedness in high places;" with which we contend when anointed and strengthened by the Holy Spirit. Of this Holy Spirit the anointing applied to the body is a sacrament, and typical of the anointing of the soul, by which we, made spiritual in the Spirit of Christ, in a spiritual battle, with spiritual arms, and against spiritual enemies, wage war in Christ, so long as we here live lawfully. At the last, when we ourselves, unvanquished, have come off safe in Christ, and our warfare is done, we are anointed at our departure; that men may know that we have finished the fight by the grace of the same Holy Spirit, in whose strength we began the contest.

Finally the body is buried, enclosed either in earth or stone or some other material, along with the men of his own order; there reserved to the day of resurrection. It was an ordinance of the primitive Church, that the corpse should be placed by itself and separate; order being preserved unbroken even among the dead, that order might everywhere appear. And as these bodies were partakers of the toil and of the contest, by endurance of ills and abstinence from pleasures, so are they laid in a sure hope that they will be

---

[1] It is worth notice how rapidly the mind of Dean Colet glances off from the mere material of the symbol to that which he takes it to signify. Some would have found matter for long disquisitions in the composition of the Chrism which he has just alluded to. As an illustration of another temper of mind, observe the spirit in which Bishop Pilkington refers to the same topic :—" Is this their sacrament of an oiling more holy than the other, because Bishops, as more holy men, are put to the doing and consecrating of the oil? Yet one doubt more. They have two sorts of oil to anoint withal, differing in holiness, consecration, and use of them, and yet both hallowed by the bishop. One is of oil and balsam blend together, which is called commonly oil and cream, wherewith bishops and priests in their consecrating, and children are anointed in christening: and that is more holy than this for sick persons is, for this is oil alone without other things blend thereto, as their master teaches. What Scripture is there for these toys, and the consecrating of them?"—*Confutation of an addition*, § v.

partakers of the glory, when by the power of God they shall be restored and joined again to their own souls. For if the whole man were not to be glorified, after the example of Christ, there would not have been instituted sacraments for the use of the body and flesh, by Christ himself and his Apostles, from whom proceeded every sacramental institution. For sacraments undoubtedly refer to the body, for its immortality, just as the Spirit works for the immortal glory of the soul; since the bread and cup of blessing, our inward food, and the anointing, which is our outward cherishing, can only mean that the body also is fed, nourished and cherished in its own fashion along with the soul, for life and glory everlasting. For by bread and drink and oil we are preserved in life both inwardly and outwardly. Among sensible signs those are used, by the ancient ordinance of the Apostles, which are most useful for this life; that hereby we may be admonished that those sacraments work eternal life for the body also, in them that believe. The soul on the other hand has its own proper food and drink on which it feeds, and its ointment, wherewith it is cherished; which the multitude and untaught people cannot see and discern. By obedience in God, by good hope, by faith in the signs, by constancy in well-doing, the multitude of Christians will be saved, although through this ignorance of theirs they will not attain to so lofty a place in heaven, in Christ all glorious, as those who through a more abundant measure of the Spirit see further, and have a deeper insight into the mysteries. Since, as men are promoted here, I do not say by their own strength, but through humility and by the leading of the Spirit, so in all cases will they be placed after the same order in heaven.

As to the sacramental words used at the Sacred rites, St. Dionysius, when treating of the sacraments,[1] is purposely silent, and would not discourse of them in writing, lest he should scatter God's pearls before swine. As I have said,

---

[1] In § 10 of Ch. vii. pt. 3 : " At vero efficientes consecrationis preces fas non est scripto interpretari," etc.

and must say again, the sacraments ought to be guarded in holy keeping from the unworthy multitude; for when handled by them they come to be held cheap. Places, vessels, robes, and whatever else pertains to the priests, being of greater sanctity, may not be looked upon by the ignorant and uninitiated multitude, except at a distance, and that too with great fear and reverence. But alas! in the unhappy state of this our age all things are in such shameful disorder, that nothing is now more profane than what ought to be most sacred.

CHAPTER VII.

PART III. SECTION II.[1]

On the Baptism of Infants.

FROM the discourse of Dionysius one may see that, from the very beginning of the rising Church, provision was made by Christ himself and his Apostles for the salvation of infants. And in the early Church I find that new-born infants were not only washed in the holy laver of regeneration and illumined, but also by participation in the most holy Eucharist (without which in the primitive Church not even the baptism of infants could take place), were joined and incorporated in the mystical body of Christ. And this, because they are at that age far from fault of their own, and clear of sins: provided only that some one took charge of them as sponsor, and promised for them that, if they lived, they would really seek for the sacraments. And although this was then had in derision by carnal men, who savour not the things that be of God, and who received and approved

---

[1] In Dionysius this subject is treated of in a single section (§ 11) of the Third Part, or *Contemplation*, of the Seventh Chapter, on the rites of the holy dead. As it appears to come somewhat abruptly there, and is expanded to much greater length by Colet, I have thought it better to distinguish it as a separate section of the present part of the chapter. The reason of its introduction, in this kind of supplementary manner, is probably from the Baptism of adults only having been discussed in Ch. ii.

of nothing save what their grovelling reason was persuaded of; yet to faithful and spiritual men the dedication of infants to God appears a great and admirable sacrament of divine compassion. By the Church also it is esteemed a matter full of piety, so it be done duly and in a lawful manner. And though the meaning of it cannot be seen by men, that is no marvel; seeing that not even the chief angels themselves know all things. But pious faith accepts and reverences all. And they who first appointed not only that sacrament, but all the rest besides, the Apostles, I mean, either possessed the reasons of them, or believed one who did so. That which has arisen, and is now performed, at the prompting of the Spirit of God, cannot be devoid of the very highest reason; and though this is not attained by poor human reason, yet it is by faith which is above reason,[1] a light full surely given us in Christ, and capable of the highest reason. Now if we are weak in this matter of faith, which even the very chief of Christ's Apostles sought to have increased, let us not on that account despise the great Sacraments of God. Nay rather let us acknowledge and truly and humbly confess the narrowness of our reason, and let us ascribe to our own perverseness our want of power to comprehend the things of God, rather than disdainfully spurn what our puny reason comprehends not; yea and let us seek to become something that is above reason, namely great in faith; and above the flesh, that is spiritual; and above men, that is divine; and let us wholly and without doubt believe that divine things cannot be received except by divine men.

But now let us see, with respect to the sacred rites of infants born in the Christian Church, what was the order and ceremony of initiating them, practised by the early men of our

---

[1] This principle was held by Dionysius as well as Colet.—"It would be impossible to affirm more distinctly than he does the absolute incapacity of man to have knowledge of anything beyond phenomena, and yet at the same time he recognises that there is a sphere beyond knowledge, to which he must look up with devout and patient adoration. Above his pantheism there is the intense belief in one God, above his positivism there is the trustful aspiration of faith."—Westcott, in the *Contemp. Rev.* No. xvii. p. 27.

religion. In the early Church, as I have said on the testimony of Dionysius, on certain conditions and rules they were admitted both to Baptism and to the Eucharist.[1] The manner of introducing them, that they might be numbered in the Church, was, according to Dionysius, as follows. A parent, when a child has been brought into the world, aware that it had been better for a son or a daughter not to be born, than not to be born again in Christ; not ignorant also that the sacrament is of little benefit, nay is certainly injurious, unless the infant's life, if he grow up, shall correspond to the sacred rites received; a parent, I say, in order that his child may be admitted by the Bishop to participate in the sacred rites, goes about and anxiously enquires where he may find a good man, and one skilled in Christian truth, to take upon himself and promise the instruction and training of his child in all things that pertain to salvation, and to be a sponsor for him before the Bishop, that, if the latter shall have signed him, and endued him with the heavenly rites, the infant, if he grow up, shall himself live according to those sacred rites, in holiness and purity in Christ. And when the father has found such a man, and entrusted his little son to him in honest faith, as to a second and greater parent in God (for the fatherly duty, and begetting of an infant, is an office preparatory to the regeneration of the same), the man then who has taken upon himself the bringing forth of the infant in Christ, that at length, if he live, he may be formed and fashioned a perfect Christian, on this great profession of fatherhood in Christ, goes to the Bishop, shews him whom he has taken to himself for regeneration, or rather for a full fashioning in Christ, and reverently asks the Bishop to admit him into the body of Christ by assimilation and sealing of the sacraments, that thereupon he may, through his sponsor's care and assiduity, grow to live a life worthy of those sacred rites. The Bishop then, on hearing the man promise and make a holy vow for the child, and perceiving that he is not unmeet to perform his promise, accepts his sponsorship, in reliance on the divine compassion; and, after the

---

[1] See above, p. 75. n.

manner and form instituted by the Apostles, provides the infant with the customary ceremonies and signs, both illumining him with baptism and perfecting him with the Holy Communion. Meanwhile the foster-father, who has undertaken the rearing of the child in Christ, gives a pledge and sacred promise, on behalf of the infant, of all things that true Christianity demands ; namely, a renouncing of all sin, and faith in the sacraments, and a life of perseverance in Christ, worthy of such a profession. And this he says not in the child's stead, since it would be a fond thing for another to speak in place of one that was in ignorance; but when, in his own person, he speaks of renouncing, he professes that he will bring it to pass, so far as he can, that the little infant, as soon as ever it is capable of instruction, shall in reality and in his life utterly renounce every principle contrary to the Christian character, and display himself in his whole life as worthy of the sacred rites, being at length in riper years aware of, and voluntarily professing, what he admitted when an unconscious infant. Then, on these terms and conditions that the foster-father perform what he has promised, the Bishop receives the infant. And when the Bishop hears him (whom I call *foster-father*, though Dionysius calls him at one time *sponsor*, at another *godfather :* by some again he is called *god-sib*, by others *surety*[1]),—when the Bishop, I say, hears him saying "I renounce,"—which means, as Dionysius explains it, "I will take care that the infant renounce and abjure all that is offered to him from a lower region, and by the devil, and desire nothing save what shall be supplied him from heaven above, by God himself;"— he, being not ignorant of the gracious mysteries of God, and looking forward to what the sponsor has promised, joyfully signs the infant with the mark of Christianity, that he may be owned to have come forth as a shoot from a faithful tree. To this scion the faith of his parents contributes something;

---

[1] I have used this term, not as exactly representing *compater*, but as the only suitable one remaining. From *compater* the French have obtained their *compère* ; but this, I believe, has now diverged in common language from its original meaning, much as *gossip* has done in English.

though it contributes not much; since the Christian tree grows and multiplies itself in branches, not by carnal generation, but by spiritual regeneration. Whence it is plain that in point of true paternity, and in Christ, the god-father is more truly a father, who completes in Christ the human being when born, than the father who has furnished the substance for his flesh. The son moreover, though he respect each parent, and him in the first place who made him a child of man, in the second place him who was the instrument of begetting him also as a child of God, has yet undoubted reason for owing more to the second, and receiving him more in the room of a parent. Since it is surely a greater thing to be perfected in God than to be begotten of man.[1] Wherefore the sponsor is of more account and in a higher position than the father; and his office and work is far more excellent and meritorious, and such as to deserve far more both of God and the little infant, than anything that is done by the parent in begetting. For he performed only the work of the flesh, rather for the sake of his own pleasure, than for the welfare of any offspring. But the sponsor, without pleasure to himself, nay even with pain, bears afresh a man to Christ, being inflamed with the love of God, for the salvation of a human being.

Thus we see how in the primitive Church, by the ordinance of the Apostles, infants were not admitted unreservedly to the sacred rites, but on condition only that some one would be surety for them, that, when come to years of discretion, they should thenceforward set before them in reality the pattern of Christ. And this surety and sponsor will hold it a matter to be seen to by him, to educate and bring up the boy in such learning and manners that, ac-

---

[1] Erasmus has a similar sentiment, though he qualifies it more than Colet:—" Atque hac quidem parte matrimonii sacramentum respondet baptismo. Per matrimonium enim nascimur huic mundo; per baptismum renascimur Christo. Præstantius quidem sic renasci quam nasci; sed tamen nisi per matrimonium nasceremur, non essent qui Christo per baptismum renascerentur."—*Christ. Matrim. Instit.* (1526), fol. c. In the *De Sacramentis*, pp. 75, 76, Colet's language is very strong on this point.

cording to the meaning of the sacraments, he may show himself a true Christian. For the infant is signed with the sacred symbols, that he may be trained up in them. And if there be one to make a solemn vow and promise that this shall be so with the boy, then the pious Church hopefully assigns the infant to him; that by the precepts and admonitions of his foster-father he may become a true man in the profession of Christ.

Mark thus how great a burden he takes upon himself who promises to be a god-father for little infants; how much he has to discharge in the infant's case; how much also both the parents and the infant himself owe to the god-father and sponsor; provided that, in pursuance of his duty, he do and perform what he has promised that he will perform. Far more, I repeat, owes the child to him, than to the sire that begat him. Here too one may see how, through this ignorance of ours, in the disorder of the times, they who undertake this office, profanely neglect what they are bound to do, to their own and the babes' great loss together. Now if, upon the temporal death of an infant through the carelessness of a father after the flesh, that be imputed as a very great crime to the sire, how great a crime does he commit, who through his negligence suffers a human being to perish everlastingly in spiritual death! How great a murderer is he, and worthy himself of what a death, by whose breach of faith a man dies in death eternal! Let every sponsor therefore acknowledge what he is, and what he promises, and what a ministry he discharges in Christ; yea and how great a father he is in this ministration of the fatherhood of God, the true regenerator of all, and how great a duty he has to perform in case of the foster-child he has undertaken. For it is no light matter for one to display himself in reality to be a righteous Christian, in keeping with the sacred rites; nor does he who promises this for some one, promise a slight matter and one easy to be discharged. And if he act in accordance with the office and duty he has professed, he does what is most acceptable to God, most profitable to the infant himself, most pleasant to the parents, gainful also to the Church, and a meritorious

CH. VII. 3, § 2. *BAPTISM OF INFANTS.* 161

cause of glory to himself. But if he neglect his duty, and suffer a man to abuse the sacred rites he has received, he then treasures up for himself on all sides death and misery everlasting. As there is nothing more beautiful than a sponsor of the former kind, and nothing better nor more profitable, if what is promised for a child be really performed; so too there is assuredly nothing either more injurious or more damnable, if he unfaithfully neglect what he promises the Bishop at the sacred font. By the carelessness of these, who are as it were the doors of the Church, there have been admitted into the Christian society those who have nothing beyond the outward signs of Christianity;[1] whence it comes to pass that under the name of Christ there is a conflux of evil doers, who under a fair-seeming name practise every kind of baseness. Of which shocking and shameful thing those godfathers and sponsors for children are in reality the chiefest cause; since to their care has been committed the training up of the little ones in Christ, and in truth of living. For such as is the plant, such is the tree; and as is the training of boys, so will be the nation.[2] Parents also are guilty of the highest folly, and partly too the cause of this plague of our Christian commonwealth, if they do not seek out circumspectly and provide for themselves such sponsors as they know can rightly instruct their children in Christ. It is the priest's duty moreover, to keep a discerning eye in this matter, that none be admitted to the sponsor's office, to whom an infant is entrusted, but worthy, holy, learned and good men; men that will bring forth the infants to be such as they are themselves; that children, imitating their holy sponsor in holiness and goodness, may at length become worthy members in Christ, and

---

[1] With this may be compared what the scholiast writes on this topic in the edition of 1498:—"Nunc vero, in hac infelicitate nostrorum temporum, ad id sacramenti pueros ducunt nullo pacto instructos, nullo preparatos modo; qui ferme sacramentum ridentes, mysteria pene cum cachinnis suscipiunt."—Fol. 45 a.

[2] Perhaps in this conviction may be discerned the germ of that purpose, of which the foundation of St. Paul's School came in due time as the fruit; the "plant," such as was afterwards the "tree."

such as will neither disappoint the promise of their sponsor, nor the hope of the Bishop, nor lastly the sacred rites they have received.

Thus much I have written, in the track of Dionysius, on our Ecclesiastical Hierarchy; from the fair fashion of which we have far degenerated. But I pray God, the framer of all things Himself, to reform, of his own great goodness, what has become deformed in us; through Jesus Christ our Lord.

END OF THE ECCLESIASTICAL HIERARCHY.

IOANNIS COLETI S.T.P.

OPUS

DE CAELESTI DIONYSII HIERARCHIA.

IOANNES COLETT, SACRÆ THEOLOGIÆ PROFESSOR, EX LECTIONE DIONISII HÆC EXCERP-SIT ET SCRIPSIT:

COGNOSCO tuam sublimem et angelicam mentem, vir optime et amice charissime, dignam sane quæ non solum de angelis audiat, sed præterea quæ cum ipsis una consocietur. Quapropter, quæ heri ac nudiustertius apud Dionysium Areopagitam, in eo suo libro qui inscribitur de celesti hierarchia (in quo magnifice et divinitus de angelis disserit) legi et memoria reportavi, ea volo tecum communicare: quum in reportatis, et in his quæ dedicimus in eo libro, id vel primum et maximum est, ut quicquid aliunde accepimus boni, id benigniter deinceps impartiamus aliis et communicemus; hoc imitati inestimabilem Dei bonitatem, qui largitur[1] se et ordine communicat universis; quique dat, quicquid dat, ut deinde, cui datur, ab eodem e vestigio traditur alii, quatenus conveniat; ut ab alio in alium distributis et dirivatis donis Dei, universi et Deum bonum agnoscant, et ipsi simul Divina bonitate concopulentur. Itaque habe nunc quæ mea memoria reservavit ex illa Dionysiaca lectione; quæ capitulorum ordinem sequutus, summatim volo et breviter perstringere.

CAP. I.

IN primo capite est: a Patre illo luminum exire et per conditas res emanare candidam quandam et spiritalem lucem, rerum omnium, quatinus sua cujusque natura patitur,

---

[1] Largiter—C.

in se revocatricem, ut sistat se quodque ordine et gradu suo, ac pro modo suæ naturæ in Deo perficiatur. Lux autem illa una per omnia et penitus eadem est, non variata quidem rerum varietate; sed magis, quæ varia sunt et diversa, quoad fieri potest, trahit in similitudinem quandam et unitatem sui. In qua unitate lucis omnino et identitate est varietas rerum, luxque eadem manet una et simplex in variis rebus; ut sine confusione semper varietatem rebus, identitatem luci tribuas. Rationales autem creaturas, divinæ ipsius naturæ capaces, mirifica illa irradiatio divini solis apprehendens quasi rarifacit et levifactas attollit sursum in se intime, atque attrahit, atque etiam secum unum facit. In hac tanta felicitate sunt spirituales illæ omnes naturæ, quas uno nomine angelos vocamus; in quos mera ipsa et nuda lux infusa est. Nam propter simplicitatem naturæ eorum, ut aperta et pura veritate perfundantur non sunt inidonii. Homines autem, qui inter racionales creaturas ultimum locum tenent, quique ipsi simplices et unius naturæ non sunt (siquidem animabus eorum gravis et tediosa adheret corporea moles; in qua anima, degenerans a sua simplicitate, nonnihil evadit corporea, ut nunc ad aspicienda mera spiritalia inepta sit sane et impotens omnino, atque adeo infirmata admixtione corporis, ut nequeat potentem aliquam lucem ferre, sed quasi valitudinaria et imbecillis exhorreat, refugiat, et offendatur) hos, inquam, homines, quum suæ lucis, veritatis et graciæ optimus et benignissimus Deus noluit omnino esse expertes, angelorum ministerio factum est, ut pro natura et capacitate eorum radius divini solis et veritas Dei a sua simplicitate quasi degeneret parumper in eam conditionem, corpoream videlicet et sensibilem; ut aspiciens mens humana, in corpore prope facta corporea, vibrationem tantæ lucis, non exhorrescat, sed cognato jam et tollerabiliori vultu admittat eam ad se, et sub sensu, quoad fieri potest, conspiciat veritatem jam etiam prope corpoream, signis eam et similitudinibus corporeis indicantibus. Quæ quum per se ipsa nuda veritas mentibus hominum non potuit sese insinuare, quumque agnovit familiaritatem quam habet anima cum sensibus, aliam est aggressa viam, et per hos sensus, utpote per opportuna media, attemptavit ad animas se introducere: ut, quod effici non potuit a priore, saltem a posteriori, aliqua ratione (ut homo veritatis particeps esset) efficeretur. Itaque quod a Deo in angelos promanat, in firmitatem, ordinem et perfectionem eorum, purum simplex et sincerum, id idem pergens in homines, in sensus eorum, a puritate et simplicitate sua cadens, angelica ministratione evadit aliquatenus sensibile; rebus ipsis sensis, quoad maxime fieri potest, similimis veritatem referentibus; ut inter sensibilia et intelligibilia collocatus homo medius, per corpora ad spiritum, per sensa ad intellectum, per umbram ad lucem, per imaginem ad veritatem adduci possit; ut eam aliquando nactus, contempta tum omnino carne, et contensus in spiritum, in spiritali sola veritate conquiescat. Sic et talibus viis mirabili benignitate bonus Deus voluit humiles homines ad suam altitudinem revocare, restaurareque tandem ad veritatem et lucem ipsam, qui ipse est noster Iesus, qui est benedictus in secula. Nam creator ille, et omnis ordinis ineffabilis causa, gloriosum et efficax exemplar est primae hierarchiae, et sacro illi principatui, qui tanto amore ardet, qui conatur totis viribus referre Deum, et quae sub se sunt deinceps ut referant impellere. Itaque, ut Deus primam hierarchiam, ita illa secundam, et secunda terciam edocet. Tertia vero deinde hierarchia angelorum, videns hominum ruditatem in terris, qui in quarto sunt loco, et ad divina agenda quam inepti erant, Deo volente consulto instituit ad tempus, ut homines suis corporibus corporumque actionibus imitentur angelos; ut, qui spiritu nequiverant, propter crassitatem corpoream, saltem in ipsa carne et corpore, quadam similitudinaria ratione, (ut fieri possit) Deum referant. Haec corporea et carnalis hierarchia et ordo in hominibus, purgans, illuminans et perficiens, immo purgationem, illuminationem et perfectionem potius significans, Hebreorum magistro Moise erat synagoga, corporibus et sensibilibus signis imitans angelos, non intellectis et spiritalibus. Moises tamen ipse non erat ignarus veritatis; ad cujus exemplar in ordine Hebreos composuit. Nec ipse Moises etiam erat ignarus fore aliquando hominem, in quo non angelus sed veritas ipsa loquiretur, qui homines ad veritatem, quam ipse adumbrarat corporibus, spiritu promoveret. Hic est noster pientissimus Iesus, justiciae sol, qui non solum indicavit quid sibi voluerunt umbrosa illa instituta moisaica, sed præterea illuminavit mentem ut revelatis credat. Interea vero factum fuit ut in terris dumtaxat inanis illa umbra ordinis et alicujus hierarchiæ appareret; ut justo ordine hominis promotio et translatio in angelicum statum proficisci videatur; ab umbra scilicet in imaginem, ab imagine in veritatem. Umbra erat sub Moyse; illustrata imago jam in terris extat in Christo: veritas aliquando nobis erit in celo. Sub Moise ea ratio hebreorum et sinagoge fuit, ut illic in plurima umbra modica lux esset. In ecclesia vero Christi hic dum sumus, plurima lux est, sed simul cum ea nonnulla opacitas et umbra; verumtamen sic victa a luce, ut color potius quam umbra nominetur. Color enim constat ex opaco et luce. Etenim ecclesia, dum adhuc in corporibus sumus, nec caret sensibilibus signis, nec potest quidem. Sed hic modica sunt, et ad retinendos infirmiores in ecclesia admodum necessaria; ut ex sensu sint admoniti quando animo spiritum capiunt. Qui spiritus non descendit in homines, dum homines sensibiles sint, nisi adhibitis signis sensilibus, quæ, dum hic vivitur, fundamenta et essencialis materia sacramentorum sunt Christianorum, sine quibus initiari et veritate sacrorum imbui non possunt. Hæc causa est, ut tradit Dionisius, sacrosancti mysterii communionis, in qua Iesu sancta societas in spiritu feliciter agnoscitur. Reliqua etiam sacramenta omnia suas habent substratas materias desenter et congrue adhibitas; in quibus dum hic vivitur, discunt ii quibus ministratur spiritus, se homines esse, adhucque etiam omnino ad nudum spiritum non esse habiles. Veniet quidem tempus in quo, corporis nostri opacitate et morte penitus extincta, nec umbra nec color sed mera illa in se et rutilans lux simplex et nuda percipietur a nobis, quando quod credimus re et effectu fiet. Sed ut ad Dionysium redeamus, id (ut summatim dicam) in hoc capite agitur et ostenditur communem quandam lucem spiritalem et divinam promanare a Deo, et procurrere per omnia suaviter, receptam a quoque pro sua cujusque capacitate. In angelos vero illos perspicuos et translucidos infusam simplicem et nudam, ad homines autem pro mirifica Dei benignitate ministratam involucris quibusdam et integumentis, ne sua nimia vibratione distringat nimium et offendat infirmos mentis oculos; utque homines per convenientia sensibilia signa ad significatam veritatem comodius adducantur.

CAP. II.

THEOLOGIA, quæ est divinæ veritatis revelatio et prophetarum sermo, magnam habet humanæ infirmitatis rationem; quam quum velit in celestem condicionem regenerare, celestes illas et spiritales naturas quodammodo degenerare facit, atque ad ipsos homines humiles deducit in sensum aliquatenus, effictionibus poeticis divinarum rerum statum et beatorum spirituum ordines discribens; non in re ficta quidem omnino, ne parum auctoritatis esset in fabula, sed in ipsis revera viventibus hominibus, et simul mutuis eorum actionibus, ut primum scena et spectaculum aliquod rude extet, representacioque obscurior, et si non ipsius absolutæ veritatis, tamen certe alicujus imaginis futuræ, quæ postea illustrior appareat, et veritatem ipsam clarius refferet, umbra aliquantisper in lucem prodita, et opacitate quæ erat quasi coloribus illuminata. Ut enim diximus supra, Judæorum sinagoga ut umbra se habet; ecclesia in sole Christo ut varie illuminata opacitas: et ut res aliqua recepta luce solis pulchre colorata, hanc ecclesiam in terris adumbravit tota illa institucio et ordo in hebreis statutus a Moyse. Quam adumbracionem exortus sol justiciæ, Iesus Christus, immissis radiis veritatis suæ pro capacitatis varietate varie illustravit, fecitque ut aperte in die spectabilis esset, umbra in claram imaginem producta, et synagoga in ecclesiam transformata, die noctis tenebras discutiente, ut non amplius in tenebris et umbra noctis, sed sub sole Christo in luce Dei, in spiritu homines ambulent hic et vivant, ut deinde aliquando in ipsam veritatem translati in dierum die et sabato sabatorum feliciter conquiescant. Ut Judei illi corporibus suis et actionibus ratione quadam compositis se exercuerunt, ita oportet quicquid illic significatum fuit Christiani animo et spiritu ex-sequantur, ut ne una quidem iota prætereat. Hæ spiritales actiones antecedentis umbræ, veritatis sequentis, et futuræ veritatis imago, ex fide proficiscuntur; videlicet ex hoc quod homines credunt Iesu Christo, qui indicavit tandem aperte quid voluit et significavit illa adumbratio Moysaica, ac tota illa sinagogalis hierarchia, corporibus non animis acta, quorsumque tenderit. Cujus evangelio et bono nuncio qui credunt, ac simul ex hac fide quod significatum est animo et spiritu peragunt, uti Iesus, qui non solem verbis sed etiam re ipsa expressius docuit, ii revera in die sunt, et incedunt quasi colorati luculentius, ac pulchro inter se ordine et mutuis actionibus admodum spiritalibus et perspicuis, cum propius tum etiam clarius veram celestium spirituum faciem representant. In quam, ut ait Paulus, transformantur a claritate in claritatem, tanquam a domini spiritu; in quaque erunt tandem in ipsa veritate, quam nunc quam melius possunt, imaginario ordine et actionibus, referunt spiritu; credentes Christo, et expectantes avide ipsam cum angelis plenam et perfectam veritatem. Hoc est quod Paulus ad Galatas scribit: Nos enim, inquit, spiritu ex fide spem justitiæ expectamus; interea fide vivimus, quæ per charitatem operatur. In qua completio est legis. Hoc est verbum abbreviatum quod posuit Deus super terram. Ita ineffabili Dei dispensatione rerum, et quasi cura humani generis, ut in felicitatem reformetur, primum antegressa est levis quædam umbra divini vultus, illiciens homines in propiorem imaginem ejusdem vultus; ut deinde in ejusdem vultus veritatem transferantur; ut non amplius nec in umbra, nec in imagine, et in ecclesia hic in terris, quasi per speculum in enigmate, sed ipsum Dei verum vultum facie ad faciem contueantur; tunc videlicet, quando apparuerit quod erunt homines (ut ait Joannes), et videbunt illum sicuti est. Nunc autem nec Deum nec divina quispiam videt: Iesu Christo magni consilii angelo credimus: unigenitus filius, qui est in sinu patris, ipse enarravit. Is enarravit tempus esse ut descriptionis Moysaicæ imago prodeat in hominibus clarior, divinum vultum et angelorum trinitates referens; atque præbens se ducem, quasi choream instituit et tripudium luculentius; ut, pressis manibus mutuo vestigia illius sectentur, fidem illi in omnibus adhibentes; sic exactius et lucidius exprimens statum celestium in terris, et Dei in hominibus imitacionem. Talibus mediis et oportunis racionibus, admirabili Dei bonitate et benignitate in homines, revocatio et retractio est ad celestia; a corpore in spiritum, a spiritu in Deum; ut ex corporeis et carnalibus facti hic in Christo spiritales, aliquando in ipso Deo beatissime deificentur. Ipsi homines vere in se promoventur gradatim in melius, a claro in clarius, ut veritatem divini vultus et justiciam perspicatius atque perspicacius discernant, ipsi magis atque magis justificati radio equitatis, et spiritu Christi; quæ hominum clarificatio eousque procedet, donec perfecte clari et plene justi justiciam ipsam contemplentur, non in enigmate et obscuro tunc, sed apertissime et clarissime; nec per ecclesiæ speculum hic, in quo divini vultus imago relucet parum expresse (quod enigma vocat Paulus) sed per ipsam ecclesiam factam faciem et veritatem, re vera facie ad faciem. Quæ ecclesia nunc imago est ejus quod ipsa erit, et nunc quoque repræsentat imaginem ejus quod tunc videbit. Quæ ecclesia quum ex speculari imagine evasit in veram faciem, tunc ipsa vera sua facie verum Dei vultum et faciem intuetur. Id plane est quod Paulus ait: Tunc autem facie ad faciem: id est, vera ecclesia verum Deum in ipso; ad exemplum Iesu, qui nunc facie ad faciem conspicit; cujus ut similes simus peragente reformatione illius spiritus in nobis, in ipsius imaginem indies magis atque magis provehimur. Quod eleganter expressit Paulus, quum ad Corinthios scripsit: Nos vero omnes, revelata facie gloriam Domini speculantes (fide scilicet), in eandem imaginem transformamur, a claritate in claritatem, tanquam a domini spiritu. Transformamur enim ut similes Iesu simus in celis, atque, una cum eo, vero vultu verum Dei trinitatis vultum conspiciamus. Quæ quum ab angelis didicit Moyses, qui indicaverunt ei quanam ratione ipsi in seipsis formam et ordinem Dei referunt, ad normam et regulam ostensi exemplaris conatus est relationem Dei, ad similitudinem angelorum, in hominibus effingere; ut quadam institutione et ordine, vita et actionibus imitati angelos, homines in ipsis nonnihil divinæ rationis repræsentent; tametsi, ut par erat pro initio rei, rudius id fecerunt et obscurius. Sed contentus erat pater ille inchoamento qualicunque, prospiciens fore qui suam obscuram ruditatem et expoliret et illustraret. Itaque hebreos illos homines parum limatos, tanquam pueros, produxit in ludum; ut, quasi ludentes pupis et fictis rebus, referant umbratiliter quod homines aliquando verius essent facturi: imitati parvas puellas, quæ in prima etate pupis ludunt, filiorum imaginibus, veros filios postea in matura etate parituras: imitati etiam puellos, qui fictos equos conscendunt, armati fictis, in veris armis veros equos aliquando conscensuri. Quum eram parvulus, inquit Paulus, sapiebam ut parvulus; quum consenuerim, evacuavi ea quæ erant parvuli.

A puerilitate et imaginibus fictisque rebus traxit nos Christus, qui illuxit tenebras, qui veritatem docuit, qui credentes in se viros fecit; ut revelata facie gloriam Dei speculantes, in eandem imaginem transformemur, a claritate in claritatem, tanquam a domini spiritu. Deus qui dixit de tenebris lucem splendescere, ipse illuxit in cordibus nostris, ad illuminationem scientiæ claritatis in facie Iesu Christi; ut veriorem illius vultum fide cernamus, qui revelavit quæ de se et ecclesia depinxit Moyses: cui verbo qui credit, credit ei verbo quod abbreviatum posuit Deus super terram. In Christo enim sunt omnia cumulate, quæ vel docere in justicia, vel in religione instituere Moyses ille voluit; quæ fuerunt prius adumbranda, tum deinde suo tempore illustranda, ut aliquando in fine seculi perficiantur omnia. In adumbracionibus illis et significacionibus a Moyse, theologo et contemplatore naturæ perspicatissimo, undeque translationes sumuntur, quod ad dicenda divina propria verba non sunt; quoniam ad Deum ipsum significandum nihil convenit, qui est omnino non solum indicibilis, sed etiam inexcogitabilis. Quocirca verissime negationibus enunciatur; quum quid non sit, non quid sit, dicere potes; de quo quicquid affirmas, mentiris, quum nihil est horum quicquid potes dicere. Tamen quia occulta Dei ratio insedet in universis, ob tenuem illam similitudinem conati sunt theologi omnium nominibus illum significare, non solum meliorum rerum, sed etiam deteriorum; ne specie pulchriorum rerum capti hebetiores, id ipsum putent Deum esse quod dicitur. Sic oportet loquaris transferendo, ut aliunde petiisse verbum, non ex re ipsa dixisse videare; utque agnoscatur aperte, te non propriis uti, sed similitudinibus. Quapropter, non solum nomine solis, celi, lucis, vitæ, intellectus, mentis, vel si quid hujusmodi sit melius; sed etiam nomine volucrum et quadrupedum et plantarum, lapidum et elementorum et reptilium, divina dicuntur. Est enim omnia in omnibus; et deteriora meliora referunt obscuriter, omnia etiam Deum, quoad possunt; a quo et per quem et in quo sunt omnia. Hoc genere scribendi usi sunt theologi veteres, patriarchæ et prophetæ, et necessario et utili. Necessario, quia aliter de Deo loqui non poterant; utili autem, quod eo et infirmior acies allicita est, et ducitur ad spectanda clariora, et impia et prophana celatur. Velamen illud contextum Moysaicum est ejusmodi quidem, ut preciosum Dei celet impios, et tamen pios nonnihil .edoceat, etsi non veritatem ipsam, saltem aliquam umbram veritatis. Quæ vero edisserit de divinis Dionysius, adjurat Thimotheum sancte celet et operta teneat, nec communicet nisi dignis, ne prophanis oculis violentur.

CAP. III.

DEUS unus, pulcher et bonus, Pater, Filius et Spiritus sanctus, illa creatrix omnium trinitas, ipsa rerum purgatio est in unum, illuminatio in pulchrum, et in bonum perfectio. Ille Deus profusa sua luce, purgante illuminante et perficiente, ineffabiliter deificat deiformemque facit triplicem illam hierarchiam angelorum; in quibus, quanquam omnia ab omnibus communicentur (nam puritas et lux et deiformitas inseparabiliter se habent), tamen sunt quasi personales attributiones; ut primæ hierarchiæ perfectio, secundæ illuminatio, tertiæ purgatio accommodetur. Item in prima hierarchia, ordini illi qui primus est, ut perficiat maxime; secundo ut illuminet; tercio ut purget, attribuitur. Hac triplici ratione triplex hierarchia trino Deo assimulatur. Totus conatus omnium spirituum est referre Deum. Deus imprimis potenter assimilat quæ vicina sunt ei; assimulata deinceps assimulant. Ita pergit derivatio deitatis ab ordine in ordinem, et ab hierarchia in hierarchiam, et a melioribus creaturis in deteriores, pro capacitate cujusque, in deificationem omnium; ut Pauli verbis utar, in laudem gloriæ graciæ Dei. In hac quoque sorte (ut in hierarchia referente Deum reformentur) homines sunt; in quibus redigendis in ordinem defatigatis angelis, ordo tunc ipse et pulchritudo Dei incarnata, speciosus forma præ filiis hominum, Iesus Christus venit in subsidium, in se constituens hierarchias tres in electis hominibus, summorum, mediorum et infimorum; atque in his singulis triplicem virtutem illam, videlicet purgatoriam, illuminatoriam et perfectoriam; ut in Christo cooperantes etiam homines in clarificationem Dei, conficiant tandem consummatam humanam hierarchiam in terris, quæ aliquando coequabitur angelis in celis.

Deus assimulat nos ei.
Impartit ut impartiamur.
In impartione accepti maxime Deo assimulamur.
Divinissima virtus est misericors liberalitas.
Benefaciendo aliis maxime Deo assimulamur.

CAP. IV.

CREAVIT omnia Deus, quia bonus; et, quia bonus, idem ad se quodque pro sua capacitate revocat, ut se illis benigniter communicet. Nihil est non communicans Deum aliquatenus; quum, quod sunt et quod bene sunt, ex Deo habent. Racionalia vero ut melius et felicius se habeant, imprimis angeli, tum homines angelorum ministerio,[1] incomprehensibili Dei bonitate, et (ut loquitur Paulus) ex divitiis Dei. Primis et summis hominibus apertiores sunt visiones, ac in mentes eorum irradiatio simplicior deitatis. Reliquis deinde crassioribus per signa commode indicantur omnia, et morum effictio, et Dei excultio, et veritatis expectatio. Harum

---

[1] Deesse videtur aliquid, forsitan *laborant*.

rerum obscura indicia lex Moysaica continet. Quare Dionysius eam vocat sacratioris legis effigiem. Dirivatio est effusæ Deitatis, quæ procedens deificat a hierarchia in hierarchiam inferiorem, et in quaque hierarchia ab ordine in ordinem vicitudinario ministerio, ut animæ et spiritus Dei fiant. Misterium illud incarnationis primum didicerunt angeli: ii tum docuerunt homines; Zachariam, Mariam, Ioseph, Pastores. In hominibus deinde vicitudinaria est eruditio a membro in membrum in Christo, quæ pergit a primis per media in ea quæ ultima sunt in ecclesia, (ut loquitur Paulus) per juncturam subministracionis. Ita a Deo per angelos, id est, ab angelo in angelum, et ab iis ad homines dirivata est quædam impartio Deitatis. Deus ipse quoque veniens in homine, Iesus, rationem subiit angeli, et magni consilii angelus vocatur; ac, quatenus homo, accepit assidue subministraciones angelorum, conceptus, natus, adolescens, moriturus et ascensurus. Erat enim ante resurrectionem homo mortalis, quasi inferior angelis, qui post resurrectionem idem homo immortalis erat omnium Deus.

CAP. V.

ANGELI dicuntur nuncii a nunciando; quia ea quæ sunt Dei superiores inferioribus denunciant, ad ipsos homines usque. Verum hominibus enunciator maximus erat Iesus Christus: hinc ab Isaia vocatur admirabilis consiliarius, et magni consilii angelus. Quanquam peculiari nomine infimi spiritus vocantur angeli, tamen, quia munus eorum perfici potest a quoque superiori (potest enim superius quicquid inferius) iccirco inferiorum nomina superioribus conveniunt; superiorum inferioribus minime. Nomina hæc non sunt inventa ab hominibus, sed ex sacris literis assumpta. Quæ varia in sacro codice necessario indicant varios spiritus in celestibus; quorum ordinem digessit Dionysius. Ultimi angeli pontifices nostros et antistites exagitant, extenuantque sursum in spiritum, ut toti scilicet spiritales fiant: ut deinceps alios sub se homines, quemque pro capacitate sua, spiritificent; ut ex hominibus (quoad fieri possit) in Christo quarta hierarchia sit bene spiritalis, qui aliquando veri spiritus erunt et angeli, spiritificacione eorum a Deo in Christo, per angelos et angelicos homines continuata.

CAP. VI.

DEUS unus trinusque, ad exemplar sui ipsius in se ordinis, triplices in beatissimis spiritibus digessit hierarchias; quas modo functiones, modo distinctiones, modo hierarchias vocat Dionysius. Ille conditor omnium rerum et ordinum Deus solus nimirum exacte novit omnia; et prophetis (quos jure theologos appellat idem Dionysius, quum proprie et vere is theologus est, qui a Deo revelata proloquitur) illis, inquam, prophetis Deus per angelos aliquatenus indicavit, quæ illi deinceps, quatenus licuit, mandarunt literis; quæ sacræ et sunt et vocantur, sacras Dei revelationes continentes; in quibus novem ordinum beatissimorum spirituum nomina audiuntur. Quæ quid voluerunt et quid significarunt, illustratus Paulus spiritu Dei probe intellexit. Is Dionysium interpretamenta divini sermonis in his rebus edocuit. Ex cujus eruditione et patefactione scripturarum, et ex ipsarum scripturarum authoritate, se ipse Dionysius omnia loqui de celestibus spiritibus profitetur. Paulum vero apostolum suum magistrum, ducem et præceptorem vocat et nominat. In quaque hierarchia scribit tres coequales ordines, personas illas in Deo, hierarchiarum hierarchia, referentes; hierarchias autem tres esse, quæ triplicatæ novem constituunt ordines, qui hisce nominibus appellantur: Angeli, Archangeli, Principatus, Potestates, Virtutes, Dominationes, Throni, Cherubin et Seraphin. Quæ nomina non sunt humanitus inventa, sed divinitus in sacro codice a prophetis Dei et theologis deprompta.

CAP. VII.

POST trinitatem primi sunt Seraphici spiritus, toti flamei et ardentes, accepto Deo pleni et perfecti. Seraphin enim incendium significat. Sunt illi quam maximi amores, in divina pulchritudine quam suavissime conquiescentes, consociati in felicitate cum amantissimo Iesu, qui est Deus ipse in secula; cujus beatitudinem contemplantes amant, venerantur, adorant; immo etiam a gloriosissimo nostro Iesu ediscunt quæ ipsi suapte natura nesciunt. Illi beatissimi amores in adhesione divinæ pulchritudini ineffabili voluptate explentur: in contuitu Iesu omni se gaudio sentiunt perfundi. Id est quod Petrus ait in Epistola: In quæ desiderant angeli prospicere. Deinde ab iis secundo loco sunt Cherubici spiritus, præclarissima quædam illustramina, longe ultra quam excogitari potest resplendentia in se omniformi Dei sapientia; quæ possunt vocari sapientiæ amantes, ut illi primi amores sapientes. In utrisque enim est et amor et sapientia. Sed in illis primis, propterea quod soli veritatis ipsi Deo sunt viciniores, longe major. Iccirco, in illis quod est, amor cognominatur. In secundis ab illis minus sunt omnia; qui, comparati ad primos, luces duntaxat videntur esse. Quapropter scientiæ cognomen habent. Sic ergo differunt illi ordines, ut in his proprioribus sit scientia amoris, in illis amor scientiæ: in his amor scientia est, in illis scientia amor. In angelis intensior sciencia est amor, remissior amor est scientia. Noli putare aut supremos non scire, aut secundos non amare; sed hos scire amanter, illos amare scienter. Cogita etiam in differentia et proprietate quasi personali recompensationem quandam et coequalitatem; ut, sicut illi primi subsistunt suo incendio amoris, ita secundi subsistunt sua scientiæ luce; tam referentes sapientiam Dei quam illi amorem. Tertio loco sunt qui ab unitate, simplicitate, constantia et firmitate, modo Throni, modo sedes, appellantur; qui hi quoque sapiunt et diligunt. Sed eis ex sua simplicitate unitas, potencia, robur, fortitudo, stabilitas attribuitur; quod ipsum quoque in Cherubicis et Seraphicis est. Sed hoc iis peculiari attributione accommodatur, quod primam trinitatis personam et Dei potenciam, cujus jactus in rebus videtur esse longior, referunt. In his enim residet potentia Dei major, atque authoritas et severitas, et quasi firma rataque sentencia, decretique immobilitas. Inde est quod in throno sedere, et exercere judicium, et irrevocabilem sententiam ferre dicitur Deus. Nam per hos angelos, imagines potenciae suae, perficiet in extremo judicio quod immobili sententia permanebit. Stabilitas est ex simplicitate, simplicitas ex purgatione. Nam expurgato quoque in suam ipsius simplicem naturam, tum incomposita res unitate sua manet indissolubilis. Ex hoc liquet purgationem thronis attribui. Purgata autem res illuminatur, illuminata perficitur. Hoc datur Seraphicis, illud Cherubicis. In omnibus omni triplici ratione est totis viribus contentio in imitacionem Dei; qui est ipsa purgatio progignens unitates, ipsa illustratio unitatum, ipsa denique illustratorum perfectio. Potentia expurgat, liquida veritas serenat, consummatus amor perficit. Tradit Dionysius angelos etiam illos supremos Seraphicos (quod pro miraculo habet) suspicere Iesum in dextera patris, et suppliciter ac reverenter eum adorare, et innuere angelicis notis se libenter velle ab illo discere; et rationem misteriorum suorum, maxime eorum quae sunt Dei inhumanati, plenius cognoscere; atque ita a benignissimo Iesu discere, quod deinde ii alios doceant inferiores. Nam intelligit ille in prophetis angelos introductos, quorum alii alios majestatem Iesu Christi glorificati docent, qui illi doctores a Iesu didicerunt; eum videlicet, qui post resurrectionem ex mortuis ascendit in celum homo glorificatus, dominum Sabaoth et exercituum esse, celestiumque virtutum, ac ipsum dominum gloriae. Nam, quis est iste rex gloriae, apud David interrogant inferiores illos super se medios, qui, ascendente Christo imperantes clamaverunt inferioribus: Attollite portas principes vestras, et elevamini portae eternales, et introibit rex gloriae. Atque interrogantibus responderunt: Dominus fortis, dominus potens in prelio, dominus virtutum; ipse est rex gloriae. Ille est qui ascendit in montem domini, innocens manibus et mundo corde, qui non accepit in vano animam, nec juravit in dolo proximo suo, quem sequitur generatio quaerentium eum, quærentium faciem Dei Jacob. Supremi illi contemplantes Iesum inter se hesitabundi rogant, Quis est iste qui venit ex Edom, tinctis vestibus de Bosra? Quibus Iesus: Ego, inquit, qui loquor justiciam. Tum animati angeli benignitate Iesu, rogant illum, Quare ergo rubrum est indumentum tuum? Quibus ille: Torcular calcavi solus. Ita secretum incarnationis plenius a glorificato Iesu didicerunt, et inferiores docuerunt, simul purgantes, illuminantes et perficientes. Sunt enim simul hæ operationes. Illi vero supremi spiritus, quam beatissima felicitate requiescentes, quam suavissime concinunt: Sanctus, Sanctus, Sanctus, dominus Deus Sabaoth.

CAP. VIII.

SUNT angelorum ordines novem, exemplarium in Deo novem imagines. Et quisque id nomen sortitur cujusmodi est id quod in Deo refert. Inde primis amor, secundis scientia, terciis thronus; stabilitatem sapientiam et amorem in Deo referentes. In Secunda Hierarchia, primis nomen Dominationis est, veri et exemplaris dominatus in Deo expressa imago. Siquidem dominatio est in eis simplex et pura, et omnino expers servitutis, omnibus præsidens, omnibus utilis, vera dominandi et mera libertas, ad formam et exemplar domini; quam divinam dominacionem non solum in se conantur referre, sed præterea in verum dominatum ubique omnia et ad imitacionem dominatus in Deo enixissime contrahere; ut quicquid quod dominationis personam suscipiat, vere in Deo dominetur. Quomodo nos homunculi imitemur dominationem Dei, dominus ipse Iesus Christus, in sua forma humana aperte edocuit: in quo didicimus dominationem in hominibus liberam esse servitutem, et spontaneum obsequium Deo et hominibus, ut ii quoque obsequantur Deo. Secundis Virtutum nomen accommodatur; quo verbo vult Dionysius in eis significari quandam virilem et masculam et inconcussam fortitudinem, valitudinemque invictam et insuperabilem, ac divinæ ipsius virtutis mirabilem imitacionem:

in qua fit nihil languide, nihil imbecilliter, nihil ignaviter. In his valitudinibus et virtutibus est studium et cura et actio; ut omnia quæ sunt in Deo fortiter et viriliter valeant quadam casta virtute et masculina; ut etiam in virtute Deus ubique repræsentetur. Virtus ipsa Dei (ut vocat Paulus) et sapientia, Iesus Christus, nos suos homunculos in se fortificatos in nostra humana effigie valitudinem et fortitudinem et invictam virtutem docuit: docuit, inquam, in hominibus veram virtutem et fortitudinem esse patientiam; quæ virtus ipsa Dei Iesus ipse exemplum ostendens, gloriose passus est usque ad mortem etiam crucis. Quæ infirmatio ad interitum robor et fortitudo erat Dei. Unde Paulus scripsit ad Corinthios: Infirmum Dei fortius est hominibus. Terciis autem potestatis cognomen attribuitur, quod divinam unitatem, simplicitatem, potentiam et authoritatem in se representant, et in se quodammodo omnipotentem statum ac majestatem quasi paternam præ se ferunt, semper imitantes Deum in progignendo quodque ad id quod magnificentius est; quod non solum ipsi nituntur, sed etiam ad potestalem (ut ita dicam) majestatem fecundam et fertilem in Deo omnia convocant; primum sibi viciniora, quæ ipsa, quod acceperunt, vicinis suis deinceps dirivant. Nam quod novem hauriunt angelorum ordines, id novinario progressu in universa diffunditur; ut nihil sit tam vile in rebus, quod sit omnino novinariæ hujus liberalitatis expers. Ut enim est promanatio trinitatis Dei in omnia, ita simul trium personarum quasi triplicitatum vel ad minima quæque profusio est; ut novinaria racione quodque constet in decimo Deo. Jesus Christus, fecunda et magnifica potestas, paterna authoritate in se statum in hominibus produxit, ut ita loquar, potestalem ex potestatibus omnibus; quarum quæque procreet in se statum indies, ad exemplum Iesu, meliorem; ut ubique divina potestate ecclesia in Christo secum constet, refulgens virtute et præsidens dominatione. Sic Deus relucet stabilis, sapiens et amans in thronis, cherubicis et seraphicis spiritibus; quæ trina ratio divini radii pergens facit ut in potestatibus, virtutibus et dominationibus divina et stabilis potestas, sapiens virtus, et amantissima dominatio resplendeat; trinitasque Dei coequalis in se jam secunda sub prima illa suffulgeat; quæ quanquam ab illa prima degeneret, unde novis appellationibus sortitur, tamen semper memento in omni degeneratione simul suboriri necessario quæ recompensantur omnia; ut in rerum serie vel dissimili et inequabili sit mirum in modum providentia Dei similitudo et equalitas; ut, quemadmodum est in dissimilitudine similitudinis quædam varietas et jucunda pulchritudo, ita in similitudine dissimilitudinis simul sit omnium ordinatorum gravis et solida constantia; ut pulchritudo non vacillet inconstans, et constantia parum pulchra non displiceat. Quod autem illustratio Dei et revelatio ordine pergit ab angelo ad angelum, docet Zacharias propheta, in cujus sermone est quendam angelum ab alio angelo didicisse quod prophetam docuerat. Ecce, inquit, angelus qui loquebatur in me egrediebatur, et alius angelus egrediebatur in occursum ejus, et dixit ad eum, Curre et loquere ad puerum istum dicens: Absque muro etc. Nam purgatio illuminatio et perfectio ab alto per media ad ima descendit. Idem Zacharias restitutionem hebreorum in patriam a babilonica captivitate, quam didicit ab angelo, vidit eum angelum ab alio excelsiori didicisse. Ita illorum theologorum testimonio probat Dionysius angelum angelo triplicem radium ministrare.

CAP. IX.

ULTIMA vero hierarchia est principatuum, archangelorum et angelorum. Qui ordines etiam habent in ipso Deo sua exemplaria quæ referunt. Quid enim est principatus aliud quam veri et excelsi principatus in Deo imago quædam, quamque spiritalis conatus per orbem trahendi omnia quæ principantur, in imitationem veri illius et principalis Dei principatus; ut, quæ in principatu sunt, cum omni amore dominentur, amentque cum dominacione? Angeli autem qui ultimum locum tenent in serie divinorum spirituum, et mundanis corporeisque rebus propiorem, quique peculiarius nomen angeli sortiuntur, quod in cura et nunciacione mundo maxime et apertissime sunt, benignam nunciationem Dei et utilem referunt maxime, et in nunciando ea inter se et hominibus denique quæ a Deo per longam angelorum seriem dirivantur (quoad possunt) vere et puriter se exercent. Quorum natura ut est nostris humanis mentibus cognatior et affinior, ita vita eorum est nobis familiarior. In hos ordines interjicitur medius qui archangelorum dicitur, qui sunt, ut situ, ita natura, viribus, officio et actione, media racione constantes inter principatus et angelos; qui referunt in Deo et imitantur principalem quandam vim et sapientem et virtute plenam nunciandi. Sunt hi ordines, ut alii in ceteris hierarchiis, suis proprietatibus distincti, et simul (quod constanter fatetur Dionysius) coequales; quod arbitror esse propter representationem trinitatis, in qua quæ sunt tres personæ equales sunt. In angelorum ordine quod prostremo exprimitur Deitatis, agunt ipsi sedulo ut id idem inferant in homines, hominesque in imitacionem sui et Dei traducant; ut sub ipsis quoque extet triplex quædam hierarchia; hominum scilicet in terris; alludens ad id quod est in angelis. Hoc moliti sunt diu angeli frustra, hominis ineptia repugnante, donec in subsidium venerit magnus ille et (ut vocat Isaias) magni consilii angelus, Iesus Christus; de cujus nativitate exultantes cecinere angeli Gloria in excelsis Deo et in terra pax hominibus. Hic virginis filius hierarchiam ad angelorum formam, ad suæ veritatis exemplar instituit, et ex quibus voluit vivis lapidibus edificavit, quos non solum digessit in ordine, sed etiam vivificavit in se, ut vivi in ipso ordine digerantur. Quod autem angeli prefecti et procuratores hominum sunt in obsequium Dei, prophetarum scripta testantur. Nam apud Danielem est princeps Persarum et princeps Grecorum, et nominatur Michael princeps Judaicæ gentis. Statuit enim altissimus terminos gentium juxta numerum angelorum Dei. Habuit Michael proconsul hebreorum provinciam sibi magis obedientem. In aliis vero omnibus improbitas humana sic reluctata est, sicque quisque sequutus est suam ipsius propriam libidinem et perversam voluntatem, ut nihil nec in ordinem nec in imaginem ordinis cogi poterat. Cujus mali (ut ait Dionysius) in causa erat et amor sui cujusque et superbia. At Michael saltem nonnihil umbræ veritatis assequutus est in hebreis, quos in figuracionibus quibusdam exercuit, ut deinde aliquando altius promoveantur. Demum magnificus Christus, dominus omnium, non solum ex omni gente convocavit in amorem Dei et obedientiam, sed preterea fecit ut amantes obedirent ministrantibus tunc universis angelis alacrius in hominum salutem in salvatore Iesu, ut ubique homines convertantur et vivant; convertantur quidem ad vivificum Dei radium, justiciæ jam sole ipso exorto Iesu. Ut autem ait Dionysius, semper lux Dei spiritalis mentibus hominum affulsit in mundo, semperque hominibus arbitrium fuisse vertendi se ad lucem, nec obstetisse quicquam nisi perversam voluntatem. Antequam Iesus natus est, Melchisedech ex gentibus convertit se ad Deum, et meruit vocari sacerdos Dei altissimi. Nato etiam Iesu, denunciaverunt angeli pacem in terra hominibus bonæ voluntatis. Sed hæc cogita adjumentum Dei cum vi voluntatis concurrere, in graciaque homines libere posse, ut ex utrisque simul nascatur libertas ad bonum; ut, nisi velit homo, non admittat lucem; et, nisi illuminetur, non velit admittere. Est voluntas in causa cur animus admittit; et est lux simul in causa cur animus velit. Anima calens gracia suapte libertate elegit bonum, quod eadem libertate potest recusare. Sine gracia vero nulla libertas, et in gracia quidem nihil nisi libertas. In diffuso radio adjumentum est, ut quisque, qui velit, se convertat ad Deum. Convertunt se hi qui sufficienter sunt adjuti ut velint se convertere. Nato Christo propior nobis advenit Sol, et in homines lux fusa efficacior, et inde conversio hominum copiosior, eorum qui positi per graciam in libertate arbitrii voluerunt se convertere. Sed mittamus hæc : hebetescit enim acies retusa sane rei et questionis duritate. Ad Dionysium revertamur, qui affirmat ubique equalem esse potentiam Dei et benignitatem, sed non ubique bonam esse voluntatem hominum; equabilem esse graciosum radium diffusum in omnes, sed homines ad eum equabiliter se non habere: omnium hominum parem esse curam Deo, et unum Deum omnium, et angelos equales prefectos suis locis universis, qui pari cura tractant provincias suas. Quid enim Egiptiorum regi Pharaoni ? Nonne bonus angelus et princeps illius regionis indicavit somnium, quod postea Ioseph edoctus ab angelo, quid voluit, exposuit ? Item

Babiloniorum regi, quod illius gentis proconsul angelus immisit in mentem, visionis nonne Daniel interpres fuit? Quid ergo est aliud dicendum quam unum Deum omnium et omnibus æque bonum? Non enim est ille acceptor personarum; sed aliqui homines sunt recusatores Dei. Item affirmat ubique distributos angelos procuratores mundi, pari potencia, studio et benignitate; hebreos illos veteres nihil præ ceteris electos fuisse; equalem sortem esse omnium, libertatem universis unam et communem: hebreos acceptiores fuisse Deo, quod proconsuli eorum Michaeli facilius obedivere. Michaelem autem habuisse prefectum Judeos, ut aliæ nationes alios archangelos, Danielis sermo plane ostendit; apud quem est in decimo capite: Et nemo adjutor meus in omnibus his, nisi Michael princeps vester. Deum autem æque omnibus Deum esse, et David testatur dicens: Rex omnis terræ Deus. Et Paulus: Num Judeorum Deus tantum? non etiam et gentium? Immo et gentium. Sed quod veteres hebreorum obsequentiores erant inspirationibus angelicis, ideo apud David est: Quoniam Jacob elegit sibi dominus, Israel in possessionem sibi.

CAP. X.

SPIRITUUM Deum contemplantium (de quibus modo dissertum est) prima hierarchia et intimius se insinuat, et in Deo candet magis ceteris, tota purgata, tota illuminata et tota perfecta. Illa maxime stabilitatem, scientiam et amorem exoperatur in humana hierarchia; ut primi in hominibus in altum rapti una cum eis puriter omnia dilucide et ardenter contueantur. Sed prima splendida et corrutilans illa hierarchia secundam sub se et proximam diradiat, ut illustrata illuminet terciam; ut deinde tercia opacos homines pulchre discoloret, faciatque ut aliquatenus divinam pulchritudinem imitantes referant; quia illuc accepta referuntur omnia. Ut autem progreditur pergitque diffusio, ita vicissim nova in distinctis gradibus nomina suboriuntur. In homines vero quæ devenerunt postremo ex imperticione Dei, propter degenerationem, alias appellationes habent: atque ita Iesu

Christo exorto, qui homo exposuit nobis homuncionibus clarius divinas raciones, radius ille ex ipso emissus qui purgat, illuminat et perficit, evangelium vocatur. In quo hominum (eorum videlicet qui tanguntur evangelico radio, qui operatur in hominis spiritu simplicitatem, perspicuitatem et perfectionem) illa simplicitas qua homo constanter vivit in Deo per Christum, spes; perspicuitas, qua sapit altius, fides; perfectio, qua recte vult et agit omnia, charitas appellatur. Similiter reliquæ graciarum donationes suis nominibus, aliis quam sunt angelorum, in hominibus, pro humana parvitate nuncupantur. In angelis vero illis omnibus, a superioribus hucusque ad nos, deorsum est mutua et vicitudinaria nunciatio, acceptis et traditis vicissim, quæ nunciant mirabili et quam pulcherrimo ordine. Quoniam in ipsis angelis est ordinatorum ordo ad omnium ordinem. Nunciant quidem suis nutibus et innucionibus angelicis, modo ab humana mente incapabili; non solum hierarchia superior inferiori, sed in quaque hierarchia ordo ordini. Omnis autem nunciatio, acceptio, eruditio, purgatio, illuminatio, perfectio et representatio est divinæ veritatis, cujus lux ordine progrediens et effulgens universis, sic singula insignit et notat mirifice, ut in ea sua quodque proprietate emicans extet et appareat sua natura, viribus et officio singulari, referens in suo gradu aliquam perfectionem in Deo, in quo summe est omnis perfectio, immo qui ipse sua cujusque est perfectio, perficiens universa, in quo nihil perfectum est nisi ipsum. Sua enim cujusque rei summa est; pro cujusque capacitate liquor implens, ex eodem dolio propinatus. Omnia enim potant ex vino qui ex Deo fonte effluit, qui unus idemque equaliter inebriat omnia, attamen varie pro cujusque capacitate.

CAP. XI.

IN eodem Deo, quem modo lucem, modo liquorem vocamus, participantium illius bonitatis singulorum sunt et extant distinctius quasi personales proprietates; ut in uno jucunda varietas, et in vario solida sit unitas. Racio spirituum dividitur in substanciam, virtutem et actionem. Sunt enim ut valeant, et valent ut agant. Hac triplici conditione constant omnes spiritus, et propter eandem nomina communicant.

CAP. XII.

ITEM sacerdos humanæ ecclesiæ a Malachia nuncupatur angelus; quod est (ut ait Dionysius) ex imitatione angelorum nunciationeque veritatis, studioque et officio purgandi illuminandi et perficiendi eos qui ejus curæ committuntur. Ut enim supra diximus, ex Dionysii sententia, omnia sunt in omnibus sed in posterioribus degeneraciori nota, in hominibus degeneratissime. Attamen in his ipsis hominibus, presertim eorum qui meliores sunt, est angelorum imitacio tanta ut homines quoque jure videantur quodammodo angeli posse appellari; [ipsis hominibus aliquo modo est causa ex imitacione cur angeli appellentur.[1]] Quinimmo etiam Dii idem in sacris literis nominantur ex mutacione et relacione quoad possunt deitatis. In quod qui omni pietate cum angelis feruntur, simul cum angelis Dii appellantur. Quod autem angeli Dii vocantur, testatur illud Geneseos, dictum Jacob a viro luctatore: Si contra Deum fortis fuisti, quanto magis contra homines. Se Deum vocavit ille angelus. Et David: Rex magnus super omnes Deos. Quod autem homines; in Exodo dominus ad Moysen: Ecce constitui te deum Pharaoni. Et David: Ego dixi, Dii estis, et filii excelsi omnes. Quod, Salvator ipse apud Joannem docet, exponendum est de hominibus ad quos sermo Dei factus est. Concludamus ergo, ut res superne, ita nomina simul ad homines dirivari.

---

[1] Ejiciendam esse hanc sententiam ex margine C. apparet, quippe in cujus locum clausulam priorem substituerit auctor.

CAP. XV.

ANGELI docti vicissim docent, vertuntur in Deum, in se stant, deorsum infundunt. Hæc angelorum figuris et similitudinibus a theologis prophetis nobis indicantur, qui libentissime utuntur ignis imagine, cujus vires nobis cognitæ sunt illis simillimæ, quaque re celestes spiritus maxime nobis demonstrantur. Ex hoc ergo sensibili et tenebrarum mundo in primis ignis sumitur, ut, quæ aguntur in luminoso mundo illo angelorum doceatur; qui sua luce hic ignis lucem illam ipsam veram, quæ inaccessibilis est, multum imitatur. Item utuntur plurimum præstanti hominis natura, quia hæc est nobis cognatissima; ac, ab omnibus ejus partibus similitudines petentes, angelos quasi homines faciunt. Præterea ex multis aliis et variis rebus, his quæ nobis sunt familiares, significant hominibus illorum beatorum spirituum naturas, vires, actiones, proprietates, similitudinem, differentiam, simplicitatem, constanciam, stabilitatem, robor, obedientiam, ordinem, pulchritudinem, lumen, sapientiam, suavitatem, benignitatem, vigorem, celeritatem, subtilitatem, libertatem, presidentiam, potenciam, authoritatem, equitatem, gubernacionem, fecunditatem, fructum, vivificationem, sanctimoniam, religionem, cultum Dei, felicitatem, beatitudinem, regnum, abundanciam, copiam, divicias, claritatem, contemplacionem denique et gaudium. Quas quidem res sensas et translaciones undique et omni ex parte petiverunt theologi veteres, magni illi prophetæ, mira prudentia et charitate, ut simul ea via et racione et doceant homunciones quæ sunt Dei, et divinarum rerum majestatem conservent.

CAP. XVI.

DEUS, immensum bonum, intrinsecus imbuens omnino, extrinsecus infinite ambiens, lux ipsa est, in quo tenebræ non sunt ullæ. Quapropter, quando lucet in tenebris, tenebræ eum non comprehenderunt. Est id ipsum quoque absolutum in se a materia, loco, tempore, gradibus, causa.

Absolutum autem ut finem illum omnia appetunt quo perficiantur, a quo erant effecta omnia,[1] et medium per quod omnia pulchre disposita sunt; et finis denique a quo omnia consummatim perficiuntur. Hoc est quod Paulus ait in Epistola ad Romanos his verbis: Ex ipso et per ipsum et in ipso sunt omnia: ipsi gloria in secula seculorum. Quia ex se et ad suum exemplar et sui gracia efficit, disponit et perficit omnia. Quatenus efficit potenter, pater est; quatenus disponit sapienter, filius est; quatenus benigniter perficit, spiritus sanctus est. Hinc in rebus existencia, ordo et appetitus; hinc creata omnia et sunt, et pulchra sunt et bona. Hoc esse, pulchritudo, et bonitas tota in principio est, et illic quiddam unum, in quo omnia sunt idem; quod ipsum ob infinitam potenciam propagat in se intime sobolem infinitam, quod infinitum in infinito est. Hic eternus pulcher filius est eterni omnipotentis patris; inter quos necessario viget eternus et infinitus amor. Quæ tria, propter communem infinitatem et inter se equalia et simillima sunt, et substancia eorum unica et simplicissima est. In his non est fas homini aliter loqui quam tres personas, et unum Deum, principium, medium et finem omnium. In quibus, exceptis relacionibus, quicquid est singulis, est in omnibus. Pater enim potencia est sapiens et bona; filius sapientia potens et bona; spiritus sanctus bonitas, potens et sapiens. Ab illa trina unitate potenter, sapienter et bene conduntur universa; in quibus est similiter propagacio et amor, essencia, sensus et appeticio in universis; quæ omnia in se principio medio et fine constant; et sunt stabiliter in se, et splendent pulchre, et bene vigent[2] quidem in illo, a quo esse, speciem et bonitatem acceperunt. In illam ineffabilem trinitatem beatissimi illi spiritus, quos angelos vocamus, assidue suæ mentis oculos intendunt. Quorum omnes sane attente tres illas personas intuentur; sed diversi racione diversa; omnes tamen omnia et omnes rerum raciones contemplantur. Se-

---

[1] Post "omnia" interponenda sunt, ex C., "a quoque eodem omnia ad sui ipsius exemplar disponuntur. Principium ergo est, a quo omnia sunt:" quæ deinde subsequuntur "et medium," etc.

[2] Agunt.—C.

raphici quidem qui in finem propius et attencius intendunt, omnia amanter et suaviter in fine speculantur, et principium et medium, et potenciam Dei et sapientiam. Verum finem ipsum attentius quam reliqua contemplantur. Cherubici eciam finem cum Seraphicis, sed in fine magis medium: Throni in fine principium speculantur magis. Itaque hii tres ordines primæ hierarchiæ magis in finem bonum, et spiritum Dei sanctum contendunt. Verum in his qui vi finis et boni corripiuntur, ut circa Deum solum versentur, quanquam in illius finis consideracione Seraphici speculantes ipsum finem maxime flammæ et amores vocantur; Cherubici in fine medium et ordinem et pulchritudinem dicuntur scientes; throni in fine maxime principium et potenciam et stabilitatem, stantes nominantur; tamen tota illa tercia et summa hierarchia, quia terciam personam maxime intendit, in qua quisque quod suum est cernit maxime, iccirco si ad alias duas hierarchias comparetur, ita se habet tota ad illas ut in eadem se habet primus ordo ad reliquos duos ordines. Atque quanquam in illo sacro principatu sunt in fine et bonitate Dei amantes, sapientes et stantes, tamen tota illa trinitas ad alias hierarchias comparata potest certe et debet cogitari amans. Item secunda hierarchia, quæ tota in medium tendit, in medioque et ordine et sapientia conspicit omnia, quanquam trina et varia racione, unde in ea quoque tres ordines locantur, secunda illa, inquam, hierarchia, ad alias comparata, tota scientia potest vocitari. Postremo tercia, quæ tota precipue in principium fertur, in quo cernunt et venerantur omnia, sed propter diversam racionem in triplici ordine, hæc tota ad illas comparata jure quasi throni et sedentes possunt nominari. In secunda autem hierarchia qui sunt spiritus omnes, etsi mirantur omnia, tamen medium et exemplar, per quod fiunt omnia, ipsum propius et ut ita dicam libentius intuentur. Sed dominationes in illo medio finem, virtutes in medio medium; potestates in medio principium. Media hæc hierarchia omnia speculatur in medio; et comparata ad alias tota scientia potest dici: quæ versatur maxime in illa racione et sapiencia per quam ordine et pulchre conficiuntur universa. Tercia hierarchia, quam maxime dependet a principio, in qua sunt principatus in finem in principio intenti;

archangeli in medium in principio; angeli in principium in principio. Ita cujusque hierarchiæ ultimus ordo in principium tendit: angeli in ipsum principium; potestates principium in medio; throni principium in fine. Media hierarchia in medium, et in quaque hierarchia omnes medii in medium: ultimi in quaque in finem.

ITAQUE videtur prima hierarchia remocior a Deo in Dei potencia esse cujusque curare: media in Dei racione speciem cujusque: ultima illa suprema perfectionem. Verum in prima qui primi sunt ordinis, maxime esse; qui secundi, maxime speciem in esse; qui tercii, maximi perfectionem in esse cujusque. In media, qui primi ordinis, maxime esse in specie; qui secundi, maxime ipsam speciem, qui tercii, maxime perfectionem in specie. In tercia illa suprema, qui primi, maxime esse in perfectione; qui secundi, maxime speciem in perfectione; qui tercii maxime ipsam perfectionem. Sic angelorum ministerio sunt, formantur et complentur omnia.

IN condenda autem ecclesia Christi aliquandiu sub angelis ex hominibus qui purgentur, illuminentur et perficiantur sub Iesu Christo; in hoc opus sunt angeli ministratorii spiritus. Prima hierarchia purgat, et quasi regignit homines ut sint spe in Deo. Media revelat et illuminat, ut homines fide clareant Deo: Ultima inspirat amorem, ut charitate perficiantur homines Deo. Sed in prima hierarchia angeli maxime agunt ut constituantur purgati in spe; archangeli operantur lumen in spe et fidem; principatus charitatem in spe. In medio, potestates spem in fide; virtutes ipsam fidem; dominationes charitatem in fide. Throni vero in tercia, spem in charitate; cherubici fidem in charitate, seraphici ipsam charitatem, perfectricem omnium. Hæc quidem ad hunc modum triplex hierarchia tripliciter in trino Deo triplicem in hominibus Christianitatem, quæ fide spe et charitate constat, assidue operatur. Purgacionem, et puram simplicem et stabilem spem, in potentia Dei throni, in thronis deinde potestates, denique in istis angeli agunt sedulo; ut ex multitudine in simplicitatem, ex feda desperatione in puram spem Deo prodeat homo, et in ea firmiter stet, speque in potente Dei radio jam sit spiraliter in Deo et Christo. In Dei omniformi sapientia tum scientes illi cherubici spiritus, et in illis virtutes, et in istis archangeli, raciones rerum et pulchras verbi Dei veritates revelant, et revelantes illuminant jam sperantem hominem Deo in fide Iesu Christo, qui est ipsa racio et verbum et nuncius veritatis: in quo omnis enunciatio lucis est ordine ab angelis mediis in homines, ut jam in spem purgati credant illi Dei verbo. Judei videntur spem habuisse magis quam fidem, ante Christi adventum. Item Christiani sub ipso Christo vivente in terris magis fidem quam charitatem, qui spiritus sanctus[1] est. In bonitate denique, amore et spiritu sancto Dei, Seraphici spiritus, toti ardentes in ipso amore, et dominaciones, toti ardentes in sapientiam, et principatus denique, toti ardentes in potentia Dei, alii in aliis ordine, inferiores in superioribus et omnes in calore spiritus Dei, perspicue lucentes homines fide, solide et graviter et suaviter et perfecte complentur[2] amore Dei; ut purgati ab angelis, potestatibus, thronis; illuminati ab archangelis, virtutibus, cherubicis; postremo a principatibus dominationibus et seraphicis in spiritu Dei perficiantur.

		DEUS		
		Principium. Pater.	Medium. Filius.	Finis. Spiritus Sanctus.
DEUS	Bonus	Prima hierarchia.	Seraphici finem in fine / Cherubici medium in fine / Throni principium in fine	
	Sapiens	Secunda hierarchia.	Dominaciones finem in medio / Virtutes medium in medio / Potestates principium in medio	
	Unus	Tercia hierarchia.	Principatus finem in principio / Archangeli medium in principio / Angeli principium in medio[3]	Speculantur.
	Bonum	Primi cujusque hierarchiæ.	Seraphici finem in fine / Dominaciones finem in medio / Principatus finem in medio[3]	
	Verum	Secundi cujusque hierarchiæ.	Cherubici medium in fine / Virtutes medium in medio / Archangeli medium in principio	
	Unum	Tercii cujusque hierarchiæ.	Throni principium in fine / Potestates principium in medio / Angeli principium in principio	

---

[1] *Leg.* sancti. [2] *Leg.* complent. [3] *Leg.* in principio, quod exhibet C.

Deus.

Pater	Filius	Spiritus Sanctus
Potentia	Sapientia	Bonitas
Throni	Cherubichi	Seraphici
Potestates	Virtutes	Dominaciones
Angeli	Archangeli	Principatus
Spes	Fides	Charitas
Judei	Christiani sub Christo	Christiani post ascensionem sub Spiritu Sancto.

Deus

Pater	Filius	Spiritus Sanctus.
Primum	Secundum	Tercium
Principium	Medium	Finis
Ortus	Progressus	Consummacio
Potencia	Sapientia	Virtus
Unum	Pulchrum	Bonum
Simplex	Verum	Justum
Vita	Scientia	Actio
Capud	Corpus	Pedes
Mens	Racio	Rectitudo
Os	Verbum	Operatio
Homo	Manus	Digitus
Radix	Rami	Fructus
Longitudo	Latitudo	Profundum
Centrum	Radii	Circumferencia
Linea	Superficies	Corpus
Sol	Lux	Calor
Nox	Mane	Meridies
Hiems	Ver estas	Autumnus
Purgatio	Illuminatio	Perfectio
Puritas	Perspicuitas	Efficacia
Constantia	Splendor	Gloria
Diabolus	Caro	Mundus
Oratio	Jejunium	Elemosyna
Obedientia	Castitas	Paupertas
Spes	Fides	Charitas
Unitas	Veritas	Justicia
Penitencia	Baptismus	Eucharistia
Desperatio	Incredulitas	Odium

Mors	Tenebræ	Frigus
Cogitatio	Verbum	Opus
Initium	Incrementum	Complecio
Paciencia	Serenitas	Misericordia
Constancia	Venustas	Gracia
Fixio	Flos	Fructus
Radix	Calamus	Arista
Ignis	Lumen	Calor
Mens	Ratio	Voluntas
Infimum	Medium	Summum
Fundamentum	Edificium	Tectum
Consilium	Decretum	Executio
Bona animi	Corporis	Fortunæ

Ut sunt novem angelorum ordines, ita similiter hominum sunt in Deo per Christum et angelorum ministerio. Omnia in his in omnibus sunt. Siquidem sperant credunt et amant omnes Deum in Christo. Alioquin in hac triplici ecclesiastica hierarchia non est nec esse potest. In ultimo loco sunt maxime sperantes; secundi sunt credentes in spe; tercii sunt amantes in spe; quarti sunt sperantes in fide; quinti sunt maxime credentes; sexti sunt amantes in fide; septimi quasi throni sunt firmiter sperantes in charitate; octavi sunt credentes in amore; noni et supremi sunt toti maximeque amantes. Qui autem sunt sine spe fide et charitate, hi in omni sunt turbulentia, in frigore, tenebris et morte, apud quos nullus est ordo, sed error quidem sempiternus. Tamen turbulenciæ infelicitatis et miseriæ sunt gradus; secundum quos statue ex opposito sub diabolo principe tenebrarum, et sub ejus ministrantes satellites, qui turbulentissime in defectu et privacione omnis bonitatis degeneruntur[1] in novem teterrimas turmas: sub illis, inquam, statue in diabolica et perditissima militia novem turbas hominum, qui sub principe diabolo, sub vexillis mortis, in armis tenebrarum gladio impietatis et odii militant hii omnes, quisque sane miserrime in suum ipsius interitum sempiternum.

ANGELI omnisque spiritalis natura creata fuit simul cum natura corporea, teste Salomone. Inquit enim,

---

[1] Degeruntur—C.

Qui vivit in eternum creavit omnia sibi. Creati fuerunt illi spiritus empyrrei celi incolæ, quod supra fundamentum splendet ut ignis. Creati vero boni: sed magna pars propria voluntate non longe post, nephanda superbia volentes se exaltare, summo deciderunt in infimum. Salvator noster Iesus id testatus est, quando dixit: Videbam Sathanam sicut fulgur de celo cadentem. Item ille in veritate non stetit. Reliqua pars suspiciens Deum, partim suapte voluntate, partim gracia coadjutrice, felices in veritate permansere; non suis quidem meritis, sed gracia beatificati Deo. Contra Lucifer ille cum suis sequacibus non corruit dedignacione Dei, sed culpa ipsius propria. Incolunt miseri hi et perditi angeli hunc circa nos aerem crassum et caliginosum, exercitatores hominum, ne negligentia et desidia torpescant; miseriores aliquando post ultimum judicium futuri. Docet nos Paulus colluctaciones nos habere cum principibus et potestatibus aeris hujus. Assidue enim conantur reddere nos eorum similes, ut parem cum eis penam sensiamus. Sed in hominum tutelam dum hic vivitur, Dei misericordia angeli deputantur. Habet enim suum quisque angelum custodem et conservatorem sui, item eundem assiduum monitorem et stimulatorem ad bonum; alioquin infirmus homo nec bono valeret insistere, nec malo resistere. Opinio quorundam est, si laborantes profecerint, etiam beatitudine profecturos; quod vocant isti disputatores meritum accidentale. Omnibus angelis sumus curæ; sed impensiori cura consulunt nobis ii quibus tutoribus commendamur. Quamobrem rectissime faciunt qui suum angelum custodem quotidie aliqua precipua oratione colunt et adorant.

DEMONES, impuri spiritus, racionales, subtiles, invidi, humano generi nocere student, fallere cupiunt, sensus deludunt, hominum affectus inficiunt. Dormientes et vigilantes inquietant mundum et elementa turbant. Hipocritæ sæpe in lucis angelos se transformant; in Idolis Dei majestatem sibi arrogant; superbi imperium affectant. Bellum in homines, tum aperte eos oppugnantes, tum occulte eisdem insidiantes, continuo movent. Vincentes exultant, victi vero abeunt confusi, ita ut amplius in eodem et ad idem peccatum temptare non audeant. De his maleficis naturis conqueritur Davyd in suis hymnis incessanter; et quasi semper in periculo, implorat sibi opem, et demonibus illis dira imprecatur. Inquit enim in quodam psalmo: Complaceat tibi, Domine, ut eruas me: domine, ad adjuvandum me respice. Confundantur et revereantur simul qui quærunt animam meam. Convertantur et revereantur qui volunt mihi mala: ferant confestim confusionem suam. Item in alio: Deus in adjutorium meum intende; domine ad adjuvandum me respice. Confundantur et revereantur qui querunt animam meam. Quinimmo nihil aliud facit universis suis psalmis fere quam deprecari Deum in Christo, ut inter tot et tantos hostes victor evadat, salvusque in Deo fiat. Ad hoc periculosum bellum vocantur homines a Deo per Iesum Christum. Ad quod non temere nec inconsiderate eundum est, sed pensitandæ sunt vires prius, et providenda discrimina. Atque antequam fiat quisque Christianus, vel in Christianitate sacerdos et religiosus, prius secum consideret prudenter quid poterit; ne apertus hostis diabolus, si vincatur, durius et infelicius agat secum quam si subjectus Sathanæ mansisset tributarius. Ob id quidem causæ Iesus Christus, dux et imperator hujus belli, quum ad se commilitones vocaret (ut Lucas refert) quanquam velit omnes homines salvos fieri, tamen ut fugientes scillam in cheribdym non incidant, nec querentes salutem in majorem damnacionem corruant, admonuit turbas, caveant et considerate prospiciant quid essent in se suscepturi; volens magis ut vivant servi diabolo, quam hostes bello occidantur; utque condemnentur potius condemnatione minore quam majore. Itaque illis dixit: Quis rex, iturus committere bellum adversus alium regem, non sedens prius cogitat si possit cum decem milibus occurrere ei qui cum viginti milibus venit ad se? Alioquin adhuc illo longe agente, legationem mittens, rogat ea quæ pacis sunt. Quando professi sumus aliquam vitam meliorem in Christo, tunc et copiosiori et instructiori exercitu se parat diabolus, ut nos aggrediatur et infestet; qui si vicerit rebelles hic tyrannus atrocius discruciabit; ut, quemadmodum Paulus scribit ad hebreos: Melius esset non cognoscere viam justiciæ, quam retrorsum converti. Sunt autem demones natura subtiles, acuta acie naturalia contemplantes, longo experimento et usu callidi, atque futurorum divinatores, revelationum superiorum etiam aliquando plurimum sapientes. Sed ipsi mali in malum omnibus utuntur, hominum interitus sempiternos ante omnia machinantur; invidi non ferentes gloriam quæ est in Christo hominibus futura. Suadent malum sub speciem boni; et si quando aliquid boni suadeant, id quoque ad malum faciunt. Dissuadent semper verum bonum, et si quando malum dissuaserint, id est ut in majus malum inducant. Corpus ledunt aliquando et membra defringunt, et morbos inferunt; sensibus vanas formulas opponunt, mentem falsis imaginibus obruunt. Quocirca Petrus ad nos scripsit: Sobrie estote et vigilate: quia adversarius vester diabolus tanquam leo rugiens circuit, querens quem devoret. Divini gracia et adjumento angelorum, precibus et expiacionibus continuis, possimus et resistere diabolo, et eundem superare; maxime imitacione ducis nostri Christi, qui temptatus vicit, et diaboli potentiam fregit.

CAELESTIS HIERARCHIÆ FINIS.

IOANNES COLET IN ECCLESIASTICAM DIVI DIONISII HIERARCHIAM.

Cap. I.

SACRA scriptura nos edocet, humanum sacerdotium ex alto divinam habere in se et sapientiam et actionem. In sacerdotio humano sunt quidem omnes qui in Christo Deo consecrantur. Sacrarum scripturarum sensus penitus spiritalis est, quem totum suis indicavit Iesus. Unde, Apostolorum institutis, sacrificia, ritus, ceremoniæ[1] in ecclesia, una cum ea, adolevisse credendum est. Post resurrectionem suam Iesus, quid velint scripturæ ad condicionem et statum novæ ecclesiæ in ipso, ipse prodibit.[2] Sensus ergo ille spiritalis, qui ut intelligatur eget spiritu prophetali, sapiencia et racio est totius fabricatæ ecclesiæ nostræ Christianæ. De Christo enim Moyses locutus est: quod etiam Leo papa, gravis author qui apostolica gubernacula tenuit, testatus est, in quodam sermone de Jejunio Penthecostes, hisce verbis: "Dubitandum non est," inquit, "dilectissimi, omnem observanciam Christianam erudicionis esse divinæ, et quicquid ab ecclesia in consuetudinem est devotione receptum, de tradicione apostolica et de sancti Spiritus prodire doctrina: qui nunc quoque cordibus fidelium suis præsidet institutis, ut ea omnes et obedienter custodiant, et sapienter intelligant." Hæc Leo ille primus, qui quadringentis et quinquaginta annis post Christum in pontificali throno sedit. De qua illustratione scripturarum non tam verbis quam factis, non tam doctrina et scriptis quam re, institucione et jussu apostolorum, scripturus divus Dionysius ad Thimo-

---

[1] *Leg.* ceremonias.   [2] *Leg.* prodidit.

theum, primum eum graviter et multis adjurat, ut sacrorum
raciones et sancta sanctorum ac mysteria Dei divinique
cultus non prodat in vulgus nepharie nec communicet, nisi
cum sanctissimis et sui similibus; memor Iesu Christi illius
precepti: Non dabitis sanctum canibus, nec margaritas
porcis: sed sancte et sobrie et seclusim custodiat omnia, et
in suæ mentis archano cum omni amore et reverencia condat
colatque religiosissime: imitatus illum Iesum, omnis sacerdotii et sacrorum authorem, qui suos tantum discipulos,
et hoc seorsum, misteria docuit, et illos quoque non omnia,
qui nondum erant perfecti et spiritales, nec poterant omnia
portare. Idem nunc lux illa ineffabilis in dextra patris et
clarius et plenius illucet angelis, naturis longe hominibus
purgatioribus, illisque revelat copiosius, ac deinde tunc per
illos talibus hominibus qui, sevocati et separati a corpore
altius extant, et naturæ angelicæ propius accedunt, purgati
illuminati et perfecti. In quo genere eximius ille erat
Joannes Zebedei filius, qui revelante angelo in die dominica
cernebat multa, quæ septem ecclesiis descripsit: quæ ut
recte intelligantur, eodem angelo revelatore sane egent;
quæ ille scriba Dei Apocalypsim vocavit. Per angelos
revelacio est hominibus sub honestate figurarum, ut * * * *
agnitio gradus et devotionis Deo per quæque homines con-
stituuntur in alio atque alio esse in Christo, ut in ipso aliter
atque aliter illuminentur, perficianturque illuminati. In
quibus omnibus in Christo vere una est quodammodo racio,
et (ut loquitur Dionysius) intensio, omnesque idem nituntur
agere pro viribus graciæ. Divisiones enim graciarum sunt
multæ, unus spiritus; unicuique datur manifestacio spiritus
ad utilitatem, alius quidem sic, alius quidem sic. Omnium
quidem conatus est ut divinis racionibus perficiantur, assimu-
lenturque Deo quam maxime fieri potest. Quod qui maxime
assequitur, is pontifex est et jure primum locum tenet ministerii, deinceps ut quod acceperit transfundat; qui quo major
est, eo inserviat pluribus charitatis officio et ministrandi.
Tum secundo id peragunt et accepta transfundunt in tercios
qui secundi sunt. Atque ita deinde pergit, procedit ve[ri]-
ficacio hominum in Christo, omnibus sursum contendentibus,
et quod superne exhauserunt tradentibus inferioribus, ut

desiderio et amore Dei et proximi in Christo perfecta membra sint; amore quidem Dei accipientes, amore etiam proximi dantes; ut utrinque amore efficti justi, ministri sint divinæ graciæ, a quo sunt omnia in Christo; in quo tam promptus debet esse quisque ut det omnia quod acceperit, ut videatur accepisse ob nullam aliam causam nisi ut daret; ut in datione declaretur acceptio, et in amore proximi amor Dei; quem tunc declaramus nos amare (ut Joannes docet in Epistola) si proximum amemus. Si quis dixerit quod diligit Deum, et fratrem suum odit, mendax est. In hac vicissitudinaria charitate est ordo, munus et officium in ecclesia, ac in ea tota ecclesiastica hierarchia consistit in amore Dei et proximi, in accepto et dato, in imitacione Iesu capitis, qui ipsa est charitas, in studio cujusque sanctificandi se charitatis igne, ut deinde sanctificet, ut sanctificandi officio tota ecclesia imitetur Iesum, ut ei aliquando omnino similes fiant; ut scribit Johannes: Omnes qui habent hanc spem in eo, santificant se sicut ille sanctus est. Et idem ait: Qui dicit se in illo manere, debet, sicut ille ambulavit, et ipse ambulare. Ille Iesus in hac ecclesiastica chorea incepit tripudium, ut omnes sertim manibus eum junctis sequantur. Ille erat plenitudo justiciæ, ut omnes in illo ipsius justitiam coimitentur, quæ consistit in datione et amore quod ex amore acceperis. Quid enim aliud est in angelis perfectionis, quam datio accepti? In qua datione magis referunt Deum quam acceptione. Nam in acceptione perfectio nulla est. Deus enim nihil accipit. Dat autem Deus maxime, et datione refertur maxime. Quapropter Paulus dicit beatius esse dare quam accipere. In Christo itaque in quo sunt omnia, qui racio est summa et diffinitio ordinis et hierarchiæ nostræ, qui nihil accepit a nobis, qui dat omnia, qui instituit nos in cursu veritatis, qui extulit nos super legem Moysaicam in lucem evangelii et revelacionis, qui fide fecit nos sapere et ex fide agere, qui spiritu suo produxit nos in melius, ut lege spiritus beatissimos illos spiritus recte imitemur, in cujus virtute incipimus esse spiritales, ut perfecti aliquando spiritus simus, quorum supra celestem vitam beatissimam quia conamur referre, ideo Paulus dixit nostram conversationem esse in celis. In hoc tamen bene felici statu in Iesu Christo, quia adhuc omnes sumus homines visibiles, certe natura hæc nostra nova, vires et actiones substratis quibusdam sensibilibus signis et indicantur utiliter et firmantur, ut monumenta sint nobis, et invitamenta ad ea quæ non videntur. Nam quamdiu nos imaginarii sumus, et per speculum videmus in enigmate, nulla nostra institutio, effictio, formacio, actio, imitacioque spirituum carere corporalibus imaginibus potest. Nam quamdiu nos corporei sumus, oportet sacramenta nostra et ecclesiastica nostra racio sit nonnihil corporea. Sub Moyse legalis hierarchia erat tota corporea et imaginaria : sub Christo (in quo nunc imitamur veritatem spirituum) constituta est ecclesiastica hierarchia, partim corporea partim spiritalis. In triumphanti vero illa hierarchia tota erit spiritalis, quando animalia nostra corpora tota erunt translata in corpora spiritalia. Ex his tunc illicibus graciæ et signaculis erumpemus in faciem et veritatem; ut cum angelis tunc veri nos et vere veritatem ipsam facie ad faciem videamus. Omnes ad unum contendere debent, et in formam illius, quoad maxime possunt. Unum vero ecclesiæ nostræ est Iesus bravium, quo currimus omnes, ut eum totum comprehendamus; quem quisque in se referre debet, et olere et sapere ipsum, tametsi non omnes eodem modo et equaliter certe, sed quisque, quatenus potest, et datum est unicuique, sicut Deus divisit mensuram fidei, et quisque, ut arbitratur se posse, nitatur referre id quod capud est et unum. Quod totum etsi non referat in summo gradu, referat tamen totum gradu quam alto potest; ne videatur nolle quantum potest, et ita abuti gracia sua, quæ data est cuique ad manifestationem spiritus; neve videatur sponte languere, quum valere potest; cujusmodi voluntaria egrotacio damnabilis est. Oblitterat enim imaginem nepharie, qui non repræsentat id quatenus percutitur. Siquidem omnes sumus ad unum sigillum signati, et unius regis character, quasi numisma illius, accepimus; ut unum, unde pendeant omnia, referamus; pro racione cujus signi et impressionis agendum est. In quo illo primo uno qui est Iesus Christus, in quo consignati sumus, figura et charactere ipsius, ut Jesuitæ simus in ipso, consignamur illi in sacerdotium consecrati in illo, ut Deo in ipso sacerdotes simus, ut sacrificemus nos Deo in illo, offeramusque hostiam sanctam, sicuti ille obtulit, qui pro nobis, ut scribit Petrus, mortuus erat, ut nos sequamur vestigia ejus: in quo si sumus, ut Johannes testatur, debemus, sicut ille ambulavit, et nos ambulare: holocaustum in Christo Deo quisque se præbeat, ut totus ardeat charitate in ara patibuli. In hoc cognoscimus charitatem Dei, quoniam ille animam suam pro nobis posuit; et nos debemus pro fratribus animas ponere.—Sed jam de ecclesiastica hierarchia disseramus.

OMNIS hierarchia sacrorum racio et comprehensio est. In christiana hierarchia pontificale munus et officium est, ut in se sacra contineat omnia, omniaque possideat. Est enim pontifex ipsum sacramentum, ipsaque in se comprehensio omnium, quæ deinceps in ecclesia sequuntur; qui scit et refert plene et clare totum in se sacerdotium, ut non sit in quoquam inferiori, quod a Deo datum est, quod non in Christo pontifice et solidius et clarius idem et modo sit etiam perfectiore: quin per ipsum in omnes ecclesiæ ordines omnia spiritalia et divina transfundi debeant; a quo non proficiscatur quippiam in ecclesia, quod non in pontifice prius contineatur, nec extet in quoquam sub pontifice quod sit laudabile et divinum, quod ab illo non agnoscatur profectum. Qui quidem si careat quod in quopiam est inferiori quod a Deo procedit, cujusmodi est sanctitas, sapientia, justicia, is profecto non est ille qui pontificalem sedem occupet. Hierarchiæ nostræ creator et conditor idem est ille unus omnipotentissimus Iesus. Pater per illum cum Spiritu sancto, adoranda illa Trinitas, pro bonitate sua, causa est certe ut sit hæc hierarchia humana militans sub duce Christo, sub vexillo veritatis, spiritalibus armis, et etiam ut bene et perfecte sit. Voluit enim bonus Deus salvetur homo; quod quidem esse non potest certe nisi homines deificentur, reformenturque in divinum statum, diique fiant assimilati Deo, ut Deum referant. Illuc enim in finem enixe et impensissime tendunt omnia, ut in divinam formam effigiantur. Ad eum finem omnes vocati in Christum Deo consecrantur, ut hic dum vivant Deum referant quatenus possunt. Quatenus autem homines possunt, Iesus Deus et homo docuit, qui voluit homo fieri, ut divinam in hominibus vivendi formam demonstret. Ad cujus similitudinem omnes in eo contendere debent. Nam qui dicit se in eo manere, debet, sicut ille ambulavit, et ipse ambulare. Ille capud est et celestis hierarchiæ et humanæ, in quo habuit terra quod imitetur, et nunc in celo habent angeli quoque quod imitentur; cujus amore ardere quisque debet; ut in illum latus nihil aliud aspectet quam ipsum, in nullam aliam partem vertat oculos, nihil omnino retrospiciat; sed (ut scribit Paulus de seipso ad Phillippenses), Quæ retro sunt obliviscens, ad ea quæ sunt priora extendens se ac persequens, ad destinatum bravium supernæ vocacionis in Christo Iesu, ut imitando illum eundem lucretur, configuratus morti ejus, ut resurgens illi glorioso configuretur; ut tandem moriens comprehendat, in quo comprehensus est a Iesu in illum; ut in unicam racionem suæ perfectionis manibus pedibusque ferantur omnes qui sunt in ipso; ut formati ab ipso referant ipsum eo quo meliori gradu possunt, alti assidue, nutriti, refecti et recreati ipso quotidie, translati a claritate in claritatem, donec penitus transformentur in ipsum. In illum, inquam, ferantur, avide charitate flagrantes, ut in ipso quasi holocausta et incensa bene redolentia Deo charitatis igne libentur et sacrificentur; fuga autem sit ab his inferioribus tam acris et solicita, ut semper a tergo hostes et mortem sibi instare putet; veritatem signi quo se dirigit et semper summum sibi proponat, assurgat, accurrat, advolet in ipsum, apprehendat, deglutiat, alatur ipso, et in ipsum Christum in Deo penitus transferatur. Hæc salutaris contencio debet esse sane cujusque in ecclesia, ut in omnibus omnes appareant, resonent, oleant, sapiant et agant Christum. Deus deificat, se impartiens angelis directe et simpliciter, hominibus indirecte et multiplici racione simulacrorum, quibus sacra scriptura plena est (quam vocat Dionysius substanciam sacerdotii nostri), vetus testamentum maxime; cui adjectum novum, conscriptum ab evangelistis et apostolis, talibus similitudinibus non caret. Qui libri tempore Dionysii authoritate tunc primæ ecclesiæ in sanctis et canonicis scriptis relati fuerint, et omni reverentia approbati. His accessit secretior quædam racio sapientiæ non mandata literis ab apostolis, sed animis et pectoribus eorum sancte et religiose servata, quæ illi didicerunt a Iesu Christo digni; qui deinceps non nisi dignis et similibus sui tradiderunt, adjurantes eos, ut literis non commendant ea, ne divina vilescant, et sancta dentur canibus, ac porcis margaritæ. Sublimitas mentis Johannis quod in illo genere cernebat, ita adumbravit suis figuris, ut nemo fere intelligat nisi ipse, nisi eodem prophetali spiritu agitetur. Instituciones etiam celebratæ in ecclesia et ab ipsis apostolis usque ad nos dirivatæ, non erant ab illis traditæ literis, sed actionibus plebeiorum commendatæ, quarum raciones tenuerunt solum primarii homines in ecclesia; quas non indicaverunt quidem nisi illis [quos] agnoverunt purgatiores, et ad pontificalem dignitatem promotos, qui illi nudas rerum rationes et sacramentorum intellexerunt. Consilio apostolorum factum fuit, ut eadem quadam racione imaginaria plebeiis propinarentur; ut rudes bibant et alantur crassiori. Nam, ut ait Paulus, non in omnibus est sciencia. Sanctus panis, salvatoris testimonio, non est dandus canibus. Ex semela sinceritatis panis sacerdotum tantum conficitur. Quo autem pascantur plebeii oportet aliquid furferis habeat imaginum et simulachrorum, ne ipsa veritate vel nimium perstringantur oculi eorum, vel illi in vanas cogitaciones concitentur. Hinc sacramenta et ceremoniæ, vel expiantes vel illuminantes vel perficientes ab ipsis apostolis optima racione et pulcherrimis simulachris descripta, plebeiis sunt instituta. Raciones autem eorum non literis sed sanctorum pontificum mentibus commendatæ et retentæ fuerint, ut, sicut in plebe signa succedant, ita in mentibus pontificum succedant raciones; quas eruere tandem plurimos post annos conatus est Gulielmus Minatensis episcopus; in quo studio vaticinatur et divinat ut potest, non aliter atque illi qui dicunt quid Joannis Apocalipsim significat. In omnibus ejusmodi, vel scriptis tanta crassitate signorum, vel mori et usui commendatis, opus est aut revelatore cui revelatum fuit, aut spiritu prophetali eodem a quo instituta fuerint, ut is indicet; alioquin humana acies hebescat necesse est. Sed quæcunque sunt in ecclesia in célebri usu, divinarum racionum symbola et signacula, ea ab apostolis instituta fuisse credendum est; quorum raciones docti a Deo ipso tenuerunt, et (ut verbis Dionysii utar) visibilibus signis celestia sacramenta texerunt, locantes apud rudiores simplex in multiplici, spiritalia in corporalibus, divina in humanis, remota in propinquis, extranea in familiaribus; de quibus quum parum scripserunt in principio, maximam partem memoriis hominum commendarunt. Nam ut profecti sunt evangelizantes et nunciantes Christum, quos nacti sunt et invenerunt credere voluisse, ulteriori doctrina quatenus visum erat effingentes, eos digesserunt ordine, prepositis ecclesiæ illi presbiteris senioribusque, quibus juniores obediant, relictis etiam obsignacionibus quibusdam sacramentalibus in verbis et signis congruis, quæ essent populo quædam quasi sustentacula et adminicula et oportuna monimenta altioris et simplicioris veritatis, quibus vulgus Christianum contineatur in religione, et religio a prophanis tutaretur. Pontifices autem in ipsam lucem tracti sunt, qui signorum veritates tenent; plebs vero coloratur Christiana; Judaica autem illa adumbrabatur. In Christiana religione pontifex Dionysius calluit mysteria sacramentorum, quæ scripturus ad Timotheum adjurat eum ut ea non communicet nisi sanctis et similibus sui doctis et bonis viris pontificiis, ea lege ut illi quoque [non] nisi talibus communicent, ne sancta (contra præceptum evangelicum) dentur canibus, et porcis margaritæ.

CAP. II. 1.

De Baptismo.

NIHIL vult aliud nostra Christianitas nisi ut Deo assimulemur. Estote perfecti, inquit Salvator, sicut pater vester perfectus est in celis. Assimulamur autem operantes et efficientes quod præcipit ille. Assimulabimur plane si illum amaverimus: amabimus quidem si ejus mandata servaverimus. Si quis diligit me, sermonem meum servat. Amor est principium omnium. Ex amore credis, ex fide speras. Antecedit amor fidem, spes subsequitur. Ut Policarpus scribit ad Philippenses: Amore regignimur in novum

esse spiritale in Deo. Amati a Deo renascimur in illo
fideles et sperantes, ut in Christo clamemus Abba, Pater.
Primum oportet regignitus sis in Deo, ut deinde adolescas
in melius. Spiritu Dei regignimur in Deum, qui calefaciens
expurgat nos, ut credamus Christo et speremus in eo. Ex
amore quum credimus et speramus credita, renascimur filii
Dei: hic baptismus est spiritu et igne. Hæc spiritalis racio
adumbratur imaginibus et significatur, ut spiritus incorpo-
retur ab eis et corpora spiritificentur ab illis; quibus signis
sumus admoniti ut memores simus divinæ regeneracionis,
qua non ex sanguinibus neque ex voluntate carnis, neque ex
voluntate viri, sed ex Deo nati sumus; ut cogitemus vivendum esse non secundum hominem sed secundum Deum
patrem, in cujus domo sumus, sumusque non ex mundo sed
ex Deo, vivamusque in hoc mundo non ut placeamus hominibus, sed Deo. Quid enim aliud vult nova nostra generatio quam ut, qui eramus, non simus? Nonne est generatio unius corruptio alterius? Nonne regignimur ut moriamur mundo et hominibus, et vivamus Deo? ut in domo
Dei conversatio nostra sit in celis, in mundo non alimentis
et, quibus tegamur, his contenti simus. Hanc perfectionem
novæ vitæ, in quam regignimur a spiritu Dei, apostoli voluerunt imaginibus significari; ut per imagines accedant
homines ad veritatem, et veritas per easdem descendat in
homines, ut imagines et sacramenta sint media quædam in
veritatem, et homines verificandos a spiritu veritatis.

CAP. II. 2.

De Baptismo.

QUUM homines erant dissimiles Deo omnino et sui
similes, voluit bonus Deus similis esse homini, ut
homines Dei similes efficeret. Verbum caro factum est et
habitavit in nobis. Qui erat in forma Dei, semet ipsum
exinanivit, formam servi suscipiens, in similitudinem hominum factus, et habitu inventus ut homo, humiliavit semetipsum, factus obediens usque ad mortem, mortem autem

crucis. Qui non noverat peccatum, pro nobis peccatum fecit, ut nos efficeremur justicia Dei in ipso. Hic erat eternus Dei filius, quem pater[mi]ttens in similitudinem carnis peccati, de peccato, damnavit peccatum in carne; ut justificatio legis impleretur in nobis qui non secundum carnem ambulamus, sed secundum spiritum, in agnitione et cultu veri Dei. Illius vicem in terris passim agunt pontifices, in illoque agunt quod egit ipse, ac pari affectu purgacionem et illuminationem hominum ac salutem, assidua veritatis nunciatione irradiacioneque evangelii moliuntur, uti molitus est ille. Paulus ait: Deus erat in Christo mundum reconcilians sibi, non reputans illis delicta ipsorum; et posuit in nobis verbum reconciliationis. Pro Christo ergo legacione fungimur. Agentes vicem Christi ignem flant, quem Christus venit mittere in terram, ut eum amplificent. Ignem, inquit apud Lucam, veni mittere in terram, et quid volo nisi ut accendatur? Baptisma habeo baptizari, et quomodo coarctor donec perficiatur? Baptizavit ille, Joannis testimonio, spiritu et igne. Ignis enim purgat, illuminat et perficit. Ignis ille spiritalis hæc facit in animis hominum. Ut hoc salutare incendium augeant in silva hominum, ministri et vicarii sunt Iesu pontifices, qui succensionem hominum in Deo quærunt. Hic autem ignis sane est sanctus amor Dei, quem amabiles pontifices dirivant in mundum, in Deo ipsi amantes homines, ut ii deinde Deum redament, amoreque Dei regeniti in Deo vivant, credentes filio misso, et omnem spem ponentes in Deo. Amor enim principium gignendi est; et sanctus amor sanctitatis, et Dei amor deitatis. Hujus autem bonitatis, misericordiæ, amoris et pietatis Dei, nuncius erat ejusdem amabilis filius Iesus Christus, qui primum amorem sapienter deduxit in homines, ut eo regeniti patrem secum celestem redament. Qui agnoscunt, admittunt, audiunt et recipiunt magni consilii angelum Iesum, dedit eis potestatem filios Dei fieri; ut nati ex hominibus, jam credentes Christo, feliciter renascantur filii Dei. Ille dum vixit mortalis in carne pontificatum agit ipse, re officium edocens. Et tum salus erat in credendo illi præsenti. Quum vero, ostensa pontificis forma, bonus et paciens sacerdos ipse se obtulit Deo sacrificium propiciatorium, tunc cepit par salus esse eis qui crediderunt illis qui vicariam operam Iesu præstiterunt, qui loco Iesu eundem nunciant, sicut ille seipsum nunciavit. Non enim prædicamus, inquit Paulus, nosmet ipsos vobis, sed Iesum Christum, dominum nostrum; nos autem servos vestros per Iesum. Ideo salvator, ut refert Lucas, illis dixit quos misit evangelisatum: Qui vos audit me audit, et qui vos spernit, me spernit. Qui me spernit, spernit eum qui misit me. Erat enim Deus in Christo, et Christus in apostolis, in apostolorumque successoribus, ad reconciliationem mundi Deo. Agit ergo pontifex quisque in sua ecclesia (beatus Ignatius martir testatus est in sua epistola ad Mag[nesi]anos) personam Dei et Christi; cui jubet obediant omnes ut Domino ipso. Sub pontifice sacerdotes apostolorum locum tenent. Sub his diaconi sunt ministri populo fideli. Episcopi officium est, Christi instar, acceptam veritatem constanter et assidue evangelizare. Est enim inter Deum et homines quasi medius angelus, qui divina, ut Christus, denunciet hominibus, ut, qualem eum Deus effecerit, ejusmodi et tales alios homines efficiat; ut quemadmodum ille Deum, ita alii deinceps ipsum imitentur; qui incessanter clamet illud apostolicum: Imitamini me, sicut ego Christum. Imitacio enim et profectio in similitudinem Dei qui est in Christo Iesu est vita hominis super terram. Pontifex, in se Christi formam præ se ferens, et prædicans et exhortans et admonens omnes ut velint se in illam formam effingi, ut similes Christo salvi sint illo, aliquos permoveat necesse est propter vim divini sermonis; qui (ut scribit Paulus ad Hebreos) vivus est et efficax et penetrabilior omni gladio ancipiti, pertingens usque ad divisionem animæ et spiritus, compagum quoque ac medullarum, et discretor cogitacionum ac intencionum cordis. Qui vero agitur spirituali Dei radio, qui commeat cum verbo Dei, is incipit spiritu regigni in filium Dei. Nam penitere incipit actæ vitæ sine Deo; etenim primus sancti spiritus effectus penitencia est vitæ illius quæ aboletur, ac depositio ejusdem et abjectio in perpertuum. Hinc clamitavit Joannes ille precursor: Penitentiam agite. Idem deinde Christus et magnificentius et sonantius acclamavit hominibus: Penitentiam agite; appropinquavit enim regnum celorum. Cujus enim non penitet præteriti mali, is futurum bonum nequit velle. Et qui, cujus penitet, non deposuit, is quod velit melius non potest induere. Qui vult mutare vestem, exuat se oportet, ut induat, et abolere in se vetustatem omnem, ut novitatem oleat. Quod prædicatur a pontifice novum est, et abraso veteri odore penitus nova vasa exposcit, ne, instar novi vini, immissum in vasa vetera, ea derumpat et ipsum effluat. Qui vult nova et immaculata tunica, quam manus et digitus Dei contexuit, decore incedere in Christo, veterem et sordidam vestem mortalitatis, quam homo sibi confecit, exutam omnino et totam abjectam oportet habeat. Nemo enim mittit commissuram panni rudis in vestimentum vetus; vel, ut Marcus loquitur, Nemo assumentum panni rudis assuit vestimento veteri. Etenim, ut addit Lucas, veteri non convenit commissura nova. Ad immortalitatem si eat homo, oportet nihil agat nisi quod spectet ad immortalitatem. Abjiciat tenebrarum opera, et induat arma lucis; sequatur pontificem ducem; sit miles sacramento ascriptus in exercitu Christiano. Quum excesserit e mundo insignitus cruce Christi, profiteatur pugnam cum hostibus veritatis, cum principe tenebrarum. Non est, ut scribit apostolus ad Ephesios, nobis colluctacio adversus carnem et sanguinem; (id est, contra homines, quorum salus quærenda est, non mors. Nolo mortem peccatoris, dicit Dominus in Ezechieli, sed ut convertatur et vivat) sed colluctacio nostra est adversus principes et potestates, adversus mundi rectores tenebrarum harum, contra spiritalia nequiciæ in celestibus. Quod bellum qui indicat hosti lucis, amore præmii quod victoribus proponitur, oportet humiliter et magno animo accedat ad ecclesiam, et roget aliquem ut ad ducem exercitus (id est pontificem) ducatur, ut militari sacramento in Christo astringatur in pugnam in ipso, profiteaturque se hostem mundi, et socium et servum et militem Christi; cujus sacramento juratus (vocat Paulus ad quos scribit suos commilitones), petat arma spiritalia, petat institui in legittima pugna. Is tum, quisquis sit ad quem talis divini spiritus ductu venit, (nemo enim, inquit Salvator, venit nisi tractus; et ad prædicationem Pauli in Antiochia Pisidiæ, ut scribit Lucas, crediderunt quotquot erant præordinati ad vitam eternam) —is, inquam, adquem præordinatus et tractus in veram ecclesiam venit, quum rogatur ab eodem ut ipsum ducat ad pontificem, ut in numero bellantum in Christo Iesu admittatur, profecto est ejus qui audit hominis votum, ut tametsi nihil magis cupit quam ut quamplurimi fideles sint, in Christoque militiam spiritalem suscipiant, tamen in principio animadvertens et colligens secum, quanta est res professio miliciæ et Christiani nominis, quantaque etiam est humana imbecillitas, exhorrescat secum et timeat homini illi, ne temere in se suscipiat plusquam præstare possit. Male enim agitur cum iis qui non militant in Christo Iesu. Verum multo pejus cum eis agitur, et mille modis infeliciores sunt, qui pro imposita persona non agunt, qui languent, qui frigent, qui locum deserunt, qui illuc unde venerint dilabuntur. Tunc, ut ait salvator apud Matheum, novissima hominis illius fiunt pejora prioribus. Ut in secunda est Petri epistola, Si refugientes coinquinationes mundi in cognitione domini nostri et salvatoris Iesu Christi, his rursus implicati superantur, facta sunt eis posteriora deteriora prioribus. Melius enim illis esset non cognoscere viam justiciæ, quam post agnitionem retrorsum converti ab eo quod illis traditum est sancto mandato. Contingit enim illis illud veri proverbii: Canis reversus ad suum vomitum, et sus lota in volutabro luti. Erat quidem in more, et consueverunt illi omnes qui introduxerint aliquem in ecclesiam Christi in celestem militiam in templum Dei primum hesitabundi secum exhorrescere: introduxerunt tamen postremo bona fide et spe in Deo simul multis fusis precibus, ut res bene succedat, et homini illi, qui voluit et cupivit Christianis sacris initiari, omnia bene et feliciter eveniant. Pontifex autem letabundus secum de lucro in Christo, Deo gracias agit, et una cum reliquo sacerdotio hymnos canit festiviter. Atque tum rogante pontifice quidnam velit? introductus respondet ille, detestans viam qua deliravit, se in semita justiciæ, in calle veritatis, institui velle; deplorat statum pristinum, desiderat novum Christi Iesu. Quam veram penitentiam agnoscens pontifex, et simplicem voluntatem approbans, asseverat ei in primis, si velit iter capere in Deum, illuc eum totum et penitus conferre oportere, purga-

P

tum omnino et perfectum. Tum exponens quæ sit recta vivendi racio, et via quam ingrediatur, ac deinde interrogans velitne libens et sponte eam subire, tum quum viderit hominem se totum in eam partem offerre, imposita manu ex more signatum quando mandavit sacerdotibus, ut ejus nomen in Christianorum cathalogo ascribant, et qui introduxerit etiam (quem Dionysius vocat succeptorem; eum, arbitror quem nunc apud nos deum patrem) hominem sacerdotibus et ministris exuendum statim tradit. Exutum et nudum ferme versus occidentem locant. Jubent ut ter exflet Sathanam, ac ore, vultu, spiritu, manibus, omnium diaboli abrenunciationem perpetuam profiteatur, denique seipsum penitus abrenunciet. Quod qui fecerit, qui efflaverit Sathanam, et ejus omnia renunciaverit, abnegaveritque denique semetipsum (juxta illud salvatoris, qui dixit omnibus suis, ut Lucas refert, Si quis vult venire post me, abneget semetipsum, et tollat crucem suam, et sequatur me) tunc hominem vertunt in orientem, et jubent tum mente tum verbis Christum ter et quæ sunt Christi profiteatur. Quem sic facientem benedicit pontifex, et precibus eum Deo commendat, manibus iterum in caput impositis. Tum, quod reliquum est tegumenti, detracto, quum ter signo crucis pontifex eum sacro oleo insigniverit, tunc totum reliquum hominem sacerdotibus deungendum tradit. Ipse pontifex interea, quum aquam, adoptionis matrem, sanctificavit more instituto ab apostolis et ritu legittimo, adductum hominem ad manus, recitato nomine ejus ex codice, ac sacerdotibus ejus nomen acclamantibus, invocans trinitatem, ter hominem aquis perfundit et obruit, ut ter emergat. Emersum autem et jam editum in lucem, quasi renatum Deo, induunt nova et candida veste; indutum ad pontificem reducunt; reductum iterum unguento insignit pontifex, et sacræ communionis participem facit, ut in corpore jam mistico ad Christum pergat indies et progrediatur in anterius, ut in suscepto itinere et habitu professo piger non judicetur. Hic erat mos et ritus baptismatis lavachrique regenerationis in prima ecclesia institutus a sanctis apostolis, quo excellentius baptisma interioris hominis significatur. Quæ forma plurimum differt a nostra qua hac ætate utimur; de quo miror sane quamobrem in una et vetustissima religione tam dispar sit ritus sacrorum; quum videamur studiosiores esse debere in conservandis nostris, quam Hebrei in suis, quanto nostra sunt, quam quæ illorum, perfectiora. Ut enim ad Ephesios scribit Paulus, Unus dominus, una fides, unum baptisma, unum corpus est: ita similiter certe unus modus et ritus sacramentorum esse debet, nihilo addito nihiloque detracto ab antiqua et veneranda institucione apostolorum, quorum statuta immutare in sacris profecto scelus nephandum est. Nam illi, edocti a Iesu Christo, mysteriis quæ sunt opportuna symbola et congrua signacula probe cognoverunt; ut liceat in additis et detractis ab institutis eorum posteritatis vel temeritatem vel negligentiam suspicari.

CAP. II. 3.

Spiritalis Speculatio Baptismi.

PRÆTER vitæ purgationem, quam decenter significat aquæ lotio illa, est etiam Anagoge in illa et significatio sublimioris intelligentiæ. Ut enim invisibilia sunt sensibilium initia, ita sensibilia sacramenta insensibilium sunt significamenta, quæ sacramentis spiritalibus, ut corpus animæ, adhibentur. Deus bonus et benignus est justiciæ sol, spiritales naturas irradians, similiter et equaliter se fundens in omnes sine intermissione, et astans ad fores et fenestras animi, pulsans ut recipiatur. Sub quibus radiis divini solis duo sunt hominum genera. Unum, quod nolit sapere quantum potest; alterum, quod velit etiam plusquam potest. Iste improbe et sponte delectatus malo et tenebris recusat lucem; hic superbius modum lucis suæ excurrit; unde sequitur non solum illum non accipere quod velit, sed etiam amittere quod habuit. Nam, ut admonet Paulus, non plus sapere quam oportet, sed sapere ad sobrietatem, ne dicentes nos sapientes esse, stulti facti fiamus, accepta divina luce si tibi confidis, incipisque molire aliqua tecum, tum extinguis omnia. Quod habes auge, qua ratione accepisti; id est, credendo confide Deo, nil tibi. Sine divinum radium in te augere; sis tu ei subjectus humilis et paciens: hoc quidem est aperire te ad lucem. In ipsa luce si confisus tibi aliqualiter superbias, claudis te ne ingrediatur lux, et in tenebris tuis ambulans, nescis quo vadis. Pontifex quem illuminavit Christus, solis instar, ex pulpito fulget luce veritatis, et diradiat evangelicum verbum pariter universis. Clamat, Surge qui dormis, et exurge a mortuis, et illuminabit te Christus. Illius oracio eloquia casta sunt, argentum igne examinatum, purgatum septuplum. Pontifex ipse ignis factus a Deo est, qui lucet veritate, qui calet bonitate, qui benignitate edocet omnes. Qui vero didicit se in tenebris esse (omnia quæ arguuntur a lumine manifestantur; omne quod manifestatur lumen est); quum is se agnoscens illuminatur, deinde quærit altius provehi in lumine, et ad illuminatiorem se accedit aliquem fidelem. Sed in hoc sensibili ordine cogita simul ordinem spiritalem. Hic accessus ad fidelem est humilitas et summissio animi divino radio. Quod quum fit suppliciter et simpliciter, e vestigio homo ille contactus divina luce consignatur in sortem sanctorum. Accipit enim lumen quoddam, signum et notam quod est ex grege dominico. Hanc Dei pastoris quasi ovis consignationem vocat Paulus in epistola ad Ephesios pignus hereditatis; in quo, inquit, et vos quum audissetis verbum Dei et veritatis, evangelium salutis vestræ, recepistis, in quo et credentes signati estis Spiritu promissionis sancto, qui est pignus hereditatis nostræ in redemptionem acquisitionis, in laudem gloriæ ipsius. Hanc insignitionem illa pontificis manus impositio denotat. Ut enim ille a pontificis manu tangitur, ita simul a Dei dextra manu, qui filius est Dei, tactus consignatur, cujus digitus in hominis capite Spiritus sanctus est. Tunc homo ille feliciter est in conscriptis ad salutem, cujus imago est illa inscriptio nominis ejus in cathologo fidelium a sacerdotibus. In prima illa ecclesia conscripti erant omnes qui per graciam in fidem consignati fuerint. Quod (postea infusa hominum turba in nomen magis Christianum quam in rem ipsam) in sinceriori ecclesiæ parte dumtaxat, ut multa alia quæ erant communia, cepit reservari. Deus pater ille, quem Dionysius vocat susceptorem, etiam conscribitur: scribitur qui se offert; scribitur qui alium offert Deo; propterea quod gaudet pater in celis super recuperatam ovem centesimam magis quam super nonaginta novem quæ non erraverunt. Is modo receptus in simplicitatem Christi unam quandam et individuam vivendi rationem sursum duntaxat profiteatur oportet. Quia, ut ait Dionysius, non est fas ut is, qui illius quod unum est ceperit consortium, dividuas habet vitas. Nam in solam unam partem tendat necesse est. Nemo enim mittens manum suam ad aratrum et reaspiciens retro, aptus est regno Dei. Nemo servus potest duobus dominis servire: aut enim unum odiet et alterum diliget, aut unum adhærebit et alterum contemnet. Divisus et simplex esse non pote[st]. Christianitas est professio simplicitatis, in quam trahitur homo, ut a multitudine in simplicitatem. Non patitur Christus simplex duplicem tunicam. In ejus nuptiali veste si vis esse, faciendum est ut nudus accedas, ut eam induas; pristinamque vivendi formam deponas, ut subeas eam quæ Christi est. Id velit et significat, quod exuit vestes omnes is qui se confert in Christum, quod exspuit et exsufflat ad occidentem, et magna protestacione abrenunciat quicquid est iniquitatis. Quod se in orientem nudum jam penitus objicit radiis exorti solis justiciæ, id, inquam, significat ut purgatus et simplex simplicem et purum divinum radium capiat, et vestem lucis et justiciæ induat, quam in Christo contexit gracia sancti Spiritus; ut in luce fulgens vestimento præclaro justiciæ, celesti majestate incedat in hac tenebrosa valle, per arma justiciæ a dextris et a sinistris, omnibus porrigens suas candidas manus, plenas bonitatis, ipse semper bonus et sui similis, nequiens aliud atque benefacere, nocentibus innocens, in malis paciencia invicta; ut continua actione boni inviolatam justiciæ vestem tenuisse videatur. Hæc est candida illa vestis quam quisque lotus sanctæ regenerationis lavachro induit; vestis sanctæ et immaculatæ justiciæ; in qua semper versus orientem magis atque magis in merementum lucis eundum est, nullo facto respectu in occidentem et mortis regionem, ne, instar uxoris Loth, in statuam salis convertamur. Quod autem totus a sacerdotibus deungitur, certamen significat et colluctationem, quam non habemus adversus carnem et sanguinem, sed adversus mundi rectores tenebrarum harum, contra spiritalia nequiciæ in celestibus, dei armatura, quam unctio illa significat, qui spiritus est sanctus, quo vegetiora membra reddantur. Dimicandum est ut vincas; vincendum ut coroneris. Pugna in illo qui in te pugnat et vincit, Iesus Christus, qui indixit bellum morti, et pugnat in omnibus. Ille est qui vincit in nobis, et nos in illo, uncti Spiritu sancto, qui, debellato et everso imperio mortis, in regno lucis ipse sit omnia in omnibus. Pugnandi regula est imitari ducem, qui dominus fortis et potens est in prælio. Nec Christianis aliud bellandi genus licet suscipere quam docuit ipse, qui non habemus hostes et inimicos nisi peccatum (quod est semper contra nos) et peccatorum suasores malignos spiritus; quibus victis in nobis, tunc armati armatura Dei ex charitate succurramus aliis, etiam si illi non paciantur, etiam si stulti non videant servitutem, etiam si liberatores suos necare velint. Ita amare hominem, ut in illius curanda salute moriare, beatissimum est. Trina vero illa immersio invocata trinitate pulchra est mortis figuratio, et depositionis carnis, carnaliumque cogitacionum a mente, et omnium peccatorum, a quibus se separari et mori in perpetuum profitetur qui Christo credit. Qui mortuus est peccato, mortuus est semel; qui autem vivit, vivit Deo. Ut mors est depositio corporis, ita spiritalis baptismus depositio est vitæ corporalis; quam obruitio illa totius hominis in aquis significat; qua admonentur se mortuos cum Christo esse, et quasi sepultos triduo cum Christo; quod vult trina illa dimersio, ut deposito Christi corpore tota nostra corporalis vita deponatur, ut resurgamus justi; in justo Christo morituri, ut aliquando etiam corpore in eodem resurgamus in gloriam. Primum emergendum est in justam vitam, tum exurgendum est in gloriosam. Mors delet mortem; gracia procreat justiciam; justicia parit gloriam. Ut moriamur peccato, oportet justus moriatur pro nobis. Ut autem vivamus justiciæ, oportet justi resurgentis gracia sustineamur. Ut denique mortui ipsi justi resurgamus, oportet divina virtute et potencia resuscitemur. Resurgunt hi quidem qui in regenerationis lavachro, in morte Christi depositis viciis, incedunt perseverantes usque in finem, in veste candida justiciæ sine macula; quique non fallunt confirmationis unctionem, quæ postremo adhibetur a pontifice, ut confirmatum in gracia et perfectum significet. Cui sic perfecto membro Christi in genere suo, in unionem cum corpore, in alimentum membri, sacrum eucharistiæ pabulum ministratur; quo intelligitur eum et in corpore esse, et in corpore ali ac spiritaliter enutriri. Nemo perfecte membrum est corporis Christi, donec sacræ communionis et vitalis alimoniæ particeps fuerit. Cujus participatione coalescit in corpus. In prima ecclesia baptizati omnes et simul confirmati sacrosancta unctione sine delatione in communionem divini pabuli adsciscebantur. Est animadvertendum Dionysium de confirmatione loqui sic, ut non id distinctum sacramentum, sed quiddam ad baptismi completionem esse doceat; ut id et baptismus solum unum sit sacramentum. Est etiam non minus notandum, quod erat in more priscæ ecclesiæ, ut omnes baptizati statim communicent, ut communi nutricione ex Christi corpore mystico esse censeantur. Alioquin, tametsi baptizati, ex corpore videntur non esse. Nam communicatio illa colligat et convincit communi nutricione, et perficit extrema completione. Ideo erat quondam impartita etiam baptizatis infantibus, de quibus hoc legitur in antiquis misteriorum voluminibus; si episcopus adest, statim confirmari oportet, postea communicari. Episcopus si præsens non fuerit, antequam lactetur infans aut aliquid gustaverit, communicet eum sacerdos de corpore et sanguine domini ante missam, etiam si necessitas ingruat, ut homo jam in Christo expurgatus illuminatus et perfectus sit. Locio purgat, crismatis posterior inunctio illuminat et nitidum facit, eucharistia implet et perficit in perfecto Christo, in quo perfecta sunt omnia, in quo esse non potest quod non est perfectum. O bone Deus, hic licet cernere, quam expurgatus quamque purus qui profiteatur Christum sit oportet, quam intimo et penitus lotus, quam candidus, quam nitidus, quam prorsus sine labe et macula, quam denique pro capacitate sua ipso Christo plenus et perfectus, in quo deinceps vigeat et valeat, integrum et sanum membrum illius. Est enim Christus capud ecclesiæ, ipsa integritas et perfectio; ex quo, ut Paulus scribit ad Colocenses, totum corpus per nexus et conjunctiones subministratum et conjunctum crescit in augmentum Dei; ut Deus reluceat in quoque simplici sereno et solido; ut constanter clare et perfecte in Christo jam agnoscant Deum et colant, utque sit quisque sic olens ac referens Christum in se solum, ut Christus in omnibus omnia esse videatur. Quapropter, si ex baptismate consurreximus cum Christo, quæ sunt Christi quæramus, ubi Christus est in dextera Dei sedens; quæ sursum sunt sapiamus, non quæ super terram. Mortui quæramus vitam nostram, quæ abscondita est cum Christo in Deo, quæ est gloria quæ apparebit nobis, quum Christus in quo spem habemus gloriosus apparuerit. Interea qui profitemur Christum, Iesus ipse Christus faciat ut simus et sapiamus et agamus omnia quæ nostra sunt professione digna.

CAP. III. 1.

De sancta Communione. Synaxi.

HÆC communio in corpore et sanguine Iesu Christi est omnium sacramentorum consummatio. Omnia quidem sacramenta in communionem trahunt; sed nihil ad hoc, in quo communicatio et convictio est admirabilis; quum plures in uno participato evadunt unum. Ad quod aliis sacramentis disponuntur homines, quæ antecedunt ut hoc compleantur. Omnia sacramenta id agunt, ut unitas in hominibus, similitudo et simplicitas extet. In hoc provehimur aliis sacramentis; eucharistia et synaxi perficimur. Quocirca quicquid magni misterii agitur, id hoc sacramento solet compleri; sine quo inchoata et imperfecta sunt omnia misteria quibus iniciantur. Quæ omnia quum id efficiant ut homines formentur in unum, ipsi ad unum uniti, quumque hoc maxime assequitur synaxis, ideo ei peculiariter id nominis sortitum est, sicut regenerationis sacramento illuminationis nomen præcipue convenit. In omnibus sacramentis hæc tria sunt, purgare, illuminare, perficere; sed perfectio synaxi, illuminatio regenerationi attribuitur. In hac enim primum lumen capit homo, quo incipit cernere veritatem. Hinc a Dionysio baptismus sacramentum illuminationis appellatur. Tactus enim divino radio revocatus in Deum respicit. Pontificis manus impositio id significat. Respicit quidem lumen resiliente in Deum: ut David inquit, In lumine tuo videbimus lumen.

CAP. III. 2.

Missa pro Communione.

PONTIFEX primum ad altare sanctam orationem facit quam arbitror dominicam fuisse. Altare fumat incenso, tum totum templum. Deinde reversus ad altare una cum sacerdotio reliquo concinit hymnos et psalmos Daviticos. Ministri deinde diaconique alius post alium ex sacra scriptura recitant quas lectiones vocavere. Hic tum ex templo abigunt cathecuminos et energuminos et penitentes, quoniam non sunt digni ut misteriis intersint. Cathecumini autem sunt qui, non adhuc iniciati sacris nec baptizati, instruuntur ut baptizentur. Catheceo autem instruo significat; unde qui instruuntur ut rite ad mysteria accedant cathecumini greco verbo nuncupantur. De quibus Paulus in Epistola ad Galathas : Communicet, inquit, is qui cathecizatur verbo, ei qui se cathecizat, in omnibus bonis. Energumini vero sunt acti a malignis spiritibus et vexati; quibus insedet magnopere potestas tenebrarum, a cujus vi et operacione actioneque energumini vocantur. Energio enim grecum verbum ago significat. Sub hoc nomine non solum sunt qui in demonicum furorem correpti insaniunt misere; sed præterea sceleratissimus quisque homo, qui vel mentitur religionem suam vel repudiat, ut apostatæ; vel quum Christum professus est, vitam tamen agit flagitiosissimam et notabilibus sceleribus contaminatam, cujusmodi sunt fornicatores, venefici, sicarii, blasphemi, et id genus reliqui; qui nominati Christiani vitam agunt impiorum paganorum, et quum appellantur a Christo quem falso profitentur, re ipsa ex regno, immo ex servitute tenebrarum sunt; in quibus plus possunt principes tenebrarum et spiritalia nequiciæ in celestibus quam Christus, qui non absunt ab illis qui a malignis spiritus et satellitibus diaboli exagitantur in furiam, nisi gradibus quibusdam. In re enim ipsa sunt in ipsaque agitacione diabolica, et vita eorum scelestorum quorumcunque in Diabolo quædam furia est. Ut autem plane insaniant et omnino sibi ipsis absint nihil deest; nisi ad consummatam insaniam aliquot gradus adhibeantur ab illo maligno spiritu, qui defectionem illam a luce inchoavit. In defectione ad deterius est inchoacio ab authore Diabolo, quæ tendit in consummationem ; sicuti in perfectione ad melius, ab authore Deo. Et quemadmodum hæc desinit in furorem divinum, ita contra illa in furorem diabolicum. Sed furor divinus sapientia et sanitas quidem est in Christo, a quo qui deciderint in seipsos in defectionem in tenebras, quique suis viis delectantur, quia tunc deserti a Deo statim et facile ad omne genus flagitii a malignis spiritibus ducuntur, energumini, id est, agitati possunt appellari. Qui non est agitatus a Spiritu Dei, ut filius Dei sit, is necessario a diaboli spiritu agitatur ut filius diaboli sit. Utrinque enim assidue trahitur homo, ut quod velit sequatur. In quam vero se partem declinat, adsunt sedulo qui tractum promovent, promotum perficiant. Sui est ipsius hominis eligere quorsum vult, audireque suasores vel bonos vel malos, inspiracionesque sequi vel has vel illas. Sed utram in partem tendit, undique sunt spiritales naturæ, qui illum quo vult conducunt. In Christo ergo quum aguntur divina misteria, non licet interesse cuiquam nisi qui agitur Spiritu Dei, qui sanctus est vita. Prophani vero, cujusmodi vero omnes possunt vocari energumini, longe a sacris et misteriis abigantur. Nam, ut David cecinit, Domum Dei decet sanctitudo. Hi ergo omnes, quorum improba vita declaravit eos in potestate diaboli esse, (ex fructibus enim eorum cognoscetis eos) in prisca ecclesia a sacris arcebantur longe, ut id honoris diabolo non tribuatur ; videlicet ut aliqui suorum divinis sacris intersint. Penitentes autem erant quos hujus errabundæ et perditæ vitæ penituit ; quique resipiscentes redierunt in ecclesiam, humiles prostrati ad pedes ecclesiæ, divinam misericordiam et graciam implorantes, et peccata deflentes sua, ac penam et mulctam peccatorum suorum flagitantes, ut publice errata sua ad omnium exemplum delugeant, utque pena temporali abeant ab eterna morte, et eternam vitam redemant. Ecclesia quæ personam Christi agit, quæ quicquid aut solvit aut ligat, ligatum id et solutum est in celis, quæ non vult mortem peccatoris, sed ut convertatur et vivat, tales quum mandatam penitenciam perfecerint, eosque satis penituerit, rursum benigniter in ecclesiam recipit, et fovet, et quoad potest in eadem conservat. Interea autem dum in mandata penitencia se exercent, adhuc habiti non satis purgati, simul cum cathecuminis et energuminis propelluntur longe et excluduntur. His autem exclusis, et templi foribus vigilanter observatis ab hostiariis et janitoribus, ne aliquis prophanus ingrediatur, tum faciente quoque diacono ministroque quod suum est, ad altare qui circa pontificem sunt principales diaconi simul cum sacerdotibus jugiter pontifici inserviunt, sanctum panem et calicem benedictionis imponunt altari. Interea universo clero laudem rei sacræ et confessionem consonante, Pontifex autem, pane et calice jam præsente, sanctissimam orationem fundit, quam credo fuisse dominicam: tum denunciata etiam a pontifice universis pace, omnes mutuo se et salutant et coosculantur. Recitatis deinde misticis verbis sanctorum, ac deinde cum sacerdotibus lotis manibus, pontifex in medio altaris, anguste circumdatus sacerdotibus et delectioribus ministris, stat et pergit ut reliqua quæ sunt in laudem et confessionem sacramenti proferat, sacramentificisque verbis tandem perficiat rem divinam et salutarem; quo facto universis confecta misteria cum omni reverentia ostendit, et tum ille primus conversus ad altare participat eam, deinde in comparticipationem communionemque ejusdem sacramenti reliquos qui sunt omnes cohortatur, ut in uno sacramenta omnes cum pontifice couniantur. Qui quum universi comparticipaverint, tum cum graciarum actione finem imponit ille pontifex, intelligens probe quid velint illa sensibilia signa, et tocius rei racionem conspiciens, quanquam alii rudiores nequiunt ultra sensa intueri. Verum quod bona fide agunt, est eis in salutem. Scientia non ducit ad vitam sed charitas. Si quis diligit Deum, hic cognitus est ab eo. Ignorans amor plus potest mille modis quam frigida sapiencia. At pontificis, et cujus est rem divinam conficere, tum summe amare tum summe sapere est; ut, quæ conficit sacra, eorum raciones intime intelligat. Ad id proculdubio obligantur et astringuntur omnes sacerdotes, quorum est divinum sacramentum conficere, ut in illo divino misterio supra plebem intelligant. In prima ecclesia (ut bonis testimoniis probat Jeronimus) quorum erat dominicum corpus conficere, ii erant omnium primi; et in principio omnes, ut hoc officio equales, ita dignitate pares. Nam ex officio et actione agnoscitur dignitas. Excellentissimum officium, qui excellentissimos et perfectissimos exposcit, est dominicum consecrare. Ex sacerdotali genere exemi et segregari non potest quisquam ad officium excellentius. Ex sacerdotibus tamen statim post apostolos, a primis illis discipulis apostolorum et sequacibus, et ex sacerdotum numero, officio et dignitate equali, unus erat delectus et prepositus ad dirimendas lites, et sedandas discordias, et sua opinione ac sententia ad terminandas dissensiones, ut in concordia commaneat ecclesia; ad quem erat delata ea auctoritas ab universali ecclesia, ut non consentientes inter se in illius sentencia conquiescant; qui officio et dignitate non tam præstat ceteris sacerdotibus, quum nihil agit quoque sacerdote excellentius, quam quadam administracione et authoritate in litibus dirimendis; ut in eo omnes qui simul cum eodem sacerdotes agunt omnia, tanquam in quodam puncto sententiæ omnibus finitis discordiis conquiescant. Hic tum peculiariter episcopus cepit vocari; quod nomen sub apostolis omnium erat sacerdotum, donec selectus is fuerat unus, de quo modo dixi, et propter causam quam dixi. Sed nunc sapiencia et speculatio veritatis depromenda est, et racio ipsa intimi archani; quam nemo sacerdos debet ignorare.

CAP. III. 3.

Significa veritas sacræ Eucharistiæ.

IN primis sacrarum literarum cantica et lectiones audiuntur a plebe, et simul ab omni ecclesia, ut in eis in quibus docetur sanctam vitam discant. Hoc est quod Paulus scribit ad Ephesios, ut impleantur illi spiritu sancto, loquentes in psalmis, hymnis et canticis spiritualibus; cantantes et psallentes in cordibus eorum domino, gracias agentes semper pro omnibus in nomine domini nostri Iesu Christi Deo Patri. Et ad Colocenses: Verbum veritatis Christi habitet in vobis abundanter, in omni sapientia, docentes et commonentes vosmet ipsos in psalmis, hymnis et canticis spiritalibus, in gracia cantantes in cordibus vestris. Illinc tractum est ut ex sacris literis passim sumpta recitentur in ecclesia; ut homines ex eis discant bene vivere. Sacra enim scriptura magistra vitae est, et veritatis regula. Item plebs et rudior multitudo, in uno pane et calice proposito, et in ejusdem alimoniae ab omnibus participatione, pulchre et commode ammonentur, ut aliti et nutriti uno, omnes in unum coalescant concordia et pace fraterna, sub Deo Patre, in mensa Dei; utque intelligant, sicuti est unus panis et unus calix quem degustant omnes et similis, ita se quoque omnes quoddam unum inter se et similes esse debere, convincirique in unitate charitatis, quod est vinculum pacis. Habet etiam illa communio venerandam repraesentacionem dominicae illius sanctae cenae cum discipulis suis, in qua seipsum tradidit eis comedendum, ut omnes uniantur in illo, et concorporati in unum cum illo eodem conficiant. Quam sacrosanctam et vivificam cenam Matheus evangelista describit, significans inter epulandum pashae panem et calicem suis proposuisse Iesum. Nam inquit, cenantibus eis accepit Iesus panem et benedixit ac fregit deditque discipulis suis, et ait: Accipite et comedite: hoc est corpus meum. Et accipiens calicem gracias egit et dedit illis dicens, Bibite ex hoc omnes; hic enim est sanguis meus novi testamenti, qui pro multis effundetur in remissionem peccatorum. Quod datum erat a Iesu Christo suis discipulis, ad eundem ritum deinde a pontificalibus personis omnibus credentibus distribuitur, ut memores illius cenae uniantur cum eis in Christo qui primi in Christo uniti erant; ut coepta vivificatio pergat et procedat, operantibus sacris mysteriis, in completionem Christi, in quo sunt et demortui et vivi, et qui credent omnes futuri, qui sacra communione et celesti cibo sustinentur in Christo, in alta societate Dei, conviventes jam non in sordida demoniorum mensa, sed in immaculata Dei. Habet vero hoc sacramentum alia et multo altiora cogitamina; sed, quod proferat dominicam cenam, et communem educationem et fraternam unitatem, si nihil in eo esset aliud, tamen hoc hominibus qui sunt humiliori sensu ad honestam societatem perutile habet monimentum. Verum nunc altiora videamus. Pontifex ille personam Dei agit, qui totus ad altare in conspectu Dei flagrat suavissimo odore incensi, quod est signum redolentissimæ charitatis suæ. Ut enim Deus suam dulcem bonitatem, utque Iesus misericordiam suam large effundat, ut cum magna hominum salute redeat in eundem, qui in se stans mirifice se amplificat in alios, ut odorifera gracia eos contrahat in ipsum, perinde ac rethe illud Petri, quod deductum in mare ab eodem piscibus plenum in navim reducitur, ad eundem ferme modum, ut minima maxima imitari possint, pontifex et vicarius Dei, ecclesiæ capud, vitalior pars, se ipsum et suam divinitatem, immo deitatem Christi in se, nihil a seipso decedens, nec suam majestatem diminuens, impartit aliis benigniter et divinitus, ut quam plurimi cum eo in Christo deificentur. Hoc certe ab altari inchoata adolitio incensi, ac deinde in universum templum progrediens, et rediens in idem unde profecta est, sancte et auguste significat rudioribus, ut in hoc, si possunt, agnoscant a summo Dei longe lateque diffundi graciam in omnes bene olentem ; ut odore capti divinæ suavitatis avide sequantur redeundam graciam in idipsum, unde gratia ipsa exierit ut rediret in idem. Gracia autem in eucharistia est quæ vocatur bona gracia, quæ ministrata a pontifice, ab ipso ad alios transit, ut redeat in eundem cum contractu aliorum in ipsum. Ipse quoque pontifex, quasi progrediens se impartit signis aliis ; nihilominus tamen recipiens se in semetipsum, et secum constans in absoluta et simplici speculatione misteriorum. Psalmorum modulatio et ex sacro codice recitacio scripturarum earum quæ canonicæ sunt, tractandis mysteriis in ecclesia abesse nec possunt nec debent. Si quidem in illis omnis sapientia et bonitas continetur, omnis naturæ cognitio, omnis metaphisicæ speculatio, omnis bonorum morum institutio, omnium præteritorum Dei recordatio, omnium futurorum expectacio, omnis denique veri et boni fides et amor: ut præterea quod recitetur auscultandum et inculcetur in auribus hominum nihil sit reliquum. Nec apostoli quidem aliud ab ecclesia audire voluerunt.

Nam Paulus semel atque iterum præcipit, et ad Ephesios et ad Colocenses scribens, ut se mutuo commoneant et consolentur, in psalmis, hymnis et canticis spiritalibus, cantantes in cordibus Deo. Itaque psalmorum modulatio et cantus in ecclesia inter agenda mysteria et sacrificandum interesse debet commode, ut auditorum mentes concinnitate demulceantur, et compositi harmonia et divina musica suaviter alliciantur in omnis concinnitatis et harmoniæ rationem; ut pacati mentibus graciæ Dei capaciores sint. Ab ipsis autem apostolis recitatio psalmorum et scripturarum, dum aguntur sacra, videtur fuisse instituta, ut venturum Christum ex veteri Testamento venisse perdiscentes et letantes, præparati hac fide pergamus in ulterius merementum graciæ, quam sacrorum confectio hominibus pie credentibus latenter et mirifice operatur. Hanc causam esse cantatorum psalmorum et scripturæ dum tractantur quævis misteria dicit Dionysius. Quamobrem decantacionem in ecclesia licet videre in nostra religione esse antiquissimam. Quattuor autem sunt genera hominum; unum, quod recusat verbum veritatis; alterum, quod admittit sed nondum iniciatur; is cathecuminus vocatur: tercium, eorum qui iniciati a potestate demonum non satis se solverint, quos veteres energuminos vocavere: quartum, quos penituit ex professione non vixisse. Hi omnes, recitatas scripturas et psalmos decantatos audiunt, ut admoniti celesti doctrina resipiscant, et redeant in perfectionem. Verum, quando prope instat tractacio sacrorum, abiguntur e templo. Vetus enim institucio voluit ut interesset nemo sacris nisi penitus perfectus. Christus enim perfectus erat, unde emanant omnia in consecratione hominum Deo in ipso; quæ non delabuntur nisi in eos qui in sancto Christi corpore mistico sunt perfecti. Itaque arcentur procul a misteriis omnes prophani, imperfecti, diminuti, delapsi, cathecumini, quos adhuc quasi informes fetus mater ecclesia parturit et eos nondum edidit in lucem. Ne ergo nimium perstringantur oculi eorum mysteriorum choruscatione, infirmitati illorum consulit ecclesia, et jubet eos abesse donec evaserint robustiores. Nam non modicam fidei lucem exposcunt sacrosancta Dei. Qui iniciati fuerint sacris, apostatæ, mali Christiani minime ex profectione viventes, et energumini qui proprie vocantur, qui maligno spiritu agitati sunt, quo perfecti nequaquam vexantur; immo ii omni maligno spiritui imperant; et denique omnis prophana turba discutitur, et a sacrorum conspectu dissipatur, etiam quos penituit peccasse, donec plene expurgentur. Relicti vero sunt in templo homines solum puri, illustres et perfecti penitus sine macula; Pontifex ille sacratissimus, sacerdotes, diaconi, ministrique et plebs sancta; qui omnes, oculis intentis in sacra, religionis symbolum (Credo in unum Deum) concinunt. In illo enim continentur omnia quæ sunt salutis nostræ in Christo, quæ summa devocione recitanda sunt, ut in graciarum actione de salute nostra divinæ misericordiæ memores et Deo videamur. Quando est altari impositus sanctus panis opertus et calix benedictionis, tum mutuo se salutant cooasculantes, et sanctorum in Christo defunctorum in memoriam nomina revocant. In uno pane proposito quem omnes comparticipent, mutuum illud osculum vivorum, et memoria mortuorum, et vivorum et mortuorum in Christo significat unitatem, concordiam, similitudinem et uniformem vivendi racionem ad imaginem Christi, quam omnes qui digne ejus sacra participant profitentur imitari. Inter recitandum etiam illa sanctorum virorum nomina, recordamur quantæ virtutis fuerint quorum memoriam tenemus, ut exemplo illorum ad parem virtutem concitemur. In illis paucis, quorum nomina audiuntur, intelliguntur qui sunt reliqui, quorum nomina præ multitudine recitari non possunt; qui pro vivis certe indubia spe recitantur.; qui (ut Salvator testatus est) transierunt a vita in mortem,[1] et in illius mente qui probe novit suos, ut in libro vitæ describitur. Proposito quidem salvatore sub speciebus panis et vini, e vestigio commemoratio sanctorum sequitur, ut in Iesu illi uniti unum quiddam cum illo esse intelligantur. Quod autem pontifex cum sacerdotibus lavat manus, significat eos totos esse mundos, nec egere lotione, nisi in extremis partibus: ut Salvator ait, Qui lotus est, non indiget nisi ut pedes lavet, sed est mundus totus. Summæ manus lavantur, ut si quis vel levis odor resideat peccati, abstergatur penitus, et pontifex cum suis totus suavis ac simplex ingrediatur sancta sanctorum, ut puriter et religiose in mysterio rem divinam agat et conficiat. Difficile est

---

[1] *Leg.* a morte in vitam

enim sic caste et integre vivere, ut nulla vel levis obfuscatiuncula affectus in nostro candore subappareat. Hinc summos pedes Petri lavit Jesus. Hinc summas manus, quod ab illa pedum lotione tractum est, Pontifex, facturus sacra lavit, ut vel quod superest, quicquid sit, in summis digitis odoris peccati, in aqua graciæ tollatur. In quo nunc in more est dicere, Lavabo inter innocentes manus meas. Sed nemo tam innocens est quin, si quippiam operetur, habeat necesse ut saltem summos digitos lavet; id est, deponat leves, a quibus difficile abstinetur, affectiones, et quasi extirpatorum relliquias peccatorum. Hic videatque quisque sacerdos per illud lotionis sacramentum quam mundus, quam tersus, quam nitidus debet esse, qui divina mysteria et præsertim dominici corporis sacramentum contrectet; qui ita lavari et tergi intime et expoliri debent, ut ne umbra quidem resideat in mente, quo superveniens lux aliquantisper obscuretur, neque quicquam vestigii ex peccatis remaneat, quod faciat quo minus in templo mentis nostræ Deus inambulet. O sacerdotes, O sacerdotium, O hujus nostræ tempestatis detestabilis audacia hominum sceleratorum, O execranda impietas eorum sacerdotilorum, quorum magnam multitudinem hoc nostrum seculum habet; qui ex popinis et lupanaribus, qui ex meretricis et olidi scorti gremio (O nephandum scelus!) in templum ecclesiæ, ad altare Christi, in mysteria Dei non verentur se ingerere; homunculi perditissimi, in quos eo gravior Dei ultio irruet aliquando, quo se illi impudentius rei divinæ immiscuerunt. Iesu Christe, nos lava non solum pedes sed et manus et caput. Ad has mysticas lotiones labrum eneum et lotio in veteri testamento instituta generi sacerdotali (uti in Exodo describitur) spectat, et eas significat, sicuti aliæ illic significatoriæ expiationes. A quibus admoneri debemus, et a nostris simul sanctis signis, quam purgati et expiati mentibus ad altare Dei astemus, ubi spectator præsens est ipse Deus judex Iesu Christus, notatores angeli, in quorum conspectu, cernente Iesu omnia, rem ejusdem sacratissimam agimus; si rite, in salutem nostram sempiternam, si illegittime, in contumeliam illius nepharie, et in perpetuam nostram damnationem. Tum pontifex, totus et penitus lotus, redit ad laudes sacratiores, ad confectionem sacramenti, ad illius in apertum ostensionem, postremo ad communicationem in eodem, quod ipsum unum una cum pontifice universi, qui adherent conparticipando; quæ quid velint, quidque significent, ut ostendatur, paulo altius repetamus. Quum vero statim post creationem stulta humana natura blandis adversarii illecebris illecta delapsa fuerit a Deo in muliebrem et moribundam conditionem, quumque fuerit in ipsam mortem celeri cursu præceps devoluta, pro omnibus malis simul omnia bona commutans, tunc aliquando suo tempore bonus, pius, benignus, clemens, misericors Deus recipere in se hominem ipse voluit, et se ei inserere et ab adversarii potestate vindicare, illius imperio everso atque deleto. Nam, ut scribit ad Hebreos Paulus, Quia pueri (id est servi) communicaverunt carni et sanguini, id est homines deserentes Deum, ideo et ipse Deus exinaniens se formam servi suscepit, et similiter participavit ejusdem carni et sanguini, id est homini, ut per mortem destrueret eum qui habebat mortis imperium, id est, diabolum; et liberavit eos, id est, qui timore mortis per totam vitam obnoxii erant servituti; destrueret quidem illum hostem, non viribus, sed (ut ait Dionysius) judicio et justicia; quod vocat occultum et mysticum. Erat enim mirabilis victoria; ut victor diabolus, eo ipso quod vicit, victus esset, et Iesus, quo victus in cruce, eodem vinceret; ut aliter re ipsa esset utrinque in victoria quam appareret. Itaque victo adversario a Deo, qui adversarius vicit hominem, restitutus est, sine querela diaboli justa, homo in libertatem et lucem Dei; cui ostensa est via in celum calcata pedibus Christi, cujus vestigia sequi debemus, si volumus quo ille ivit pervenire. Paciens Christus, inquam, et moriens (miraculum!) quasi victus vicit, et ejectus ejecit, quando audita erat vox patris illa, Et clarificavi, et iterum clarificabo; quæ propter alios facta est. Tunc Iesus, ostendens quænam erat illa clarificatio, dixit: Nunc judicium est mundi; nunc princeps mundi hujus ejicietur foras. Et ego, si exaltatus fuero a terra, omnia traham ad meipsum. Hoc autem dicebat, significans qua morte esset moriturus. Morte enim illa erepti a mortuis servimus Deo, et memoriam illius mortis celebramus iniciati sacris illius, qui moriturus dixit præcipiens: Hoc facietis in memoriam mei. Item Paulus: Quociensquunque bibetis calicem hunc, mortem Domini annunciabitis, donec veniat. Inter sacrificandum illa recordatio mortis sane efformat nos in imaginem Christi, et sacramenta nos trahunt et abducunt a mundo, et disponunt atque devinciunt Deo, ut Dei forma in nos reluceat. Quapropter (ut ad rem redeamus) pontifex ille et sacerdotes, quum quod fecit Iesus filius Dei pro nobis commemoraverit, tum pergit reliqua conficiens signis idoneis a Deo institutis. Excusat se ex animo, et indignum ad tantum misterium se proclamat; petit digne conficiat, rite distribuat ecclesiæ astanti, ecclesia recte participet. In prima ecclesia in missa pendentes a sacerdote simul cum illo immolatum Christum comparticiparunt, quibus confecta sacramenta proponit ante oculos, et sanctum panem conscindit in frusta, et distribuit simul cum calice, et sic multiplicat unum multis ut multos unificet in uno. Voluit individuum manens se quodammodo multiplicare, ut multi comparticipantes ipsum unum verbum Dei uniantur in illo, similes illi facti, toti sancti in ipso.

Oportet spectemus (ut scribit Dionysius) vitam illius Iesu in carne, quæ erat tota pro nobis, et ostensum exemplum illamque vitam imitemur, si volumus gloriæ suæ comparticipes esse. Prodiit ex occulto in apertum hominibus, invisibilis factus est visibilis, unus quodammodo multus, ut in suam rationem contrahat omnia. Et id est mysterium quod ex abdito et occulto depromptus unicus panis et calix et ostensus et distributus comparticipatusque significat; quæ ut sensibilia una multiplicantur, in unitionem, ita intelligamus invisibilia et Iesum unum dimultiplicatum esse, ut quam plurimi in ipso uniantur. Illi videlicet qui Iesu (ut Dionysii verbo utar) impeccantiam imitantur, quique non peccant, sicut ille non peccavit. Primus pontifex participat, quod is propior est Deo, qui debet longe omnium esse sanctissimus et sapientissimus. Nam indigna tractatio illius tanti sacramenti ex ignorantia est. Discant igitur pontifices mysteria Dei, et dignos ad sacra sacerdotes promoveant, ne longa indignitate digna ultio provocetur tandem in nos Dei; qui pro sua maxima pietate faciat nos dignos mysteriis suis.

CAP. IV. 1, 2.

De Consecratione Unguenti.

IN omnibus sacramentis est deductio unius ad multa, et simplicis ad multiplicia, et invisibilis unitatis ad sensibilia signa; ut his cognatis racionibus homines capti a multiplicitate ad unitatem contrahantur. Sic constat sacramenta omnia esse opportuna media inter unum Deum et multos homines, ut multi in Deo deificentur. Unguentum autem consecratur, quo ad omnia fere utitur sacerdotale officium, et habet ferme eas ceremonias quas Synaxis, incensum, psalmos, lectiones, cantus. Illud quoque dum consecratur, cathecumini, apostatæ, energumini, penitentes abiguntur. Opertum et tectum unguentum vult et significat secretam custodiam divinarum inspirationum in sanctam mentem, quæ nec ostentari insolentius nec prophanari temere debent, ne tum bonum odorem amittant. Fragrantia rei et nitor divinæ graciæ velamine sanctæ custodiæ tutari debet. Nihil enim nec preciosius nec odoratius infuso dono in hominis mentem a Deo. Ad quam infusionem si perstet homo, intenduntur graciæ gradus; ut tandem mens ad Dei similitudinem evadat non dissimilis. Depingit Deus plenam suam imaginem, si in illum totus homo intendat assidue. Quod accepit Deitatis non invulget, ne vilescat evanescatque divinæ rei odoris fragrantia. Suo jure secreto divina celari velint, quæ si invulgentur, divinitatem amittunt. Non enim vult Deus communicare se multis; quia non sunt multi quibus se communicet. Nitor, species, virtus, odor abest, si archana invulges; quæ ita celare debes, ut non solum sapientiam, et quæ cognoscis per revelationem, non publices, sed etiam opera (salvatoris præcepto) publicitus non facias, ut ab hominibus videare. Ut enim Deus secretus est, ita divini homines abducti, secreti et solitarii, et intimi in seipsis sunt, longe a vulgo separati; et sapientia eorum tota et vita ac opera sunt abscondita, spectata a Deo et angelis, non ab hominibus. Quærunt et sapiunt quæ sursum sunt, ubi Christus est in dextera Dei sedens, non quæ super terram. Mortui sunt et vita eorum abscondita est in Christo. Hinc solitudinem amant, et, Dei instar, omnia quæ bene faciunt, occulte agere cupiunt, ut laudetur Deus non ipsi; utque opera eorum luceant coram hominibus non ipsi, et glorificetur pater celestis, non ipsi. Si vis divinus esse, late ut Deus: appare in celo, et sit conversatio tua in celis. In veritate ipsa si sis, sacramentis sensibilibus non eges; habes ipsam Dei graciam, quo omnia tendunt sacramenta. Sic habuerunt quondam monachi in Egipto, non habentes in usu illa omnia sacramenta quæ nos habemus ut trahamur ad Deum; propterea quod tracti in Deum eis non eguerunt. Ut intelligamus divina secreta et tecta esse oportere, alæ illæ integunt et tutantur sacrum crisma, quo omne sacerdotale munus perficitur et completur. Est enim sanctum crisma eucharistiæ pene par, et usu necessitateque equalis. In cujus consecratione est eadem ceremoniarum celebritas, in quo etiam per multiformes colores homines trahuntur ad ipsam simplicem lucem quæ in se intime lucet, et in opacitate signorum non evadit colorata; in quo unguento, sicuti in eucharistia, in qua a corporis oculis veritas Dei in signis spectatur, a spiritali acie simplex illa veritas, ut a sole justiciæ funditur, conspicitur. Qui nequeunt cernere ipsum solem, cujus potentis lucis vibracio diffringit aciem teneram in umbris, tamen colores ferre possunt. Unguentum autem illud et sacrum crisma ex multis et variis et bene odoriferis materiebus concinnatur; quo imbuti homines bene et suaviter redoleant, naresque reficiant dulcissime. Hoc unguentum est Iesus ipse Christus, unctio et odor divinus; in quo ex omnium virtutum concinnitate spirat spiritalibus hominibus odor quidam ineffabiliter delectans, et nares mentis reficiens; qui ipse Iesus, nostrum crisma, nos imbuit seipso, et inungit suo ipsius vivifico oleo letitiæ, quo vegeti, fortes, nitidi, suavesque simus. Id est oleum, de quo Paulus in secunda Epistola ad Corinthios sic scribit: Qui Deus confirmat nos vobiscum in Christo et qui unxit nos Deus, et dedit nobis pignus spiritus in cordibus nostris. Hic spiritus Christi est quod ipsum crisma est; qui ubi est, odorem spirat suavissimum. Hæc unctio est a sancto illo quod docet omnia, ut Joannes scribit: Christiani sumus in Christo; id est, uncti in unctione ipsa.

Tota mollicies, lenitas, suavitas, voluptas, delectacio, sapor, odor, harmonia, lux, et leticia exultans Deus est. Deus homo, Iesus, omnes spiritales sensus omni voluptate perfundit, et animam sponsam quæ cum illo coit, præ voluptate rapit in exstasim, ut in voluptate Dei tota sit voluptas, non voluptatem jam sentiens, sed ipsa voluptas magis aliis voluptatem præbens. Hæc mollitudo implens tactum, et sapor recreans gustum, et odor delectans olfactum, et harmonia aures concilians, et lux oculos reficiens, est Iesus, sponsus noster, totus delectabilis. Cui qui propior astat, is fragrat olentius. Omnes nos odoratores et odorisequi esse debemus, ut odoratum templum Dei, et odori simus, ut in Christo odorabiles jucunda fragrantia totum templum Deum oleat. Crisma itaque nostrum Christus est, quo sumus imbuti ut odorati simus. Duodecim alæ seraphicæ obtegunt Christum crismaque, a prophanisque tutantur. Ipsi quoque illi spiritus priores et sine intermissione ex Iesu odorem hauriunt. Ideo circa Christum crismaque depinguntur. Per angelos deinceps ad nos omnia a Iesu veniunt, qui illi assidue et indesinenter reficientes se in plenitudine Iesu, incessanter exultant, concinentes sine fine: Sanctus, sanctus, sanctus; præ ineffabili leticia nequeuntes cohibere; tam summe in summo letantur. Quum duodecim alas legis, duas seraphin intelligite, quarum sex alæ alteri et sex alæ alteri alta et profunda celant, media aperiunt, et in media Dei feruntur. Invicem ad se clamant, ut gloriam invicem communicent. Astant crismali Iesu, ut intelligamus Christum incarnatum a majestate sua et angelis non decessisse, et inunctum præ consortibus suis ac sanctificatum, ipsum esse qui inungens sanctificat. Christus Iesus unctio est ipsa, quam angeli venerantur; ideo in omnibus sacris juste adhibetur. Est ejusmodi ad nares spiritales, cujusmodi ad aures verbum Dei, et ad oculos eucharistia.

$$\text{Anima} \begin{cases} \text{Videt} \\ \text{Audit} \\ \text{Olfacit} \end{cases} \text{Deum in} \begin{cases} \text{Eucharistia.} \\ \text{Verbo evangelico.} \\ \text{Sacro unguento.} \end{cases}$$

$$\text{In his tribus est Iesus Christus ipsum sacramentum} \begin{cases} \text{Eucharistiæ.} \\ \text{Evangelii.} \\ \text{Unctionis.} \end{cases}$$

Et signa crucis facta unguento sancto sacramentum est semper Christi et crismatis nostri crucifixi et mortui pro nobis. In baptisterio ad crucis modum oleum infunditur, quo signatur unctum ipsum crucifixum et mortuum fuisse pro baptizatis in eo, et baptizatos in cruce Christi mori, mergique in morte Christi, ut in vitam illius immergant. Id est quidem quod Paulus ad Romanos scribit: An ignoratis, fratres, quia, quicunque baptizati sumus in Christo Iesu, in morte et cruce illius baptizati sumus, qui erat in carne pro nobis, ut nos in ea peccabundam vitam deponamus, obruamurque aquis mortis illius, consepulti cum illo per baptismum in mortem. In quo baptismo credentes in cruce Christi, quasi simul crucifixi, morimur ad eam vitam pro qua Christus mortuus est. Ideo ait: consepulti cum illo Christo per baptismum in mortem; ut, quomodo Christus resurrexit a mortuis in gloriam patris, ita nos emergentes lauti in novitate vitæ ambulemus. Ille Iesus mors est nostra sanctificans: ideo ille adest crucifixus aquis nostris. Ille etiam altare nostrum est; ideo crisma ipsum altari infunditur dum consecratur. In omnibus est Christus, qui est omnia nostra, qui factus est nobis sapientia et justicia, sanctificacio et redemptio; ut (quemadmodum scriptum est) qui gloriatur, in Domino glorietur. Ille est revera omnia sacramenta nostra, et purgantia et illuminantia et perficientia. Ille templum, ara, sacerdos, sacrificium, sanctificatio est nostra; qui se sanctificavit pro nobis, ut nos sanctificemur in eo ipso domino nostro Iesu Christo.

CAP. IV. 3.

DEUS quidem est in Christo, Christus in sacramentis, sacramenta in hominibus, ad mortem eorum hic temporalem, ut homines in sacramentis ipsis iniciati sint in Christo et Deo in vitam eternam. Omnis descensio deitatis est ad ascensionem humanitatis: omnis descensio ad mortificationem est, ut sit resurrectio ad vitam. Deus factus est homo, ut moreretur pro hominibus, utque constitueret mortificantia sacramenta in ipso credentibus; mortificantia, inquam, mortem fidelium hominum, ut immortales vivant Deo. Omnia sacramenta, ut docet Dionysius Areopagita, agunt assimilationem nostri Deo, quod non potest esse, nisi simul agant mortificationem nostri in nobismet ipsis, ut Deus vivat in nobis. In sacramentis ergo morimur ipsi, ut vivat in nobis Christus: per mortem itur in vitam; per mortem scilicet mortis, in vitam vitæ; per sacramenta mortificantia, in quibus omnibus est mors et crux Christi, in vivificantem ipsum Christum; ut in ipsis crucifixi, mortui, et consepulti cum Christo, purgati illuminati et perfecti in ipso extemus, quasi resurgentes a mortuis, viventes in Christo, expurgati sacramentis illius, in quibus est virtus mortis Christi et crucis, per quæ sacramenta crucifigimus carnem cum viciis et concupiscenciis, ut virtus spiritus vivat in nobis. Omnia erant prius in Christo, et ab illo ad nos sunt omnia. In illo humilitas, mors, sanctificatio sui, exemplum aliis, ut justi moriantur. Apud Ioannem ait: Ego pro eis sanctifico meipsum, ut sint et ipsi sanctificati in veritate. Sanctus ille sanctificavit alios, ut sancti illi alios sanctificent: exemplum sanctitatis præbuit hominibus. Ab illo fluunt omnia quæ sunt prius in ipso. Ille purgatus purgat, sanctificatus sanctificat, et perfectus perficit. Ille est *teleta* nostrum, id est sanctificatio et perfectio. Quod perficit unguentum, idcirco a majoribus *telete* vocatum fuit. Extrema unctio consummata christianizatio est. In unctione est significatio christianizationis: a plenitudine unctionis Iesus vocatur Christus, in quo omnes illius sunt uncti.

CAP. V. 1.

EST functio sacerdotalis muneris ut ad ordinem honestatem et decus trahantur omnia. Omnis hierarchia tripharia distribuitur. Omnis sacri ordinis functio in teletas dividitur, id est, in perfectiones. In perficientibus et perfectis consistit sacerdotalis muneris omnis functio; ut superiores perfecti inferiores perficiant, et hi deinceps si qui sunt inferiores; ut sint primi perficientes, secundi qui perficiuntur et perficiunt, tercii postremo qui perficiuntur. In dirivatione deitatis divinarumque racionum hominibus functio omnis et labor sacerdotalis est; ut accepta tradantur in perfectionem omnium. Telete autem et ipsa perfectio perficiens omnia ipse Deus est unus et trinus, qui triphariam agit hominum perfectionem. Hinc tres sunt sub trinitate Dei hierarchiæ spirituum; et earum quæque triplex tribus ·distinctis ordinibus. Aperte et dilucide omnes illi ordines suscipiunt gloriosissimam trinitatem a primis per medios ad infimos angelos, divina luce accepta et transfusa deorsum. Hæc benigna perfusio divinæ lucis et bonitatis; qua perficiantur omnia, pergit per simplices illos spiritus ad homines usque. Sed superioribus seculis adhuc, quum homines parvuli erant et sensibus teneri, subiit simplex ille divinus radius veritatis et justiciæ, ministrante Moyse, quam plurimas et varias umbras, qu[ibus] quasi degenerans a se simplex illa lux Dei in multos et diversos colores evasit; ut tenella acies, quæ meram ipsam et simplicem veritatis et justiciæ lucem, vi et operacione potentem, ferre non potuit, deluciores et quasi debiliores colores ad tempus intueatur; donec vigorosior aliquando et lucipotens oculus in ipsam veritatem sine umbris intendere poterit. Hæc est quidem sub angelis a sacro Moyse instituta hierarchia, et sacerdotium legale; qui Moyses sub angelis in monte expositus ipsi luci simplici, quod excepit veritatis, quum eam non ausus est imbecillitati hominum committere, congruis sane, qui novit singula singulis accommodare, sed tamen crassis admodum et denso filo contextis velaminibus, quod cernebat in monte deposuit humili hominum conspectui; et quasi pratum veritatis et justiciæ subjecit oculis eorum, ut lucem in pictis Mosaicis floribus despiciant, qui in celo summum justiciæ solem suspicere non valuerunt. Quum enim totus mundus jacuit prorsus sine luce, immo sine imagine, immo etiam sine umbra omnino veritatis, adumbrandus erat celicus ordo, quasi in nuda tabula primum, ac homines quidem instituendi in frigidis umbris mutua inter se actione, opere et cultu umbratico; quod in epistola ad Colocenses elimenta vocat Paulus; quæ adumbracio expectaret illustracionem futuram, ut splendida imago extet aliquando suo tempore, quæ clarius et evidentius illam, quæ in celis est veritas, exprimeret. In hac tabula mundi ita opus Dei processit ab umbra in imaginem, ab hac deinde in veritatem. In hoc mundi theatro Christianam hierarchiam retulit illa legalis hierarchia. Nunc Christianus ludus illam cel[estem] civitatem representat. Sunt hæc tria quæ se ordine habent, et unum infra aliud subapparet, superioris imago; celestis scilicet hierarchia, christiana, et Moysaica.

> Deus omnis ordinis causa.
> Ordo ipse omnis ordinis conditor.

Hierarchia { Celestis . . . . . Veritas luculenta.
Christiana . . . . Illustris imago veritatis.
Moysaica . . . . Adumbratio imaginis.

Mundus materies operis, et quasi tabula picturæ.

Humanum genus materies, lutum, unde quod velit Deus ipse effingat: ex his hominibus componit et, ministro Moyse, umbratica constructura, adumbrat in terris hierarchiam celestem. Tunc ex quibus vult illius adumbracionis claram, Iesu ministro, constituit imaginem; ut celum in terra evidenter appareat. Aliquando totum erit celum et omnia veritas. Ita quod subito decidit, longo ordine revelatum est; et quod demolita est creatura subito, creator longo temporis successu reedificat; ut restauret omnia in Iesu Christo. A nihilo in umbram, ab umbra in imaginem, ab imagine in veritatem promovet, ut in veritate aliquando verificentur omnia. Quum autem homines debuerant ad Deum revocari, ut illum angelico more contemplentur, tam humiles ad tam altam contemplacionem, fuit necesse prius trahere eos imaginariis quibusdam racionibus aliquousque, ubi consistentes aliquandiu, deinde tollantur altius, unde postremo in ipsam veritatem promoveantur. Erant post casum hominis tenebre in mundo: sol justiciæ et veritatis per angelicam [hierarchiam] suos radios defendens, ejusdem hierarchiæ umbram jacuit in terras. Suo tempora deinde sol ipse descendit, ut per se immediate eam umbram angelicæ hierarchiæ illustret coloribus, infunderetque lucem veritatis suæ, unde colorata imago et angelicæ civitatis clarius spectetur in terris. Sublata vero tandem umbra, penitus mera lux aliquando apparebit in gloria Christi, quæ vita est nostra, abscondita in celis, quæ apparebit quum apparuerit ille in gloria sua. Interea ingemiscit et parturit usque adhuc omnis creatura, adoptionem filiorum Dei [expectans]. Ex hoc ordine licet cuique videre rationes quattuor sensuum in veteri lege qui in ecclesia celebrantur. Litteralis est, quando quid actum fuit ab hominibus illis veteribus narratur. Quando cogitas de illa imagine et ecclesia Christiana quam adumbrat, tunc capis sensum allegoricum. Quando attolleris in altum, ut ex umbra veritatem ipsarum conjicias, tum suboritur tibi sensus anagogicus. Quando unius hominis institutionem ex signis animadvertis, tunc omnia tibi sonant moralia.

Hierarchia
{
Celestis significatur Anagoge, id recessu remotiori.
Christiana significatur Allegoria.—Totum.
Particularis hominis sensu morali.—Pars.
Moysaica rebus gestis tota significans est
{
Celestem veritatem.
Christianam imaginem.
Christiani hominis justam vitam.
}
}

Res gesta umbra est trium
{
Lucis.
Totius.
Partis.
}

In novi testamenti scriptis, nisi quando in parabolis placuit domino Iesu et apostolis loqui, quod Christus sæpe facit in evangeliis, Ioannis in Apocalipsi omnia, totus reliquus sermo, quo vel salvator apertius edocet discipulos, vel apostoli instituunt ecclesias, habet eum sensum quem præ se fert; nec aliud dicitur, aliud significatur; sed id ipsum significatur quod dicitur; et literalis est sensus totus. Tamen quia ecclesia Dei est imaginaria, semper in eo quod audis in dogmatibus ecclesiæ cogita Anagogen, cujus significatio non cessabit quidem, donec imago fuerit veritas. Ex his etiam conclude, non semper ubi literalis sensus est, ibi simul esse allegoricum; sed contra, ubi est sensus allegoricus, semper ibi subesse sensum literalem.

Vel potest aliquis cogitare in nocte hujus mundi et tenebrec[ulis] hominum, stellas lucentes absente sole fuisse patriarchas et prophetas, Moysen, et erant delecti septuaginta seniores, quibus erat cum Moyse spiritus communicatus. De quibus est illud Petri in epistola secunda: Et habemus, inquit, firmiorem propheticum sermonem, cui bene facitis attendentes, quasi lucernæ lucenti in caliginoso loco, donec dies elucescat, et lucifer oriatur in cordibus vestris. Dies est veritatis Christi, in quo nos Christiani ambulamus. Imagines stellarum in aquis lucentes fuisse reliquam plebem, qui veritatem non cernebant, nisi in fluxis signis. Dies autem ille qui peculiariter vocatur domini dies, est ille dierum, ubi dominorum dominus in majestate sua summum tenebit emisperium, et illustrabit omnia.

Dies sub sole. Dies est verus ille dominicus, sole justiciæ illustrante omnia.

In nocte ⎧ Stellæ lucentes in celo, sub Christo, sancti illuminati a sole.
⎨ Conversatio in celis.
⎩ Stellæ lucentes in aquâ, sub lege, imago ecclesiæ aquea.

Nox caliginosa, penitus sine luce, ante legem.

Nam dum hic vivimus, in matutinis et antemeridianis horis, peregrinamur in meridiem, cum domino cenaturi. Exorti quidem a plaga septentrionali in meridiem tendimus.

Dies ⎧ Plenus domini, discussis omnibus nubibus et subjectis hostibus, quum erit Deus omnia in omnibus.
⎩ Inchoatus in Christianis: cernentes solem justiciæ exortum.

Nox ⎧ Lucentes stellæ in celo prophetæ; intelligentes quid velint signa.
⎨ Lucentes in aqua plebeii; adherentes signis.
⎩ Penitus sine luce gentes, errantes in vanitate sensus sui.

Moyses quidem non tantum legem, quam exaratam quinque libris posteritati reliquit, sed etiam certe in monte Syna divinitus accepit totius legis secretam et veram enarrationem interpretacionemque, et sensum spiritalem apertæ; quem præcepit Deus ne traderet literis ullo modo, nec invulgaret, sed revelaret et traderet Iesu Naue tantum, qui deinceps sancto, severo et religioso [silentio u]suris primis sacerdotibus indicaret. Legem autem scriptam jussit Deus ut populo publicaret; in qua per simplicem historiam nunc Dei potencia ostenditur, hic ira in improbos, illic clemencia in bonos, ubique in omnes justicia; ut potentem, bonum et justum Deum populus agnoscat et veneretur. In quaque etiam lege per salutaria et divina præcepta instituitur multitudo ad bene beateque vivendum, et cultum veræ religionis. Itaque in lege scripta spectatur duntaxat quanto in successu rerum est et bonitas et potentia Dei; quomodo quisque vivat; qua ratione Deum colat. At vero secretiora illa mysteria et sub cortice legis rudique prætextu verborum latitancia, archana videlicet illa altissimæ divinitatis, si veteres illi stultæ plebi patefecissent; id, te quæso, quid fuisset aliud quam sanctum dare canibus, et inter porcos spargere margaritas. Quapropter sapientes illi veteres in lege profundissimam secretissimarum rerum contemplacionem et abstrusioris veritatis recessum non communicaverunt, nisi, clam vulgo, solis sapientibus; inter quos tantum se loqui sapientiam ad Corinthios scribit Paulus. Erat hoc sanctum institutum apud omnes sapientes veteres, ut mistica dogmata per enigmatum nodos a prophana multitudine inviolata custodirent. Magister vitæ Iesus discipulis suis revelavit multa, quæ illi [qui]dem, ne communia fierent vulgo, scribere noluerunt. Dionysius tradit, secretiora mysteria Christiana a nostræ religionis authoribus sine literis, medio intercedente solo verbo, ex animo in animum transfusa fuisse. Eodem modo ex Dei præcepto vera illa legis interpretacio Moysi deitus revelata et tradita, Cabala est dicta, hebreo verbo, quod latine receptio est; propterea quod illam doctrinam non per literarum monimenta, sed ordinariis revelacionum · successionibus alius ab alio quasi hereditario jure recepit. Verum postquam hebrei a babilonica servitute restituti per Cyrum, et sub Zorobabel instaurato templo ad reparandam legem animum appulerunt, Esdras tunc ecclesiæ præfectus, post emendatum Moyseos librum, quum plane cognosceret per exilia, cædes, fugam, captivitatem gentis Israeliticæ, institutum a majoribus morem tradendæ per manus doctrinæ servari non posse, futurumque ut sibi divinitus indulta celestis doctrinæ archana [perirent], quæ, eorum commentariis non intercedentibus, durare diu memoria non poterant, constituit ut, convocatis qui tunc supererant sapientibus, afferret unusquisque in medium quæ de legis mysteriis memoriter tenebat, et adhibitis notariis in septuaginta volumina (tot enim fere in Synedrio erant sapientes) redigerentur.

De qua re sic Esdras ipse loquitur quarto suo libro capite decimo et tercio: Exactis quadraginta diebus loquutus est altissimus, dicens, Priora quæ scripsisti in palam pone: legant digni et indigni: novissimos autem septuaginta libros conservabis, ut tradas eos sapientibus de populo tuo. In his enim est vena intellectus, sapientiæ fons, scientiæ flumen. Atque ita feci. Hi libri sunt Cabalæ receptionisque, qui apud Hebreos tanta religione coluntur, ut eos [attingere] præterquam quadragenarios liceat nemini. In illis omnia sunt nostra aperte; quos libros studiose curavit Sixtus quartus, Pontifex Maximus, docti alicujus opera transferre in latinitatem: quo vivente tres libri legebantur. Itaque constat præter legem quam dedit Deus Moysi in monte Syna, et quam ille quinque libris scriptam contentamque reliquit, revelatam quoque fuisse eidem Moysi ab ipso Deo veram legis expositionem, cum manifestacione omnium misteriorum et secretorum, quæ sub cortice et rudi facie verborum legis continentur; duplicemque accepisse legem Moysen in monte, litteralem et spiritalem. Illam literalem scripsisse, et ex præcepto Dei populo tradidisse; hanc spiritalem sapientibus solum, qui erant septuaginta, communicasse, quos ex præcepto Dei elegerat Moyses [ad] legem custodiendam, quibus præcepit ne eam scribere[nt], sed successoribus suis viva voce revelarent, et illi deinde aliis; a qua vicitudinaria receptione fuit vocata Cabala; quæ scientia postea in scripta venit, qui libri aperte continent omnia secreta et mysteria quæ in lege litterali velantur. Quæ secreta, ut sentit Origenes, vocat Paulus eloquia Dei, quæ vivificant legem; sine quo spiritu vivificante lex mortua jacet. Illa expositio et spiritalis sensus, quem accepit Moyses a Deo totius legis, ut diximus, literalis, erat is quem nos vocamus Anagogicum. Sicut enim apud nos est quadruplex [ratio] exponendi bibliæ, quadruplexque sensus, literalis, Misticus Allegoricusque, Tropologicus et Anagogicus; ita apud Hebreos. Sed Cabala anagogicum sensum persequitur, qui erat traditus Moysi ab ore Dei; qui est sublimior et divinior, sursum nos trahens et ducens a terrenis ad celestia, a sensibilibus ad intelligibilia, a temporalibus ad eterna, ab infimis ad suprema, ab humanis ad divina, a corporalibus ad spiritualia. Sectantur Iudei terrena, sensibilia, temporalia, infima, humana, corporalia; quæ sunt omnia in litera occidente. Qui vocantur in spiritum Christianum, ii celestia, intelligibilia, eterna, superna, divina, spiritalia sectantur, et id plane, quod revelatum fuit Moysi a Deo, et ab eodem Moyse septuaginta delectis traditum; qui sensus celestis et supernus est. [Ad] quam divinam veritatem propius vocati sunt homines a Christo, ut altius sapiant quam Iudei, et rectius vivant; qui sensus est anagogicus. Ad quem scribit Dionysius duces esse eos, qui a Moyse sanctum tabernaculum sacratius didicerunt, quos intelligamus fuisse septuaginta sapientes, quos delegit Moyses ut eos expositionem legis doceret. At ut cum fide et charitate credamus celestia, dux erit nobis Iesus Christus, qui eduxit nos de egipto, et extra etiam terrenam promissionem terrestremque Ierusalem, constituitque nos sub se hierarchiam clariorem, quæ ad legalem hierarchiam se habet ut finis et perfectio. Cujus hujus nostræ deinde finis, et extrema perfectio, celestis est illa et superna; inter quam et legalem (ut tradit Dionysius) media est nostra; quæ, ut medium decet, aliquatenus utraque extrema in se comprehendit, habens tum ex superiori spiritalem et lucentem intelligentiam, tum ex inferiori carnalem corporalemque et sensibilem significationem. Nam quamdiu homines sumus, vel spiritalissimi signis omnia carere non possumus. Inferior superiorem refert, ut possit, modo suo. Omnia quæ sunt in celesti hierarchia, eadem sunt in Christiana, modo imaginario; omniaque quæ sunt in Christiana, præcesserant in legali, modo umbratico.

Celestis	Angelica. Luculenta.			Superior.
Christiana	Angelica; luculenta.	Spiritus Deus.	Celum.	Media.
	Humana; umbratica.	Caro Homo.	Terra.	
Legalis	Humana. Umbratica.			Inferior.

Itaque cogitemus in Christiana ecclesia tres hierarchias, et has quoque triplices; ut sint in nobis, sicut in angelis, novem ordines, angelicos gradus imitantes, quorum umbræ in literali lege antecesserunt; quorum omnis functio versatur in sanctificatione, ut homines Deo, qui sanctus est, assimilentur; in quibus sunt sancti quidam primi et summi sanctificantes, quidam sanctificati, quidam inter hos medii, sanctificati simul et sanctificantes. Omnes autem ministri Dei in dirivationem Deitatis, in plenam tandem hominum sanctimoniam. Omnes student imitari angelicos ordines; ut prima trinitas purget, secunda illuminet, tercia perficiat et compleat; ut tota ecclesia sit purgata, illuminata et perfecta in Deo. Purgatio est in depositione quicquid erat nostri, etiam maximæ spei in nobismet ipsis; ut versi in Deum speremus in ipso. Illuminatio in fide est revelatis, quæ est sapientia nostra. Perfectio in completione charitatis est, quæ plenitudo legis et justiciæ est. Purgant, illuminant et perficiunt summi; purgantur, illuminantur et perficiuntur infimi, jam iniciati sacris, baptizati et conf[ir]mati. Purgantur et purgant etiam medii, ipsi lucentes jam et illuminantes purgatos ad completionem. Complent et perficiunt supremi in ecclesia, in quibus debet esse summa vis stabiliendi homines in spe, et illuminandi in fide, et denique perficiendi in charitate. Illic et ab illis primariis in ecclesia aguntur eadem quæ a mediis; et ab his eadem quæ a primis. Ab omnibus enim agitur simul purgatio, illuminatio et perfectio. Hæc enim tres operationes ab una causa operatæ separari non possunt quidem; sed a mediis ad illustriorem notam efficiuntur illa eadem quæ a primis; ab ultimis postremo illis et supremis ad illustrissimam. Tota illa operatio divina in celestibus tendit in assimilationem Deo, in representacionem trinitatis, unitatem, pulchritudinem et bonitatem illius. Hinc tres sunt operationes; purgatio, illuminatio et perfectio. Effectus purgationis est unitas, simplicitas, potencia, constantia, stabilitas, quæ in illis unum quiddam est, quo firmiter se sistunt in Deo. Effectus illuminationis est speciosa varietas, veritas, ordo, pulchritudo, sapientia, claritas; quæ verba idem quiddam significant, et in angelis multiformem quandam divini verbi scientiam. Perfectionis demum effectus est bonitas, benignitas, amor, perfectio, charitas. Hæ operationes in nobis etiam habent suos effectus, ad similitudinem unitatis, veritatis et bonitatis in angelis. Unitas enim nostra, quo tendit purgatio nostri, est spes, quæ certe est simplicitas et stabilitas nostra. Veritas nostra est fides veritati omniformi quæ erat in Iesu Christo. Bonitas et perfectio nostra est amor boni. Ad hæc tendit omne munus et functio in Christi ecclesia. Potest in his sperantibus[1] cogitari tria genera, et tria genera credentium, et amantium tria genera; non quod quisquam est in ecclesia non amans, aut non credens: omnia enim sunt in omnibus: sed quod hæc secundum gradus distinguuntur, et secundum majorem et minorem participationem divini radii variantur; qui est unus et idem, quodque agens in omnibus; sed pro distinctione graduali varia est nominum sorti[tio], et suum cuique proprium. Quisque in gradu suo pro dato munere fungitur officio; omnes collaborant in abstractione ab hoc mundo, et sanctificatione hominum Deo. Nunc, inquit Paulus, liberati a peccatis, servi facti Deo, habemus fructum nostrum in sanctificationem, finem vero in vitam eternam. Apud Dionysium tres sunt nominati ecclesiastici ordines; pontificum, sacerdotum et ministrorum. Pontificum munus est amplissimum, potens quicquid inferius potest, habens præterea et suum proprium officium, quod est eucharistiam conficere, unguentum sanctum consecrare, sacerdotes efficere; unde constat eum illos appellare pontifices, quos posterior ecclesia vocat sacerdotes; sacerdotes ferme eos qui diaconi vocantur. Sacerdotum apud illum officium est purgatos a ministris sacris iniciare, et illa quæ ads[ueta] sunt præbere, indicationem mysteriorum relinquere pontifici. Nam vult ministros secernere, et separare homines a mundo et seipsis, et quasi exuere eos pristina consuetudine penitus et denudare; ut nihil habeant contrarii quominus illuminentur a sacramentis, sed sint excusso et exterso pulvere puri tanquam tabula rasa, apti jam ut in eis celestis imago depingatur. Qui quum ita a ministris parantur, tunc offeruntur sacerdotibus. Hi quum eos nihil maculæ habere inspiciunt, nihilque olere gravis vetustatis, summeque esse dispositos ut effingantur et formentur in Christo, ut, sicut portaverunt imaginem terreni, ita portent imaginem celestis, eos quasi depingit sacramentis, iniciatus eosdem sacerrimis signis, cum quibus, saltem credentibus, operatur spiritus Dei. Hic in

---

[1] *Leg.* sperantium.

manibus sacerdotum illuminantur, ut perficiantur et compleantur a pontifice. Completio autem omnis pontificis est, qui plenus censetur: is eucharistiam præbet, et sacro unguento confirmat, et signaculorum mysteria dignis indicat, ut in manibus pontificis, si habeantur idonei, in omnibus perficiantur, ex illoque perfecti proficiscantur in locum et gradum muneris sui, uti pontificis sapientia juste disponit. Per diaconos ministrosque introducuntur puri in ecclesiam; per sacerdotes promoventur sacramentis illuminatoriis; a pontifice perficiuntur mysteriis perfectoriis. Pontifex omnium sacrorum scius, et divinarum rerum contemplator, rite sub se disponit ecclesiam; ut quisque in ipso aliquid agat divinæ actionis, ad Dei et divinorum spirituum imitacionem. Quia (ut docet Dionysius) omnis actio in ecclesia cujuscunque oportet imitetur divinam actionem. Nam, ut idem ait, divinarum operationum imagines sunt sacerdotales functiones. Ad exemplar enim celestis hierarchiæ angelorum, qui assidue Deum imitantur, a Christo ecclesiastica societas conditur in terris; et in Christo a pontificali munere omnia disponuntur; qui pontifex personam Dei et Christi gerit in terris, ut quisque in ecclesia in publicam utilitatem totius societatis in aliqua divina operatione pro virili sua se sedulo exerceat; ut ipse unum et sanum et perfectum in Christi corpore mystico membrum esse agnoscatur. Unicuique, inquit Paulus, sicut Deus divisit mensuram fidei. Divisiones gratiarum sunt multæ; unicuique datur manifestacio spiritus ad utilitatem; scilicet ut ecclesia perficiatur spiritu tandem, et immortalitate, in quam vocata totis viribus, servato ordine, distinctis officiis sub pontifice, sub [angelis], sub Deo, contendat necesse est, si aliquando immortalis velit esse.

CAP. V. 2.

PONTIFEX autem dum consecratur, prostratus ad altare dextram manum pontificis et evangelia supra capud habet. Invocatur trinitas in eum; insignitur cruce; nominatur a toto sacerdotio; deosculatur. Eadem fiunt veteri ritu in sacerdote, excepta impositione evangelii in capud. Eadem denique ministro; sed is unico duntaxat genu flexo consecrationi se substernit. Solus pontifex evangelia gestit in capite. Omnes consecrati ad eucharistiæ communionem cientur.

CAP. V. 3.

UT autem dicamus quidnam quæ videntur significant, ut simul spiritalis oculus cum corporeo sua objecta cernat, primus ille accessus ad pontificem, et ad altare prostracio, subjectionem Deo et pontifici suo loquitur et admonet. Genuflexio enim significatio est subjectionis et obedientiæ; quo verbo usus Paulus in epistola ad Philippenses omnia Iesu subjecta esse affirmat, dicens: Propter quod et Deus exaltavit illum, et dedit illi nomen quod est supra omne nomen; ut in nomine Iesu omne genu flectatur, celestium, terrestrium et infernorum. Itaque, charissimi mei, obedite. Hæc subjectio in ecclesia est, et debet esse, cujusque inferioris personæ superiori in sanctificationem sui Deo in Christo; in quo etiam præsidentia est superiorum in inferiorum sanctificationem, sub quocunque nomine præsident; etiam in plebeis patres, domini, mariti; ut docet Paulus in epistola ad Ephesios, et in epistola ad Collocenses scripta; in quibus præcipit filiis, servis et uxoribus subjectionem et obedientiam, quod intelligendum est in omnibus ut sanctificentur ab illis. Idcirco Paulus notanter semper adhibet et inculcat "in Domino." Ad Ephesios est: Viri diligant uxores, ut Christus ecclesiam, et tradant se pro uxoribus, ut eas sanctificent lavachro graciæ in verbo vitæ; ut exhibeant ipsi sibi gloriosas uxores, non habentes maculam neque rugam, aut aliquid ejusmodi; sed sanctas et immaculatas. Impositio autem illa manuum pontificis in capud prætendit illum consecratum Deo, quisquis sit, totum comprehensum esse a Deo, ut in eo sit et agat omnia, illius etiam potestate se speret defensum et tutum esse. Manus enim est potestas Dei in homine. Quod si Deus nobiscum sit, quis contra nos? Defenditur autem contra spiritales nequiciæ in celestibus. Quia, ut scribit ad Ephesios apertius, non est nobis colluctacio adversus carnem et sanguinem, sed adversus principes et potestates, adversus mundi rectores tenebrarum harum, contra spiritalia nequiciæ in celestibus. Insigniri autem crucis caractere prædicat et protestatur, crucem nos bajulare Iesu, ut illius discipuli simus. Nam ille dixit: Qui non tollit crucem [suam] et sequatur me, meus non potest esse discipulus. Tollere autem et accipere crucem revera est, fide in morte Christi, vitam peccatricem omnino et in perpetuum deponere, ac cum mortali Christi carne sepelire; atque deinde oculis in Christum intentis constanter illius sanctissimam vitam imitari; ut configurati morti illius occurrant ad resurrectionem quæ est ex mortuis, ad eundem modum quo de se scribit Paulus ad Philippenses: Unum, inquit, scio; quæ quidem retro sunt obliviscens, ad ea vero quæ sunt priora extendens meipsum, ad destinatum persequor bravium supernæ vocationis Dei in Christo Iesu. Ad Galathas scribit idem: Qui sunt Christi, carnem suam crucifixerunt cum viciis et concupiscentiis. Id denotat crucis signaculum, impressum in hominem profitentem Christum; ut, quum caracter sanctæ crucis a pontifice acceperit, dicat cum Paulo: Christo crucifixus sum cruci; vivo autem, jam non ego; vivit vero in me Christus: in quo certe est membrum homo, ut capiti conformis sit, et surculus in arbore Christi; ut in omnibus radicem sapiat; ut non suo jam judicio, quod crucifixum est, sed, ex radice hausto vitali succo, qui Christus est, in omnibus vivat (ut ita dicam) Christianiter. Recordetur ergo graviter secum quisque, quid velit impressio signi crucis, quæ est peccatricis personæ in homine ipsa mors in sempiternum, ut ea deinde nunquam reviviscat. Nam, ut docuit ille magister vitæ, accipienda est crux illius, et sequendus est ipse; id est, relinquenda est vita nostra propria, et illius imitanda. Nominatim deinde consecratus a pontifice denunciatur, quo certe indicatur divina electio et sors, cujus arbitratu et voluntate fiunt quæ recte fiunt in ecclesia omnia. Sed hic nonnullus est locus ut de divina sortitione aliquid dicamus, si prius, quid sors est, dixerimus; quod nomen in scripturis multum usurpatum est. Sors quidem fortuitus alicujus rei eventus est, a quo fit verbum sortior, quod est, sortes facio, sive, sortes recipio, seu, per sortem aliquid decerno vel eligo. Qui aliquid eligunt per sortem, sortilegi vocantur. Item qui per sortes futura prænunciant. Capitur tamen aliquando sors pro fatali necessitate, aliquando pro judicio. Sors etiam pro patrimonio accipitur, unde consortes et consortia dicuntur. Apud Christianos, certe illos quidem priscos viros et apostolos, magnum erat sortis sacramentum; sortisque jactio apud homines certissimam apud Deum indicavit electionem. Est quidem sors apud homines expectantes omnia a Deo, credentesque cum eorum signis Deum operari, argumentum et signum et quasi sacramentum, in quo agnoscitur in quem incidit divina voluntas et certissima electio. Sortes, ait Salomon, mittuntur in sinum, sed a domino temperantur. Itaque sorte electus erat in apostolatum Mathias, ut scribit Lucas; multa oracione antecedente, quæ spiritum sanctum invocaret, ut ex sortis sacramento divina voluntas in electione reverenter approbetur. Verba in Actibus Apostolorum hæc sunt: Et statuerunt duos; Josephum, qui vocatur Barsabas, qui cognominatus est Justus, et Mathiam; et orantes dixerunt: Tu, domine, qui corda nosti omnium, ostende quem eleg[eris] ex his duobus unum, accipere locum ministerii hujus et apostolatus, de quo prevaricatus est Judas, ut abiret in locum suum. Et cecidit sors super Mathiam, et annumeratus est cum undecim in apostolis. Sors etiam habet suam significationem in scripturis nonnunquam pro fatali necessitate, pro judicio, et pro patrimonio, unde consortes nominantur et consortia. Quos enim divina prædestinatio indicat filios et heredes patrimonii sui, hi in sorte Dei dicuntur, et consortio cum Christo. Omnia autem in ecclesia Christi, cujus quasi anima est Deus ipse, agi debent ab ipso Deo, hominibus interea credentibus et expectantibus. Quicquid, vel qui vocetur in ecclesiam, vel in eadem ad aliquem gradum et dignitatis locum promoveatur, vel ab eodem promoto ex ejus officio agitur;—quicquid (inquam) agitur vel in constructione vel ordinatione vel completione ecclesiæ, si id divini spiritus instinctu non fiat, nihil est. Nisi Dominus, ait David, edificaverit domum, in vanum laboraverunt qui edificant eam. Nisi dominus custodierit civitatem, frustra vigilant qui custodiunt eam. In opere suo, quæ est ecclesia, æquum est ut ille temperet omnia. Quod si humanum se temere immisceat ingenium, disturbari et confundi omnia necesse est. In hominibus nihil est aliud quod requiratur, nisi oratio instans et peticio, fides indubia, spes firmissima, quæ (ut ait Paulus) non confundit. Quia vero latentes sunt actiones et operaciones Dei, non sine divino præcepto credendum est apostolos, et apostolicos viros in prima ecclesia sortibus nonnunquam fuisse usos; ut per illas de Dei judicio doceantur, quem ad aliquod munus et officium ex Dei voluntate nominent, credentes plane illic esse voluntatem Dei ubi sors cecidit. Quæ statim in quem obtigit sors, omnes quasi uno ore Dei connominent, credentes indubitanter, qui nominatus est in terris, eundem a Deo nominatum esse in celis. Soluta enim et ligata in terris, Salvatoris testimonio, solvuntur et ligantur in celis; quoniam congregatis in illo ille medius est. Id est quod Dionysius ait, nominationis sacramentum significare delectum et approbationem Dei in celis. Quam nominationem cujusvis, vel in membrum, vel in ministerium aliquod in Christo Jesu, in ecclesia illius fieri sane nephas est, nisi id fiat quidem a summis et sanctissimis viris, et locis quoque augustissimis, et præterea cum longissimis et religiosissimis jejuniis, votis, sacrificiis et precibus; ut non ab homunculis, sed a magno Deo factum esse videatur. Quocirca hic licet execrari illum detestabilem mo[rem] qui jam diu inolevit in ecclesia, et nunc prope in interitum reipublicæ Christianæ inveteratus est, quo temporales principes, insani quidem et sub Christiano nomine hostes et inimici Dei, blasphemi Christi, eversores ecclesiæ, non humilibus et piis animis, sed superbis et temerariis, non sacris et castis locis, sed in cubiculis et conviviis, episcopos, qui Christi ecclesiam gubernent, nomi[nan]t, et eos quoque (O nephandum scelus) homines omnis sacræ rei ignaros, omnis prophanæ scios, quibus jam ante flagitiose eosdem episcopatus vendicarunt. O seculum nequam, O perditi mores, O principum insania, O ecclesiasticorum hominum cecitas et stultitia, deridendane an deflenda magis ignoro : pervertitur ordo, caro tumet, spiritus extinguitur, deforma et feda extant omnia. Nisi Christus misereatur ecclesiæ suæ, mors, quæ jam prope instat, occupabit omnia. Nam quo pacto durabit quod tractatus pestifero consilio et veneficis manibus? Bonus Iesus, nihil sibi ascribens, humiliter omnia retulit ad patrem. Si ego glorifico me (inquit apud Johannem) gloria mea nihil est. Est pater meus qui glorificat me; de quo non ipse sed pater dixit, Tu es sacerdos in eternum, secundum ordinem Melchisedech. At isti principes nequitiæ, nomine Christiani, re vero ipsa ministri diaboli, arroganter ascribentes sibi quæ Dei sunt, opus quod sanguis Christi construxit, et templum Dei, nepharia libidine demoliuntur; quibus dabit Deus aliquando secundum opera eorum. Sed nos ad id de quo loquebamur redeamus. Sacra illa omnia, ut diximus, sacramentum est nominationis in celis. Nomine sacramenti non solum dicuntur illa septem notissima in ecclesia; sed præterea quicquid sensibili signo et notis spectabilibus remotius significatur, sacramentum vocatur. In sorte Mathiæ magnum notat sacramentum Dionysius, quum in ea dicit indicium fuisse apostolis in quem latens divina electio incidit. Ita in connominationis sacramento patefacta est, ut creditur sine dubio, si ab idoneis viris fit, nominatio illa divina in celis; a quo, quem ille vult, is in ecclesia nominatur; a quo qui non est nominatus, is credat se non esse quem se profitetur; quod velim audiant episcopi qui tales a temporalibus regibus nominantur. In cons[aluta]tione vero et coosculo ejus qui nominatur, similitudo, amor et gaudium innuitur, quod est omnibus in assimulato, et ei quoque cum illis quibus assimulatur. Sed quid velit illa sacrosanctorum evangeliorum impositio capiti pontificis consecrati? Nempe ut pontifex ille omnia sacra et divina in suo capite et p[ectore] contineat, sitque omnium in divinis rebus longe sapientissimus, et omni virtute ac sancta actione longe optimus, ad exemplum illius Christi qui in evangeliis prædicatur; quem quodammodo innuit quum sacerrima illa evangelia in capite accipit, ut quoad possit ipsum in se Christum præ se ferat vita, sanctimonia et bonitate, et illius veritatis ac religionis sapientia. Minister vero uno genu flexus purgatorum sacramentum habet; sacerdos duobus flexis, purgatorum et illuminatorum; pontifex præter duorum genuum flexus, in capite sacra evangelia habet, in sacramentum et purgationis et illuminationis et perfectionis; quod is evangelica mysteria ostendit rite, ut eis impleti homines pro capacitate perficiantur. Ita tota ecclesiastica institucio, purgatione illuminatione et perfectione in Christo, molitur hominum constantem simplicitatem, et sapientem ordinem, et perfectam bonitatem, ad clarum illud exemplar angelorum; ut super cahos confusionis et mundi, aliquorum hominum in Deo simplicium et perfectorum luculentus ordo extet, quæ sit civitas in monte posita, quæ sit lux mundi et sal terræ; quæ, fide, spe et charitate sub sole Christo resplendens, illuminet et vivificet mundum. Sed, proh dolor, fumus et caligo tetra ex valle hominum tenebrosorum tanta jam dudum et tam spissa spiravit sursum, ut civitatis lumen fere obruit; ut nunc ecclesiastici homines, involuti tenebris, ignorantes quo vadant, stulti commiscuerunt et confunderunt se cum omni [?], ut nunc rursus in mundo nihil sit, quam hominum turba, confusius. In quo mundo, quod impressit, sigillum Christi turbulenta collisione hominum in tanta rerum confusione oblitteratum est prope et deletum. Misericors Iesus pro tua omnipotencia, te precor, cito discussis tenebris in tua ecclesia restitue ordinem et serenitatem.

CAP. VI. 1.

UTI sunt a Deo instituti qui purgent, illuminent et perficiant, quæ sunt causæ agentes, et quasi jam viri masculina virtute, ita contra ex opposito oportet sint qui purgentur et qui illuminentur et qui perficiantur; qui sint quasi materies ecclesiæ, et virili parte quasi substernenda femina, ut in viro perficiatur. In hac parte sunt obstetricandi cathecumini, apostatæ revocandi, energumini exorcizandi, penitentes detergendi. In his officiis sunt ministri, quorum officium purgare est, et parere, quoad possunt, simplicem unitatem in hominibus; ut delabentes et defluentes et jactati se sistant in Deo, in puncto spei, ut sperantes in Deo jam radicentur. Ut autem sunt varii qui purgentur, ita varii ministri sunt. Cathecuminis contendentibus exire mundum, manum porrigunt et assidua instructione ad Deum trahunt cathecizantes ministri. Adversarius incessanter oppugnat ecclesiam, ut quod per ministros construit Deus, demoliatur. Itaque quosdam evertit et diruit apostatas; quosdam quassat et vexat energuminos. Contra soliciti labore et diligentia oportet sint ministri Dei, ut damnum illatum ab hoste reficiant, restaurentque ecclesiam omnibus viribus, tum a civitate diaboli avocantes, tum qui a civitate Dei deciderunt revocantes, tum si qui sunt moti firmantes. Itaque contra eorum apostatas sunt ecclesiæ cathecumini; contra illorum energuminos, quos turbant ut cadant, sunt ecclesiæ penitentes, quos expurgant ministri ut sistant. Verum, quod suum est, indesinente labore studet ecclesia servare, et quod modo erat suum recuperare; dico apostatas et energuminos; sicut contra, quod suum est et erat, nititur contra retinere adversarius; cathecuminos videlicet et penitentes. Ita mutuis excursionibus et crebris conflictibus, cum damnis vicitudinariis dimicant dominio isti exercitus Dei et diaboli: spiritus contra spiritus, et spiritales homines contra carnales. Maligni spiritus diligunt carnem, boni spiritum concupiscunt. Caro, inquit Paulus, adversus spiritum, et spiritus adversus carnem. Sed quia, Salvatoris testimonio, spiritus promptus est, caro autem infirma, ideo aliquando spiritus vincit carnem et lux tenebras, et vita mortem, et Deus diabolum, per dominum nostrum Iesum Christum, cui subjicie[ntur] omnia, ut Deus sit omnia in omnibus. Ecclesia Dei quæ supra mundum in monte Dei sita est, in liquido aere et spiritu luculento, suppeditatam sibi et suæ felicitatis materiem habet ex valle miseriæ hujus mundi; quæ inferiori sua parte virili et activa, superiorem et magis passivam mundi partem, non aliter ferme atque solis radii summas aquæ partes, suo calore eas extenuans et rarifaciens, attollit in altum, ut ex ea primum construat sibi quasi corpus, quod ipsum, quanquam spiritaliori parte ecclesiæ crassius est et corpulentius, tamen est toto mundano corpore spiritalius. Ex quo corpore deinde, et crassiore ecclesiæ parte, sano et integro, ex ejus videlicet summa et sereniore regione, et talibus qui jam prope evaserint spiritales, qui sunt corporis ecclesiæ quasi purior serenior et vitalior sanguis,—ex talibus hominibus in passiva parte ecclesiæ, qui maturiores sunt, trahuntur in racionem spiritalem; ut jam activæ sint partes et spiritus sint; sed primum purgatorii, quorum munus et officium totum versetur in purgatione et recreatione et nutricione corporis, quæ est humilior et crassior ecclesiæ pars; inter quam quidem, et Deum ecclesiæ animam, sunt spiritales homines, operatores et effectores omnium. Ut in homine inter ejus animam et corpus medii sunt spiritus puri, subtiles, lucidi, calidi, ab ipso cordis calore et subtiliore sanguine procreati; ita similiter inter Deum et ecclesiam convocatorum hominum sunt ex ipsis convocatis hominibus, ex sinceriore ejus parte et quasi deificatiori sanguine, a calore Dei et amore procreati spiritales homines, qui sunt medii inter Deum et reliquos homines, qui per eos a Deo dependent. Atque etiam, ut inter animam hominis et corpus spiritus sunt triplici in genere, alii enim naturales, alii vitales, alii animales; hi summe animæ inserviunt, vitales sensibus, naturales generacioni, nutricioni, auctioni, expurgationi, refectioni, sanacioni, et ejusmodi operibus in parte corpulentiori hominis; sic ferme ad eundem modum in Christo, inter Deum et partem popularem, sunt tria genera hominum spiritalium; quorum quidam, instar animalium spirituum, maxime inserviunt Deo, animæ ecclesiæ; quidam, qui humiliorem ecclesiæ partem curant maxime, ut eam reficiant, nutriant, foveant, augeant, expurgent, conservent; quidam inter hos medii, qui subserviunt quasi sensibus, et eos, ut sensibiles qualitates sacramentorum in ecclesia agnoscant, illuminant. Primi hi, et viciniores carnali parti ecclesiæ, vivificant carnem purgatoria virtute; fedam eorum mortem abluentes, ut in spe Dei vivant. Secundi, qui sensus spiritales faciunt, purgatos sperantesque in Deo illuminant, ut sacramenta ecclesiæ et omne sacratius signum perfecte sentiant credentes, et eo summa fide delectentur. Tercii illi quidem et summi, qui in Deum toto desiderio intenti sunt, qui simplicem cujusque sensus racionem perspicue intelligunt, eos qui senserunt signa et fide sacramenta, qui idonei ex eis et maturi ad se accedunt, mysteriorum et sensibilium rerum simplices raciones, quatenus capaces sunt, speculatores faciunt; ut quod fide senserint jam dudum sub sacerdotibus, jam tandem sub pontifice cum summo amore intelligant, ac pro capacitate impleti mysteriis perficiantur. Lux enim res rara et tenuis est, si non quasi condensetur calore; et spectacio sensibilium rerum pæne inanis est et vacua, si amore intellectorum mysteriorum non impleantur. Mysteriorum visio, amor et cultus complet et perficit omnia. Supremi ergo illi perficientes sunt pontifices; medii illuminantes sacerdotes; primi purgantes ministri. Qui autem purgantur in simplicem Deo spem, ut se sistant in ipso, et sperantes jam respirent in eo, ac renati nova creatura [fiant] nunc creatura nova penitus, hi in primo ecclesiæ gradu sunt et vestibulo, et quasi ossa ejus crassa firmitate, parum in se sensus habentes, sed stabiles spe, in omnibus quæ agunt in mundo pro sustentacione superioris ecclesiæ ex Deo pendentes; qui sunt certe conquisitores necessariorum vitæ, ministri non callidi ingenii sed boni Dei et solertis naturæ † Dei et naturæ † suppeditacionem excipientes, et eam subministrantes aliis; ut in temporalibus ministri sint ministris spiritalium. Omni enim sunt Dei. Nemo habet quod det suum, nemo possidet quod non accepit. Domini est terra et plenitudo ejus. Illius sunt quidem jure et temporalia omnia et spiritalia, qui creavit omnia. Temporalia ex terra sunt, spiritalia ex celo. Humilior et terrestrior ecclesiæ pars ministra est temporalium Dei opera et racione simplici; celestis vero illa et sublimior elargitur spiritalia, ministra magnæ benignitatis Dei. Hi sunt ministri corpulentiori et crassiori ecclesiæ parti in vitam sempiternam, spiritale eis pabulum largiter præbentes. Humilior vero pars, quæ spe ex Deo pendet, et sedulo ex terra trahit quo pascatur ecclesia, hæc pars spiritaliori illi subministrat vitam temporalem. Ita mutuis officiis et beneficiis ecclesia, dum hic militat, dumque est partim temporalis, partim et maxime spiritalis, utrinque et ex superiori et ex inferiore loco in divitiis Dei et temporalibus et spiritalibus; Dei servis et ministris se sancte exercentibus in utraque vita sustinere et temporali et spiritali; superiori parte inferiori viventi temporaliter, et inferiori ex superiori vivente et valente spiritaliter; ut tota ecclesia in hoc mundo necessariis dumtaxat, et ea quoque leviter in diem, conquisitis, in spiritalem hic contendat vitam, in vitam eternam. In hac humilima ecclesiæ parte sunt vocati cathecumini et jam instructi, et revocati penitentes, et exorcizati energumini, et recuperati apostatæ. Horum est opere et labore corporis in terrenis Dei diviciis corporalem ecclesiæ victum quæritare; ut in terrenis se exerceant in omni simplicitate et veritate, ministri jam Dei in his terrestribus, in refectionem caducæ et corporeæ partis ecclesiæ. Hi sunt quos in sua prima epistola ad Corinthios scripta, concordiam suadens Paulus toti ecclesiæ, assimilat vilioribus corporis membris, quæ quo minus speciosa sunt aliis, eo magis sunt necessaria, et sui, ut integra conserventur, majorem curam habe[nt]. Ex hoc hominum genere, si quando aliqui eorum ex summa et seriore parte, ministrorum assiduitate et opera, evaserint tandem deificaciores, omni peccati sorde detersa penitus, ut jam dyaphinitate perspicui et lucis alicujus capaces a perspicacibus ministris censeantur, tunc sacerdotibus offeruntur, ut ab eis perfusi copiosiore luce majore fide splendeant; quibus offeruntur spectacula fidei, ut claro mentis oculo sensibilia sacramenta quibus a sacerdotibus iniciati erant, jam purgati discernant; iniciatique jam sacris Christianis et sacerrimis signis insigniti sine offensione in sensu spiritus speculatores sint divinarum et illustrium in Christo imaginum; ipsi quoque modo lucentes eisdem simulachris, et ostentantes in omni humilitate signa in se et notas et caracteres humano ministerio sed divino sigillo impressos, sublimioris certe et simplicioris lucis veritatisque dignissimi testes. Hi januam modo ingressi sunt templi Dei, et vulgatiorem supellectilem domus Dei contemplantur; non admissi adhuc ad eas quæ secretiores sunt opes et reconditiores in penetrabilibus Dei, quæ in sua archa sapientiæ sancte et religiose custodit pontifex, quas non est phas prodere, nisi amore Dei divinarumque rerum perfectis et consummatis Christianis. Dionysius eos a sacerdotibus sacramentis illuminatos, quos nunc sacris interesse et ea spectare licet, sub nomine sanctæ plebis comprehendit, qui fide maxime vigent. Alii interea, tales qui in purgatione sui præsentes sacris esse non possunt, si non sint, cujusmodi †non† esse facile non possunt, tum in parando victu ecclesiæ iniciati sacris et sancta plebs se occupet. Potest enim superior in ecclesia quicquid inferius; non contra quidem. Summa vero et serenior pars sanctæ plebis, quæ nunc aspiravit quasi in regionem ignis, et amore calet presto ut inflammetur, ea a sacerdotibus tradatur pontifici, ut ei opportune in perfectionem extremam manum imponat, eamque, quatenus capere potest, simplicibus nudis mysteriis perimpleat, quibus conspectis fragret amore. Hi super plebem sunt, quos Dionysius vocat Monachos, quæ plebis pars liquidior est, jam inflammata amore ut ignis instar celestibus orbibus adhereat; in quo loci ita proficiant ut in ministrorum ordinem possunt promoveri, ut qui sunt summi in pacientibus sint infimi in agentibus. Cujusmodi autem est pontifex inter spiritales, tales sunt monachi singulares et solitares inter corporales; et inter illos quales sunt sacerdotes, tales inter hos sunt qui in sancta plebe numerantur. Et inter illos denique qui sunt ministri, tales sunt in his ii qui in manibus sunt purgantium.

Spiritus	Pontifex.	Monachus.	Perfectio.
	Sacerdotes.	Sancta plebs.	Illuminatio.
	Ministri.	Qui purgantur.	Purgatio.
Corpus	Monachi perfecti.	Pontifex, perficiens bonitate.	
	Plebs discens.	Sacerdotes, illuminantes doctrina.	
	In purgatione penitentes.	Ministri, purgantes potencia.	

CAP. VI. 2, 3.

MONACHUS ex purissima plebis parte procreatus est, jam totus simplex in se et unus, ac uni Deo omnino et penitus deditus, quatenus quisque ex populo dedi et tradi potest. Ut illuminati baptismate suum habent consecrationis ritum, ut hæc plebs sancta sacra signa speculetur, ita ex populo consummati in unitatem ac in alium perfectionis gradum provecti, illius rei ceremonialem consignationem habent, ut sensibilis habitus spiritalem processionem admoneat et indicet. Itaque monachus aliquis ut unitatem quam modo assecutus est, et indivisibilem vivendi racionem profiteatur, ad aliquem ex genere sacerdotali, qui mihi videntur tenuisse eum locum in prima ecclesia quem apud nos dyaconi, accedit, et pone illum ante altare stat erectus in Deum unus, simplex, solitarius. Sacerdos postquam Deo gracias egit, versus [ad] hominem audit illum severissima professione omnem divisionem ac dispertionem vitæ abrenunciare in perpetuum; in unum se collectum tenere oculum simplicem, ut totum corpus suum sit lucidum; in unam partem duntaxat tendere; Deo soli inservire. In hac magna professione insignitionem sanctæ crucis patitur, ut quæ prædicat se abrenunciare, in Christi cruce mortua esse intelligantur, nunquam amplius in ipsum revictura. Tonditur cæsaries, ut omni diviso et superfluo abraso quam mundissimus in conspectu Dei appareat. Mutat vestem, mutans vitam; ut vitæ simpliciori simplicior vestis congruat. Hoc observatum est in omni sancta mutacione, ut quum se interior homo ab habitu spiritali in alium se spiritalem habitum transmutat, tum simul exterior homo idem faciet, ut habitus exterior interiori respondeat. Hinc a sanctis apostolis vitæ hominis vestis et tunica appellatur. Osculum autem habet significacionem suavissimæ conjunctionis. Ad eucharistiam denique admittitur, sed modo sacratiori quam plebs reliqua, qui nunc mysteriorum gnarus est. Ita monachus quasi populi monadon consummatur rite et perficitur. Qui vetus mos iniciandi et consecrandi non modo monachos sed omnes alios quoscunque ordines, qui propter institucionem apostolorum summam authoritatem habuit, et sanctissime in prima ecclesia observatus fuit, posterioribus seculis nescio qua pontificum abolevit mos vetus, et alius deinde etiam nescio qua temeritate hominum novis signis et ceremoniis inolevit, et invaluit jam tantum, ut reverendissimæ antiquitatis et apostolorum sanctissimæ institucionis, in ecclesia quæ nunc est, ne vestigium quidem appareat. Quod si divus Dionysius, (qui mihi videtur in nostra ecclesia qualis erat Moysaica synagoga Esdras, qui voluit mysteria veteris legis mandari literis, ne turbatione rerum et hominum tantæ sapienciæ memoria deperíret) quod si ad eundem modum, quasi divinasset hominum futuram negligentiam, divus Dionysius, quae tenuit memoria ex statutis apostolorum in disponenda et ordinanda ecclesia suo felici calamo descripta non reliquisset, nihil recordacionis veteris moris habuissemus. Quod jam a consuetudine decessisse ingemendum est sane, quum nos in conservandis institutis patrum nostrorum multo studiosiores esse debemus, quam erant hebrei in suis traditionibus retinendis; quanto nostra excellentiora et clariora sunt quam quae erant illorum, et majoris veritatis purioris significamina; quorum rationem et congruitatem maxime nimirum noverunt apostoli, qu[ibus] spiritus revelavit omnia, ut non poterat esse, quin illi sapienter intellexerint quae singula singulis apte accommodarent, et justa concinnitate depingerent spiritales veritates in propriis signis; quae postea demutata esse haud scio quomodo sine nephario scelere contigit, quum credendum est illos a spiritu sancto doctos omnia in ecclesia instituisse. Nam apud Ioannem sunt haec Salvatoris verba: Quum autem venerit ille spiritus veritatis, docebit vos omnem veritatem: non enim loquetur a semetipso; sed quaecumque audiet loquetur, et quae ventura sunt annunciabit vobis. Quorum sanctissimae tradiciones quia posthabitae sunt et neglectae, quiaque homines a spiritu Dei ad proprias inventiones deciderunt, hinc profecto omnia misere conturbata sunt et confusa. Et, ut ante dicebamus, si Deus non misertus fuerit, interibunt omnia.

CAP. VII. 1.

EST indubitanter credendum, qui regenerati sunt in Christo, quorum peccatrix vita interiit, quique juste vixerunt ut justi moriantur, sicut Christus justus mortuus fuit, tales pro propugnatione iniquitatis et pro tutacione justiciae Dei in ipsis, justiciae praemium, excedentes ex hac vita, primum in sancta eorum anima habituros, ac deinde suo tempore in carneque etiam, quae erat comes in itinere ad Deum et in bello socia: ut quisque justus homo totus ipse in Christo et animo et corpore in gloria beatus sit. Quod saduceis, non credentibus resurrectionem, omnis veritatis conscius Iesus affirmavit, dicens : Quum a mortuis resurrexerint, neque nubent neque nubentur, sed erunt sicut angeli Dei in celis. Qua spe sustentati boni, qui sanctam hic vitam in Christo egerint, libenter et letabunde moriuntur; partim gaudentes se evasisse periculum casus, in quod forsan inciderent si vita eorum longius produceretur; partim vel maxime gaudebundi, expectantes perfuncti laboris præmium, et Christianæ militiæ coronam gloriæ, quæ legittime certantibus sine dubio reservatur; de quo illorum sanctorum felici exitu et morte etiam simul amici et propinqui valde gaudent, gratulanturque, et sibi parem vitæ consummacionem in Christo exoptant, ut, justiciæ semita servata usque ad mortem, in ipsa morte vitam temporalem et erumnosam pro felici et eterna commutent, in Christoque sine fine vivant; qua spe gaudentes in defuncto, ac plane persuasum habentes illum migrasse ad Christum, funus exultantes efferunt, et deferunt ad pontificem, et id offerunt illi, sanctæ sepulturæ committendum. Nihil enim est magis indignum Christiana professione, in qua est certissima spes resurrectionis et gloriæ ad Christi similitudinem, quam paganorum more, quod jam quoque turpiter in ecclesia fere ubique faciunt, maxime vero in Italia, ubi viri in amicorum et propinquorum funeribus muliebres ejulatus fedissime edunt, tantis lachrimis deflere mortuos, quasi nobis esset opinio cum illis male actum esse, et non cum Christo beatissime vivere. Sed est is mos eorum tantum proculdubio, qui sic vixerint vita hic Christi vitæ tam dissimili, ut consciencia perditæ vitæ non habeant apud illum quod expectent, unde merentur valde et dolent se hinc decessuros, vel desperantes futuram vitam, vel expectantes eternam miseriam. Quos ad hunc modum alloquitur Paulus in sua epistola ad Tessalonicenses: Nolite, inquit, fratres, ignorare de dormientibus, ut non contristemini sicut et ceteri qui spem non habent. Si enim credimus quod Iesus mortuus est et resurrexit, ita et Deus eos qui dormierunt per Iesum adducet cum eo. Quod quidem mali Christiani desperant, desperantesque miseri moriuntur. Boni autem multis de causis letabundi obeunt mortem; et quod tedet eos hujus turbulentæ et erumnosæ vitæ, et securitatem velint, et requiem cupiunt, et cum Christo esse desiderant; id quod Paulus in se dixit: Cupio dissolvi et esse cum Christo. Item Ignatius ille, fortissimus martir, Amor meus, solitus est dicere, crucifixus est; Christum significans, cum quo in celo esse cupiebat. Deliramenta quæ nata sunt hominibus etiam post Christum ex ascultacione philosophorum (quæ Dionysius commemorat), a magnanimis Christianis et meliora sperantibus longe repudianda sunt; videlicet vel animas interire cum corporibus; vel superesse, sed corpora non resumpturas; vel superstites migrare in alia corpora; vel in campis (nescio quibus) elysiis omni amenitate et jucunditate plenis degere. Omnes has nebulosas opinatiunculas claritas Christi longe discussit, et veritatem credendam aperuit.

CAP. VII. 2.

SACERDOTIS si sit quod mortuum est cadaver, ante altare locetur interea, dum exequiæ funebreque officium agitur. Sin sit ex plebeo genere, dum inferiæ sacraque mortuorum fiunt, statuatur dimortui corpus ante sacrarium, eo loco ubi est plebis stare, in medio omnium, ut Dei sacramenta universi conspectent. Sacrarium autem sive sanctuarium sceptum est illud quod cancellis secernitur et sacerdotium separat a plebe, in quo chorus sacerdotum sacra officia celebrat, qui locus a nostris quoque jam chorus vocitatur. Cantus graciarumque actio a sacerdotio incipit. Recitantur a ministris quæ resurrectionis confirment. In dimortuos laus dicitur, si prius archidiaconus cathecuminos ejecerit. Ille quoque mortuus modo in Christo beatus prædicatur. Ab archidiacono qui adsunt omnes admonentur ut curent in Christo bene moriantur. Pontifex in demortuum, prope quasi ad aurem se admonens, bene precatur et orat, commendatque illum Deo, salutat cum suis et tota ecclesia, in eum oleum infundit. Quum sic parentatum fuerit rite, et justa facta, reliquiæ tum sepulturæ inter alios sui ordinis sanctos commendantur. In hac parentacione nihil est nisi spes, leticia, gaudium, et congratulacio de mortuo in Christo Iesu, quod creditur iniisse in cetum sanctorum, et in vitam beatiorem in celis, ubi Christo suo fruetur feliciter evo sempiterno.

CAP. VII. 3.

SED jam quid velint sacra ceremoniæque mortuorum videamus. Omnis nostra actio hic in ecclesia est significatio eorum quæ fiunt in celis. Nam in fide fundamur et credimus ita esse in celis ut in terris agimus, divinarum rerum dispensationem imitantes. Dixit Petro fide insigni, quod solveris vel ligaveris in terris, solutum ligatumque fore in celis. Tota nostra vita Christiana contentio est, ut Deo quam maxime fieri possit assimilemur. Erat Deus ipse factus homo quodammodo sui dissimilis. Nam, ut Paulus scribit, exinanivit se, formam servi accipiens, ut homines suo patri assimularet. Et quum docuit suos discipulos Iesus in monte celestem pietatem, sermonem suum hac sentencia conclusit, dicens: Estote ergo vos perfecti, sicut et pater vester celestis perfectus est. Sed in hac contentione in Deum per Christum, id assequitur quisque quod datæ vires paciuntur. Quod scripsit apostolus ad Corinthios: Unusquisque proprium donum habet; alius quidem sic, alius vero sic; pro mensura fidei sunt merita; pro racione meritorum sunt præmia. Diversitas et ordo hic in ecclesia militante imago est ordinis illius quem ecclesia triumphans est habitura in celis. Sacerdos itaque quia habetur justior laico, is mortuus dum parentatur, in medio choro inter sacerdotes statuitur. Extra cancellos vero ante chorum in plebeorum regione laicus defunctus, vel monachus ille sanctior, inter laicos collocatur; ut hoc ordine ammoniti alium in celis sacerdotibus locum, et sacratiorem multo, quam laico, datum esse credimus; quum hic ordo in ecclesia ex supracelesti illo ordine dirivatur; apostolis divino spiritu præditis rite et celitus disponentibus omnia, qui a spiritu paraclito omnem veritatem didicerunt. Dei virtute electi in Christianum exercitum pugnamus, vincimus, evadimus, morimur justi in Christo, justorum gloriam accepturi, quisque pro racione justiciæ suæ. De justo mortuo gaudet ecclesia, et cum festivali pompa victorem defunctum certa spe Deo tradunt coronandum. Quæ canit ecclesia in sacris mortuorum, cantica leticiæ sunt, ad consolationem et exhortacionem vivorum; ut ii sperantes mortuum migrasse ad Deum, parem sibi exitum exoptent; ut sibi gloria et ecclesiæ gaudium esse possit. Fletus vero, lachrimæ, ejulatus, feditas est in ecclesia, et eorum plane hominum qui gloriam Christi resurgentis ex mortuis justis post mortem fore parum credunt. Quod si credidissent Iesum Christum, quia justus mortuus est, gloriosum resurrexisse, exemplum resurrectionis justorum, et ad eandem formam in illo per potentiam Dei omnes justos resurrecturos, sine dubio amicorum mortem tam miserabiliter non lugerent. Quoniam preciosa est in conspectu Domini mors sanctorum ejus. Mors autem peccatorum pessima. Quocirca, si quid dolendum esset, profecto de injustorum morte dolendum esset; quoniam cum illis pessime agitur, quorum vermis non extinguetur. Verum in Christiana ecclesia, quæ fide et spe magnanima in Deo, nihil turpius et dedecore plenius quam mortuorum, saltem quos cognoverunt non injustos fuisse in Christo, defletio. Ecclesia in justis mortuorum decantat laudes; gratulatur de mortuo; ex scripturis spem resurrectionis jucundam profert; in præsenti commodo amici et fratris, quod sancta morte liberatur a malis, letatur; in spe futuri boni justis exultat. Electa, sapiens, pia in Christo ecclesia hæc facit ut ostendat Christianis hominibus jucundiorem diem nullum esse posse, quam eum in quo justus aliquis moritur; maxime si pro justicia etiam vim paciens moriatur. Illi homini tanta erit gloria, ut tota ecclesia præ leticia exultet. Iesus quum sua sanctissima mors instaret, de ea suos discipulos ita alloquutus est, ut Ioannes refert: Audistis quia dixi vobis, vado et venio ad vos. Et, quia vidit eos mæstos, addidit: Si diligeretis me, gauderetis utique quia vado ad patrem; ut illi de Iesu morte gauderent; ita et tota ecclesia et singulus quisque in ea gaudeat de justo homine commortuo cum Christo in gloriam, ut officium Christianæ pietatis videatur præstitisse, utque fratrem demortuum etiam dilexisse videatur:—gaudeat (inquam) quisque de fratris commodo in morte, et illi valde gratuletur; alioquin non fratris in Christo speranter, sed sui ipsius et in mundo desperanter amicus et amator judicetur. Quod autem cathecumini a sacris funeribus propulsantur et abiguntur, est id quidem quod ii sine regenerationis lumine, quod in baptismate a Deo ministrantibus sacerdotibus datur, sunt, et ceci adhuc, ut mysteriorum spectacula inspicere nequeant. Alii autem qui illuminati fuerint, et se sua ipsorum improbitate obcecaverunt, apostatæ et penitentes; item energumini, qui adhuc molliores malignas diaboli agitaciones ferre non possunt; quanquam aliis sacris non sinuntur interesse, parentacionibus tamen et justis interesse possunt, ut ecclesiæ officio et spe futuræ vitæ quam cernant in sacris mortuorum, commoneantur ut resipiscentes futuram vitam desiderent. Est præterea, uti diximus, in ceremoniis et sacris mortuorum, ut pontifex in funere prope feretrum oret pro mortuo, et eum quasi sensu habentem salutet, omnes deinde reliqui consalutent.[1] Orat autem Deum ut, si quæ sint peccata, in quæ ille vivus humana imbecillitate inciderit, ut id ei agnoscat, et misericors veniam det, recipiatque in luculentam illam suam regionem vivorum, ut feliciter in patriarcharum sinubus conquiescat, ubi est leticia et gloria sempiterna, et ea quoque tanta et tam solida, ut Paulus asserat, ad Corinthios scribens, nec oculum vidisse, nec audivisse aurem, nec in cor hominis ascendisse, quæ præparavit Deus diligentibus se. O quanta voluptas erit quamque exultans delectacio illis filiis hominis, bone Deus, qui speraverunt in tegmine alarum tuarum, ut cecinit regius propheta tuus David. Inebriabuntur ubertate domus tuæ, et torrente voluptatis tuæ potabis eos, quoniam apud te est fons vitæ et in lumine tuo videbimus lumen. Dominus ipse, ut in alio psalmo est, spes nostra est, et porcio nostra in terra viventium. Sed rogat quispiam quidnam opus sit ut pro defuncto oretur? Nam de eo actum est, vel in bonam vel in malam partem. Etenim ex vitæ meritis justo Dei judicio aut sursum aut deorsum tendit. Post mortem nullus cuique est locus promerendi. Dionysius illi respondens primum significat oracionem non prodesse cuiquam,

---

[1] Consultent. MS.

nec vivo nec mortuo quidem, nisi et digno et etiam a digno. Qui oret dignus, sanctus est. Dignus pro quo oretur is est solum, qui velit et omnem dat operam ille imprimis ut sanctus sit, quique agnoscens suam indignitatem, veretur precibus divinam majestatem adire, et in illius conspectu (nisi intercedat quem arbitratur plus apud Deum [valere], qui simul cum eo supplicet) apparere, quique postremo humilime quærit sibi ex primariis ordinibus in ecclesia unum, qui inter Deum et se medius sit, cujus fretus suffragio, et comprecatione adjutus, ipse simul cum illo maxime et intentissime deprecans tandem exaudiatur. Hac via et modo inita oracio res est omnium potentissima et efficacissima sane, ut si incessanter cum spe pergat humilis flagitacio (salvatoris ipsius doctrina, in exemplo illius qui petiit panes media nocte, et illius mulierculæ, quæ postulavit sententiam ab iniquo judice), non potest certe non exaudiri. Quod si quispiam negligat suam causam, et frigeat ipse intime in salute sua, ac ex more ut solitus erat, male vivat, non incipiens et agens ipse imprimis [1] ut cum Deo in graciam redeat, sed mandat aliis (uti nunc mos est secularium hominum data exigua stipe) ut pro se orent, habens spem in aliorum oracionibus se salvum esse posse; is profecto in his est qui sunt indigni ut pro eis oretur, et ipse quoque homo est unus omnium stultissimus; qui putat in sua negligentia aliorum diligentiam sibi prodesse posse, seque per alios salvum fore, qui nihil curat ipse ut salvus sit; qui perinde agit ac ille egrotus aliquis, qui luxuriose vivens velit a medico curari; et, ut Dionysii exemplo utar, qui aliquis erutis sibi oculis velit solem intueri. Desipit ille insane qui nihil ipse agens quum potest, aliorum externa actione putat se utilitatem adipisci posse; quique redire in graciam cum eo principe a quo alienatus erat confidit per aliorum operam, quum ipse nihil agit cur graciam sibi principis reconciliet. Si qui ergo sint tales qui non ipsi imprimis et maxime agunt ut bene cum eis fiat, ii in numero eorum sunt quibus oracio nihil prodest, quique indigni sunt ut pro eis oretur. Qui vero agunt ipsi omnibus viribus ut salvi fiant, talibus sanctorum oracio non potest

---

[1] Imprimens. MS.

non maxime prodesse. Huic sentenciæ subscribit Ioannes apostolus in epistola canonica, dicens, Qui scit fratrem suum peccare peccatum non ad mortem, petat et dabitur ei vita peccanti non ad mortem. Est peccatum ad mortem: non pro illo dico ut roget quis. Juvat certe oracio orantem; non orantem vero, si possit orare, nihil juvat. Frustra sperat, Dionysii sentencia, in bonorum precibus, qui ipse male vivit. Deprecatio illa pontificis super defunctum, ut is in gloria sit, non tam est peticio ut ita fiat, quam indicacio ita esse. Est enim pontifex, ut Malachias appellat, angelus Dei, et interpres divinæ voluntatis, divino spiritu agitatus. Ideo deprecatio illa est narratio ex sacro ore pontificis, quid sine dubio cum justo mortuo agitur; ut in verbis pontificis discat ecclesia quid præmii est justis qui mortui sunt in Christo; et pontifici qui pendet ex ore Dei, et qui habet spiritum sanctum (Accipite, inquit, Spiritum sanctum) ex fide loquenti aliquid in ministerio Dei credat. Qui non ex se loquitur, sed ex Spiritu; et quod summa fide credit esse et testatur in terris, id factum est in celis, ubi prius agitur quam revelatur ut credatur. Est ille, ut ait Dionysius, angelus et interpres voluntatis Dei, et loquitur agitque omnia, uti monetur a Deo; et quorum vult Deus misereri, eorum pontifex in Deo, illius voluntatis divinator, miseretur. Quorum non miseretur pontifex, argumentum spiritum Dei non monere eos ut misereatur, taliumque Deum ipsum in celis non misereri, qui ad suam voluntatem spiritu sancto ministrum suum pontificem agit, ut quod in celo decretum est, in terris pontificali officio exequatur. A celo enim et a Deo dirivantur omnia; et ille est qui agit in omnibus; et homines veri in illo sunt ministri voluntatis illius a quo habent spiritum; ut quasi instrumenta sint actionis Dei; non agant quidem ipsi aliquid, sed Deus in eis agat omnia. Ad hoc post suam resurrectionem Deushomo Iesus Christus ut dilectiores suos discipulos ad quos intravit januis clausis, et dixit eis semel atque iterum Pax vobis, ut eos sibi apta instrumenta efficeret voluntatis suæ, ut quod fecerit ipse in celis illi exsequerentur in terris, insufflans in eos dixit, Accipite Spiritum sanctum. Sicut misit me Pater, ego mitto vos. Quorum remiseritis peccata (exequentes scilicet voluntatem Dei isto Spiritu accepto) remittuntur eis; et quorum retinueritis, retinentur: modo ex Spiritu dato fiat, et justa dispensatione voluntatis Dei: alioquin non a Deo sed ab homine fit, cui credendum est. Quapropter Paulus ad Corinthios scribens, quum se apostolos et qui talem personam gerunt dixit ministros Christi et dispensatores misteriorum Dei, subjunxit e vestigio: Hic jam quæritur inter dispensatores, ut fidelis quis inveniatur. Non omnes enim justi sunt ministri, nec recte dispensant, nec prudentes a Deo Spiritu aguntur divino; sed confisi sibi efficiunt quod volunt ipsi spiritu proprio, qui inimicus est Deo. Qui vero a Deo per Christum electi in ipsum sursum tracti ex illo pendent, et quasi instrumenta in manu illius, illuc semper et in eam partem et in eum affectum sunt versa quo dirigit Deus; qui sunt indicia et declaramenta et executores voluntatis Dei, et mentis illius, diffinientis prius et formantis omnia. Hi certe non agunt ipsi, sed Deus in eis, nec authores sunt ipsi cujuspiam facti, sed Deus; qui quicquid fecerint, id a Deo factum esse credendum est: qui sunt sane loco Dei habendi et colendi, ut ipse Deus; non ipsi sed Deus in eis, in cujus spiritu monentur ut divinitus cogitent, agant et loquantur omnia. De id genus hominibus est illud Iesu apud Lucam dictum: Qui vos audit, me audit; et qui vos spernit, me spernit: qui autem spernit me, spernit eum qui misit me. Quia est Deus in Christo, et Christus in illis qui vere sunt sui; maxime in ecclesiæ primariis, si illi vere sunt Christi. Vultisne experimentum ejus, inquit Paulus, qui in me loquitur Christus? Hi Spiritu Christi agunt omnia, ut Christus Spiritu Dei: hi alti in Deo revelatas veritates accipiunt et revelatis credunt; et quod indicatum est a Spiritu Dei latenter monente, cujus motus non noscunt nisi sublimes in Deo, id indubia fide et agunt et dictitant. Hæc est fides magnifica qua Petrus agnovit Iesum Christum filium esse Dei vivi, et verbis confessus est. Hæc est illa fides cui tantam potestatem tribuit Deus, ut quodcunque ligaverit in terris, idem erit ligatum in celis; et quod solverit in terris, solutum erit idem in celis. Ligata sunt autem proculdubio antea in celis quam ligentur omnia, et solvuntur illic prius quæ hic deinde solvuntur. Non enim Deus ex hominibus, sed homines ex Deo pendent. Nec ille quasi postea confirmat nostra, sed homines exequuntur quæ prius erant Dei. Et hominum ministerio patet tandem in terris, quod a Deo prius diffinitum in celis erat occultius. Quod revelatum et creditum a legitimo Dei ministro prodit in apertum, oportuno tempore et servi Dei officio patefactum est; cui, ut nuncio et interpreti divinæ voluntatis, credendum est. Hinc est quod Dionysius pontificem, qui est in ecclesia summus et Deo proximus, angelum et Dei interpretem vocat; qui quod ligatum est in celis, credens revelanti Deo, idem ligat in terris; et quod solutum est in celis, idem solvit in terris; id est, divinam ligacionem et solucionem quatenus ei indicatur, ecclesiæ demonstrat et in Deo hoc volente notificat. Quia est valde annotandum, ut pontifices non insolescant, non esse hominum remittere peccatorum vincula; nec ad eos pertinet potestas solvendi et ligandi quicquam. Solvit enim et ligat solus Deus, et apud se in celo solvit et ligat omnia. Qui primi sunt in ecclesia, sicuti sunt pontifices, quod illic ligatum et solutum est accipiunt ex revelatione, et acceptum denunciant, et verbis divinam mentem exsequuntur, non propriam. Quod si non procedant ex revelacione, acti spiritu Dei in omnibus quæ agant dicantve, delirant stulti tunc necessario ex seipsis, et potestate data tum in blasphemiam Dei tum in perniciem ecclesiæ abutuntur. Ex quibus licet cernere, quam altus, quam sublimis, quam totus in celo positus debet esse pontifex; maxime ille quidem qui summus est, quem nos papam vocitamus, ut sua authoritate quod in ecclesiam dirivet, vivificans eam in vitam eternam, id totum ex Deo hauriat, haustumque decoquat, et rite ac legittime per omnia membra distribuat; ut hæc refecta divino pabulo in pontifice convivant illo, qui maxime vivit Deo; utque omnia ex Deo procedant in ecclesiam, in revocationem omnium in ipsum, qui ipse in sana et casta ecclesia est omnia in omnibus; qui vivificat, illuminat et perficit pontificem, maxime illum qui summus est; ut is deinceps sapientiam et voluntatem Dei in omnibus in vitam et salutem omnium fideliter et sinceriter ministret; nihil quærens nisi lucrum hominum in Deo, et approbationem sui a Deo, in dispensacione ministeriorum Dei. Qui si sit legittimus, non ille agit quippiam sed Deus in illo. Quod si quippiam ex semetipso attemptet, venenum tunc parturit. Si idem proferat, et suam ipsius voluntatem exsequatur, in ecclesiæ interitum perdite venenum infundit. Quod nunc quidem abhinc annis multis factum est, et jam ita se auxit et omnes ecclesiæ artus ita potenter occupat, ut nisi mediator ille qui solus potest, qui ecclesiam sibi creavit et condidit ex nihilo (idcirco eam sæpe creaturam vocat Paulus); nisi, inquam, mediator ille Iesus quam cito manus apponat, egrotissima ecclesia longe a morte abesse non potest. Relaxant et retrahunt, solvunt et ligant homines, non ex fide Deo, quæ ligata sunt in celis, sed quæ ipsi volunt, unde omnia disturbantur in terris. Non sunt executores voluntatis Dei, sed actores propriæ. Non testificant quid Deus vult, quod facere debent (nam eorum officium nihil aliud est quam testificacio voluntatis Dei), sed quod ipsi appetunt, demonstrant. Non consulunt Deum in agendis oracione assidua, sed cum hominibus consultacionem capiunt; quo labefactant et demoliuntur omnia. Quærunt (quod dolendum est, quodque ego et dolens et flens scribo) quæ sua sunt omnes, non quæ Iesu Christi; terrestria non celestia; quæ ferent eos in mortem, non in vitam eternam. Sed, ut redeamus ad propositum, Verus pontifex et antistes legittimus et fidelis dispensator ministeriorum Dei, non agit quicquam nisi ex Deo; manus, minister, instrumentum Dei; cui ut Deo ipsi credendum est. Quamobrem in officio funerali, dum precatur eternam vitam sanctis demortuis in Christo, reverenter Dei certam voluntatem eloquitur, ex fide et effectu id rogans ut fiat quod plane scit fore; ut verbis deprecatoriis, quæ in omnibus debent pontificem, testetur ecclesiæ astanti justiciam et graciam Dei hominibus; eis scilicet qui in Christo bene moriantur. Est enim Pontifex testificator voluntatis Dei, et quasi os et mentis Dei verbum, quæ præscripta sunt a Deo, quæ fide cernit, exprimens. Deus ipse est qui bene agit omnia in omnibus. Quod autem deinde pontifex et universa ecclesia salutet defunctum, et ei quasi ultimum vale dicat, est significatio non mortui omnino, sed hominis in aliam regionem, et veram suam et propriam patriam commigrantis. Salutatum cadaver sacro oleo perfundit pontifex, ut hoc illum certamen confecisse denotet. Annotandus est vetus mos ab ipsis apostolis institutus, iniciandos primum symbolo eruditos fuisse, instructos, et nudatos; et jam iniciatos oleo in certamen perunctos fuisse: postremo egregios pugnatores defunctos extremam et perfectoriam unctionem accepisse. Unguenti usus est frequens in Christiana ecclesia, quæ ab unctione cognomen habet, et vocatur Christiana. Unguentum vero est diversorum odorum commixtio, addito oleo aut balsamo, aut alio hujusmodi pingui. Ecclesia in hoc genere propriam suam habet compositionem. Quod unguentum Spiritum sanctum significat, quo roborantur omnes in Christo, et ad certamen spectat quod imus sub duce Christo cum spiritalibus nequiciæ in celestibus, cum quibus Spiritu sancto inuncti et roborati dimicamus; cujus sancti Spiritus sacramentum est quæ corpori adhibetur unctio, quæ est unctionis animæ significatrix, qua spiritales in Spiritu Christi, in spiritali pugna, armis spiritalibus cum spiritalibus hostibus, quamdiu hic vivimus legittimi, in Christo confligimus. Postremo invicti ipsi tuti in Christo quum evaserimus perfuncta milicia, defuncti ungimur, ut intelligatur cujus virtute pugnare cepimus, ejusdem Spiritus sancti gracia nos bellum confecisse. Postremo corpus sepelitur, circumceptum vel terra, vel lapide, vel quavis alia materia, cum sui ordinis hominibus, in diem resurrectionis reservatum. Primæ ecclesiæ institutum fuit, ut seorsum et distinctum locaretur cadaver, etiam in cadaveribus non disturbato ordine, ut ubique ordo appareret. Quæ corpora ut erant participia laboris et certaminis, paciencia malorum et abstinencia a voluptatibus, ita certa spe ponuntur in participacionem gloriæ, quando Dei potencia reintegrata suis animabus revincientur. Nam si totus homo ad exemplum Christi non glorificaretur, ab ipso Christo et apostolis, unde omnis sacramentorum institucio profecta est, in ipsum corpus et carnem non instituta fuissent sacramenta; quæ se habent certe ad corpus, in immortalitatem illius; quemadmodum spiritus in gloriam animi immortalem. Panis enim et benedictus calix, internum pabulum, et unctio, extrema[1] fotio, quidnam vult aliud

---

[1] *Leg.* externa.

quam etiam corpus ali, nutriri et foveri suo modo una cum anima in vitam et gloriam immortalem ? Pane enim et potu et oleo servamur in vita et intus et extra. In sensibilibus signis quæ sunt in usu maxime ad hanc vitam adhibentur veteri instituto apostolorum; ut hoc admoneamur sacramenta illa etiam in corpus vitam credentibus operari sempiternam. Anima autem suum proprium panem et potum habet, quo vescitur, et unguentum quo fovetur; quod vulgus et rudis plebecula nequit videre et cernere. Obedientia in Deo, bona spe, fide in signis, assiduitate bene agendi, salvabitur vulgus Christianum, quanquam hac ruditate tam excelsum in celo locum in glorioso Christo non assequentur, sicuti illi qui copiosiori Spiritu longius prospiciunt et mysteria altius discernunt. Quoniam, ut homines hic promoventur, non dico viribus propriis, sed humilitate et tractu Spiritus, ita omnino ad eundem ordinem locabuntur in celis. Quæ in sacris sacramentifica verba fiunt, divus Dionysius de sacramentis consulto tacet, et de illis literis disserere noluit, ne spargeret in porcos Dei margaritas. Uti diximus, et dicendum est sæpius, ab indigno vulgo sancta custodia vindicanda sunt sacramenta, quæ ab illis attrectata vilescunt. Sacratiora loca, vasa, vestes, et quicquid est sacerdotale, imperitæ et prophanæ multitudini non nisi ex remoto licet aspicere, et id quoque magno timore et reverentia. Sed, proh nephas, in hujus tempestatis nostræ infelicitate confunduntur omnia ita turpiter, ut nihil jam magis sit prophanum quam quod debet esse sacerrimum.

CAP. VII. 4.

EX sermone Dionysii videre licet, saluti infantum statim ab inicio nascentis ecclesiæ ab ipso Christo et apostolis provisum fuisse. In primaque ecclesia ipsa infantulos modo natos, propterea quod longe tum a culpa propria et nudi a viciis sunt, dummodo susceperit aliquis eorum curatum, et pro illis spoponderit, si vixerint, in re fore quod sacramenta exposcunt, non tantum regeneracionis sancto lavachro lotos et illuminatos, sed præterea sacrosanctæ eucharistiæ (sine qua in prima ecclesia ne infantum quidem baptismus esse potuit) participacione annexos et Christi corpori mystico consertos fuisse.[1] Quod quanquam carnales homines, qui non sapiunt ea quæ Dei sunt, tunc pro ridiculo habuerint, qui nihil admiserunt nec probarunt nisi quod humilis racio sibi persuasum habuit, tamen hominibus fidelibus et spiritalibus infantum consecratio Deo magnum et admirandum divinæ misericordiæ sacramentum videtur. Et ab ecclesia habetur res plena pietatis, modo rite fiat et modo legittimo; cujus rei racio etsi cerni ab [hominibus non] possit, nil mirum est quidem, quando nec ipsi quidem primi angeli omnia cognoscant. Verum pia fides admittit et colit omnia. Et qui primum instituerunt non modo illud sacramentum, sed præterea reliqua omnia, illi scilicet apostoli, eorum vel raciones tenuerunt vel crediderunt tenenti. Quod instinctu divini spiritus exortum est et fit, racione vel summa carere non potest, quam non attingit humilis humana racio, sed super hanc racionem fides, lumen certe nobis datum in Christo divinæ racionis capax. In qua re fideque, quam vel ipsi præcipui Christi condiscipuli sibi exaugeri petierunt, si nos parvi sumus, idcirco magna Dei sacramenta non contemnamus. Quinimmo agnoscamus, et vere ac humiliter confiteamur angustiam racionis nostræ, atque quod nescimus quæ Dei sunt comprehendere, nostræ pravitati ascribamus; potius quam statim quæ non capit pusilla racio dedignanter aspernemer; ac studeamus supra racionem majores fieri fide, et supra carnem spiritales, et supra homines divini; credamusque omnino et indubitanter divina, nisi a divinis hominibus, capi non posse. Sed jam de sacris parvulorum qui in ecclesia Christiana nati sunt, quisnam fuerat eorum iniciandorum ordo et ritus apud priscos illos nostræ religionis viros videamus. Apud [priscam ecclesiam], ut diximus Dionysii testimonio, quadam condicione et lege tum ad baptismum tum ad eucharistiam admissi erant. Modus inducendi eos ut annumerarentur in ecclesia, sicuti refert Dionysius, hic quidem fuit. Parens edito in lucem nato, intelligens non nasci filio filiæve

---

[1] *Deest* reperio, *vel aliquid simile.*

melius fuisse, quam in Christo non renasci; non ignorans etiam parum prodesse sacramentum, immo obesse certe, nisi vita, si infans adolescat, acceptis sacris responderit:—ut ergo a pontifice in participacionem sacrorum admittatur, parens circuit et sollicite quærit, ubinam locorum reperiat bonum virum ac peritum Christianæ veritatis, qui recipiat in se et promittat instructionem filii et eruditionem in omnibus illis quæ spectant ad salutem, quique apud pontificem, si ille eum insigniverit et induerit divinis sacris, pro infante spondeat ex racione sacrorum, si adoleverit, ipsum sancte et puriter in Christo victurum. Cujusmodi virum quum nactus fuerit pater, quumque ei suum filiolum bona fide commendaverit, quasi altero et majori parenti in Deo: (nam paternum officium et generatio infantis regeneracioni ejusdem antecedens ministerium est) is tum vir qui susceperit in se parturitionem pueruli in Christo, ut tandem, si vixerit, perfectus Christianus formatus effigiatur, hac magna professione paternitatis in Christo, adit pontificem, illi ostendit quem in regeneracionem, vel potius in quandam plenam formationem in Christo, sibi accepit, petit reverenter a pontifice ut eum Christi corpore asciscat similitudine et consignatione sacrorum, ut ex ipsis in vitam sacris dignam sua assiduitate et cura coalescat. Pontifex tum quum audiat hominem spondere sancteque promittere pro puero, quumque eundem videat ut promissa præstet non esse inidoneum, accepta sponsione, confisus divinæ misericordiæ, more et ritu instituto ab apostolis, justis formulis et signaculis infantem exornat, tum illuminans baptismate, tum sacra communione perficiens. Interea illo alumno, qui puerum in Christo educandum suscepit, dante fidem, et sancte promittente pro infante omnia ea quæ vera Christianitas exposcit; abrenunciacionem videlicet omnis iniquitatis, et sacramentis fidem, et vitam perseverantem in Christo, tanta professione dignam; quod non pro infante loquitur, quod esset ridiculum ut alius pro ignorante loquatur; sed quum dicit abrenunciacionem loquens ipse profitetur se, quoad poterit, effecturum ut infantulus ille statim quum eruditionis capax fuerit, re ipsa et vita omnem racionem Christianæ personæ contrariam longe abrenunciet, exhibeatque se in omni vita dignum sacris, sciens tandem in adolescentiore etate, et sponte profitens quæ ipse infans inscius accepit. Tum hac lege et condicione ut alumnus præstet quod promiserit, ad sacra pontifex infantem admittit. Quando audit illum (quem ego alumnum, Dionysius vero modo susceptorem, modo divinum patrem appellat: ab aliis patrinus, compater ab aliis vocatur) pontifex, inquam, quando audit dicentem Abrenuntio, quod est quidem, ut exponit Dionysius, efficiam ipse ut infans omne ei oblatum ex inferiori loco et diabolo abrenunciet repudietque, nihilque velit nisi quod ei superne ex celo ab ipso Deo delatum fuerit; illi promisso habens fidem pontifex, bona non ignorans mysteria Dei, et quod pollicitus est susceptor ille expectans, libenter infantem Christian[itatis] nota distinguit, ut agnoscatur quasi surculus ex fideli arbore prodiisse. Cui nonnihil affert fides parentum, tametsi etiam non multum affert; siquidem Christiana arbor surgit et se multiplicat in ramos, non carnali generacione sed regeneracione spiritali. Unde constat vera paternitate, et in Christo, magis et verius patrem alumnum illum esse, qui natum hominem in Christo complet, quam genitorem qui carni materiam sumministravit: filium etiam, tametsi utrumque parentem colat, et illum primum qui eum hominis filium fecit, et hunc secundum qui minister eundem Dei filium procreavit, tamen profecto est quod plus debeat secundo, et eum parentis majori loco suscipiat. Quoniam plus est quidem perfici in Deo, quam progigni ab homine. Quamobrem pluris est et in superiori loco susceptor quam pater; et ejus officium actioque multo est excellentior et magis meritoria, atque ea quæ et a Deo et ab illo infantulo longe plus meretur, quam quicquam quod est in generatione a parente factum; qui opus carnis fecit, suæ voluptatis magis causa, quam prolis utilitate. Susceptor vero sine sua voluptate, etiam cum dolore reparturit hominem Christo, Dei charitate incensus, in hominis salutem. Sic videmus in prima ecclesia, apostolorum instituto, non simpliciter infantes ad sacra admissos fuisse, sed ea lege tantum ut fide jubeat aliquis pro eis, quum per etatem racione uti poterint, illos in re hinc Christi formam præ se laturos. Qui fidejussor et sponsor habebit sibi in curam, ut erudiat et educet puerum ea doctrina et moribus, ut pro sacramentorum racione præstet se verum Christianum; qui infans est insignitus sacris, ut educetur in ipsis. Quod si sit qui spondeat sancte et promittat in puero id futurum, tunc bona spe pia ecclesia adjungit sibi infantulum, ut alumni præceptis et monitis in professione Christi vir evadat. Sic vide quantum onus in se suscipit qui alumnum infantulis se polliceatur esse; quantum habet quod in infante præstet; quantum etiam et parentes et infans ipse debet alumno et susceptori suo, modo ex officio agat perficiatque quod spopondit se facturum. Longe plus, dico, ei debet, quam illi qui genuit genitori suo. Hic etiam licet videre quam ob ignoranciam hanc nostram, temporum confusione, qui hoc munus subeunt, quod obligantur facere, impie negligant; simul cum et ipsorum et infantulorum maximo dispendio. Quod si carnalis genitoris incuria infans secundum carnem moriatur, id genitori maximum scelus imputetur, quantum tunc scelus committit is, qui sua negligentia sinit hominem sine fine perire spiritu? Quantus est hic homicida, et quanta morte dignus ipse, cujus perfidia moritur homo morte sempiterna? Agnoscat ergo susceptor quisque, quis ipse est, et quid spondet, et quod ministerium gerit in Christo, atque quantus est pater in ministerio paternitatis Dei, qui verus est regenitor omnium, quantumque habet quod præstat in suscepto alumno. Non [levis] enim est res, pro racione sacrorum aliquem se in re justum Christianum exhibere; nec qui hoc pro aliquo spondet, rem parvam et factu facilem spondet. Quod si ex professo munere et officio faciat, rem gratissimam Deo, ipsi infanti utilissimam, jucundissimam parentibus, ecclesiæ etiam lucrum, et sibimet merementum gloriæ facit. Sin negligat officium, et sinat hominem susceptis sacris abuti, undique tunc sibi mortem et miseriam accumulat sempiternam. Ut est isto susceptore nihil pulcrius, nihilque melius nec fructuosius, si fideliter fit in re pro puero quod promittitur; ita quoque eodem certe nihil est nec detrimentosius nec damnabilius, si quod ad sacrum lavachrum promittit pontifici, perfide negligat. Ex quorum incuria, qui sunt quasi januæ ecclesiæ, in Christianam societatem introducti sunt qui nihil præter signa habent Christianitatis; unde fit ut sub nomine Christiano confluctuacio sit peccatorum, qui sub specioso nomine omne genus exercent feditatis. Cujus horroris et turpitudinis sane in causa sunt vel maxima susceptores illi et sponsores pro pueris, quorum curæ commissa est educatio in Christo et veritate vivendi parvulorum. Quoniam qualis plantacio est, talis est arbor; et puerorum qualis est educatio, talis est civitas. Parentes etiam in summa stulticia sunt et partim etiam in causa pestis hujus Christianæ civitatis, si non circumspecte conquirant et comparent sibi tales susceptores a quibus rite in Christo suos liberos sciunt institui posse. Sacerdotis est etiam perspicacem in hac re oculum habere, uti non admittantur in susceptoris officium cui commendetur infans, nisi tales qui sunt digni, sancti, docti et optimi viri, qui, quales ipsi sunt, tales parturiant ipsos infantulos; ut sanctum suscepto[rem infantes] sanctimonia et bonitate referentes, tandem in Christo digna membra extent, et tales qui nec sponsionem susceptoris, nec pontificis spem, nec denique suscepta sacra fallant.

HÆC Dionysii vestigia secuti scripsimus de ecclesiastica nostra hierarchia; a cujus pulchra forma longe degeneravimus. Sed Deum precamur, ipsum formatorem rerum, ut pro sua maxime pietate deformata in nobis reformet, per dominum nostrum Iesum Christum.

FINIS EORUM QUÆ SCRIPSIT IOANNES COLET IN ECCLESIASTICAM
HIERARCHIAM DIONYSII.

INDEX.

⁎ *The Roman numerals refer to the pages of the Introduction.*

ALCUIN quoted, 56 n., 76 n.
Altars, consecration of, 100.
Angels, meaning of name, 17; nine Orders of, 18, 24; called Gods, 34; fallen, 44; guardian, 45.
Anointing, 152.
Apostates, 127, 131.
Archangels, 27.
Archdeacon, origin of, 140 n.
Atonement, Dionysius on the, 55 n., 61 n.

Baptism, 59; triple immersion in, 74; of infants, 155.
Bishop, office of, 50, 62 n., 116, 150; origin of, 84; consecration of, 118.
Burial, solemnities of, 140.

Cabala, account of the, 110.
Cabalistic names of Angels, 20 n.
Catechize, meaning of, 79.
Catechumens, 88, 127, 144.
Chancel, meaning of, 140, 142 n.
Chrism, composition of the, 97, 152; consecration of the, 95.
COLET, DEAN, Treatises of, xiii, xiv, 3 n.; his inaccuracy of style, xiii; power of memory, 2 n.; fondness for children, 12 n.; disapproval of innovations, 69, 123, 135; Convocation sermon, 90 n.; on the Mosaic writings, 103 n.; complaint of disorders, 126, 136, 151, 155, 162; Will, xiii; 146 n.

Confirmation, the completion of Baptism, 75.
Cross, sign of the, 99, 120.

Dead, prayers for the, 145.
Demoniacs, 80.
DIONYSIUS, Trithemius's account of, xix; resembles Plotinus, xxx; character of writings of, xxxiii; external evidence against their genuineness, xxxiv; internal do., xxxv; probable date of, xxxvii; sources of, xxxix; resemblance to Proclus, xli; incompleteness of his system, xlvi; compared to Ezra, 135.
Diptychs, meaning of, 82 n.
Durandus, account of, 57 n.

East, turning to the, 68, 72.
Education, importance of, 161.
Egypt, monks in, 97.
Elysian fields, 139.
Emanations, notion of, xliii.
Empyrean, the, 43 n.
Energumens, 79, 127, 131.
Erasmus, his Life of Colet, x; opinion concerning Dionysius, xxxiv; on the Episcopal office, 62 n.; complaint of innovations, 69 n.; on parents and sponsors, 159 n.
Eucharist, Holy, 84.
Evil, existence of, xlvi.

Faith, above reason, 156.

Ficino, Marsiglio, manuscript of, xviii n.; account of, xxiv; letter of, to Mirandola, xxiv; inclined to astrology, xxviii; quoted by Colet, xviii, xxxi n., 36 n.
Free will, man's, 29.
Funerals, lamentation at, 138, 143.

Gaguin, Robert, xvi, xxix n.
Ganay, Germain de, xvii.
God, best expressed by negations, 13.
Godfathers, 67, 158; responsibility of, 160.
Grammars, early Latin, xxi n.
Greswell, W. P., opinion of Ficino, xxviii n.

Heywood, Thomas, his *Hierarchie*, 19 n.
Hierarchy, definition of, xliv n.; office of, 15, 37-41; the Legal, 52, 103; the Christian, 104; the Heavenly, 104.
Holdsworth, Dr. Richard, xiv n.

Ignatius, quotation from, xxxv, 63, 139.
Incarnation, Dionysius on the, xlv.
Incense, meaning of, 86.
Indulgences, 151 n.
Infants, admitted to the Eucharist, 75; Baptism of, 155.
Initiation, 126.
Isaiah ix. 6 explained, 9 n.
Italy, funerals in, 138.

Jerome, St., quoted, 83.
Jesuits, 53.
Jonas, Justus, x.

Kennett, Dr. White, collections of, for a Life of Colet, x; account of, xii n.
Knight, Dr. Samuel, his Life of Colet, xii.

Leo I., Pope, quotation from, 48.

Lots, use of, 121.
Love, more powerful than knowledge, 83.

Mass, meaning of, 81 n.
Medici, Lorenzo de', fondness of for Plato, xxxii.
Mirandola, Pico della, account of, xxii; his *Conclusiones*, xxii, 110 n., 111 n.; his *Apologia*, 109 n.; his Commentary on Benevieni, xliii n., 133 n.
Monks, consecration of, 134.
More, Sir Thomas, his translation of Pico, xxviii.
Moses, reference to, 109.
Multiplicity and simplicity, 72, 95.
Mysticism, xvi, xxxix.

Neo-Platonists, the, xix.
Nomination, sacrament of, 123.

Ordination, manner of, 118.
Origen, quotation from, 112.

Penitents, 81, 127, 131.
Pico, see Mirandola.
Plato, read in 14th century, xx; his *Symposium*, xxxix.
Platonic banquets, xxi.
Platonic revival, xxxi.
Plotinus, Mirandola's opinion of, xxiv; influence of, xxx; quoted, xl.
Politian, Angelo, 1 n.
Pope, responsibility of the, 150.
Porphyry, quotation from, xli.
Postlethwayte, Mr. John, xi.
Priest, office of the, 116.
Proclus, quotation from, xli.
Psalm xxiv. 3-6 explained, 23 n.
Purgatory, doctrine of, not in Dionysius, 146 n.

Redemption, Dionysius on, xlvi.
Romans ix. 28 explained, 9 n.

INDEX.

Sacraments, utility of, 154.
Sacramentaries, 76.
Savonarola, influence of, xxv, xxvi n., xxx; quotation from, 1 n.
Scripture, fulness of, 87; manifold senses of, 105 n., 112.
Simony, 123 n.
Sixtus IV., Pope, 111.
Smith, Thomas, his translation of Erasmus's Letter, xi.
Sponsors, see Godfathers.
Symbols, use of, 7, 35.
Synagogue, Jewish, 5, 7.
Synaxis, meaning of, 77.

Tabernacle, inner meaning of the, 113.
Telete, *i.e.* Perfection, 101-2.
Theology, definition of, 7.
Tonsure, clerical, 135 n.
Tradition, 56.
Trittenheim, John, xix.

Vergil, Polydore, quotation from, 138 n.
Vitrier, or Vitrarius, John, x n., 151 n.

Wafer bread, no authority for, in Dionysius, 93 n.
Wirtzung, on Colet's memory, 2 n.

THE END.

www.ingramcontent.com/pod-product-compliance
Lightning Source LLC
Chambersburg PA
CBHW050609300426
44112CB00013B/2148